Latest Intelligence

An International Directory of Codes
Used by Government, Law Enforcement,
Military, and Surveillance Agencies

Latest Intelligence

An International Directory of Codes Used by Government, Law Enforcement, Military, and Surveillance Agencies

James E. Tunnell,
Edited by Helen L. Sanders

TAB BOOKS

Blue Ridge Summit, PA

Published by **TAB BOOKS**
FIRST EDITION/FIRST PRINTING

© 1990 by **TAB BOOKS**
TAB BOOKS is a division of McGraw-Hill, Inc.

Library of Congress Cataloging-in-Publication Data

Tunnell, James E.
    Latest intelligence: an international directory of codes used by government, law enforcement, military, and surveillance agencies / by James E. Tunnell.
       p.   cm.
    Includes index.
    ISBN 0-8306-7531-0   ISBN 0-8306-3531-9 (pbk.)
    1. Ciphers—Dictionaries.   2. Law enforcement—Abbreviations--Dictionaries.   3. Intelligence service—Abbreviations--Dictionaries.   4. Military surveillance—Abbreviations--Dictionaries.   5. Administrative agencies—Abbreviations--Dictionaries.   I. Title.
Z104.T89 1990
652'.8—dc20   90-37042
                                        CIP

TAB BOOKS offers software for sale. For information and a catalog, please contact TAB Software Department, Blue Ridge Summit, PA 17294-0850.

Questions regarding the content of this book should be addressed to:

Reader Inquiry Branch
TAB BOOKS
Blue Ridge Summit, PA 17294-0850

Acquisitions Editor: Roland S. Phelps
Book Editor: Eileen P. Baylus
Production: Katherine G. Brown
Cover Design: Lori E. Schlosser

Contents

Dedication

This book is dedicated to Helen, Steve, Jimmy, Keith, Brian, Lynn, and David, who have taught the author to love and smile. It is important that we learn to make our world a more peaceful one, and an everlasting one, if not for ourselves, then for them.

Acknowledgments

This book could not have been written without a great deal of assistance from friends in the government, law enforcement, intelligence agencies, and the military. I am grateful to them all. Some organizations and individuals are acknowledged throughout the book, but most are not. They wanted it that way. Special thanks is due to Robert Kelty of Mobile Radio Resources and Bob Grove, Publisher of *Monitoring Times* for insight and advice.

Introduction

Latest Intelligence: An International Directory of Codes by Government, Law Enforcement, Military and Surveillance Agencies is a concise international directory covering communication codes, radio frequencies, and descriptions used by government, law enforcement, military, and surveillance agencies.

This book contains about 35,000 entries, arranged in alphabetical order, of codes, terms used in covert communications, acronyms, abbreviations, and descriptions used by intelligence agencies and police organizations worldwide. *Latest Intelligence* has been written with the assistance of the U.S. Department of Defense, INTERPOL, NASA, the Soviet Union, and law enforcement agencies and intelligence groups in America, Asia, and Europe.

The object of the book is to provide fundamental information on subjects discussed in law enforcement, military, and government radio communications, not only to experts but also to the general public. The book will prove useful to hobbyists and professionals in the communications field, as well as a valuable resource in police departments, criminal justice training centers, editorial offices of the media, and other institutions of this nature.

Topics range from radio codes used by law enforcement agencies to street slang for narcotics. A directory of worldwide law enforcement agencies is supplemented by an extensive listing of hostage rescue and antiterrorism units in more than 200 countries. *Latest Intelligence* has been prepared as a ready-reference guide to shortwave radio and scanner listening wherever you are in the world. It is the most comprehensive and up-to-date communications tool you can have on your bookshelf.

Communications listening is a discipline, a skill, and an art. It involves learning, an encyclopedic memory for facts both basic and arcane, discovery, practice, and the pleasure that comes from getting better and better at a complex task.

If you own or use a scanner or shortwave radio, you are standing at the threshold of unimagined capabilities. With other publications offered by TAB BOOKS and *Latest*

Intelligence, your radio receiver can become the gateway to thousands of hours of listening pleasure. This reference book will escort you across the threshold into the world of codes, special radio frequencies, surveillance applications, law enforcement procedures, and details on all branches of the military and government with the guide to frequencies and the unique language these agencies use.

You do not need a technical background to use *Latest Intelligence*. It has been written for the curious who want to know what's going on around him. In *Latest Intelligence* you'll discover background and specialty codes used by private and insurance investigators; microfiche service codes; command, control, communications and intelligence (C3I) codes from the military, terrorist groups and hostage rescue units; specialized law enforcement agencies and terms used in intelligence and surveillance activities; and unique facts to help you stay in tune. Without a doubt, *Latest Intelligence* is one of the most useful communications tools you'll ever use. If you are now using a frequency guide for your area of interest but have not understood all you hear, you are missing out on one of the most useful and exciting applications for your radio receiver. If you are already searching for definitions, *Latest Intelligence* will quickly make you more aware. Either way, your scanner or shortwave receiver is a ticket to ride and the reference book you have in your hands is not only the latest intelligence in the professional communications field but is also your roadmap to better listening. Happy travels.

Index Codes

Preceding the majority of terms, codes, acronyms, abbreviations, and definitions is an index code that can be used to identify the source. Those index codes are:

[A]	Aviation
[B]	Commercial broadcasting
[C]	Communications
[C,G&PS]	Criminal, gang related, and police slang
[CW]	Chemical Warfare
[C3I]	Command, Control, Communications, Intelligence
[D]	Definitive (self-explanatory)
[E]	Electronics
[EW]	Electronic Warfare
[GOV]	Government
[HRU]	Hostage Rescue Unit(s)
[I]	Intelligence
[LE]	Law Enforcement
[M]	Military
[NASA]	National Aeronautics and Space Administration
[NATO]	North Atlantic Treaty Organization
[S]	Satanism
[Speciality Codes]	Private and insurance investigators
[TRG]	Terrorist or Radical Group
[UK]	United Kingdom
[US]	United States
[USSR]	Soviet Union

A-6 Designation for a military airplane used by the United States Navy and Marines, the A-6 Intruder and EA-6B Prowler produced by Grumman Aircraft Corporation as a carrier-based all-weather attack aircraft. A modified version of the A-6, known as the KA-6D is a two-seat air-refueling tanker.

A-10 USAF close-support attack aircraft, also known as the Thunderbolt II, produced by the Fairchild Republic Company. Armament is a seven-barrel GAU-8/A Avenger rapid-firing cannon that fires high explosive steel-fence-post-sized projectiles of depleted uranium at controlled rates of 2,100 or 4,200 per minute (*See* DU). The A-10 (also known among its pilots as the "Warthog," not the Thunderbolt II) also can carry a 16,000-pound combined bomb and rocket load hung on 11 external pylons.

A's [C,G&PS] Slang for amphetamines. (*See* QUICK REFERENCE.)

AA 1. [D] Abbreviation for Arabic. 2. [M] Anti-Aircraft. 3. [I] Abbreviation for Accommodation Address—a mailing address, usually a post office box, used as a message drop for communication between intelligence agents or a law enforcement agency and an undercover operative.

AAA 1. [M] Abbreviation for Anti-Aircraft Artillery (flak). 2. [LE] Abbreviation for Argentine Anticommunist Alliance.

AAAM [C3I] Abbreviation for Advanced Air-to-Air Missile.

AABNCP [US] Abbreviation for Advanced Airborne National Command Post.

AAC [US] Abbreviation for Alaskan Air Command.

AAC [UK] Abbreviation for (British) Army Air Corps.

AAC [A] Abbreviation for Australian Aircraft Consortium.

AACOMS [US] Abbreviation for Army Area Communications System.

AAM [M] Abbreviation for Air-to-Air Missile.

AASM [C3I] Abbreviation for Advanced Air-to-Surface Missile.

AAWS [C3I] Abbreviation for Anti-air Warfare System.

AB [C,G&PS] Abbreviation for an abscess, open sore on a human body.

ABC [LE] Slang for a ruled sheet used in horse race betting.

ABC-C [B] Abbreviation for American Broadcasting Company Contemporary Network.

ABCCC [US] Abbreviation for Airborne Battlefield Command and Control Center.

ABC-D [B] Abbreviation for American Broadcasting Company Direction Network.

ABC-E [B] Abbreviation for American Broadcasting Company Entertainment Network.

ABC-F [B] Abbreviation for American Broadcasting Company FM Network.

ABC-I [B] Abbreviation for American Broadcasting Company Information Network.

ABC-R [B] Abbreviation for American Broadcasting Company Rock Radio Network.

ABC-T [B] Abbreviation for American Broadcasting Company Talkradio Network.

ABM 1. [C3I] Slang for Anti-Ballistic Missile. 2. [M] Abbreviation for Air Breathing Missile.

ABMA [US] Abbreviation for Army Ballistic Missile Agency.

ABRACADABRA [D] A term used in satanism to actually invoke an act of black magic. (*See* BLACK MAGIC.) The term dates from early Greece and Persia. It comes from the Greek word *abraxas*.

The Greeks gave each letter of their alphabet a numerical value—abraxas adds up to 365. The Persians worshipped 365 gods and avoided having to make mention of each one when praying by simply saying the word abraxas—365. This gave the word its supposed magical powers.

ABRAXAS [D] *See* ABRACADABRA.

Abu Abbas [TRG] Designation for the Palestine Liberation Front—Fatah faction, headquartered in Syria.

Abu Musa [TRG] Abbreviation for a small but very active Fatah faction terrorist group headquartered in Syria.

Abu Nidal **1.** [TRG] Alias for Sabry al-Banna, also known as Sobhia Murad, a renegade Palestinian terrorist who broke away from the Palestine Liberation Organization and who attacked Israeli, American, and moderate Palestinian targets with seemingly equal fervor. He and his small group of international terrorists are believed to have been behind the simultaneous December 1985 attacks at the Rome and Vienna airports that left 20 dead and 121 injured, and the Boeing 747 crash of Pan Am flight 103 in Lockerbie, Scotland, where 258 passengers died and 22 more were killed on the ground in late December 1988. In late 1989, it was reported by Abdulrahman Issa, a former member of the council's 10-man politburo, that more than 150 members of Abu Nidal's group, including 20 top officials, had been murdered by Sabry al-Banna in his own home, "lured to Abu Nidal's house near Tripoli on the pretext of discussing policy matters, taken by surprise and killed in the house," in a bloody internal power struggle. "Then, they were buried right there. Sabry al-Banna and his hirelings dug a pit and poured cement over the bodies," Issa said. **2.** [TRG] The Fatah Revolutionary Council with headquarters in Libya and Syria.

A/C [A] Abbreviation for Aircraft.

AC **1.** [LE] Abbreviation for Aided Card. The initial reporting card of a crime or specific incident completed by a law enforcement officer. Also called an incident report. **2.** [B] Abbreviation for Adult Contemporary. **3.** [CW] Designation for the blood agent cyangen chloride. This chemical warfare agent is used by the military and was developed to cause quick convulsions in humans and animals, asphyxiation, and death. **4.** Specialty code for accident investigation. **5.** [LE] Abbreviation for Anti-Crime. **6.** [I] Designation for accommodation address, an address used in counterintelligence to receive communications or mail that is held for pickup. An accommodation address is sometimes used as a relay point for data to be forwarded to another intelligence agent. **7.** [C,G&PS] *See* AREA CODE.

Acapulco gold [C,G&PS] A high-grade, golden-colored marijuana that is grown near Acapulco, Mexico.

ACC Specialty code for accident reconstruction or evaluation of an accident site.

ACCS **1.** [C3I] Abbreviation for Army Command and Control System. **2.** [US] Abbreviation for Airborne Command and Control System or Advanced Communications Control System.

ACD [US] Abbreviation for Automatic Call Distribution System.

ACE [C,G&PS] Slang for a twelve-month jail or prison sentence.

ACE-ACCIS [NATO] Abbreviation for Allied Command Europe Automated Command Control and Information System.

Ace high [NATO] Slang for tropospheric scatter communications network.

ACI [C3I] Abbreviation for Adjacent Channel Interference.

Acid [C,G&PS] Slang for LSD-25, lysergic acid diethylamide. (*See* QUICK REFERENCE.)

Acid head [C,G&PS] Slang for an LSD drug user.

Acid test [C,G&PS] Slang for a party where LSD is an added ingredient in the punch.

ACK [C3I] Abbreviation for Acknowledge.

ACLICS [US] Abbreviation for Airborne Communications Location Identification and Collection System.

ACM **1.** [C3I] Abbreviation for Advanced Cruise Missile. **2.** [US] Abbreviation for Air Combat Maneuver.

ACOUSTINT   [I] Abbreviation for Acoustic intelligence.

across the board   [LE] In horse racing, to place the same amount of money for (a) a win (the horse comes in first) or (b) place, the horse that is bet on comes in second, and (c) show, where the horse bet on comes in third. This process is used at the majority of tracks in the United States.

across the river   [GOV] A term common to offices of the Pentagon and in other military establishments of the U.S. military to indicate the White House, Congress, and the State Department.

ACS   **1.** [US] Abbreviation for Aegis Combat System, the United States Navy's sophisticated shipboard air defense system. **2.** [M] Abbreviation for Artillery Computer System.

ACSI   [M] Abbreviation for Assistant Chief of Staff for U.S. Army Intelligence. This individual authorizes and controls intelligence operations for all divisions of the United States Army.

ACT   [M] Abbreviation for Air Combat Training.

action   [C,G&PS] Slang for drug dealing or offering narcotics for sale.

ACTS   [C3I] Abbreviation for Advanced Communication Technology Satellite.

ACU   [C3I] Abbreviation for Antenna Control Unit.

AD   [A] **1.** Abbreviation for Airworthiness Directive. The Federal Aviation Administration (FAA) issues an AD when it considers a design for a specific aircraft type to be defective or a threat to flight safety. A plane then can be legally grounded until the modification is carried out. Naturally, aircraft manufacturers want as few ADs as possible. ADs basically are seen as black marks on a manufacturer's design and manufacturing record. Also, product liability and hull insurance cost increase with the number of ADs against a particular design. **2.** Specialty code for adjusting when referring to insurance. **3.** [TRG] Abbreviation for Action Directe, an active terrorist/radical group headquartered in France.

A/D   [C3I] Abbreviation for Analog-to-Digital.

Ada   [C3I] A Department of Defense standardized computer programming language.

ADACS   [C3I] Abbreviation for Attitude Determination and Control Subsystem.

Adam   [A,LE,MIL] Designation for the letter *A*.

ADC   **1.** [M] Abbreviation for Assistant Division Commander. **2.** [US] Abbreviation for Aerospace Defense Command. **3.** [A] Abbreviation for Air Data Computer.

ADCAP   [M] Acronym for Advanced Capability (torpedo).

a-detachment   [M] Designation for the basis special forces operational unit of the United States Army. Usually it is comprised of twelve men; also known as an A-Team. (*See* B-DETACHMENT and C-DETACHMENT.)

ADEWS   [C3I] Abbreviation for Air Defense Electronic Warfare System.

ADF   [C3I] **1.** Abbreviation for Atmosphere Defense Initiative. **2.** [A] Abbreviation for Automatic Direction Finding (also referred to as radio compass). ADF generally are used to pinpoint a specific position.

ADI   [C3I] Abbreviation for Airborne Defense Initiative.

ADLIPS   [US] Acronym for Automatic Data Link Plotting System.

ADM   [C3I] Abbreviation for Adaptive Delta Modulation.

ADP   [C3I] Abbreviation for Automated Data Processing.

ADPA   [C3I] Abbreviation for American Defense Preparedness Association.

ADPCM   [C3I] Abbreviation for Adaptive Differential Pulse Code Modulation.

ADPE   [M] Abbreviation for Automatic Data Processing Equipment.

ADS   [C3I] Abbreviation for Area Detection System.

ADSAF   [US] Abbreviation for Automatic Data System for the Army in the Field.

ADSCOM   [US] Acronym for Advanced Ship Communications.

ADSP   [C3I] Abbreviation for Advanced Design Special Processor.

ADT   [US] Abbreviation for Airborne Data Terminal.

Aduana [LE] Name of the Mexican custom authorities.

advanced class [C] The second highest class of amateur radio operator, as far as privileges are concerned.

aegis [M] U.S. Navy's sophisticated combat air defense system.

AEW [M] Abbreviation for Airborne Early Warning (radar).

AF [D] Abbreviation for Audio Frequency, the band of frequencies a human being can hear. The range is from 20 to 20,000 Hz.

AFA [M] Abbreviation for Air Force Association.

AFAP [M] Abbreviation for Artillery-Fired Atomic Projectile.

AFATDS [M] Abbreviation for Advanced Field Artillery Data System.

AFB [M] Abbreviation for Air Force Base.

AFCS 1. [M] Abbreviation for Air Force Communications Service. **2.** [A] Abbreviation for Automatic Flight Control.

AFD [C3I] Abbreviation for Automated Frequency Deconfliction.

AFF [M] Abbreviation for Army Field Forces.

AFLC [US] Abbreviation for Air Force Logistics Command.

AFOAT-1 [US] Acronym for Office of the Air Force Assistant for Atomic Energy, Section 1.

AFOSR [US] Abbreviation for Air Force Office of Scientific Research.

AFP-42 [A] Abbreviation for Air Force Plant 42, located in the Mojave Desert, near Palmdale, California. This is where stealth aircraft are assembled and flight tested.

African black [C,G&PS] Slang for marijuana that is deep black in color. (*See* QUICK REFERENCE.)

AFSA [M] Abbreviation for Armed Forces Security Agency.

AFSATCOM [US] Acronym for Air Force Satellite Communications.

AFSC [C3I] Abbreviation for Air Force Systems Command.

AFSCF [US] Abbreviation for Air Force Satellite Control Facility.

AFTAC [US] Abbreviation for Air Force Technical Applications Center.

afterburner [A] A device onboard an aircraft engine designed to augment the thrust of a turbojet or turbofan by burning extra fuel in the jet pipe.

AFV [M] Abbreviation for Armored Fighting Vehicle.

AG Specialty code for Armed Guards.

AGC [C] Abbreviation for Automatic Gain Control (radio).

AGE [US] Abbreviation for Aerospace Ground Equipment.

agent [I] An individual who gathers information in law enforcement, usually as a member of an intelligence operation. In the field of espionage an agent acts as a saboteur or spy.

agent meeting [I] A prearranged meeting between agents representing the interests of an intelligence agency, or between a case officer and an informant.

agent net [I] An intelligence-gathering unit of agents.

agent of influence [I] An intelligence agent or individual working with an intelligence agency who covertly can influence an organization, foreign official, or in some way do good for his government.

agent provocateur [I] A person who urges illegal acts by those who are under suspicion. An agent provocateur is a trained and experienced professional.

AGER [US] Abbreviation for Auxiliary General for Environmental Research ship.

AGF [M] Abbreviation for Army Ground Forces.

AGI [US] The western intelligence security classification designation for any ship used to collect intelligence data.

AGR Specialty code for agricultural and farm machinery.

AGTR [US] Abbreviation for Auxiliary General for Technical Research ship.

A-head [C,G&PS] Slang for a heavy user of amphetamines.

AHR [C3I] Abbreviation for Ampere-Hour.

AHS [C3I] Abbreviation for Autonomous Helicopter System.

AI **1.** Specialty code for Aviation Investigator. **2.** [C3I] Abbreviation for Artificial Intelligence.

AIAA [C3I] Abbreviation for American Institute of Aeronautics and Astronautics.

A.I.C. [I] Abbreviation for the Agent In Charge of surveillance and intelligence-gathering operations.

AID [GOV] Abbreviation for Agency for International Development.

AIDS [US] Abbreviation for Advanced Integrated Display System.

aileron [A] The movable surface located at the outer trailing end of the wing on an airplane. The aileron provides roll control in flight.

AIM [M] Abbreviation for Air-Intercept Missile.

aircraft band [A] The radio frequency range from 108 to 135 MHz that is dedicated to aircraft communications.

air defense [M] The system designed to intercept intruding missiles, bombers, and reconnaissance or fighter aircraft.

airplane [C,G&PS] Slang for the butt end of a marijuana cigarette.

air superiority [M] Control of the air, through the destruction of enemy aircraft or missiles.

AJ [M] Abbreviation for Anti-jamming.

AJM/C [C3I] Abbreviation for Anti-Jam Modem Controller.

AK [D] Postal abbreviation for Alaska.

AK-47 [M] Designation for a rugged, compact assault rifle of Soviet origin. As a modified semi-automatic weapon, it fires 40 rounds per minute; unmodified, up to 600 rounds per minute.

AKA [LE] Abbreviation for Also Known As.

AKO [TRG] Abbreviation for Anarchistische Kampforganization, a small anarchist and terrorist group based in Zurich, Switzerland.

AL **1.** Specialty code for Asset/Locating. **2.** [A] Abbreviation for Air Interception (radar).

ALC [C3I] Abbreviation for Automatic Level Control.

ALCC [C3I] Abbreviation for Airborne Launch Control Center.

ALCM [C3I] Abbreviation for Air Launched Cruise Missile.

Al Amal [TRG] A Shiite terrorist group headquartered in Lebanon. English translation: Islamic Hope.

Al Daawa [TRG] A small but active terrorist group headquartered in Iraq. English translation: The Call.

Alfa [A,LE,MIL] Designation for the letter *A*.

Alfatah [TRG] A Palestinian terrorist group closely related, by specific activities, with the Black September movement.

alias [LE] Slang for an assumed name.

alley juice [C,G&PS] Slang for methyl alcohol that is consumed as a drink.

ALMV [M] Abbreviation for Air Launched Miniature Vehicle.

ALN [TRG] Designation for Brazilian Action for National Liberation. More of a radical (noise-making) group than actual terrorists. Also known as the Acao Libertadora National.

ALOFT [US] Abbreviation for Airborne Light Optical Fibre Technology.

ALPS [M] Abbreviation for Accidental Launch Protection System.

ALS **1.** [M] Abbreviation for Advanced Life Support. **2.** [NASA] Advanced Logistics Spacecraft.

altar [S] In the practice of satanism, the membership of a clan use a nude woman in the position of a table to worship Satan. This is called the altar. (*See* CLAN, SATAN.)

alternate meet [I] A prearranged meeting held in the event that a regular meeting scheduled on a regular basis is somehow missed.

ALV [C3I] Abbreviation for Autonomous Land Vehicle.

Al Zulfiqah [TRG] A small but very active Pakistani terrorist/radical group opposed mostly to officials of their government.

AM [C] Abbreviation for Amplitude Modulation, the common way of transmitting voice and other signals with radio transmission.

AMA [US] Abbreviation for Air Material Area.

Aman [I] The Israeli defense branch of the Mossad (Office of Intelligence and Special Missions) that reports directly to the Chief of Staff, Defense Forces. The Aman is responsible for all military and strategic intelligence and electronic intercepts.

amateur radio [C] The system of radio communications used between licensed (ham) radio amateurs.

amateur radio prefix callsign codes international The following are radio prefix call sign codes:

Prefix	Country
A2	Botswana
A3	Tonga
A4	Oman
A5	Bhutan
A6	United Arab Emirates
A7	Qatar
A9	Bahrain
AA	United States of America
AL	United States of America
AP	Pakistan
BV	Taiwan
BY	China
C2	Nauru
C3	Andorra
C5	The Gambia
C6	Bahamas
C9	Mozambique
CE	Chile
CE9	Antarctica
CE9	South Shetland Islands
CE0A	Easter Island
CE0X	San Felix
CE0Z	Juan Fernandez
CM	Cuba
CN	Morocco
CO	Cuba
CP	Bolivia
CR3	Guinea
CR3	Bissau

Prefix	Country
CR5	Principe
CR5	Sao Tome
CR9	Macao
CT	Portugal
CT2	Azores
CT3	Madeira Island
CX	Uruguay
D2	Angola
D3	Angola
D4	Cape Verde
D6	Comoros
DA	Federal Republic of Germany
DF	Federal Republic of Germany
DJ	Federal Republic of Germany
DK	Federal Republic of Germany
DL2	Federal Republic of Germany
DM	German Democratic Republic
DT	German Democratic Republic
DU	Philippines
EA	Spain
EA6	Balearic Island
EA8	Canary Island
EA9	Ceuta & Melilla
EI	Ireland
EL	Liberia
EP	Iran
ET	Ethiopia
F	France
FB8W	Crozet
FB8X	Kerquelen Island
FB8Y	Antarctica
FB8Z	Amsterdam Island
FB8Z	Saint Paul Island
FC	Corsica
FG	Guadeloupe
FG	Saint Martin
FH	Mayotte
FK	New Caledonia
FL8	Djibouti
FM	Martinique
FO	Clipperton Island
FO	French Polynesia
FP	Saint Pierre

Prefix	Country	Prefix	Country
FP	Miquelon	IT	Italy
FR	Glorioso Island	J2	Djibouti
FR	Juan de Nova, Europa	J2	Abu Ail
FR	Reunion	J2	Jabal at Tair
FR	Tromelin	J2A	Abu Ail
FS	Saint Martin	J2A	Jabal at Tair
FW	Wallis Island	J3	Grenada
FW	Futuna Island	J5	Guinea-Bissau
FY	French Guiana	J6	Saint Lucia
G	England	JA	Japan
GC	Jersey	JD	Minami Torishima
GC	Guernsey	JD	Ogasawara
GD	Isle of Man	JN	Japan
GI	Northern Ireland	JT	Mongolia
GJ	Jersey	JW	Svalbard
GM	Scotland	JX	Jan Mayen
GU	Guernsey	JY	Jordan
GW	Wales	K	United States of America
H4	Solomon Islands	KA	Japan
H5	South Africa	KA1	Minami Torishima
HA	Hungary	KA1	Ogasawara
HB	Switzerland	KB6	Baker Island
HB0	Liechtenstein	KB6	Howland Island
HC	Eucador	KB6	Am Phoenix Island
HC8	Galapagos islands	KC4	Navassa Island
HF0	South Shetland Islands	KC4	Antarctica
HF4K	South Shetland Islands	KC6	Federal States of Micronesia (East Caroline Islands)
HH	Hati		
HI	Dominican Republic	KC6	Republic of Belau (West Caroline Islands)
HK	Colombia		
HK0	Malpelo Islands	KG4	Guantanamo Bay
HK0	San Andres	KG6	Guam
HK0	Providencia	KG6R	Mariana Islands
HL	Korea	KH1	Baker Island
HM	Korea	KH1	Howland Island
HP	Panama	KH1	Am Phoenix Island
HR	Honduras	KH2	Guam
HS	Thailand	KH3	Johnston Island
HT	Nicaragua	KH4	Midway Island
HV	Vatican	KH5	Palmyra Island
HZ	Saudi Arabia	KH5	Jarvis Island
I	Italy	KH5K	Kingman Reef
IS	Sardinia	KH6	Hawaiian Islands

Prefix	Country	Prefix	Country
KH7	Kure Island	OR4	Antarctica
KH8	American Samoa	OX	Greenland
KH9	Wake Island	OY	Faroe Island
KH0	Mariana Island	OZ	Denmark
KJ6	Johnston Island	P2	Papua New Guinea
KL7	Alaska	PA	Netherlands
KM6	Midway Island	PD	Netherlands
KP1	Navassa Island	PE	Netherlands
KP2	Virgin Islands	PI	Netherlands
KP4	Puerto Rico	PJ2	Netherlands Antilles
KP4	Desecheo Island	PJ3	Netherlands Antilles
KP5	Desecheo Island	PJ4	Netherlands Antilles
KP6	Palmyra Island	PJ5	Saint Maarten
KP6	Jarvis Island	PJ5	Saba
KP6	Kingman Reef	PJ5	Saint Eustatius
KS6	American Samoa	PJ6	Saint Maarten
KV4	Virgin Islands	PJ6	Saba
KW6	Wake Island	PJ6	Saint Eustatius
KX6	Marshall Islands	PJ7	Saint Maarten
LA	Norway	PJ7	Saba
LA	Antarctica	PJ7	Saint Eustatius
LB	Norway	PJ8	Saint Maarten
LF	Norway	PJ8	Saba
LG	Norway	PJ8	Saint Eustatius
LJ	Norway	PJ9	Netherlands Antilles
LU	Argentina	PP	Brazil
LU-Z	Antarctica	PR	Brazil
LU-Z	South Georgia Islands	PW	Brazil
LU-Z	South Orkney Islands	PY	Brazil
LU-Z	South Sandwich Islands	PY0	Fernando de Noronha
LU-Z	South Shetland Islands	PY0	Saint Peter & Saint Paul Rocks
LX	Luxembourg	PY0	Trindade & Martin Vaz. Island
LZ	Bulgaria	PZ	Surinam
M1	San Marino	S	Mariana Island
N	United States of America	S2	Bangladesh
OA	Peru	S4	South Africa
OD	Lebanon	S7	Seychelles
OE	Austria	S8	South Africa
OH	Finland	S9	Sao Tome
OH0	Aland Island	S9	Principe
OJ0	Market Reef	SK	Sweden
OK	Czechoslovakia	SL	Sweden
ON	Belgium	SM	Sweden

Prefix	Country	Prefix	Country
SP	Poland	UK1	European Russian SFSR
ST	Sudan	UK1	Franz Josef Land
ST0	Southern Sudan	UK1	Antarctica
SU	Egypt	UK2A	White R.S.S.R.
SV	Greece	UK2B	Lithuania
SV	Crete	UK2C	White R.S.S.R.
SV	Dodecanese	UK2F	Kaliningradsk
T	Mariana Island	UK2G	Latvia
T2	Tuvalu	UK2I	White R.S.S.R.
T4	South Africa	UK2L	White R.S.S.R.
T5	Somali	UK2P	Lithuania
T7	San Marino	UK2Q	Latvia
T19	Cocos Island	UK2R	Estonia
T30	W. Kiribati (Gilbert & Ocn Islands)	UK2T	Estonia
T31	C. Kiribati (Brit. Phoenix Island)	UK6C	Azerbaijan
T32	East Kiribati (Line Island)	UK6D	Azerbaijan
TA	Turkey	UK6F	Georgia
TF	Iceland	UK6G	Armenia
TG	Guatemala	UK6K	Azerbaijan
TI	Costa Rica	UK60	Georgia
TJ	Cameroon	UK6Q	Georgia
TL	Central African Republic	UK6V	Georgia
TN	Congo	UK7	Kazakh
TR	Gabon	UK8	Uzbek
TT	Chad	UK8H	Turkoman
TU	Ivory Coast	UK8J	Tadzhik
TY	Benin	UK8M	Kirghiz
TZ	Mali	UK8N	Kirghiz
UA	European Russian SFSR	UK8R	Tadzhik
UA	Asiatic R.S.F.S.R.	UK20	White R.S.S.R.
UA1	Franz Josef Land	UK2S	White R.S.S.R.
UA1	Antarctica	UK2W	White R.S.S.R.
UA2	Kaliningradsk	UK3	European Russian SFSR
UB	Ukraine	UK4	European Russian SFSR
UC2	White R.S.S.R.	UK6	European Russian SFSR
UD6	Azerbaijan	UK50	Moldavia
UF6	Georgia	UL7	Kazakh
UG6	Armenia	UM8	Kirghiz
UH8	Turkoman	UN1	European Russian SFSR
UI8	Uzbek	UO5	Moldavia
UJ8	Tadzhik	UP2	Lithuania
UK	Asiatic R.S.F.S.R.	UQ2	Latvia
UK	Ukraine	UR2	Estonia

Prefix	Country	Prefix	Country
UT	Ukraine	VP8	South Shetland Islands
UV	European Russian SFSR	VP9	Bermuda
UV	Asiatic R.S.F.S.R.	VQ9	Chagos
UW1	European Russian SFSR	VR1	W. Kiribati (Gilbert & Ocn Islands)
UW9	Asiatic R.S.F.S.R.	VR1	C. Kiribati (British Phoenix Island)
UW0	Asiatic R.S.F.S.R.	VR3	East Kiribati (Line Island)
UY5	Ukraine	VR4	Solomon Islands
V2	Antigua Barbuda	VR6	Pitcairn Island
V3	Belize	VR8	Tuvalu
V9	South Africa	VS5	Brunei
VE	Canada	VS6	Hong Kong
VE1	Sable Island	VS9	Maldive Islands
VE1	Saint Paul Island	VU	India
VK	Australia	VU7	Andaman Island
VK	Lord Howe Island	VU7	Nicobar Island
VK9	Willis Island	VU7	Laccadive Island
VK9	Christmas Island	VY1	Canada
VK9	Cocos-Keeling Islands	W	United States of America
VK9	Mellish Reef	XE	Mexico
VK9	Norfolk Island	XF4	Revilla Gigedo
VK0	Antarctica	XP	Greenland
VK0	Heard Island	XT	Upper Volta
VK0	Macquarie Island	XU	Kampuchea
VO	Canada	XV	Vietnam
VO	Canada	XW	Laos
VP1	Belize	XZ	Burma
VP2A	Antigua Barbuda	Y2-9	German Democratic Republic
VP2D	Dominica	YA	Afghanistan
VP2E	Angullia	YB	Indonesia
VP2G	Grenada	YC	Indonesia
VP2K	Saint Kitts	YI	Iraq
VP2K	Nevis	YJ	New Hebrides
VP2L	Saint Lucia	YK	Syria
VP2M	Montserrat	YN	Nicaragua
VP2S	Saint Vincent	YO	Romania
VP2V	British Virgin Islands	YS	El Salvador
VP5	Turks Island	YU	Yugoslavia
VP5	Caicos Island	YV	Venezuela
VP8	Antarctica	YV0	Aves Island
VP8	Falkland Islands	Z2	Zimbabwe
VP8	South Georgia Island	ZA	Albania
VP8	South Orkney Island	ZB	Gibraltar
VP8	South Sandwich Islands	ZC	Cyprus

Prefix	Country	Prefix	Country
ZD7	Saint Helena	4U	Headquarters, United Nations
ZD8	Ascension Island	4W	Yemen
ZD9	Tristan de Cunha Island	4X	Israel
ZD9	Gough Island	4Z	Israel
ZE	Zimbabwe	5A	Libya
ZF	Cayman Island	5B	Cyprus
ZK1	North Cook Island	5H	Tanzania
ZK1	South Cook Island	5N	Nigeria
ZK2	Niue	5R	Malagasy Republic
ZL	New Zealand	5T	Mauritania
ZL	Auckland Island	5U	Niger
ZL	Campbell Island	5V	Togo
ZL	Chatham Island	5W	Western Samoa
ZL	Keradec Island	5X	Uganda
ZL5	Antarctica	5Z	Kenya
ZM7	Tokelau Island	6O	Somali
ZP	Paraguay	6W	Senegal
ZS1	South Africa	6Y	Jamaica
ZS1	Antarctica	7O	People's Democratic Republic of
ZS2	Prince Edward Island		Yemen
ZS2	Marion Island	7P	Lesotho
ZS3	South West Africa (Namibia)	7Q	Malawi
ZS6	South Africa	7X	Algeria
1A0	Soviet Military Order of Malta	7Z	Saudi Arabia
1S	Spratly Island	8J	Antarctica
3A	Monaco	8P	Barbados
3B6	Agalega	8Q	Maldive Islands
3B6	Saint Brandon	8R	Guyana
3B7	Agalega	9A	San Marino
3B7	Saint Brandon	9G	Ghana
3B9	Mauritius	9H	Malta
3B9	Rodriquez Island	9J	Zambia
3C	Equatorial Guinea	9K	Kuwait
3C0	Annobon	9L	Sierra Leone
3D2	Fiji Islands	9M2	West Malaysia
3D6	Swaziland	9M6	East Malaysia
3V	Tunisia	9M8	East Malaysia
3X	Republic of Guinea	9N	Nepal
3^	Bouvet	9Q	Zaire
3Y	Peter Island	9U	Burundi
3Y	Antarctica	9V	Singapore
4K	Antarctica	9X	Rwanda
4S	Sri Lanka	9Y	Tobago
4U	I.T.U. Geneva	9Y	Trinidad

AM/BB [B] Abbreviation for AM Broadcast Band, the commercial broadcast band used in the United States. The frequency range is from 550 KHz to 1600 KHz.

amber deck [US] Naval aviation voice brevity code meaning flight deck is in standby condition.

AMMIES [C,G&PS] Slang for amyl nitrate. (*See* QUICK REFERENCE.)

amphetamines [LE] General term for any of several controlled substances that are considered stimulants. (*See* QUICK REFERENCE.)

amps [C,G&PS] Slang for amphetamines. (*See* QUICK REFERENCE.)

AMRAAM [C3I] Abbreviation for Advanced Medium Range Air-to-Air Missile.

AMTOR [C] Acronym for Amateur (ham) Teleprinting Over Radio.

Amytal [LE] Brand name for amobarbital, a controlled substance that is a sedative. (*See* QUICK REFERENCE.)

analog receiver [C] A radio receiver that tunes in radio stations by converting a mechanical movement into a frequency change. (*See* SYNTHESIZED RECEIVER.)

analysis [I] A stage in the intelligence process whereby the information that has been collected is reviewed to identify significant facts and useful details.

analysis paralysis [GOV] A term used, especially in the upper levels of the military, to define the effects on an individual who studies and evaluates a problem or situation to excess. Analysis paralysis is considered by those who have experienced it as an obsession in developing a solution—the obsession becoming an overwhelming mental process that can cause loss of sleep, mental breakdowns, and related medical problems.

ANAVS-6 [US] Slang for night-vision goggles. The older goggles (*See* ANPVS-5) have been used since the early 1970s, while the newer version (ANAVS-6) have been in service since 1987. These goggles are used primarily by the Marine Corps and the Army and were originally designed for night driving. Night-vision goggles electronically amplify moonlight and starlight, partly improving night vision, but also sacrificing peripheral sight and reducing normal 20-20 vision to 20-50 or worse. Use of these goggles can lead to eye fatigue and illusions. When used by aircraft or helicopter pilots, under certain conditions, the images viewed tend to strobe causing disorientation to the user. At least 62 helicopters have crashed and 134 servicemen have died in the past decade in accidents where the pilot was looking through night-vision goggles. The newer goggles have been modified for night flying. It has been reported that image resolution is sometimes not in sync with realtime events.

ANC [D] Abbreviation for The African National Congress, headquartered in South Africa.

ancient one [S] The priestess who officiates at a satanism Black Mass. (*See* BLACK MASS.)

ANDVT [US] Abbreviation for Advanced Narrowband Digital Voice Terminal.

ANG [M] Abbreviation for Air National Guard.

angel dust **1.** [C,G&PS] Slang for the drug phencyclidine, or PCP. The usual method of ingestion is to mix with marijuana and smoke. **2.** [LE] Slang for a controlled substance that is an hallucinogen. (*See* QUICK REFERENCE.)

angles [US] Naval aviation voice brevity code meaning the altitude in thousands of feet ("angels 12" indicating an altitude of 12,000 feet).

angle of attack [A] The inclination of the airfoil to the direction of the airflow.

angle of incidence [A] The setting of the wing angle relative to the fuselage axis. The term is sometimes used to indicate the angle of attack.

anhedral [A] In aviation, the downward angle of a wing viewed from the front.

Anpo Kenkyu [M] The Japanese Navy code research section. The Anpo Kenkyu has supplied data to the US on Soviet communications received in Asia.

ANPVS-5 [US] Designation for night-vision goggles (*See* ANAVS-6). The ANPVS-5 goggles have been in use since 1970.

antenna [C] A wire, rod, dish, or array that transmits or can receive radio waves.

antenna tuner [C] A device that can match the

impedance of an antenna to the impedance of a radio transmitter or receiver.

anthropomancy [S] A method of human sacrifice in satanism.

antifreeze [C,G&PS] Slang for heroin. (*See* QUICK REFERENCE.)

AOA **1.** [C3I] Abbreviation for Advanced Optical Adjunct. **2.** [M] Abbreviation for Angle Of Attack.

AOD [USSR] Abbreviation for Administrative Organs Department.

AOR [B] Abbreviation for Album-Oriented Rock.

AOS [C3I] Abbreviation for Airborne Optical System.

AP **1.** [M] Abbreviation for Armor Piercing. **2.** [LE] Abbreviation for Auxiliary Police.

APACHE [US] Acronym for Analysis of Pacific Area Communications for Hardening to Electromagnetic Pulse (EMP).

APC **1.** [C3I] Abbreviation for Adaptive Predictive Coding. **2.** [M] Abbreviation for Armored Personnel Carrier.

APCO [C] Abbreviation for Associated Public-Safety Communications Officers.

apogee [NASA] The highest point reached by a satellite that is positioned in an elliptical orbit. The apogee is the position of a satellite at that point when it is farthest away from the earth's atmosphere.

APOMS [A] Abbreviation for Automated Propeller Optical Measurement.

apparatchik [USSR] A Soviet official who has power within the government administration and is feared because of that power base.

APP CON [A] Acronym for Approach Control.

Apple [C,G&PS] Slang for a nondrug user or nondrug addict.

APR [B] Abbreviation for Associated Press Radio Network.

APS [A] Abbreviation for Aircraft Prepared for Service.

APSE [C3I] Abbreviation for Ada Program Support Environment.

APT [LE] Abbreviation for Age Progression (technology) Technique, one of the most ad-

vanced tools available to law enforcement in their search for missing or lost children. Developed at the University of Illinois by scientist Scott Barrow, APT is a computer technology that enhances existing photographs of children to produce pictures of what a child might look like years after the child was kidnapped. Along with the Center for Lost and Exploited Children (1-800/THE LOST), the age progression technique has given new hope in recovering missing children.

APU [M] Abbreviation for Auxiliary Power Unit.

aquacade [I] One of the code names used for the Rhyolite satellite project. (*See* RHYOLITE.)

aquatone [I] The original code word for the development of the U-2 surveillance aircraft.

AR [TRG] Abbreviation for Azione Revoluzionaria, an Italian terrorist group closely associated with the Red Brigades.

ARB [TRG] Abbreviation for Armee Revolutionnaire Bretonne, a radical/terrorist organization based in France, associated with the Breton Liberation Front (BLF) and a known supporter of the IRA.

ARC **1.** [M] Abbreviation for Aerial Resupply and Communications (special wings of the US Air Force). **2.** [C] Abbreviation for Amateur Radio Club. **3.** [TRG] Abbreviation for a small French terrorist organization about which little is known. Members of this group are on the watch list of agents of Interpol throughout Europe.

archives [USSR] The KGB term for all central files.

area rule [A] The lengthwise distribution of an aircraft's cross-section area to minimize wave drag.

Are you holding? [C,G&PS] Slang for do you have any drugs with you?

area code [C,G&PS] Slang for gang members who are being identified by their telephone number area code. For example, "He's a 213 (Los Angeles) member of the Crips."

area-30 [M] Certain areas of military installations that are often classified as off limits. Nellis Air Force Base near Tonopah, Nevada has more than the normal share. Current intelligence indicates that Area-30 at Nellis, also known as the Mellon Strip or Sandia Strip, is the major base of operations for the F-117A stealth fighter in the United States, and headquarters to the 4450th Tactical Group, assigned to flight test the aircraft. (*See* AREA-51.)

area-51 [M] A super-secret military weapons test zone located in Nevada. Area-51 is located to the north of Nellis Air Force Base in a valley protected by surrounding high mountains and extensive military patrols.

ares [C] Abbreviation for Amateur Radio Emergency Service.

argus [M] One of the code names used to identify an advanced version of the Rhyolite satellite series. (*See* RHYOLITE.)

ariane [C] The Ariane rockets have been developed by a 13-member European Space Agency for the launching of commercial satellites. Ariane rockets are launched by Arianespace, a private French-based consortium from the Kourou space center on the Atlantic coast of French Guiana. The Ariane program now has 40 satellites set for future launches.

ARINC [A] Acronym for Aeronautical Radio, Inc., a communications link to commercial airlines.

ARIS [M] Abbreviation for Advanced Range Instrumentation Ship.

ARM **1.** [M] Abbreviation for Anti-Radar Missile. **2.** [M] Abbreviation for Anti-Radiation Missile.

army disease [C,G&PS] Slang for the addiction to opiates. The term dates from before World War I, when wounded soldiers were given morphine and cocaine to ease their pain. Many became addicted.

Army mobilization sites and American Red Cross support network In the event of a national or local emergency, most citizens of the United States mistakenly believe the American Red Cross (ARC) stands ready with support teams prepared to move into disaster areas with food,

clothing, and communications. The foundation of emergency services from the ARC is based on a volunteer program. The reality of any such given situation is that the responsibility for emergency repatriation or evacuation of U.S. citizens has been assigned to the Department of Health and Human Services (DHHS) and redelegated to the Social Security Administration's Office of Family Assistance (OFA). The ARC will most likely serve as a local conduit for the distribution of food and clothing, supporting the National Guard or active military in any mobilization effort. The communications network servicing such an operation will be the link of amateur radio volunteers organized by the ARC working with members of the Military Amateur Radio Services (MARS) groups at the military installation listed in TABLE A-1. Communication services for DHHS, OFA, ARC, and MARS stations will use the same frequencies in a national emergency situation. States not shown in this listing will rely on established internal programs or neighboring states for assistance. Most state and city governments are not prepared or staffed for a major emergency. Food and water are not being stockpiled by agencies, such as local police departments, who will need them over the long term. That same factor holds true for the majority of households in the United States. The pace and organization in major emergency and rescue efforts that involve the lives of hundreds of people always leaves a great deal to be desired. Individual preparedness and a scanner will carry you a long way toward personal survival. (*See* EMERGENCY FREQUENCIES; REPATRIATION MATRIX.)

ARPA [M] Abbreviation for Advanced Research Projects Agency. (*See* ARPANET.)

ARPANET **1.** [M] The computer network of the Advanced Research Projects Agency; a Pentagon research agency. This computer network is used by most research centers in the nation and has a sophisticated (restricted) entry code system. **2.** [US] Designation for packet switched data communications network.

Table A-1. Army Mobilization Sites and American Red Cross Network

ALABAMA

Fort McClellan — Calhoun County Chapter
407 Noble St.
Anniston, AL 36201

Fort Rucker — Dale County Chapter
215 South Merrick Ave.
Ozark, AL 36360

ALASKA

Fort Richardson — South Central Alaska
P.O. Box 1139
Anchorage, AK 99501

ARIZONA

Fort Huachuca — Huachuca Area Chapter
430 North 7th St.
Sierra Vista, AZ 85635

ARKANSAS

Fort Chaffee — Sebastian County Chapter
1709 South Greenwood Ave.
Ft. Smith, AR 72901

Camp Robinson — Pulaski County Chapter
401 South Monroe
Little Rock, AK 72205

CALIFORNIA

Fort Irwin — Victorville Police Dept.
Victorville, CA 92310

Camp Roberts — San Louis Obispo Chapter
1216 Morro St.
San Louis Obispo, CA

Fort Ord — Monterey County Chapter
942 Lupin Dr.
Salinas, CA 93906

Letterman Army Medical Center — Golden Gate Chapter
1550 Sutter St.
San Francisco, CA 94109

COLORADO

Fitzsimons Army Medical Center — Mile High Chapter
P.O. Box 6989
Denver, CO 80206

Fort Carson — Pikes Peak Chapter
1600 N. Cascade Ave.
Colorado Springs, CO 80907

FLORIDA

Camp Blanding — Northeast Florida Chapter
P.O. Box 40809
Jacksonville, FL 32203

GEORGIA

Fort Gordon — Augusta Chapter
811 12th St.
Augusta, GA 30901

Fort Benning — Muscogee County Chapter
P.O. Box 8009
Columbus, GA 31908

Fort Stewart — Georgia Lowcountry
P.O. Box 242
Hinesville, GA 31313

HAWAII

Fort Shafter — Hawaii State Chapter
P.O. Box 3948
Honolulu, HI 96812

IDAHO

Gowen Field — P.O. Box 8168
Boise, ID 83707

INDIANA

Fort Benjamin Harrison — Indianapolis Area Chapter
441 East Tenth St.
Indianapolis, IN 46202

Camp Atterbury — Indianapolis Area Chapter
441 East Tenth St.
Indianapolis, IN 46202

ILLINOIS

Fort Sheridan — Mid America Chapter
43 East Ohio St.
Chicago, IL 60611

KANSAS

Fort Riley — Geary County Chapter
116 West 8th St.
Suite #1
Junction City, KS 66441

KENTUCKY

Fort Knox — Louisville Area Chapter
P.O. Box 1675
Louisville, KY 40201

Fort Campbell — Clarksville-Montgomery
1300 Madison St.
Clarksville, TN 37040

LOUISIANA

Fort Polk — Central Louisiana Chapter
1808 Jackson St.
Alexandria, LA 71301

MARYLAND

Aberdeen Proving Ground — Baltimore Regional
2701 N. Charles St.
Baltimore, MD 21218

Fort George G. Meade — Baltimore Regional
2701 N. Charles St.
Baltimore, MD 21218

Table A-1. Continued

MASSACHUSETTS	
Camp Edwards	Cape Cod Chapter 286 South St. Hyannis, MA 02215
Fort Devens	Central Mass. Chapter 61 Harvard St. Worcester, MA 01608
MICHIGAN	
Camp Grayling	Crawford County Chapter P.O. Box 649 Grayling, MI 49738
MINNESOTA	
Camp Ripley	Morrison County Chapter Police Department HQ Swanville, MN 56382
MISSISSIPPI	
Camp Shelby	South Central Chapter 606 Hutchinson Ave. Hattiesburg, MS 39401
MISSOURI	
Fort Leonard Wood	Pulaski County Chapter c/o County Courthouse Waynesville, MO 65583
NEW JERSEY	
Fort Dix	Burlington County 254 West Union St. Burlington, NJ 08016
NEW YORK	
Fort Drum	Jefferson County 1020 State St. Watertown, NY 13601
NORTH CAROLINA	
Fort Bragg	Cumberland County Chapter P.O. Box 35041 Fayetteville, NC 28303
OKLAHOMA	
Fort Sill	Comanche County Chapter 401 Gore Blvd. Lawton, OK 73501
PENNSYLVANIA	
Fort Indiantown Gap	Lebanon County 740 Cumberland St. Lebanon, PA 17042
PUERTO RICO	
Fort Buchanan	Puerto Rico Chapter S.P.O. Box 1067 San Juan, PR 00902

SOUTH CAROLINA	
Fort Jackson	Central South Carolina P.O. Box 5495 Columbia, SC 29250
TEXAS	
Fort Hood	Killeen SMF Office 600 South Gray Killeen, TX 76541
Fort Bliss	El Paso Chapter 609 Montana St. El Paso, TX 79902
Fort Sam Houston	San Antonio Chapter 90 Brees Blvd. San Antonio, TX 78209
VIRGINIA	
Fort Belvoir	Alexandria Chapter 401 Duke St. Alexandria, VA 22314
Fort Lee AP Hill Military Reservation	Caroline County Bowling Green, VA 22427
Fort Eustis	Hampton Roads Chapter 4915 W. Mercury Blvd. Newport News, VA 23605
Fort Lee	Southside Area 120 East Washington St. Petersburg, VA 23803
Camp Pickett	Nottoway County Chapter East Irving St. Blackstone, VA 23824
Fort Story	Tidewater Chapter P.O. Box 1836 Norfolk, VA 23501
WASHINGTON (State)	
Fort Lewis	Tacoma-Pierce County 306 South 7th St. Tacoma, WA 98402
WISCONSIN	
Fort McCoy	Monroe County Chapter P.O. Box 253 Tomah, WI 54660

ARQ [C3I] Abbreviation for Automatic Repeat Request or Automatic Retransmission upon Request.

ARRADCOM [US] Acronym for Army Armament Research and Development Command.

ARRCOM [US] Acronym for Army Armament Material Readiness Command.

ARRL [C] Abbreviation for American Radio Relay League.

ARS Specialty code for arson.

Arsenal [C,G&PS] Slang for a large quantity of drugs offered for sale.

ARTADS [US] Acronym for Army Tactical Data System.

artichoke [I] The code word in the tradecraft jargon of an intelligence agency used to indicate hypnotism, drugs, or methods that are applied in a psychological evaluation.

artillery [C,G&PS] Slang for the equipment used for injecting drugs.

AS Specialty code for Answering Service.

ASA [M] Abbreviation for Army Security Agency, one of the Service Cryptologic Agencies. Its collection activities are under the authority of the director of the National Security Agency (NSA) in his capacity as the chief of the Central Security Service (CSS) of the United States government. The work of the ASA is most secret in nature and requires the highest security clearance.

ASAL [TRG] Abbreviation for Armenian Secret Army of Liberation, an Armenian terrorist group whose sole purpose is to kill Turks because of past atrocities directed toward Armenians.

ASALA [TRG] Designation for Armenian Secret Army, also known as the Armenian Secret Army of Liberation, a small, but well-trained and active group.

ASARS [C3I] Abbreviation for Advanced Synthetic Aperture Radar System.

ASAS/ENSCE [C3I] Acronym for All Source Analysis System/Enemy Situation Correlation.

ASAT [C3I] Acronym for Anti-Satellite weapon. An ASAT can be a direct-ascent missile, a coorbital satellite, a missile fired by an aircraft, or a directional energy weapon, such as a high-energy laser.

ASB Specialty code for asbestos, or asbestosis case.

ASCII [C3I] Abbreviation for American Standard Code for Information Interchange.

ASCL [US] Abbreviation for Advanced Sonobuoy Communications Link.

ASCON [US] Acronym for Automatic Switched Communications Network.

ASD [I] Abbreviation for the Administrative Survey Detachment, which creates false identification by way of references, background checks, job history, and birth records, as well as cover stories for covert operatives and intelligence agents of the United States Army.

ASI [A] Abbreviation for Air Speed Indicator.

ASIO [I] Abbreviation for Australian Secret Intelligence Organization, the secret intelligence organization of the government of Australia.

ASIOE [M] Abbreviation for Associated Support Items of Equipment.

ASL [US] Abbreviation for Atmospheric Sciences Laboratory.

ASM [M] Abbreviation for Air-to-Surface Missile.

aspect ratio [A] The ratio of the wing span to average chord in an airplane, which governs the drag caused by lift and the best glide angle.

ASPJ [C3I] Abbreviation for Airborne Self Protected Jammer.

ASRAMM [C3I] Abbreviation for Advanced Short Range Air-to-Air Missile.

ASROC [M] Acronym for Anti-Submarine Rocket.

assets **1.** [I] Technical or human resources that are made available for a security or intelligence purpose. **2.** Agents or sympathizers positioned in a target country. An asset can be trained, then sent to a country and told to wait until called upon when needed.

assessment [I] A part of the intelligence process where an analyst determines the reliability of a piece of information.

AST Specialty code for asset check.

ASU [C3I] Abbreviation for Acquisition and Synchronization Unit.

ASV [M] Abbreviation for Air-to-Surface Vessel (radar).

ASV [M] Abbreviation for Anti-Surface Vessel (missile).

ASW [C3I] Abbreviation for Anti-Submarine Warfare.

AT Specialty code for Anti-Trust.

ATA [M] Abbreviation for Advanced Tactical Aircraft.

ATAC [I] Abbreviation for Anti-Terrorist Alert Center, operated by the United States Navy. ATAC has agents at most of the U.S. Navy installations worldwide. ATAC is an intelligence-gathering arm of the Navy and works closely with the Navy SEAL Team counterterrorist units. In 1985, Jonathan Jay Pollard, an employee of ATAC, was arrested for breaching the security of this agency for selling highly classified information to the government of Israel. Pollard is serving a life sentence in a federal prison. Israel has never acknowledged Pollard was a spy.

ATACS [US] Acronym for Army Tactical Communications System.

ATACCS [C3I] Acronym for Advanced Tactical Command and Control System.

ATACMS [M] Acronym for Army Tactical Missile System.

ATARS [C3I] Acronym for Advanced Tactical Air Reconnaissance System.

ATB [M] Abbreviation for Advanced Technology Bomber (stealth).

ATBM [C3I] Abbreviation for Anti-Tactical Ballistic Missile.

ATC [US] Abbreviation for Air Training Command.

ATC 1. [C3I] Abbreviation for Adaptive Transform Coding. 2. [A] Abbreviation for Air Traffic Control. 3. [UK] Abbreviation for (British) Air Training Corps.

ATCAP [US] Acronym for Army Telecommunications Automation Program.

ATDES [C3I] Abbreviation for Adaptive Threshold Detection with Estimated Sequence.

ATDS [US] Abbreviation for Airborne Tactical Data System.

ATE [M] Abbreviation for Automatic Test Equipment.

a-team *See* A-DETACHMENT.

ATF [M] Abbreviation for Advanced Tactical Fighter (stealth).

audio frequencies for television Certain scanning receivers have the provision for wideband FM reception. The audio portion of television transmissions in the United States fall into the spectrum listed in TABLE A-2 and are defined by channel as issued by the Federal Communications Commission (FCC).

AT&F [LE] Abbreviation for Alcohol, Tobacco, and Firearms. (*See* FEDERAL LAW ENFORCEMENT NATIONWIDE COMMUNICATIONS FREQUENCIES.)

athame [S] In satanism, an athame is a ceremonial knife used in a black mass. (*See* BLACK MASS.)

ATIS [C] Abbreviation for Automatic Terminal Information Service.

atlas [HRU] Atlas, located on the Mediterranean Sea, is considered to be the best antiterrorist and hostage rescue training center in the world. Both military and civil police organizations from the western block countries have sent their senior experts to this facility to practice the latest techniques, sharpen skills, and share intelligence information. Attendance is highly selective and only by invitation.

ATM [M] Abbreviation for Anti-Tactical Missile.

ATO [M] Abbreviation for Ammunition Technical Officer.

ATT [M] Abbreviation for Army Training Test.

attitude (Bad) [C,G&PS] Slang for a sudden hostile or aggressive feeling that is outwardly expressed.

AUT Specialty code for automobiles and small trucks.

AUTODIN [C3I] Acronym for Automatic Digital Network.

AUTOP [TRG] Acronym for Workers Autonomy, based in Italy.

autopatch [C] A telephone communications linkup.

AUTOSEVCOM [US] Acronym for Automatic Secure Voice Communications.

AUTOVON [US] Acronym for Automatic Voice Network.

AUW [M] Abbreviation for All-Up Weight.

Table A-2. Audio Frequencies for Television

Channel	Audio Frequency	Channel	Audio Frequency
2	59.75	55	721.75
3	65.75	56	727.75
4	71.75	57	733.75
5	81.75	58	739.75
6	87.75	59	745.75
7	179.75	60	751.75
8	185.75	61	757.75
9	191.75	62	763.75
10	197.75	63	769.75
11	203.75	64	775.75
12	209.75	65	781.75
13	215.75	66	787.75
14	475.75	67	793.75
15	481.75	68	799.75
16	487.75	69	805.75
17	493.75		
18	499.75		
19	505.75		
20	511.75	**UHF Translator Channels**	
21	517.75	70	811.75
22	523.75	71	817.75
23	529.75	72	823.75
24	538.75	73	829.75
25	541.75	74	835.75
26	547.75	75	841.75
27	553.75	76	847.75
28	559.75	77	853.75
29	565.75	78	859.75
30	571.75	79	865.75
31	577.75	80	871.75
32	583.75	81	877.75
33	589.75	82	883.75
34	595.75	83	889.75
35	601.75		
36	607.75		
37	612.75		
38	619.75	**RCI Subchannels**	
39	625.75	01	11.25
40	631.75	02	17.25
41	637.75	03	23.25
42	643.75	04	29.25
43	649.75	05	35.25
44	655.75		
45	661.75		
46	667.75		
47	673.75		
48	679.75		
49	685.75		
50	691.75		
51	697.75		
52	703.75		
53	709.75		
54	715.75		

Table A-2. Continued

CATV Midband Channels		CATV Superband Channels	
Channel	Audio Frequency	Channel	Audio Frequency
A	125.75	J	221.75
B	131.75	K	227.75
C	137.75	L	233.75
D	143.75	M	239.75
E	149.75	N	245.75
F	155.75	O	251.75
G	161.75	P	257.75
H	167.75	Q	263.75
I	173.75	R	269.75
		S	275.75
		T	281.75
		U	287.75
		V	293.75
		W	299.75

AVB   [I] Abbreviation for *Allami Vedelmi Batosag,* the Hungarian (secret) Intelligence Service.

AVD   [C3I] Abbreviation for Alternate Voice Data.

AVESCOM   [HRU] Acronym for The Philippine Aviation Security Commando group that serves as a hostage rescue and anti-hijacking unit.

AVGAS   [A] Acronym for Aviation Gasoline; that is, fuel for aircraft piston engines.

aviation band   [A] *See* AIRCRAFT BAND.

AVRADCOM   [US] Acronym for Army Aviation Research and Development Command.

AVTUR   [A] Acronym for Aviation Turbine (fuel).

AVN   Specialty code for aviation (general aviation).

AWACS   [C3I] Abbreviation for Airborne Warning and Control System.

AWOS   [M] Abbreviation for Automated Weather Observation System.

AWS   [C3I] Abbreviation for Advanced Warning System.

AXAF   [M] Abbreviation for Advanced X-ray Astro-physics Facility, a 15-ton satellite currently under development. It is scheduled to be launched by the space shuttle in 1996 to provide data about quasars, black holes, and other bodies whose x-ray emissions give clues to the underlying cosmic process. The x-ray telescope and high-resolution mirror assembly are being built by Eastman Kodak's Federal System Division.

AZ   [C3I] Abbreviation for Azimuth, an arc of the horizon measured between a fixed point.

B

B [C] Designation for base station. Mobile transmitters are not used on this channel/frequency.

B-1B Designation for USAF bomber aircraft. The four-engine, swing-wing B-1B is the first new addition to America's manned bomber force in more than 25 years. The wings normally are swept back for high-speed attack runs, and swept forward for takeoffs and landings. Built by the Rockwell International Corp., the B-1B has a maximum speed of about 1,000 miles per hour and a range of more than 7,000 miles. Each bomber costs $280 million. The Air Force built 100 of the planes during the Reagan administration to modernize the B-52 bomber force while it developed the B-2 Stealth bomber. Several B-1B bombers have crashed for mechanical reasons, reducing the size of the fleet. The B-1B continues to have electrical problems with its radar-jamming gear. The Pentagon "black" budget gives the current estimates of comparative ranges without refueling as 6,400 miles for the B-1B and 6,000 miles for the B-2. This gives the B-1B a slightly greater edge in an actual combat situation. (*See* B-2.)

B-2 Designation for USAF Stealth bomber aircraft. The B-2 is a flying wing, superficially resembling the B-49 flying wing Northrop Aircraft built after World War II. The B-2 is powered by four General Electric F-118-GE-100 engines similar to those currently installed in the F-16 fighter; each engine produces 19,000 pounds of thrust. The height of the B-2 is 17 feet, the length is 69 feet, and the wingspan is 172 feet. The cockpit windows are gold plated to deflect any radar signal. Conspicuously absent from the design are the external pitot tubes used for measuring air speed, weapon pylons, external fuel tanks, and other protuberances usually found on combat aircraft. All such equipment strongly reflects radar. Aircraft flying at high altitude tend to create trails of vapor condensation that make them easily visible to an enemy. A highly classified development in wing cooling of the B-2 has solved that problem. The B-2 design calls for two crew members with a tentative provision for a third.

All fuel and weapons systems for the B-2 are carried internally to preserve its smooth radar-evading contours. The Air Force plans to order 132 of the B-2s for deployment in the mid-1990s at a cost the General Accounting Office estimates at about $520 million per plane. That is not likely to happen, according to members of the United States Congress who authorize military spending, because funding has already been reduced from the $520 million estimate. It is even more unlikely to happen with the world political picture changing so rapidly and borders being opened. Some planners in government believe additional B-2s will be constructed for test purposes, and as modifications are made, the testing phase will move forward with approximately a dozen aircraft.

Intelligence reports indicate an operational status of the B-2 by the mid-1990s will be superseded by funds going to maintaining existing weapon systems rather than developing new and unproven ones. Another view exists within the military: One B-2 can deliver more conventional ordnance than all the cruise missiles carried by a 688-class submarine (or a battleship)—and a submarine needs two weeks to rearm and return to station so the cost of a B-2 returns a high combat value. Supporters also contend that by using 900 new materials and processes to construct the B-2 —and with 200 on-board computers and radar nullifying technologies that give it the radar cross section of a small bird or, some say, a moth—the B-2 can defy most modern air defense systems, including those with a look-down, shoot-down capability. The B-2, which the Air Force is now flight testing, was designed as a flying wing partly to achieve better fuel efficiency. Experts have said the B-2's four engines lose some efficiency because the exhaust must be ducted and cooled to reduce the chance of detection by radar or heat-seeking defense systems. (*See* B-1B.)

B-52 Designation for currently operational Strategic Air Command (SAC) bomber aircraft. It is scheduled to remain in service until replaced by adequate numbers of the B-1B or the B-2 bomber.

BA **1.** Specialty code for burglar alarm. **2.** [A] Abbreviation for British Airways.

baby [C,G&PS] Slang for someone new in drug/narcotic usage. The term also is used as an indication of a small habit.

baby gangsters [C,G&PS] Slang for younger gang members, usually ages 11–14.

babysitter [C,G&PS] An LSD user sometimes has a bad trip. A babysitter is the person who takes care of the user who is on a bad trip.

BAC [LE] Abbreviation for Blood Alcohol Concentration.

back briefing [LE & GOV] The passing on to others of the highlights or special factors discussed at a meeting or the sharing of contents of a document containing classified information. Use of the term means that this process has the necessary security clearance or approval.

back channel [GOV] The sharing of information between members of military, or the military and the news media, by other than official channels. Back channels often are created by an agency of the military or government as a means to mislead one agency into believing certain details or information is true when, in reality, it is untrue.

backstop [I] The arrangements made through a variety of resources that support a cover story by an intelligence agent.

backtrack [C,G&PS] Slang for the process of drawing blood into a syringe during the injection of narcotics into the body.

bad [C,G&PS] Bad is good in the drug/narcotics trade. When someone says "This is really bad stuff!" he is really saying "This is really very good marijuana!"

BAe [A] Abbreviation for British Aerospace.

BAe Harrier U.S. Navy and Marine short take-off, vertical landing (VSTOL) tactical attack and reconnaissance aircraft produced by the British Aerospace Corporation. Best known in the States as the Harrier, it also is described as the GR.3 'Jump Jet.'

BAe Hawk U.S. Navy trainer, light interceptor, and light attack aircraft produced by British Aerospace. It is known in the U.S. Navy as the T-45A Goshawk. That version is produced in the United States by McDonnell Douglas.

Baader-Meinhof [TRG] Name of a terrorist/radical group that started in Germany. The group also is known as the Red Army Faction (RAF). The ideology and aims of the group are supported by a limited number of people in the U.S. The group is still under FBI investigation as "most wanted." (*See* RAF AND RED ARMY FACTION.)

back-to-back [D] In the card game of stud poker, two cards (one face up and the second face down) that are the same denomination.

backer [D] Slang for an individual who supplies gamblers with their bankroll.

bad go [C,G&PS] Slang for an insufficient amount of drugs for the money offered.

bad paper [C,G&PS] Slang for stolen or counterfeit money or securities.

bad seed [C,G&PS] Slang for the drug peyote.

bad scene [C,G&PS] Slang for a bad (unpleasant) experience.

BAFO [C3I] Abbreviation for Best And Final Offer.

bag [C,G&PS] Slang for a $5 or $10 bag of heroin. Another term sometimes used is a "nickel" ($5) or "dime" ($10) bag.

bagman 1. [C,G&PS] An individual involved in an illegal activity who collects money and delivers it to those who offer protection or some criminal act, such as the sale of drugs. 2. [GOV] An agent who pays bribes to individuals to have certain things accomplished that are usually illegal.

Bahamian Island Drug traffickers have all but taken over the Bahamian island of South Bimini, chasing off U.S. patrol boats with gunfire and intimidating the Bahamian military, according to Customs Service reports and law enforcement officials. Drug officials are reluctant to talk on the record about the situation for fear of endangering joint U.S.-Bahamian drug interdiction efforts, but say privately that the island is out of control. South Bimini is only about 45 miles from Florida. It has been raided by the Royal Bahamian Defense Force on a number of occasions. That force has been met by snipers using machine guns, according to Coast Guard and Customs Service intelligence reports. Intelligence reports indicate that drug runners have mined parts of the island.

Baikonur [I] Name of the major Soviet launch station for all Cosmodrome man-related space flights. Baikonur Cosmodrome is comparable to the Florida site of the Kennedy Space Center.

Bakuto [LE] Name of one of the three major gangster organizations involved in blackmarket operations in Japan. Other groups are the *Gurentai* and *Tekiya*.

balaclava [LE] The knitted black hood that is worn by most members of police/military hostage rescue units. It is a simple means of camouflage and hides the identity of the wearer.

bale [C,G&PS] Slang for a one-pound brick of marijuana.

ball 1. [C,G&PS] Slang term meaning to have intercourse and/or a good time. 2. [C,G&PS] Slang for the injection of cocaine into the genitals.

balloons [C,G&PS] Slang for narcotics/drugs sold in small rubber balloons or contraceptives.

bambi [C,G&PS] Slang for a mixture of heroin and desoxyn.

bamboo [C,G&PS] Slang for the paper used to make a marijuana cigarette.

bamboo tree [US] The code name for a classified communications and location system.

bancroft [US] The code name for a classified radio communications system with encryption.

bandwidth [C] The total width of a radio signal. The bandwidth can vary from a few hundred Hz when applied to continuous wave (CW) which usually is coded transmissions, to five or six MHz for television.

bandit [US] Naval aviation voice brevity code meaning an enemy aircraft ("bandit at 11 o'clock").

bang [C,G&PS] Slang for an injection of some drug.

bangalore [M] A form of pipe-bomb—sometimes called a bangalore torpedo—used to destroy a defense surrounding a building or protecting a roadway (i.e., barbed wire). A bangalore can be made by a commercial process, but usually is constructed from existing materials at hand.

bank [C,G&PS] Slang for the location where a bagman turns in his collections. This is not a bank in the usual sense of the word, but rather has to do with a collection point for illicit monies. (*See* BAGMAN.)

banker [C,G&PS] Slang for an individual or group of people who finance an illegal act.

baphomet [S] The Goat God of satanism that represents the symbols of Satan in ritual acts.

bar [C,G&PS] Slang for a blend of honey, chocolate and marijuana made into a candy bar.

barbs [C,G&PS] Slang for barbiturates. (*See* QUICK REFERENCE.)

barf [C,G&PS] Slang that means to vomit or be very sick.

barnacle [US] The code name used to define a highly classified joint Navy/CIA submarine intelligence gathering and photographic surveillance operations of Soviet military activities.

barometric chamber [LE] A pressure chamber used at some airports to check luggage for barometric bombs. Luggage is placed inside the chamber, and the pressure of the air in the chamber is then increased to simulate that pressure at high altitudes. If a bomb with a barometric fuse has been placed in the luggage, the process might explode the bomb. (*See* DOUBLE TRIGGER.)

barometric fuse [LE] A mechanical device used to detonate a bomb. The fuse is set for a specific altitude. When the aircraft or vehicle reaches that altitude, pressure by the atmosphere causes the bomb to explode.

basehead [C,G&PS] Slang for a dope user.

base station [C] The permanent location of a radio transmitter or transceiver.

bash [C,G&PS] Slang for marijuana. (*See* QUICK REFERENCE.)

BASIC [C3I] Acronym for Beginners All Purpose Symbolic Instruction Code, used in computer language.

basuco [LE] Slang for a low-grade cocaine produced in Columbia and used throughout the country by the working class people who cannot afford cocaine in a more pure form. Basuco costs approximately one-tenth of the going street price for cocaine smuggled into the United States. Widespread usage of basuco in Columbia is turning a majority of the working population into drug addicts, who then crave more powerful extracts of cocaine.

batted out [C,G&PS] Slang for being taken into custody or arrested by law enforcement officials.

baud rate [C] A unit of signal speed. A baud rate of 9600 means 9600 bits of information can be transmitted or received in one second.

BC [C] Abbreviation for broadcast or broadcasting.

BCAR [A] Abbreviation for British Civil Airworthiness Requirements.

BCD [C3I] Abbreviation for Binary-Coded Decimal.

BCRA [D] Abbreviation for Bureau Central de Renseignements et Action (French).

BCS **1.** [M] Abbreviation for Battery Computer System. **2.** [US] Battlefield Computer System.

BDCS [C3I] Abbreviation for Below Deck Communications System.

B-detachment [M] A 23-man command-and-control element of U.S. Special Forces. The B-Detachment staff normally is charged with controlling and supporting four A-Detachments.

BDLC [C3I] Abbreviation for Bissync Data Link Control.

beacon [C] A radio transmitter that operates continuously. The beacon indicates the exact location of an aircraft in flight, a static navigational aid, a ship at sea, or a satellite as it circles the earth.

beam [C] A beam is a directional antenna system that is composed of several elements that are parallel to each other.

beans [C,G&PS] Slang for amphetamines. (*See* QUICK REFERENCE.)

beard [LE] Slang for an individual who makes bets with a bookie for a syndicate. A beard is also an individual who works with doped horses.

beat **1.** [C,G&PS] Slang for physically tired. **2.** [C,G&PS] Slang for out of narcotics. **3.** [C,G&PS] Slang for to cheat someone.

beat for dough [C,G&PS] Slang for when a drug dealer steals the money given to him for dope or narcotics.

beaut music [B] Slang for beautiful music.

be away [C,G&PS] Slang term meaning to be incarcerated—put into jail or prison.

bedbug letter [GOV] Slang for a response to a government letter of complaint that generally is nonresponsive to the actual situation. The term comes from early letters written by members of Congress who traveled to various cities and found bedbugs in the hotel rooms where they slept. The term has remained active in government usage for more than 100 years.

bells and whistles [GOV] A term closely related to government and military spending for items that appeal to the buyer because of accessories or devices that make the product more appealing, rather than better or of a higher quality.

belly [C,G&PS] Slang term meaning to ingest drugs by mouth.

belong [C,G&PS] Slang term meaning to have a serious narcotic or drug habit.

belt [C,G&PS] Slang for the euphoria resulting from narcotic usage.

belted [C,G&PS] Slang for an individual who is under the influence of some narcotic.

bender [C,G&PS] Slang for a drug or drinking orgy.

Benji [C,G&PS] Slang for a $100 bill, referring to Benjamin Franklin on the face.

bennies [C,G&PS] Slang for benzedrine tablets.

bent 1. [C,G&PS] Slang for an individual who is addicted to narcotics and is depressed by them. 2. [US] A naval aviation voice brevity code meaning whatever the item under discussion (aircraft, weapon system, etc.,) is inoperative.

benzedrine [LE] A controlled substance that is a stimulant. (*See* QUICK REFERENCE.)

BER [C3I] Abbreviation for Bit Error Rate, used when referring to computers.

Beredskapstrop [HRU] The Readiness Troops of the Norwegian National Police for any hostage rescue requirement in Norway.

Bernie [C,G&PS] From Bernhard Goetz, the New York City subway self-styled vigilante who shot some thugs who approached him, a street slang term used by police to refer to a crime victim who could be armed and ready to use a weapon.

Bernie's flakes [C,G&PS] Slang for cocaine. (*See* QUICK REFERENCE.)

Bernice [C,G&PS] Slang for cocaine. (*See* QUICK REFERENCE.)

BFO [C] Abbreviation for Beat-Frequency Oscillator, an internal receiving oscillator in a radio receiver that enables clear reception of Morse code and single sideband signals.

BfV [I] Abbreviation for *Bundesamt fur Verfassungsschutz*, the Federal Internal Security Office and Headquarters for all West German counterespionage units. Responsible to the Minister of the Interior, the BfV is the domestic counterintelligence branch of the West German government.

BFV [US] Abbreviation for Bradley Fighting Vehicle.

bhang [C,G&PS] The ground (powdered) version of hashish that is eaten in pill form or used to make marijuana tea.

BI [I] Abbreviation for Background Investigation. For a government or military security clearance at the lowest level, a BI consists of verification of birth, education, citizenship, employment for the past five years, and passport usage/travel outside the United States. In addition, a review is made of the files of all federal agencies for derogatory information. The BI is known as a National Agency Check (NAC). A review of records kept by the National Crime Information Center (NCIC) is made to determine if a criminal record exists. A check of the individuals credit history also is a part of the background investigation.

BICES [M] Abbreviation for Battlefield Information Collection and Exploitation System.

big C [C,G&PS] Slang for cocaine. (*See* QUICK REFERENCE.)

big chief [C,G&PS] Slang for peyote. (*See* QUICK REFERENCE.)

big D [C,G&PS] Slang for LSD. (*See* QUICK REFERENCE.)

big guy [LE] Slang for the primary suspect used in intelligence/surveillance.

big harry [C,G&PS] Slang for heroin. (*See* QUICK REFERENCE.)

big house [C,G&PS] Slang for a penal institution such as a prison or jail facility.

big John [C,G&PS] Slang for law enforcement officer, that is a policeman or a policewoman.

big man [C,G&PS] Slang for an individual who supplies narcotics.

big O [C,G&PS] Slang for opium. (*See* QUICK REFERENCE.)

big one [I] Slang for a major street or intersection used in intelligence/surveillance.

big ribbon [I] Slang for a major highway involved in an intelligence or a surveillance operation.

bigot list [GOV] A list of the individuals who have access to a particular and highly sensitive class of information. *Bigot* is an indicator meaning narrow.

bind [S] In satanism, to cast a spell on a person, place, or thing.

bindle [C,G&PS] A small quantity of narcotic usually packaged for street sale in a folded sheet of paper is called a bindle.

bing 1. [C,G&PS] The slang term for isolation cells in a penal institution or jail. 2. [C,G&PS] A slang term that means to inject narcotics.

bingle [C,G&PS] Slang for an individual who supplies narcotics.

bingo 1. [C,G&PS] Slang term that means to inject narcotics. 2. [US] Naval aviation voice brevity code meaning a minimum of fuel remains for a safe return to base.

bingo field [US] Naval aviation voice brevity code meaning an alternate landing field.

bio lever [I] Abbreviation for biographic leverage, a term used in covert intelligence to indicate that because of someone's past activities he or she might be a target for blackmail.

biometrics [LE] Shortened form of biometrics technologies, a way to identify people by using a physical characteristic that is unique to each individual. Biometrics is used to make sure that unauthorized persons cannot enter restricted areas of buildings or get personal or sensitive information from computers. Law enforcement and government agencies, banks, research laboratories, and airlines are now using biometrics. The physical characteristics used as biometric identifiers include fingerprints, voice patterns, signature styles, and retinal patterns. (*See* RETINAL PATTERNS.)

biphetamine [LE] A controlled substance that is a stimulant. (*See* QUICK REFERENCE.)

BIR [US] Abbreviation for the Bureau of Intelligence and Research, a principal intelligence gathering agency of the United States government. Responsible for strategic intelligence, the BIR evaluates weapons and tactics of foreign governments.

bird dog [LE] Slang for surveillance aircraft.

birds [US] Naval aviation voice brevity code meaning guided missiles.

birdseye [C,G&PS] Slang for a tiny amount of drugs or narcotic.

biscuits [C,G&PS] Slang for methadone tablets that have been broken into small pieces.

bistatic radar [M] Radar that uses transmitters and receivers that are not together but placed in different locations, possibly both on the ground or one on the ground and the other on a satellite. The receiver thus could "see" reflections that are deflected away from the transmitter by Stealth aircraft. (*See* CARRIER-FREE RADAR.)

bit [C,G&PS] Slang for a term in jail or prison.

bite 1. [M] Abbreviation for Built-In Test Equipment. 2. [C,G&PS] In the drug/narcotics trade, a bite is a bribe or a piece of the action.

biz [C,G&PS] Slang for the needle and syringe used for the injection of drugs.

BKG Specialty code for background investigation.

black 1. [I] Of or referring to a reliance (or usage) of concealment involving a specific activity. A black operation might be concerned with an illegal method or tactic or could be considered covert. 2. [C,G&PS] Slang for opium. (*See* QUICK REFERENCE.)

black acid [C,G&PS] Slang for LSD. (*See* QUICK REFERENCE.)

black bag job [I] Slang for the warrantless and surreptitious entry of a building, individual office, or facility complex for purposes other than electronic surveillance where the actual reason is to conduct a physical search of the premises and take photographs, documents, or personal property. A black bag job also is any act of bribery to accomplish an illegal activity.

black beauties [C,G&PS] Slang for biamphetamines, also known by drug chemists as amphetamine sulphate.

blackbird [M] Designation for the SR-71A high-altitude reconnaissance aircraft called the Blackbird because of its black epoxy surface. The SR-71A is 107.4 feet long with a wingspan of 55.6 feet and a fuselage 5.34 feet in diameter.

The engines are Pratt & Whitney J-58 turbojets. The JT-7 fuel is unique to the SR-71. It is nonvolatile (does not burn). The engines must be started chemically using a substance known as polyethyl bromide (PEB). Once airborne, the SR-71A is completely computer controlled (*See* SR-71.)

blackbirds   [C,G&PS] Slang for amphetamines. (*See* QUICK REFERENCE.)

black bombers   [C,G&PS] Slang for amphetamine sulphate.

black box   [A] An aircraft's flight data or cockpit voice recorders. The information from these devices is considered so crucial that the U.S. Federal Aviation Administration made them mandatory on commuter and commercial aircraft in 1988. Although the devices sound mysterious, they are actually quite simple. Contained in a tough metal and plastic casing and mounted in a shockproof base, the black boxes—they actually are painted bright orange to make them more visible in an aircraft's wreckage—are just glorified tape recorders. The flight data recorder receives information about airspeed, direction, altitude, acceleration, and engine thrust from sensors that are scattered around the aircraft. It translates the data into numbers and records it on a type of magnetic tape similar to that used in a home videocassette recorder. This digital information can be recovered after a crash to determine why the plane went down. For example, a sudden loss of speed, engine thrust, and altitude would indicate that the problem was mechanical. The cockpit voice recorder records the voices of the flight crew before a crash and compares it with information gathered by the data recorder.

black gold   [C,G&PS] Slang for distilled and concentrated heroin.

blackhawk   A military helicopter favored by federal drug enforcement agencies as a chase aircraft of narcotic smugglers.

Black June   [TRG] Nickname for Black June Organization, a radical terrorist Palestinian group.

black magick   [S] In the practice of satanism, black magick is the evil believed to kill or injure. The word *magick* is usually spelled with a *k* to indicate the difference from common usage and the magic of sleight-of-hand.

black mass   [S] An unholy gathering of satanists where prayers to Satan are said backward, the candles used are black rather than white, and communion can include the eating of human flesh and the drinking of blood.

black molly   [C,G&PS] Slang for diet pills sold in the form of black capsules.

black mote   [C,G&PS] Slang for marijuana that is mixed with honey.

black propaganda   [I] Propaganda that can include photographs, documents, news releases, and other information that purports to come from a source other than the true one.

black rain   [CW] Slang for an unknown compound developed by the Soviet Union that causes instant death when dispersed by low-flying aircraft. Black Rain was first reported used by Soviet troops in Afghanistan.

black Russian   [C,G&PS] Slang for black opium.

Black September   [TRG] A radical Palestinian group best known for its involvement in the massacre at the Olympic Games in Munich, Germany. The Black September organization took its name from the month in which King Hussein ordered his Arab Legion to attack the Palestinians in Jordan. The Black September movement is known to have financial supporters in the western United States.

black stuff   [C,G&PS] Slang for opium. (*See* QUICK REFERENCE.)

black tabs   [C,G&PS] Slang for LSD. (*See* QUICK REFERENCE.)

black tar   [C,G&PS] Slang for distilled and concentrated heroin.

black tar heroin   [LE] Slang for Mexican black heroin, which is sold in lumps and accounts for about 75 percent of the heroin sold in the United States. The rest is a white or golden powder, often imported from Southeast Asia. The strength of black tar heroin can vary greatly from batch to batch. Solid heroin is liquefied over a flame and injected by syringe. Sometimes it is smoked or sniffed. The majority of black tar heroin is cut or diluted with a variety of inert materials. Used uncut, it is highly dangerous. If someone normally needs two injections to get high, he might choose instead to double his first injection, without being aware of what he is putting in his system. A typical experience is a rapid feeling of euphoria and then, if the dosage is high enough, a stoppage of breathing, suddenly. Black tar heroin destroys the user's entire impulse to breathe within seconds of administering the drug intravenously. If the victim is not given artificial respiration and an injection of naloxone hydrochloride within minutes he will die. Naloxone hydrochloride counteracts many of heroin's neurological effects.

black trainee   [I] A foreign student or businessperson receiving training in undercover/covert methods employed by the Central Intelligence Agency (CIA) at one of its facilities in the United States. When the black trainee graduates, he or she is returned to his or her country to serve as a mole or intelligence agent.

blade   [C,G&PS] Slang for a knife.

blanca   [C,G&PS] Slang for heroin. (*See* QUICK REFERENCE.)

blanco   [C,G&PS] Slang for Mexican heroin.

blank   1. [C,G&PS] Slang for a packet of nonnarcotic powder that is sold as heroin. 2. Low-grade drugs or narcotics.

blast   [C,G&PS] Slang for the strong effect on an individual from the uses of a narcotic.

blast a stick   [C,G&PS] Slang meaning to smoke a marijuana cigarette.

blast party   [C,G&PS] Slang for a marijuana party involving several people.

blasted   [C,G&PS] Slang for an individual who is under the influence of alcohol or drugs.

blaster   1. [C,G&PS] Slang for an expert on explosives. 2. [C,G&PS] Slang for a marijuana smoker.

bleed air   [A] An aviation term indicating the extraction of gas from a turbine engine to provide power or heat.

bleep box   [I] A multifrequency simulator designed to recreate tones and frequencies used in the telephone systems of various countries. With this device, the secret telephone numbers of many organizations, criminal operations, and spy networks around the world have been decoded. There are a variety of bleep box designs used, including those that act remotely.

BLF   [TRG] Abbreviation for Breton Liberation Front, a Marxist separatist (terrorist) movement with headquarters in Paris. They also are known in France as the FLB (Front de Liberation de la Bretogne) or the ARB (Armee Revolutionnaire Bretonne). The BLF has a number of factions, each with a different name, as much to confound the police as to show their individuality. All the factions are known to have links to the Irish Republican Army (IRA).

blind munchies   [C,G&PS] Slang for the hunger for food that is frequently brought on by the use of marijuana.

BLIS   [C3I] Abbreviation for Buried Line Intrusion Sensor.

block   [C,G&PS] Slang for a bundle of morphine.

blocked   [C,G&PS] Slang for an individual high on drugs.

Bloods   [C,G&PS] A predominantly black gang formed in the mid-1970s in Compton, California. Membership in the southern California area is estimated at 12,500 and growing daily. Membership beyond the southern California area is unknown but does exist. There are more than 70 offshoot groups (sets) of the Bloods in the Los Angeles area alone. Members are easily identified by their red bandanas, red warm-up suits, red shoelaces, Cincinnati Reds baseball caps, khakis, and track shoes. Another indicator of membership is a heart tattoo to symbolize a circulating blood.

blow   1. [C,G&PS] Slang for a lost opportunity. 2. [C,G&PS] Slang for cocaine. (*See* QUICK REFERENCE.) 3. [C,G&PS] Slang meaning to inhale a drug. **4.** [I] Slang meaning to expose—often unintentionally—some personal information, or other elements of a clandestine operation.

blow a stick [C,G&PS] Slang meaning to smoke a marijuana cigarette.

blow a vein [C,G&PS] Slang for the failure to enter a vein when injecting drugs or narcotics.

blow away [C,G&PS] Slang meaning to kill a person.

blow charlie [C,G&PS] Slang for the process of snorting cocaine up the nose. The most common (and flashy) way to blow charlie is with a rolled up $100 bill.

blow horse [C,G&PS] Slang term meaning to snort heroin, rather than inject it.

blow up [C,G&PS] Slang term meaning to kill a person.

blown [I] Slang for being discovered, either as a person or group.

blown flap [A] A wing flap on an aircraft with bleed air discharged over the upper surface to draw with it the surrounding flow, and thus prevent separations.

blue acid [C,G&PS] Slang for LSD. (*See* QUICK REFERENCE.)

blue angels [C,G&PS] Slang for the barbiturate amytal.

blue birds [C,G&PS] Slang for barbiturates. (*See* QUICK REFERENCE.)

blue bullets [C,G&PS] Slang for barbiturates. (*See* QUICK REFERENCE.)

blue cheer [C,G&PS] Slang for LSD and methedrine blended together.

blue devils [C,G&PS] Slang for various barbiturates.

blue dolls [C,G&PS] Slang for barbiturates. (*See* QUICK REFERENCE.)

blue heavens [C,G&PS] Slang for barbiturates, usually sodium amytal tablets.

blue light [M] The interim antiterrorist unit formed by the Special Forces branch of the United States Army until Delta Force became operational. Many of the Blue Light experts continue to serve as consultants to antiterrorism

organizations (within government and law enforcement) on a worldwide basis.

blue lightning [LE] Slang for a high-speed patrol and chase boat used by drug enforcement agencies.

blues [C,G&PS] Slang for barbiturates. (*See* QUICK REFERENCE.)

blue sky [C,G&PS] Slang for heroin. (*See* QUICK REFERENCE.)

blue thunder [LE] Slang for a high-speed patrol (thunder) boat used for drug enforcement by the U.S. Coast Guard and DEA.

blue tips [C,G&PS] Slang for barbiturates. (*See* QUICK REFERENCE.)

blue velvet [C,G&PS] Slang for a mixture of paregoric and pyrobenzomine.

blue water [C,G&PS] Slang for LSD. (*See* QUICK REFERENCE.)

blue X [CW] The composition of this chemical warfare agent developed by the Soviet Union is unknown. It was created to incapacitate human beings for periods estimated at 1 to 2 and 8 to 12 hours. It can be dispersed by entry into a water system or sprayed from low-flying aircraft.

BMD [C3I] Abbreviation for Ballistic Missile Defense.

BMEW [C3I] Abbreviation for Ballistic Missile Early Warning.

BMEWS [M] Abbreviation for Ballistic Missile Early-Warning System.

BMO [C3I] Abbreviation for Ballistic Missile Office.

BND [I] Designation for West German Federal Intelligence Service. The BND is responsible for all military and strategic intelligence operations, electronic intercept, and foreign counterintelligence.

BNE [US] Abbreviation for Board of National Estimates.

BNK Specialty code for bank and accounting fraud.

BOA Specialty code for boating accident.

boat [I] A term used in intelligence/surveillance operations to indicate a specific automobile.

bobo bush   [C,G&PS] Slang for marijuana. (*See* QUICK REFERENCE.)

body armor   [LE] Slang for a bullet-proof vest.

bogart a joint   [C,G&PS] Slang meaning to cup a marijuana cigarette in the hand so as to hide it and not to share the cigarette with others.

bogey   [US] Naval aviation voice brevity code meaning unidentified air contact—assume hostile.

bogie   [LE] Slang for someone who is a visitor at a facility in the law enforcement community and is not known by the agency.

BOM   [LE] Abbreviation for Beginning of Month.

Bombay black   [C,G&PS] Slang for a very powerful Indian-made hashish.

bomber   1. [C,G&PS] Slang for an oversized marijuana cigarette. 2. [C,G&PS] Slang for a very powerful and highly skilled attorney.

bombitas   [C,G&PS] Slang for desoxyn, an amphetamine that is used with heroin. This blending gives the user a much more powerful high than heroin alone.

bona fides   [I] Various materials, such as information or supporting documents, that form a foundation of good faith and establishes a mutual trust between a contact and an intelligence agent.

bong   [C,G&PS] Slang for a smoking pipe with hashish or marijuana used by drug addicts.

bonita   [C,G&PS] Slang for the milk sugar used to cut heroin.

boo   [C,G&PS] A popular term for marijuana used among musicians.

boo coo   [C,G&PS] Slang for an excessive amount of drugs or money.

boogie   [C,G&PS] Slang term meaning to move on. The term also is used among the college crowd for narcotics/drug running.

book   [LE] Slang for bookmaker or bookie.

bookie   [LE] Slang for an individual who accepts bets.

boost   [LE] Slang term meaning to steal, usually shoplifting.

boostering   [LE] Slang term meaning to sell or give to someone property that has been stolen.

boot   [C,G&PS] The process by which a heroin user injects heroin into a vein, draws his blood back into the syringe and mixes it with the heroin, and then reinjects the blend into his body. Drug users have said this method of injection creates a more powerful and lasting effect.

boryokudan   [LE] Japanese meaning "groups that promote violence." This term is used by law enforcement agencies in Japan referring to the *yakuza*, Japan's criminal underworld. Members of the yakuza have infiltrated the activities of Japanese businessmen in the United States and have resorted to extortion in west coast cities. (*See* YAKUZA.)

bocso   [LE] A synthetic form of heroin produced in South America, also known as P-funk.

bosozoku   [LE] The young motorcycle gangs in Japan. The bosozoku are young thugs who ride motorcycles and rob people in the streets, then ride away.

boss   1. [C,G&PS] Slang for an individual who is in control of a drug or narcotics sales operation. 2. Abbreviation for Bureau of State Security of the Government of South Africa. The actual name of the State Security branch is the National Intelligence Service, but the old initials are still used.

botanica   [LE] An underground shop that offers animals, herbs, and ritual devices used by members of the cult of Santeria. (*See* SANTERIA, THE CULT.)

bouncing powder   [C,G&PS] Slang for cocaine. (*See* QUICK REFERENCE.)

box   [I] In intelligence/surveillance operations, a specific van-type vehicle that is suspect or under surveillance.

boxed   [C,G&PS] Slang term meaning to be examined by a polygraph, that is, a lie detector.

boxman   [LE] Slang for the individual in a gambling operation that places the house winnings in a secure area, such as a locked box.

boy   1. [C,G&PS] Slang for heroin. (*See* QUICK REFERENCE.) 2. [A,LE,MIL] Designation for the letter *B*.

BPC [HRU] Abbreviation for *Bataillon de Parachutistes de Choc*, a crack French military paratroop unit also known as Berets Rouges, (Red Berets) active in counterterrorist operations in Europe.

BPSK [C3I] Abbreviation for Binary Phase Shift Keying.

B/R [M] Abbreviation for Bistatic Radar. (*See* BISTATIC RADAR.)

bracero Literally, the Mexican term for someone who works with his arms. The word has come to designate the migrant farm workers who come from Mexico to the United States searching for work. Often they will bring marijuana across the border in place of pocket money.

brainwashed [D] Of or referring to the object of any psychological technique that alters the human thought processes, loyalty, and personal motivations.

Bravo [A,LE,MIL] Designation for the letter *B*.

breaching [LE] Gaining entry into a confined area where criminal elements conduct their activities or a hostage situation exists. To breach an area can involve something as simple as a shoulder against a door or explosives to blow it down.

bread [C,G&PS] Slang for money or stolen property. This term has come to mean anything of value.

break a needle [C,G&PS] Slang term meaning to break a drug or narcotic habit.

break off [I] Slang meaning to terminate surveillance.

brick [C,G&PS] Slang for a kilogram of marijuana in brick form.

bridge [C,G&PS] Slang for a device used to hold a marijuana cigarette so it can be smoked to the very end.

briefing [LE] Term for a meeting that describes a situation that will be encountered, the methods that will be used, and the objectives of the enforcement agencies involved.

Brigate Rosse [TRG] The Red Brigades faction headquartered in Italy. (*See* RED BRIGADE.)

brilliant pebbles [M] Slang for a tiny satellite equipped with a communication system, small supercomputer, maneuverable propulsion engine, wide-angle television cameras, and electronic sensors. The design does not call for a weapon or warhead of any kind. If a missile strike were launched against the United States, the pebbles in the closest orbit would come to life and—traveling at more than 6 miles per second—would crash into the missile, guided by the TV system and tracking on the hot exhaust that is the calling card of a nuclear-tipped ballistic missile early in its flight pattern. Prototypes of the brilliant pebbles interceptor satellite are undergoing testing at the Air Force Astronautics Laboratory at Edwards Air Force Base in California. It is reported that each satellite weighs approximately 150 pounds and is about four feet long.

bring down [C,G&PS] Slang for the feeling an individual has when the effect of a drug or narcotic has worn off.

Broadcast Media Frequency Assignments, nationwide Although individual television and radio stations in your area probably have a communications network used by their working staff, a specific number of frequencies have been set aside for live remote operations, network feeds, news gathering, and airborne traffic reports. Those unique nationwide frequency assignments are listed in TABLE B-1.

brody [C,G&PS] A term used by addicts to refer to the process of pretending they are ill in order to get drugs from an unsuspecting physician.

broken arrow [M] The coded term used by the Navy to describe accidents involving nuclear weapons.

broker [C,G&PS] Slang for a narcotics or drug dealer.

brother 1. [C,G&PS] Slang for a police officer who is black. Most black law enforcement officers dislike the usage of this term because it can refer to an officer who might or might not be friend or associate. 2. [CW] Slang for a chemical or device that appears to be dangerous when, in reality, it is not. 3. [US] Naval aviation voice

Table B-1. Broadcast Media Frequency Assignments, Nationwide

25.87	450.050	455.050
25.91	450.0875	455.0875
25.95	450.100	455.100
25.99	450.1125	455.1125
26.03	450.1375	455.1375
26.07	450.150	455.150
26.09	450.1625	455.1625
26.11	450.1875	455.1875
26.13	450.200	455.200
26.15	450.2125	455.2125
26.17	450.2375	455.2375
26.19	450.250	455.250
26.21	450.2625	455.2625
26.23	450.2875	455.2875
26.25	450.300	455.300
26.27	450.3125	455.3125
26.29	450.3375	455.3375
26.31	450.350	455.350
26.33	450.3625	455.3625
26.35	450.3875	455.3875
26.37	450.400	455.400
26.39	450.4125	455.4125
26.41	450.4375	455.4375
26.43	450.450	455.450
26.45	450.4625	455.4625
26.47	450.4875	455.4875
	450.500	455.500
	450.5125	455.5125
	450.5375	455.5375
161.640	450.550	455.550
161.670	450.5625	455.5625
161.700	450.5875	455.5875
161.730	450.600	455.600
161.760	450.6125	455.6125
	450.650	455.650
	450.700	455.700
	450.750	455.750
166.250	450.800	455.800
	450.850	455.850
	450.900	455.900
170.150	450.925	455.925

brevity code meaning an attack is underway on ships of surface antisubmarine warfare (ASW) unit.

brown 1. [C,G&PS] Slang for amphetamines. (*See* QUICK REFERENCE.) 2. [C,G&PS] Slang for Mexican-made heroin.

brown dot [C,G&PS] Slang for LSD. (*See* QUICK REFERENCE.)

brownie [US] Naval aviation voice brevity code meaning a photo mission. The term derives from the Brownie camera produced by the Eastman Kodak Company.

brown shoes [C,G&PS] Slang for an individual who is not a drug user.

brush contact [I] Slang for a quick prearranged meeting between intelligence agents where materials often are exchanged.

BSC [C3I] Abbreviation for Binary Synchronous Communications.

BSTS [C3I] Abbreviation for Booster Surveillance and Tracking System.

BTP [C3I] Abbreviation for Burst Time Plan.

bubble machine [I] Slang for a voice scrambler used in telephone and radio communications. Two or more units are required to create scrambled communications in a radio or telephone system.

buckets [C,G&PS] Slang for a small caliber handgun or a shotgun.

bug 1. [I] Slang for a hidden listening device, usually a radio transmitter. The audio surveillance of someone can mean to install a bug, which can be a microphone or recording system. 2. [LE] A term used by some police officers indicating a criminal who they believe has little or no feelings toward a victim.

bugged [I] Slang term meaning to contain a hidden listening or recording device for the purpose of eavesdropping.

bulldog [C,G&PS] Slang for a rough operator—a really tough thug.

bumble bee [LE] Slang for surveillance helicopter.

bummer [C,G&PS] Slang for a bad experience using narcotics.

bundle [C,G&PS] Slang for five-dollar bags of heroin, Bundles usually consist of twelve to fifteen packets of heroin.

burakumin [LE] In Japan, the *burakumin* are members of the class of ancestral outcasts and a primary source of recruits for the *yakuza*, Japan's criminal underworld. (*See* YAKUZA.)

Bureau of Prisons [US] Nationwide radio frequencies used by the federal Bureau of Prisons are listed in TABLE B-2. (*See also* LEVEL 6/5/4/3/2/1.)

Table B-2. Bureau of Prisons Radio Frequencies

Type	F	Input	Output	Tone
Operations	1		170.875	none
Operations	2		170.925	none
Emergency	3		170.650	none
Repeaters T2		163.8125	163.200	none
Repeaters T3		163.8125	163.200	none
Repeaters T4		163.8125	163.200	none
Repeaters T5		163.8125	163.200	none
Court Security 1			170.850	none
Court Security 2			170.750	none

burn [C,G&PS] In the marijuana trade, to **1.** the peddling of phony grass after good grass has been promised. **2.** being paid for the marijuana and then not making a delivery. The theft of money or drugs.

burn(ed) [LE] Slang term meaning to be identified during surveillance.

burnt [I] Slang term meaning to be compromised.

burst transmission [M] Messages that are transmitted rapidly by some mechanical or electronic means to thwart any hostile direction-finding surveillance effort.

bury [I] To conceal source-sensitive intelligence information within the body of a conversation or written report.

bus [LE] Slang for ambulance.

bush [C,G&PS] Slang for marijuana. (*See* QUICK REFERENCE.)

business [C,G&PS] Slang for the hardware used for the injection of drugs.

businessman's special [C,G&PS] Slang for dimethyltryptamine, DMT, a synthetic chemical similar to psilocybin and LSD.

bust [C,G&PS] Slang term meaning to arrest an individual.

busted [C,G&PS] Slang for arrested.

buster **1.** [C,G&PS] Slang for an individual (considered by both law enforcement authorities and gang members as a phony) who goes from one gang to another. **2.** [US] Naval aviation voice brevity code meaning to fly at a continuous maximum speed.

butter [C,G&PS] Slang for marijuana. (*See* QUICK REFERENCE.)

buttons [C,G&PS] Small sections of the peyote cactus plant.

buy [C,G&PS] The purchase of drugs, usually made by an undercover police officer, when used in the course of a conversation.

buzz **1.** [C,G&PS] Slang for a chemical high that is drug induced. **2.** [LE] Slang term meaning to quickly arrest someone on the street. **3.** [C,G&PS] Slang for an hallucinogenic LSD derivative developed for the U.S. military for chemical warfare applications. (*See* BZ.)

buzzing [C,G&PS] Slang for searching for someone interested in selling drugs.

BVR [M] Abbreviation for Beyond Visual Range, used when referring to engagements or missiles.

BW **1.** [C3I] Abbreviation for bandwidth. **2.** [M] Abbreviation for Bacteriological Warfare.

BWA [C] Abbreviation for Backward Wave Amplifier.

BWO [C] Abbreviation for Backward Wave Oscillator.

bypass ratio [A] In aviation, the ratio of the air that bypasses the basic gas generator of a turbofan to the flow that goes through it. The higher the bypass, the more economical the engine.

BZ [US] A chemical agent, also called buzz, that is a hallucinogenic LSD derivative which, most likely, would be dispersed into the water system.

C

C [C,G&PS] Slang for cocaine. (*See* QUICK REFERENCE.)

CA [CW] Designation for tear gas, (brombenzyl cyanide) a chemical agent used by law enforcement agencies and the military. It is long acting, and causes the eyes to tear and smart.

C3 [M] Abbreviation for Command, Control, and Communications.

C3CM Abbreviation for Command, Control, and Communications Countermeasures.

C3I Abbreviation for command, control, communications, and intelligence.

C-4 **1.** [M] Designation for plastic explosive used by the U.S. military. **2.** [M] Designation for Trident I missile.

C-130 Designation for a four-engine transport aircraft used for multipurpose applications by military and government agencies. The C-130 is manufactured by Lockheed Aircraft and also is called the Lockheed Hercules.

C-141 Designation for the Lockheed StarLifter, which is much larger than the C-130 and was designed to carry heavy loads of troops and cargo. The C-141 requires extensive runway space.

CAA [A] Abbreviation for Civil Aviation Administration (British).

CAB [US] Abbreviation Civil Aeronautics Board.

caballo [C,G&PS] Slang for heroin. (*See* QUICK REFERENCE.)

cacklebladder [I] An intelligence term used by a variety of agencies that denotes a method used to make a living human being appear dead.

cactus [C,G&PS] Slang for peyote or mescaline.

CAD/CAM [C3I] Abbreviation for Computer Aided-Design/Computer Aided-Manufacturing.

CAE [C3I] Abbreviation for Computer-Aided Engineering.

Caesar [I] The code name that defines the initial Sound Surveillance System (designed to detect submarines) along the East Coast of the United States. (*See* COLOSSUS.) This system involves the installation of sensors underwater.

CAI [C3I] Abbreviation for Computer-Aided Instruction.

CAL [TRG] Abbreviation for Commandos Armados de Liberacion, a terrorist group headquartered in Puerto Rico.

California sunshine [C,G&PS] Slang for LSD. (*See* QUICK REFERENCE.)

caller ID [I] An electronic device that enables the receiver of a telephone call to view on a display the telephone number of the caller's phone, even if that number is unlisted. The device is currently in use by some law enforcement agencies and is available from commercial telephone stores for personal use at a cost of about $70 and a monthly service charge.

callsign codes *See* AMATEUR RADIO PREFIX CALLSIGN CODES, INTERNATIONAL.

CALS [M] Abbreviation for Computer-Aided Acquisition and Logistics Support.

CAM [M] Abbreviation for Computerized Alert Monitor.

CAMP [LE] Abbreviation for Campaign Against Marijuana Planting, a joint state-federal-local effort to eradicate the growing of marijuana on private land or in the National forests.

CAMP [M] Abbreviation for Computer-Aided Message Processing.

CAMPS [NATO] Abbreviation for Computer-Assisted Message Processing System.

Canadian quail [C,G&PS] Slang for methaqualone. (*See* QUICK REFERENCE.)

can of 'M' [C,G&PS] Slang for roughly 1½ ounces of marijuana.

can of 'O' [C,G&PS] Slang for approximately 3¹/₂ ounces of opium.

canard [A] A term used in aviation meaning a fore-plane, or an aircraft with a foreplane or wing in the very front of the craft.

canary [C,G&PS] Slang for an individual marked as an informer.

candy [C,G&PS] Slang for cocaine. (*See* QUICK REFERENCE.)

candyman [C,G&PS] Slang for a dealer of drugs or narcotics.

canehead [C,G&PS] Slang for a user seeking crack cocaine for personal use.

canned [C,G&PS] Slang term meaning to be placed under arrest.

cannon **1.** [C,G&PS] Slang for a hypodermic syringe and needle. **2.** [C,G&PS] Slang for a firearm, usually a handgun. **3.** [I] Slang term for a professional thief employed by an intelligence agency.

Cap **1.** [C,G&PS] Slang for a capsule of some narcotic or drug. **2.** [C,G&PS] Slang term meaning to shoot someone.

CAP [M] Abbreviation for Combat Air Patrol.

capman [C,G&PS] Slang for an individual who supplies drugs.

Capo Bastone [I] The word *Capo* means head. In the Mafia, a Capo Bastone is the head boss.

Capo Crimini [I] A term used in the Cosa Nostra (Mafia) to denote the highest-ranking boss.

capping someone [C,G&PS] A slang term meaning to shoot (kill) an individual. The term is used in an aggressive (hateful) manner.

carburetor [C,G&PS] Slang for a handcrafted smoking pipe used with marijuana.

CAREME [FRANCE] Abbreviation for *Centre Automatique de Reception et d'Emission de Messages*.

carpet place [LE] Slang for a very posh and illegal gambling establishment.

carrie [C,G&PS] Slang for cocaine. (*See* QUICK REFERENCE.)

carrier-free radar [M] Normal radar waves travel on a single frequency that undulates like a normal radio wave and therefore is easy to defeat with currently applied Stealth technology. Carrier-free radar generates a pulse with a large range of frequencies that produce "square" waves of radio-frequency energy. These are reflected and are not absorbed by radar-absorbing material on Stealth aircraft, thus a Stealth airplane could be detected in flight. (*See* BISTATIC RADAR and IMPULSE RADAR.)

cartwheels **1.** [C,G&PS] Abbreviations for Amphetamines (*See* QUICK REFERENCE.) **2.** [C,G&PS] Abbreviation for silver dollars (U.S. money).

case [I] In an intelligence or law enforcement capacity the case is the operation in its entirety.

case officer [I] A subordinate intelligence officer that directs the activities of agents in the field. A case officer with agencies such as the CIA also have the responsibility of making contact with prospective agents—someone who might be a military officer with a foreign government or a household employee of a high official with access to classified materials. Case officers who are employed by an intelligence agency tend to change their ethics if they stay in the profession of an intelligence agent. By the very nature of their work, they must, more often than not, lie to and deceive those around them.

cash room [LE] Slang for a place where bets are taken and the results determined.

casket [US] Naval aviation voice brevity code meaning an aircraft about to crash or crash land.

CASMS [I] Abbreviation for Computer-controlled Area Sterilization Multi-sensor System. Tiny seismic detectors that resemble small rocks, lumps of mud, or twigs are placed in enemy territory either by air drops or insertion teams that detect the movement of people and vehicles in the area. Federal narcotic task force groups also have installed CASMS units in marijuana fields in the national forests to catch the growers. The CASMS are pretuned to a specific frequency and are kept frozen until ready for use because of the limited life of the battery. They come to life as they warm up and have a life span of approximately 20 days.

CAT **1.** [C,G&PS] Slang term meaning that individual. **2.** [I] Abbreviation for Civil Air Transport, the covert/undercover air service operated by the CIA.

catcher [LE] Slang for an individual inside or outside a racetrack who relays the results of a race to someone outside and away from the track.

catching [LE] Slang for the review of a criminal or civil complaint. This review is the first step in the investigative process following any incident.

cat house radar [I] Slang for the Soviet intermediate-range radar system surrounding Moscow, supporting the Galosh/ABM-IB missile batteries. The cat house radar system supplies initial tracking data to early missile/aircraft engagement radar. (*See* TRY ADD RADAR.)

catnip [C,G&PS] Slang for fake marijuana. This does not refer to generic catnip, but rather something appearing to be marijuana.

catting [LE] Slang for an individual who is destitute and living on the street.

cave [LE] Slang for a Surveillance Headquarters.

CB [C] *See* CITIZENS BAND.

C-BD [NASA] Abbreviation for C-Band.

C band [C] The radio frequency band of 3.9 to 6.2 gigahertz-per-second.

CBS [B] Designation for CBS Radio Network.

CBS R-R [B] Designation for CBS 'Radio Radio' Network.

CBTR [C3I] Abbreviation for Carrier and Bit Timing Recovery.

CBU [M] Abbreviation for Cluster Bomb Unit.

CC **1.** Specialty code for Communications Center. **2.** [D] Abbreviation for Chinese.

CCAU [LE] Abbreviation for Career Criminal Apprehension Unit.

CCC [TRG] Designation for Belgian Fighting Communist Cell. This terrorist group is known to be KGB controlled. The major activity of this group are anti-NATO operations. This group is also known as the Cellules Communistes Combatants.

CCC (C3) [US] Abbreviation for Command, Control, and Communications.

CCCI (C3I) [US] Abbreviation for Command, Control, Communication, and Intelligence.

CCD [C] Abbreviation for Charge-Coupled Device.

CCS [C] Abbreviation for Clear-Channel Station, an AM broadcast band radio transmitter that shares its authorized channel only with very distant stations.

CCTV [C] Abbreviation for Closed Circuit Television.

CCV [M] Abbreviation for Control-Configured Vehicle.

CD **1.** Abbreviation for Concealment Device. Some inconspicuous device or object that has been designed or modified for the purpose of secreting photographic film, microfiche, (prints) or documents. **2.** [GOV] Abbreviation for Civil Defense.

C-detachment [M] An eighteen-man command-and-control element of Army Special Forces, which, in effect, functions as the Special Forces company headquarters (HQ) controlling three B-Detachments and men attached to A-Detachments of Special Forces.

CE Specialty Code for Criminal Evidence technician.

cecil [C,G&PS] Slang for cocaine. (*See* QUICK REFERENCE.)

CECORE [FRANCE] Abbreviation for Centre de Commandements du Reseau.

ceech [C,G&PS] Slang for hashish. (*See* QUICK REFERENCE.)

CELD [I] Abbreviation for Central External Liaison Department, a branch of the mainland Chinese Secret Service. This division of the CSS is concerned with the collection and evaluation of foreign intelligence data gathered by their agents. The CELD has extensive files on political malcontents (students and professional people) in China, one of the first lists to be computerized.

cell [I] Slang for the basic unit of an espionage network.

CELV [M] Abbreviation for Complementary Expendable Launch Vehicle.

CEM [M] Abbreviation for Combined Effects Munitions.

Center [I] An intelligence service headquarters.

Center for Missing Children The phone number for the center is 1−800−843−5678.

centering [US] The project code name for the Air Force's Long Range (nuclear explosion) Detection Program (AFLRDP).

CEP 1. [M] Abbreviation for Circle of Equal Probability, the radius of a circle containing half the bomb/bullet/missile strikes, thus giving a measure of accuracy. 2. [M] Abbreviation for Circular Error Probability.

CERCOM [US] Acronym for Army Communications and Electronics Material Readiness Command.

CERES [UK] Abbreviation for Computer Enhanced Radio Emission Surveillance.

CESE [M] Abbreviation for Communications Equipment Support Element.

CETAC [UK] Acronym for Communications Control System.

CEWI [C3I] Abbreviation for Combat Electronic Warfare and Intelligence.

CFAR [M] Abbreviation for Constant False Alarm Rate.

CFR 1. [M] Abbreviation for Carrier-Free Radar. (*See* CARRIER-FREE RADAR.) 2. [GOV] Abbreviation for Code of Federal Regulations.

CFRP [M] Abbreviation for Carbonfibre-reinforced Plastics.

CG 1. [A] Abbreviation for Center of Gravity. 2. [M] Abbreviation for Command Guidance. 3. [CW] Designation for a choking agent (phosgene). This chemical agent is used by the military and is reported to be in storage for law enforcement agencies to use in emergency (massive riot) situations. CG causes severe coughing and choking. Extended use can result in asphyxiation.

chaff [M] Slang for strips of metallic-coated material cut to a variety of wavelengths. When disbursed into the air (usually by high-flying aircraft) chaff reflects radar signals. In Europe recently, the USSR created a chaff barrier during a military exercise that covered hundreds of miles and made radar interpretation of the activities by western countries impossible. The process of chaff usage also tends to make any radio communication—except at very short range—next to impossible. Chaff is usually dropped by an aircraft to produce spurious radar returns.

chalk [C,G&PS] Slang for cocaine. (*See* QUICK REFERENCE.)

chalk bettor [LE] Slang term for a horse racing gambler who tends to place bets on the most popular or favored horses.

chalet [US] The code name used to define a class of geosynchronous-orbiting sigint satellite operated by the United States military over territories of the Soviet Union. Chalet satellites have proven to be effective in gathering troop movement data.

channel [C] A predetermined frequency that usually is given a number for reference.

charged up [C,G&PS] Slang for a person affected by narcotics.

Charles [A,LE,MIL] Designation for the letter *C*.

Charlie 1. [C,G&PS] Slang for cocaine. (*See* QUICK REFERENCE.) 2. [US] Naval aviation voice brevity code meaning correct. 3. [C] Stands for clean (unscrambled) communications. 4. [A,LE,MIL] Designation for the letter *C*.

chasing a bag [C,G&PS] Slang term for looking for the best possible heroin.

chasing a dragon [C,G&PS] A method of taking heroin. Heroin is placed on a small piece of tinfoil and heated. Fumes are inhaled, usually through a straw or by some other means. (*See* V8 COOKER.)

chatter [US] Naval aviation voice brevity code meaning communications jamming.

cheba cheba [C,G&PS] Slang for marijuana. (*See* QUICK REFERENCE.)

check cop [LE] A mechanical device used in gambling that affords the user a method of stealing chips.

check up house [LE] Slang for a location in an

illegal gambling organization where money is counted.

cheese eater   [C,G&PS] Slang for an informant.

Cheka   [USSR] Abbreviation for *Vserossiyskaya Chrezvychaynaya Komissiya po Bor'be s Kontrrevolyutsiyey i Sabotazhem* (All-Russian Extraordinary Commission to Combat Counterrevolution and Sabotage). Also abbreviated VChKa, VCheKa, VeCheKa.

chekist   [USSR] A member of the KGB, after *Cheka*, the first Soviet security service organization. Also the name of an internal and secret KGB magazine containing the latest intelligence information and terms like those appearing in this book.

cherubs   [US] Naval aviation voice brevity code meaning altitude in hundreds of feet.

chesty   [C,G&PS] Slang for a criminal element who is headstrong or acts as the leader or authority figure in a group.

Chicago sugar   [C,G&PS] As the story goes, some marijuana was shipped to Chicago in used sugar bags. The dealer sampled some of the grass and found it left a sweet taste in his mouth. The marijuana sold at a premium price because of its uniqueness, and the name stuck. Marijuana is now sometimes dried with a light coating of honey or dusted with sugar to enhance the flavor. That process is known to increase the selling price from the wholesaler, as well as at the street level, by as much as 200 percent.

Chicano   [LE] A term used mostly at the street level that means to be politically conscious in the Mexican-American community. To say someone is chicano is to acknowledge that person is more aware than the norm.

chick   [C,G&PS] Slang for a young girl.

chicks   [US] Naval aviation voice brevity code meaning friendly fighter/bomber aircraft.

chicken   [LE] Slang for a male teenaged homosexual prostitute.

chicken hawk   [LE] Slang for an adult male homosexual with a preference for having sex with young boys.

chief   [C,G&PS] Slang for LSD. (*See* QUICK REFERENCE.)

chillin'   [C,G&PS] Slang for an individual just hanging around.

China white   [C,G&PS] Slang for a powerful synthetic heroin. China White's chemical name is 3-methylfentanyl or methyl analog of fentanyl. It is several times more powerful than heroin, and even extremely small amounts can be fatal. It is marketed on the street as a powerful heroin—not a chemical blending—which is untrue. Users usually have no idea of its potency; three granules are a common dose. It is sometimes mixed with cocaine. China White can be manufactured by anyone with a background in basic college chemistry, according to the National Institute on Drug Abuse in Rockville, Md.

chip   [C,G&PS] Slang for an individual who tends to use small amounts of heroin on an occasional basis.

chipper   [C,G&PS] *See* CHIP.

chipping   [C,G&PS] *See* CHIP.

chippie   [C,G&PS] Slang for a female prostitute who elects to have sex with men for little or no money, sometimes in exchange for drugs.

chippy   [C,G&PS] Slang for an individual who uses drugs but claims not to be addicted.

CHL   Specialty code for children's rights/child abuse.

cholly   [C,G&PS] Slang for cocaine. (*See* QUICK REFERENCE.)

cholo   [C,G&PS] Slang for a hispanic (Mexican) gang member.

chop   [US] Naval aviation voice brevity code meaning a change of operational control.

chopper   [A] Slang for helicopter.

choppers   [C,G&PS] Slang for guns (usually automatic weapons).

chord   [A] In aviation, the lengthwise dimension of an airfoil.

CHR   [B] Abbreviation for Contemporary Hit Radio.

Christmas tree   [C,G&PS] Slang for a bag or pocketful of barbiturates.

CHU [B] Designation for Canadian time and frequency station.

chuck-a-luck [LE] Slang for a gambling game played with several dice. The roll that wins is the highest poker hand.

Chukakuha [TRG] A middle core faction of the Japanese Red Army. Also known as the *Chukaku-Ha*.

chullum [C,G&PS] Slang for a pipe used to smoke hashish.

CI **1.** Specialty code for Criminal Investigation. **2.** [LE] Abbreviation for Case Informant. **3.** [LE] Abbreviation for Confidential Informant. **4.** [I] Abbreviation for Counterintelligence, which includes acts and activities devoted to the destruction of foreign intelligence operations. **5.** [I] Abbreviation for Clandestine Intelligence—intelligence of any kind that is collected by covert sources.

CIA [US] Abbreviation for Central Intelligence Agency, an agency responsible for military, strategic, domestic, and foreign intelligence. Like the military, awards are given to intelligence agents for exceptional acts.

[CIA] Awards The following is a listing of CIA awards:

- *D.I.C.* Distinguished Intelligence Cross, awarded for a voluntary act or acts of exceptional heroism involving the acceptance of existing dangers with conspicuous fortitude and exemplary courage.
- *D.I.M.* Distinguished Intelligence Medal, awarded for the performance of outstanding services or for an achievement of a distinctly exceptional nature in a duty or responsibility.
- *I.S.* Intelligence Star, awarded for a voluntary act or acts of courage performed under hazardous conditions or for outstanding achievements or service rendered with distinction under conditions of grave risk.
- *I.M.M.* Intelligence Medal of Merit, awarded for the performance of especially meritorious service or for an act or achievement conspicu-

ously above normal duties. This medal usually is given for intelligence-gathering assignments.

- *C.I.M.* Career Intelligence Medal, awarded for a cumulative record of service that reflects exceptional achievement with the agency.
- *I.C.M.* Intelligence Commendation Medal, awarded for the performance of especially commendable service or for an act or achievement significantly above normal duties that results in an important contribution to the agency.
- *E.S.M.* Exceptional Service Medallion, awarded for injury or death resulting from service in an area of hazard.
- *S.R.M.* Silver Retirement Medallion, awarded for a career of 25 years or more with the agency.
- *B.R.M.* Bronze Retirement Medallion, awarded for a career of at least 15 but less than 25 years of service with the agency.

CIA/C-TC [I] Central Intelligence Agency/Counter-Terrorism Center, a little-known CIA agency-within-an-agency that serves as a vital nerve center in the nation's war against terrorism. The Counter-Terrorism Center, like its parent agency, does not conduct criminal investigations within the United States. The center's mission is much broader than merely learning about terrorists and assisting investigators. Its job is nothing short of disrupting, countering, and assisting in the arrest of terrorists, and interfering with relations between terrorists and sponsoring countries. The Counter-Terrorism Center will not disclose its precise number of employees (fewer than 200), the variety of equipment employed (it draws heavily on computers, spy satellites, and National Security Agency intercepts), or its budget. It has at its disposal everything from covert operatives to translators, bomb-analyzing scientists to bomb-sniffing dogs.

CIAV [GOV] Designation for United Nations International Support and Verification Commission in Central America.

cibas [C,G&PS] Slang for doridens, a nonbarbiturate hypnotic sedative. Dependence potential is high.

CIC [GOV] Abbreviation for Counter Intelligence Corps.

CID [US] Abbreviation for Criminal Investigation Division, the internal branch of the United States Army's investigative operations. Agents of the CID are stationed at every Army installation.

CIG [GOV] Abbreviation for Central Intelligence Group.

CINC [M] Acronym for Commander-IN Chief. CINC denotes the highest-ranking military officer in each of the United States military commands.

CIP [GOV] Abbreviation for Classified Information Procedures Act, a process by which classified documents, photographs, or related intelligence or classified information is reviewed by the controlling agency and the decision made at what level the information should be made available, and to who, specifically, it will be made available.

CIPA [GOV] Abbreviation for Classified Information Procedures Act.

cipher [I] A number of methods developed to conceal a message.

cipher pad [I] A small pad of printed sheets containing a nonrepetitive key. Each sheet is used for sending a coded message. Cipher pads also are known as *one-time* pads.

circle [S] The black magick, in satanism, conducted inside a circle that offers protection or directs the energy and power of the group. (*See* BLACK MAGICK.)

citizens band [C] The bandwidth at approximately 27 MHz. This bandwidth has been set aside by the Federal Communications Commission for

Table C-1. Citizens Band Channels and Frequencies

Channel	Frequency	Channel	Frequency
1	26.965	21	27.215
2	26.975	22	27.225
3	26.985	23	27.225
4	27.005	24	27.235
5	27.015	25	27.245
6	27.025	26	27.265
7	27.035	27	27.275
8	27.055	28	27.285
9	27.065	29	27.295
10	27.075	30	27.305
11	27.085	31	27.315
12	27.105	32	27.325
13	27.115	33	27.335
14	27.125	34	27.345
15	27.135	35	27.355
16	27.155	36	27.365
17	27.165	37	27.375
18	27.175	38	27.385
19	27.185	39	27.395
20	27.205	40	27.405

general use by the public. This same bandwidth also is used for the radio control operation of model boats and airplanes. TABLE C-1 is a listing of citizens band channels and frequencies.

citizens band nationwide emergency channel: Channel 9

citizens band nationwide road conditions channel: Channel 19

civil aircraft markings, international Aircraft of every country has individual identification markings. These markings (identifiers) can be mentioned in the course of communications with the aircraft or by U.S. Customs or the Coast Guard who have a particular aircraft under surveillance. An aircraft from Pakistan, as an example, has the identifier AP followed by the aircraft registration number (000000). The following are the aircraft identifiers for every country in the world:

Aircraft Identifier	Country
AP	Pakistan
A2	Botswana
A3	Tonga
A5	Bhutan

Aircraft Identifier	Country
A6	United Arab Emirates
A7	Qatar
A9C	Bahrain
A40	Oman

Aircraft Identifier	Country	Aircraft Identifier	Country
B	China (People's Republic)	HK	Colombia
B	China/Taiwan	HL	Republic of Korea
BNMAL	Mongolia	HP	Panama
C	Canada	HR	Honduras
CC	Chile	HS	Thailand
CCCP	Soviet Union	HZ	Saudi Arabia
CN	Morocco	H4	Solomon Islands
CP	Bolivia	I	Italy
CR-C	Cape Verde Island	JA	Japan
CS	Portugal	JY	Jordan
CU	Cuba	J2	Djibouti
CX	Uruguay	J3	Grenada
C2	Nauru	J5	Guinea Bissau
C5	Gambia	N	United States
C6	Bahamas	OB	Peru
C9	Mozambique	OD	Lebanon
D	Federal Republic of Germany	OE	Austria
DDR	German Democratic Republic	OH	Finland
DQ	Fiji	OK	Czechoslovakia
J6	St. Lucia	OO	Belgium
J7	Dominica	OY	Denmark
J8	St. Vincent	P	Korea (DPRK)
LN	Norway	PH	Netherlands
LV	Argentina	PJ	Netherlands Antilles
LX	Luxembourg	PK	Indonesia
LZ	Bulgaria	PP/PT	Brazil
MI	Marshall Islands	PZ	Surinam
DZ	Angola	P2	Papua New Guinea
D6	Comoros Island	RDPL	Laos
EC	Spain	RP	Philippines
EI	Eire	SE	Sweden
EL	Liberia	SP	Poland
EP	Iran	ST	Sudan
ET	Ethiopia	SU	Egypt
F	France	SX	Greece
F-O	French Ov. Dept/ Protectorates	S2	Bangladesh
G	Great Britain	S7	Seychelles
HA	Hungary	S9	Sao Tome
HB	Switzerland & Liechtenstein	TC	Turkey
HC	Ecuador	TF	Iceland
HH	Haiti	TG	Guatemala
HI	Dominican Republic	TI	Costa Rica

Aircraft Identifier	Country	Aircraft Identifier	Country
TJ	Cameroon	ZS	South Africa
TL	Central African Republic	3A	Monaco
TN	Congo Brazzaville	3B	Mauritius
TR	Gabon	3C	Equatorial Guinea
TS	Tunisia	3D	Swaziland
TT	Chad	3X	Guinea
TU	Ivory Coast	4R	Sri Lanka
TY	Benin	4W	Yemen Arab Republic
TZ	Mali	4X	Israel
T3	Kinbati	5A	Libya
VB	Brunei	5B	Cyprus
VH	Australia	5H	Tanzania
VN	Vietnam	5N	Nigeria
VP-F	Falkland Islands	5R	Madagascar
VP-LKA/LZ	St. Kitts-Nevis	5T	Mauritania
VP-LMA/LUZ	Montserrat	5U	Niger
VP-LUA/ZZ	British Virgin Islands	5V	Togo
VQ-T	Turks & Cacos Islands	5W	Western Samoa
VR-B	Bermuda	5X	Uganda
VR-C	Cayman Islands	5Y	Kenya
VT-G	Gibraltar	6O	Somalia
VR-H	Hong Kong	6V	Senegal
VT	India	6Y	Jamaica
V2	Antigua	7O	People's Dem. Rep. of Yemen
V3	Belize	7P	Lesotho
XA/B/C	Mexico	7Q	Malawi
XT	Upper Volta	7T	Algeria
XU	Kampuchea	8P	Barbados
XY	Burma	8Q	Maldives Republic
YA	Afghanistan	8R	Guyana
YI	Iraq	9G	Ghana
YJ	Vanuatu	9H	Malta
YK	Syria	9J	Zambia
YN	Nicaragua	9K	Kuwait
YR	Romania	9L	Sierra Leone
YS	El Salvador	9M	Malaysia
YU	Yugoslavia	9N	Nepal
YV	Venezuela	9Q	Zaire
Z	Zimbabwe	9U	Burundi
ZA	Albania	9V	Singapore
ZK	New Zealand	9XR	Rwanda
ZP	Paraguay	9Y	Trinidad & Tobago

CIWS [M] Abbreviation for Close-In Weapons System.

CK [CW] Designation for blood agent (a hydrogen cyanide). This chemical agent is used by the military. It causes convulsions, choking, gasping, and asphyxiation.

CL [CW] Designation for a choking agent (chlorine). This chemical agent is used by the military and is designed to cause choking, severe coughing, asphyxiation, and severe membrane (eyes, nose, throat, and lung) burns.

clansman [UK] The code name for British Army tactical communications equipment.

clarifier [C] Slang for an incremental tuning control for the radio reception of single-sideband signals.

clarinet [US] Code name for communications security.

class [B] Classical.

classification [I] The determination that materials are in the interest of the national security and thereby mandate a specific degree of protection from unauthorized disclosure.

CLASSIC [I] Abbreviation for Covert Local Area Sensor System for Intrusion Classification.

classic wizard [US] The code name for Navy/CIA ocean surveillance teams that keep track of Soviet naval activities and missile testing.

clean 1. [C,G&PS] Slang for someone not using narcotics or drugs or cured of an addiction. 2. [A] Of or referring to an aircraft with undercarriage and flaps retracted, or with nothing on the external body of the aircraft that might disturb the airflow. 3. [US] Naval aviation voice brevity code meaning no remaining external ordnance.

Clearance Command Codes *See* TABLE C-2.

Clickbeetle [US] Code name for the military signal intelligence units gathering data in the Sea of Japan.

Clipped [C,G&PS] Slang for someone who has been arrested.

Clnc del [I] Abbreviation for Clearance Delivery.

Cluckhead [C,G&PS] Slang for a user, seeking crack cocaine for his personal consumption.

CM [EW] Abbreviation for Countermeasure.

CMS [I] Abbreviation for Classified Materials System.

C/N [M] Abbreviation for Construction Number.

CN [CW] Designation for tear gas (choracetophenone). This chemical agent is used by law enforcement agencies and the military in riot control situations. It is short acting, and causes the eyes to tear and the skin to smart. It is in common usage as a backup defense for police officers.

CNCE [M] Abbreviation for Communications Nodal Control Element.

CNI [US] Abbreviation for Communications, Navigation, and Identification.

CNN [B] Abbreviation for Cable News Network.

CNO [US] Abbreviation for Chief of Naval Operations.

C-note [C,G&PS] Slang for $100 dollar bill.

CO 1. Specialty code for consulting. 2. [I] Abbreviation for Case Officer, as it refers to the profession of the intelligence agent.

coast to coast [C,G&PS] Slang for amphetamines. (*See* QUICK REFERENCE.)

coasting [C,G&PS] Slang for someone under the influence of drugs.

coating [C,G&PS] Slang for being high on drugs or narcotics.

coaxial cable [C] A two-conductor, shielded cable.

cobbler [I] Slang for an individual acting as a forger (usually of false documents or identification papers).

Cobra dane [US] Code name for phased array land-based radar installed on the remote Shemya Island in Alaska and operated by U.S. military. The Cobra Dane installation provides intelligence and Soviet space tracking data of atmospheric and ballistic targets. The Cobra Dane Cyber computers installed in the early 1970s are scheduled for replacement in the early 1990s. The system was originally designed as the early warning of a missile attack against the United States and Canada and is the primary sensor for tracking Soviet missiles launched over the North Pole.

Table C-2. Clearance Command Codes Used by Police

Code 1*(MCU)	Acknowledge this call
Code 1	Report or report and citation
Code 1	Contact *(person)* A.S.A.P.
Code 1	Subject is armed, use caution
Code 2*(MCU)	Proceed to assignment with red lights but no siren
Code 2	Proceed to this assignment with no lights or siren
Code 2	Party advised and no report required
Code 2	Arrest made
Code 2	Drunk driver
Code 3*(MCU)	Emergency, respond with red lights and siren
Code 3	Arrest was made and individual is being transported to jail
Code 3	Ticket issued
Code 3	Abandoned vehicle
Code 4*(MCU)	No further assistance needed
Code 4	No further assistance required here; subject is still at large
Code 4	Unit/officer going to or from medical center
Code 4	Subject was gone when unit arrived on scene
Code 4	Reckless driver
Code 5*(MCU)	Law enforcement stakeout. Uniformed officers stay away from this area
Code 5	Parking complaint clearance requested
Code 5	Unable to locate *(location*, *subject*, *complaining party)*
Code 5	Obstruction on highway
Code 6*(MCU)	Out of service/or out of unit for investigation
Code 6	Out of unit for investigation. Assistance might be required
Code 6	Personal property or automobile being impounded
Code 6	Civil matter
Code 6	Property damage—accident blocking roadway
Code 7*(MCU)	Out of service for meal or break
Code 7	Circumstances warrant no arrest
Code 7	Situation handled by officer
Code 7	Property damage—accident is not blocking roadway
Code 8*(MCU)	Message has been delivered
Code 8	Fire alarm activated at *(location)*
Code 8	Turn over to *(person)*
Code 8	Personal injury accident—roadway is not blocked
Code 9*(MCU)	No action taken
Code 9	Other units are busy, can *(person)* take the call?
Code 9	Following ambulance to hospital
Code 9	Personal injury accident—roadway is blocked
Code 10*(MCU)	Bomb threat
Code 10	Request clearance to *(location)*
Code 11*(MCU)	Incident/report number is *(number)*
Code 11	Send ambulance (code 3) dispatch number is *(number)*
Code 12*(MCU)	Act as media/press contact
Code 12	Patrol your district. Report extent of damage

Table C-2. Continued

Code 12	Act as personal escort for *(person)*
Code 12	Send wrecker and ambulance
Code 13*(MCU)	Disaster *(flood or earthquake)*
Code 13	All units respond to *(location)* for *(reason)*
Code 14*(MCU)	*(Unit number)* resume normal operations
Code 14	*(Unit number)* return to your assigned duty
Code 15*(MCU)	*(Number of unit)* is in service
Code 15	*(Number of unit)* is standing by for instructions
Code 20*(MCU)	Officer needs assistance at *(location)*
Code 20	Officer wounded
Code 20	Notify press
Code 22*(MCU)	Use this channel only for emergency communications
Code 30*(MCU)	All available units—trouble at station—emergency!
Code 33*(MCU)	Emergency on this channel—hold any other communications
Code 34*(MCU)	Emergency is over
Code 666*(MCU)	Unit/number establish roadblock at *(location)*
Code 1000*(MCU)	Aircraft crash
Code 1000	Bank robbery
Code 2000*(MCU)	Prison or jail break
Code 2000	Aircraft crash

---

*(Most Common Usage)

Cobra shoe   [US] Code name for an intelligence gathering radar imaging receiving installation operated by the CIA and U.S. military personnel at Pirinclik Air Force Base in Turkey. Pirinclik is considered to be the most important U.S. intelligence gathering facility in that part of the world. The U.S. also operates a satellite receiving station at the *Diyarbakir* Air Station in Turkey.

Cobra unit   [HRU] Cobra unit is officially known as the Gendarmerieeinsatzkommando, (the Gendarmerie Special Unit). It is the elite antiterrorist and hostage rescue unit for the government of Austria.

Cobra x-ray   [US] The code name for deployment of advanced-ranged instrumentated naval vessels that monitor Soviet missile testing. Each vessel also has a code name, so communications might be from Cobra X-Ray Papa to Cobra X-Ray Golf.

cocaine   1. [LE] Cocaine is usually white and odorless and is extracted from the leaves of the coca bush. Cocaine is sometimes called snow because of its crystalline appearance. Cocaine is often cut down from its original (full) strength by the addition of powdered sugar. In this form, it is cooked to create flakes or rocks. Uncooked cocaine in crystal form can be snorted through the nose, injected, or ingested into the mouth.

Cocaine prices continue to drop in the world market and street purity is increasing amid signs that worldwide production of the drug has reached record levels. Cocaine sold for as little as $11,000 a kilogram in 1989 compared to $30,000 in 1985. **2.** [LE] A controlled substance that is a stimulant. (*See* QUICK REFERENCE.)

cocked [C,G&PS] Slang for someone who is high on cocaine.

COCOM [C3I] Abbreviation for Coordinating Committee.

code 1. [I] A method of communication in which arbitrary symbols represent units of text. Codes have a number of applications, but generally are for brevity or security. **2.** [M] Ranking officers in the U.S. military are referred to (mostly during travel) by code. An in-flight reference to ground control will indicate a ranking officer or government official aboard. Here are some examples:

Code 1	Secretary of Defense
Code 2	Ranking Cabinet Official(s)
Code 3	General
Code 4	Lieutenant General
Code 5	Major General
Code 6	Brigadier General
Code 7	Colonel

codeine [LE] A morphine-derived controlled substance that is a narcotic. (*See* QUICK REFERENCE.)

code name [I] A substitution for the actual name of a person, place, or thing to ensure secrecy. A code name also can designate a specific operation.

code word [I] A word that is prearranged to be used in a conversation or communication to signal an identity of an individual. The purpose of code words is to safeguard the actual intention or meaning of an action.

COE [HRU] Abbreviation for *Comando de Operaciones Especiales*, the tough hostage rescue and antiterrorist unit of the Honduran Special Forces Command.

coke [C,G&PS] Slang for cocaine. (*See* QUICK REFERENCE.)

coked up [C,G&PS] Slang term meaning to be under the influence of cocaine.

cokie [C,G&PS] Slang for a cocaine addict.

colas [C,G&PS] The top part of a marijuana plant; the flower.

cola de zorra [C,G&PS] Most of the resin in the cannabis (marijuana) plant concentrates itself in the colas. The foxtails (flowers) are the most prized part of the plant. The cola de zorra, or the tail of the fox is usually separated from the rest of the marijuana plant when it is harvested.

cold 1. [US] Naval aviation voice brevity code meaning antisubmarine warfare (ASW) contact lost. **2.** [C,G&PS] The term cold in the drug/narcotic trade means without heart or feelings. If to get money means killing another person—anyone who happens to cross your path—that's cold.

cold bust [C,G&PS] Slang for an arrest or raid on the part of a group of narcotic or customs agents without any prior planning. A cold bust usually is prompted by an act of bad judgment on the part of a drug dealer. (*See* HOT BUST.)

cold, I'm [US] Naval aviation voice brevity code meaning that live ordnance is not being used.

cold popping [C,G&PS] Heroin is usually heated prior to injection. Cold popping is to inject heroin cold.

cold turkey [C,G&PS] Slang term meaning to abruptly be subjected to the withdrawal of drugs, usually from heroin.

collar [LE] Slang term meaning to place an individual under formal arrest.

collection [I] The acquisition of information by any means and its delivery to an intelligence group for processing and initial evaluation.

Colombian [C,G&PS] Of or referring to a high-quality grade of marijuana grown in the South American country of Colombia.

Colors 1. [C,G&PS] *See* CRIPS; BLOODS. **2.** [S] In satanism, specific colors have certain meanings in the ritual ceremonies. The colors can apply to dress or the environment of a meeting place. Black means evil, Satan, and darkness, while white indicates innocence, goodness, and purity.

Red is used to denote life forces, blood, forceful energy, and magick involving sex and children. (*See* BLACK MAGICK.)

Colossus [I] The Sound Surveillance System (SOSUS) that is deployed along the Pacific coast of the United States for the purpose of detecting Soviet submarines. Colossus also has been used by the DEA and Coast Guard for long-range, offshore surveillance of ships involved in suspected drug running operations near San Diego, San Pedro, Los Angeles, and San Francisco, CA.

COM Specialty Code for computer crime fraud.

Comacchio Company [HRU] The antiterrorist unit of the Special British Royal Marine Commandos.

COMECON [USSR] Abbreviation for Council of Mutual Economic Assistance.

come down [C,G&PS] As the effects of drugs wear off, the user feels sick. This is to come down from whatever feeling the drug has given. Usually, at this point, the addict wants (needs) more drugs.

COMINT [C3I] Abbreviation for Communications Intelligence, information based on intelligence that is obtained from a communications intercept. (*See* SIGINT.)

COMIREX [US] Abbreviation for Committee on Imagery Requirements and Exploitation.

common carrier [D] Slang for a telephone company.

communications receiver [C] Any radio receiver that is designed to receive code, single sideband, and/or AM broadcasts with equally high quality.

COMOR [US] Abbreviation for Committee on Overhead Reconnaissance.

COMPAC [UK] Designation for man-portable satcom terminal.

company, The [I] Slang for the Central Intelligence Agency (CIA).

compartmentation [I] The management of intelligence information so that personnel involved in one aspect of an operation have data available to them that pertains to their specific responsibilities.

composites [D] Materials produced by bonding together filaments of very high strength. This process sometimes is used in aircraft construction and has been used in the development of bullet-proof vests and armored vehicles used in law enforcement.

compromise [I] Slang for the public exposure of classified information to unauthorized persons.

COMSEC [C3I] Abbreviation for Communications Security. COMSEC includes electronic emissions security, (TEMPEST) all crypto messages, and radio transmissions. It also involves classified documents, physical hardware and individual (site) security. The National Security Agency (NSA) has overall responsibility for all COMSEC activities.

CON 1. Specialty code for construction sites law. 2. [C,G&PS] Slang meaning to manipulate another individual.

CONAD [US] Abbreviation for Continental Air Defense Command.

confetti [US] Naval aviation voice brevity code meaning radar chaff. (*See* CHAFF.)

confidential [GOV] Of or referring to the lowest United States security classification used by government and the military. The transmission or revelation of any federal material marked confidential to an unauthorized person is prohibited within the meaning of the Espionage Law, Title 18, 18 U.S.C., Sections 793 and 794.

connected [LE] Slang for an individual who is somehow connected to, or has ties with, organized crime.

connection [C,G&PS] Slang for an individual who sells drugs or is connected with organized crime and is willing to bring individuals together who have a mutual interest such as drugs, the sale of stolen property, and so on.

consiglio [LE] Term used in the Cosa Nostra (Mafia) that describes the sitting council or ruling body.

consumer [I] An individual or internal agency using any information supplied by its own members or by another agency.

contact high [C,G&PS] An individual who becomes high without the benefit of narcotics because he is interacting with other people who are actually under the influence of real drugs.

Contrabandista [C,G&PS] Name for a drug/narcotic smuggler operating from south of the border of the United States, usually from Mexico or Colombia.

Contras [US] Shortened form of *Contra Revolutionarios,* counterrevolutionaries in Nicaragua, supported and funded by the United States government and trained by the CIA.

control [I] The physical and/or psychological pressure exerted on an individual to ensure he responds to the exact directions given by an intelligence agency. This control often is carried forward under some threat.

CONUS [D] Abbreviation for Continental United States.

converter [C] An electronic device that can convert one frequency band to another frequency bandwidth. These devices shift the receiving frequency.

convertible [LE] Slang for a transport aircraft used by law enforcement or the military that can be adapted to take either passengers or freight.

cook 1. [C,G&PS] Slang for a drug chemist. 2. [C,G&PS] Slang for heating opium for smoking.

cooker [C,G&PS] Slang term for anything that will hold a blend of water and heroin for heating, usually a spoon.

cookie [C,G&PS] Slang for a cocaine addict.

cook-up [C,G&PS] Slang for heating (cooking) heroin for an injection. The heroin usually is mixed with lemon juice or water.

cool [LE] Slang for being in control, someone who is not a troublemaker.

coopted worker [I] Slang term for a resident of a country who assists a foreign intelligence agent.

COP 1. [LE] Slang for a police officer. 2. [LE] Slang for someone looking for a source of drugs. 3. [LE] Slang term meaning to admit to, to acquire, to buy, to get. Cop is a term used most often in connection with drugs or narcotics.

copilots [C,G&PS] Slang for amphetamines. (*See* QUICK REFERENCE.)

cop killers [LE] Slang for bullets coated with Teflon that make them so slick that they easily penetrate the bulletproof vest used by law enforcement officers. Banned from legal sale in the United States, they are still sold by some dealers under the counter.

cop out [C,G&PS] To cop out is slang meaning to not take care of narcotic or drug business in a proper manner or to tell the police about the activities of another individual that might result in their arrest.

COPUOS [US] Abbreviation for Committee on the Peaceful Uses of Outer Space.

COR 1. Specialty code for corporate investigation. 2. [C] Abbreviation for Carrier Operated Relay.

coralls [FRANCE] Code name for packet-switching system.

CORANDCOM [US] Abbreviation for Army Communications Research and Development Command.

corona [I] Code name for certain CIA photographic reconnaissance satellite systems.

cosmic [US] Code word for nuclear secrets that are more restricted than top secret information.

cosmos [USSR] A Soviet satellite surveillance system. In early 1989, the Soviet Union deployed its 2,000 Cosmos-series satellite from a Cyclone rocket in an orbit that will allow it to photograph the Arctic (North Pole) and Antarctica (South Pole). The Soviets hold the record of 10 satellites placed into different orbits from a single rocket launch.

COSRO [C] Abbreviation for Conical Scan Receive Only.

cottons [C,G&PS] Slang for cotton balls that are saturated with a narcotic.

cottonseed [US] Code name for the Air Force's project for the Long Range Detection Program of nuclear explosions anywhere in the world.

count [C,G&PS] Slang for a large amount of narcotics.

counterespionage [I] An aspect of counterintelligence involving a variety of aggressive operations against another intelligence group. Counterespionage usually is conducted to penetrate, deceive, or manipulate those suspected of conducting espionage activities.

counterinsurgency [I] Actions taken by a government to defeat subversion or rebellion in a country.

counterintelligence [I] Specific and well-planned activities that are conducted to destroy the effectiveness of a foreign intelligence operation.

counterspy [I] An individual who is in a position to betray or forestall the actions of others.

county hotel [C,G&PS] Slang for a local (small) jail.

courier 1. [C,G&PS] Slang for a drug/narcotic delivery person. 2. [I] Slang for an individual who serves as a messenger—usually responsible for the transmission of materials and supporting documentation in an intelligence operation.

course [D] Term for the desired direction of travel used in law enforcement, the military, and in aircraft navigation.

cousin [LE] Slang for an arrest that usually is made to cool down a situation.

cousins [D] The British Secret Intelligence Service (SIS) name for the CIA.

coven [S] A group of followers in satanism, of the occult. Usually thirteen people are involved.

covendom [S] The dome of energy that satanists believe the strength of their activities radiate outward in. (*See* BLACK MAGICK.)

covenstead [S] A place where members of a satanic group meet.

cover 1. [I] A disguise that is adopted by an individual to avoid discovery in a covert or intelligence operation. 2. [C,G&PS] In the drug/narcotic trade, to cover means to have things under control.

cover name [I] Slang for an alias used by an individual, group, or covert operation.

cover story [I] Slang for a false background history supplied to an individual who is involved in an intelligence operation and wants his real history to remain secret.

covert [I] Of or referring to the activities that are conducted in a manner to make detection impossible.

covert action [I] Any action that designed to influence a foreign government.

cowboy 1. [LE] Slang for an individual who is impersonating a police officer or is an unlicensed private investigator. 2. [US] Naval aviation voice brevity code meaning a pilot who is less than polished and lacks skill.

coyote [LE] Term used by agents of the United States Immigration Service and U.S. Border Patrol to identify smugglers of illegal aliens into the United States.

CP [M] Abbreviation for Circularly Polarized.

C.P. [M] Abbreviation for Command Post (military/police operation).

CPS [HRU] Abbreviation for The Cobras Political Squadron of the Honduran Public Security Forces. The Cobras Political squads have been highly trained in antiterrorist and hostage rescue operations.

CPU [C3I] Abbreviation for Central Processing Unit.

CPUSA [USSR] Abbreviation for Communist Party of the United States of America.

CQB [LE] Abbreviation used by law enforcement and military antiterrorist units meaning Close Quarters Battle. CQB is very dangerous and usually involves knives, close-range gun fire, or unarmed hand-to-hand combat.

CR [B] Abbreviation for Contemporary Rock.

crabs [C,G&PS] A derogatory term for members of the Crips street gang.

crack [C,G&PS] A form of cocaine. Crack is a 50-50, heated mixture of cocaine and baking soda. When it dries, it is like Plaster-of-Paris and is cracked into chunks. Crack is a highly addictive smokable cocaine. Crack cocaine costs about $100 a gram. A rock the size of a small fingernail costs about $25. With a $10 rock, there is enough to get high four or five times. People smoke it, typically in a heat-resistant pipe or in cigarettes. The vapors, when inhaled, quickly reach the brain, causing an intense, short high. (*See* COCAINE.)

crack cocaine   [LE] A controlled substance that is a stimulant. (*See* QUICK REFERENCE.)

crack a crib   [C,G&PS] Slang term meaning to rob a store or burglarize a residence.

crack house   [C,G&PS] Slang for a place where cocaine is sold and used frequently.

crackpot   [C,G&PS] Slang for a marijuana cigarette laced with cocaine dust.

crank   [LE] A controlled substance that is a stimulant. (*See* QUICK REFERENCE.)

crash   [C,G&PS] Slang term meaning to go to sleep—most often applies when drugs are used.

crash pad   [C,G&PS] Slang for a place to sleep.

crazy cat   [US] Code name for optical communications jamming system.

crazy dog   [US] Code name for battlefield communications jamming system.

CRB   [TRG] Abbreviation for Croatian Revolutionary Brotherhood, known to have conducted terrorist operations—including bombings and hijackings—against the Yugoslav government. The CRB membership is also known as the *Hrvatsko Revolucionarno Bratstvo* (HRB).

creep joint   [C,G&PS] Slang for a drug party or gambling that goes on at a different place every day, usually operated by the same people.

Crips   [LE] A predominantly black gang formed in 1969 in the southwest area of Los Angeles. There are an estimated 25,000 members in the southern California area. An estimated 200 offshoot (sets) groups exist in Los Angeles. The choice of clothing for members of the Crips are blue bandanas, blue warm-up suits, blue shoelaces, Kansas City Royals baseball caps, khakis, and track shoes. Another indicator of membership is a teardrop tattoo(s) usually on the face near an eye that symbolize the number of people the member has killed.

CRITCOM   [US] Abbreviation for Critical Intelligence Communications.

CRM   Specialty code for criminal defense (general).

croaker   [C,G&PS] Slang for a physician or druggist who sells prescription drugs.

croaker joint   [C,G&PS] Slang for a hospital emergency room.

cross roader   [LE] Slang for someone who cheats at gambling.

crossing him off   [C,G&PS] Getting "rid" of a gangbanger (*see* GANGBANGER), usually by killing him.

CRT   [C3I] Abbreviation for Cathode Ray Tube.

cruise missile   [M] A long-range guided weapon, normally powered by a turbine engine and flying at a very low level.

crutch   [C,G&PS] Slang for a holder for marijuana cigarette butts so the lips of the smoker are not burned. Sometimes called a roach holder.

crypto   [I] The designation applied to classified information (usually in cryptographic form) that involves specific rules for handling.

cryptoanalysis   [I] The conversion of an encrypted message into text that can be clearly understood without the use of a code key.

cryptography   [I] The enciphering of text so it is unintelligible to an unauthorized reviewer.

cryptology   [I] The science of secret communications. Cryptology is the craft of writing ciphered (secret) messages.

cryptonym   [I] The symbols and/or code words that define a classified project but never actually describe it.

cryptosystem   [I] The various items of cryptomaterial and the procedures and methods that as a unit provide the single tool for encryption as well as decryption.

crystal   [C,G&PS] Slang for methedrine. (*See* QUICK REFERENCE.)

crystal ball   [US] Naval aviation voice brevity code meaning a radarscope.

crystal filters   [C] An electronic circuit that is designed into a radio receiver that produces very high selectivity by the incorporation of quartz crystals.

crystal set [C] A simple radio receiver that uses a crystal detector to receive a transmitted signal.

crystals [C,G&PS] Slang for methedrine. (*See* QUICK REFERENCE.)

CS 1. Specialty code for courier service. **2.** [LE] Designation for tear gas (Choracetophenone in Chlorpicrin). This chemical agent is used by law enforcement and the military. It causes smartness and tearing of the eyes, deep-lung choking, and shortness of breath. It is generally used for riot control.

CSCG [US] Abbreviation for Communications Security Control Group.

CSIS Abbreviation for The Canadian Security Intelligence Service.

CSOC [NASA] Abbreviation for Consolidated Space Operations Center.

CSSR [C3I] Abbreviation for Communication System Segment Replacement.

CSTAL [US] Abbreviation for Combat Surveillance and Target Acquisition Laboratory.

CSU [LE] Abbreviation for Crime Scene Unit.

CT 1. [LE] Abbreviation for Counterterrorism. **2.** [LE] Abbreviation for Communist Terrorist.

CTAF [A] Abbreviation for Common Traffic Advisory Frequency, a system at uncontrolled airports designed to transmit information to vehicles and aircraft on a single (common) frequency.

CTASC [C3I] Abbreviation for Corps Theater Automatic data processing (ADP) Service Center.

CTBT [US/USSR] Abbreviation for Comprehensive Test Ban Treaty.

CTOL [C3I] Abbreviation for Conventional Take-off and Landing.

CTW [LE] Abbreviation for Counter-Terrorist Warfare.

CUBES 1. [C,G&PS] Slang for LSD or morphine. **2.** [C,G&PS] Slang for LSD ingested by mouth on a cube of sugar.

cube head [C,G&PS] Slang for an individual who is known to frequently use LSD.

CUDIXS [US] Abbreviation for Common User Digital Information Exchange System.

Culiacan [LE] A city in the state of Sinaloa, Mexico, that in recent years was a major marijuana distribution center. Raids by Federale patrols have made Culiacan an unsafe place to offer marijuana for sale.

Culiacan garbage [LE] Mexican marijuana growers around the city of Culiacan have been forced by federale patrols to plant and harvest too early in the season. The result is a very low quality marijuana that has gotten the street name of Culiacan garbage because it is so bad that only hard-up marijuana smokers will buy it.

cultivate [C,G&PS] Term meaning to plant something, marijuana, and watch it grow.

cultivation [I] A casual but deliberate act on the part of an intelligence agent to gain control over an individual and induce the individual to supply information, usually classified, to a foreign power.

CUS Specialty code for child custody.

Customs Shortened form of U.S. Customs Service, which protects the borders of the United States against illegal entry and the smuggling of drugs or narcotics into the country. They have more authority than any other U.S. law enforcement agency. They are the only U.S. law enforcement agency that can pump a suspect's stomach against his will. United States customs agents operate clandestinely in Mexico, usually in concert with Mexican narcotics agents.

cut [C,G&PS] Slang term meaning to reduce the original strength of narcotics and extend the quantity. Powdered milk and/or a variety of other substances are used to cut heroin and cocaine. This is a common practice of drug dealers to make their supply go as far as possible.

cutout 1. [I] When an intelligence agent wishes to avoid direct contact in an operation, a third party is involved that might not know either person. That individual is referred to as a cutout. The cutout is a go between used to protect the identity of other members of an intelligence or espionage network. **2.** [LE] Slang term meaning to leave a location.

cutting blade [C,G&PS] A razor blade that is used to separate cocaine into lines for snorting up the nose.

Cuz [C,G&PS] Term of greeting (from cousin), for a fellow (or sister) gang member.

CV Specialty code for civil investigation.

CVL Specialty code for civil rights.

CVR [C] Abbreviation for Crystal Video Receiver.

C&W [B] Abbreviation for Country & Western.

CW 1. [C] Abbreviation for Continuous Wave, usually a code transmission. 2. [C,G&PS] Slang China White, a high quality heroin. One of the most potent examples of heroin in the narcotic marketplace. 3. Abbreviation for Chemical Warfare.

CWI [M] Abbreviation for Continuous Wave Illuminator.

CWIED [M] Abbreviation for Command Wire Improvised Explosive Device.

CX [CW] Designation for blister agent (phosgene oxide) a chemical agent used by the military. CX destroys the skin and membrane tissue.

cyclone [USSR] The Soviet launch system used most often to place photo-surveillance satellites into orbit around the earth. Using the Cyclone rocket, the Soviet Union holds the record for 10 Cosmos-series satellites placed into orbit from a single launch.

cypher [I] A process that involves a variety of techniques for secret-message writing.

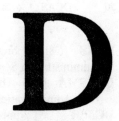

D [I] In intelligence/surveillance operations, a departure time.

D-4 Designation for the Trident II, a submarine launched, missile.

D-11 [HRU] designation for The London Metropolitan Police anti-terrorist and hostage rescue unit.

dabble [C,G&PS] Slang term meaning to have a small drug habit.

DACT [M] Abbreviation for Dissimilar Air Combat Training (i.e., with different aircraft types).

DA 1. [LE] Abbreviation for District Attorney. 2. [CW] Designation for the nausea gas diphenylchlorarsine, a chemical agent used by law enforcers and the military that causes depression, nausea, and sneezing in people. 3. [I] Abbreviation for Damage Assessment, an evaluation of the impact of a compromise in intelligence gathering. It refers to the loss of actual intelligence information, methods used, contacts made, and government sources.

D/A [C3I] Abbreviation for Digital to Analog.

DAB [C3I] Abbreviation for Defense Acquisition Board.

dagga [C,G&PS] A slang name for marijuana that originated in Vietnam.

dalmane [LE] Name of a controlled substance, a sedative. (*See* QUICK REFERENCE.)

DAMA [C3I] Abbreviation for Demand Assigned Multiple Access.

daN [D] Designation for decaNewton, a measure of force roughly equal to 2.25 lb.

dangle [I] Slang for one who intentionally draws the attention of a hostile intelligence or law enforcement agency so that, through mere contact, information can be learned about that agency.

DAR [US] Abbreviation for Defense Acquisition Regulation.

DARCOM [M] Acronym for Department of the Army Material Development and Readiness Command, also known as the Army Development and Readiness Command.

DARCOM/DARISSA [M] Designation for the classified weapons and development division of DARCOM.

DARPA [C3I] Abbreviation for Defense Advanced Research Projects Agency, the little-known research and development arm of the United States Department of Defense. Based at the Pentagon, DARPA has about 150 workers including scientists and research staff, and a budget for fiscal year 1990 of more than $1.5 billion and not a single laboratory. Despite its small size, it plays a key role in developing some of the nation's most advanced military and law enforcement technologies.

DARS [US] Abbreviation for Defense Acquisition Regulation System.

DART [M] Abbreviation for The Disaster Assistance and Relief Team, made up of Army Special Forces (ODA) Operational Detachment A and additional medical personnel. DART groups stand ready worldwide to assist in the aftermath of disasters.

DASS [C3I] Abbreviation for Demand Assignment Signalling & Switching.

David [A,LE,MIL] Designation for the letter *D*.

DB [I] Abbreviation for Drop Box, usually a mail-forwarding service used to process stolen documents—often to a foreign government in return for payment of services (espionage).

dB [C3I] Designation for Decibel.

DC [LE] Designation for Deputy Police Commissioner (Chief).

DCA 1. Abbreviation for Dual-Capable Aircraft. 2. [C3I] Defense Communications Agency.

DCAS [C3I] Abbreviation for Defense Contract Administration Services.

DCASMA [US] Abbreviation for Defense Contract Administration Services Management Area.

DCASR [US] Abbreviation for Defense Contract Administration Services, Region.

DCDS [LE] Abbreviation for Deceased (*person*) Confirmed Dead (*at*) Scene (*site/location*).

DCI [US] Abbreviation for Director of Central Intelligence (Agency). An individual appointed to office by the President of the United States.

DCID [US] Abbreviation for Director of Central Intelligence Directive.

DCIM A directive issued by the DCI that outlines the procedures, policies, and general guidelines for agency operation.

DCIS [I] Abbreviation for Defense Criminal Investigative Service, the responsibility of which is to investigate U.S. defense contractors suspected of fraud/theft/conspiracy against the government.

DCM [I] Abbreviation for Deputy Chief of (diplomatic) Mission.

DCS [C3I] Abbreviation for Defense Communications System.

DCSOPS [M] Abbreviation for Deputy Chief of Staff for Operations and Plans.

DCPI [LE] Abbreviation for Deputy Police Commissioner (chief) for Public Information.

DCU [C3I] Abbreviation for Deviation Control Unit.

DDA [I] Abbreviation for CIA Directorate of Administration; also, the Deputy Director of CIA's DDA.

DDCI [I] Abbreviation for Deputy Director of Central Intelligence.

DDCMP [C3I] Abbreviation for Digital Data Communications Message Protocol.

DDG [M] Designation for Guided Missile Destroyer.

DDI **1.** [I] CIA Directorate of Intelligence; also, the Deputy Director of DDI. **2.** [C3I] Abbreviation for Direct Digital Interface.

DDN [C3I] Abbreviation for Defense Data Network.

DDO [I] Abbreviation for CIA Directorate of Operations; also, Deputy Director of DDO.

DDP [I] Abbreviation for CIA Directorate of Planning.

DDR Specialty code for Drunk Driving Defense.

DDS&T [I] CIA Directorate of Science and Technology; also, the Deputy Director of DDS&T.

DEA **1.** [LE] Abbreviation for Drug Enforcement Administration of the United States Department of Justice. (*See* FEDERAL LAW ENFORCEMENT NATIONWIDE COMMUNICATIONS FREQUENCIES.) **2.** [HRU] Abbreviation for *Dimoria Eidikon Apostolon*, is the Special Mission Platoon of the Athens City Police Force. The DEA unit specializes in antiterrorist and hostage rescue operations throughout Greece.

DEA salary [LE] Agents of the DEA earn little more than half of what their counterparts make on some local police departments. The gap begins at the entry level. All DEA agents are required to have college degrees, but the starting salary in 1990 is $24,366 a year. College-educated rookies earn $38,000 in the Los Angeles Police Department; an LAPD officer with a high-school diploma starts at $32,400 a year.

dead drop [I] Slang term for the location where documents, covert equipment, or communications are left by agents in a special operation for pick-up by a second individual without the two people meeting.

dead presidents [LE] Slang term used in drug deals for dollar bills.

deal [C,G&PS] Slang term for selling narcotics.

dealer [C,G&PS] Term for someone who deals or sells dope.

DEB [C3I] Abbreviation for Digital European Backbone.

DEB TROPO MODEM [C] Acronym for Digital European Backbone Troposcatter Modem.

debriefing [I] The interviewing of an individual who has just returned from an intelligence-gathering assignment. The purpose of a debriefing is to gather information from as many sources as possible who have worked in the same area to determine small details that might be of some aid in future missions.

decibel [C] Abbreviated dB, the smallest detectable change in an audio level. That change is used to detect and measure electrical signals.

deck [C,G&PS] Slang for a packet of heroin.

DECM [C] Abbreviation for Digital Electronic Countermeasure.

deep six [NASA] Code name for a space shuttle mounted blue-green laser system designed to communicate with submarines deep undersea. Until now, all submarines have had to come near the surface to communicate.

DEF [C3I] Abbreviation for Development Evaluation Facility.

defector [I] An individual who, for political and/or personal reasons, repudiates the rules of his government and/or flees his country, usually to become an adversary.

defense cuts [C,G&PS] Slang for cuts on the fingers and forearms of an individual who has been in a knife fight or the victim of a knife attack.

DEFSMAC [US] Abbreviation for Defense Special Missile and Astronautics Center.

derated [A] Of or referring to an aircraft engine in which the maximum power is reduced to improve its life.

DELTA 1. [M] *See* DELTA FORCE. **2.** [A,LE,MIL] Designation for the letter *D*.

Delta force [M] A special forces (antiterrorist) group, also known as the 1st Special Forces Operational Detachment—Delta (SFOD-D). This is one of the elite fighting forces of the U.S.

demerol [LE] Name of a controlled substance, a narcotic. (*See* QUICK REFERENCE.)

DEMS [C3I] Abbreviation for Digital Electronic Message Service.

DEP CON [A] Acronym for Departure Control.

desoxyn [LE] Name of a controlled substance that is a stimulant. (*See* QUICK REFERENCE.)

Detachment 81 [HRU] The Special Commando Team of the Indonesian Army Special Forces. The main responsibility of Detachment 81 is anti-terrorism.

detail [LE] A detail is an assignment in law enforcement that is not routine in nature.

deuce [C,G&PS] Slang for a two-year prison sentence, used by someone convicted of a crime.

devils [US] Naval aviation voice brevity code meaning depth.

Dev-Sol [TRG] A Turkish left-wing revolutionary terrorist organization with links to Syria and Libya. This group is also known in Turkey as Devsol.

DEW 1. [C3I] Abbreviation for Distant Early Warning. **2.** [M] Abbreviation for Directed-energy Weapon, such as a laser.

Deuxieme Bureau [I] The intelligence section of the French military, under the direction of the Minister of Defense of France.

Dexedrine [LE] Brand name for a controlled substance that is a stimulant. (*See* QUICK REFERENCE.)

dexies [C,G&PS] Slang term for amphetamines. (*See* QUICK REFERENCE.)

dextroamphetamine [LE] A controlled substance that is a stimulant. (*See* QUICK REFERENCE.)

DF [M] Abbreviation for Direction Finding.

D-F [M] Abbreviation for Direction Finder.

DFAT [C3I] Abbreviation for Destination Final Acceptance Test.

DGM [C3I] Abbreviation for Digital Group Multiplexer.

DGS [GOV] Designation for *Policia Internacional e de Defensa do Estado*, formally known as PIDE, the Portuguese secret police in Mozambique.

DGSE [I] Abbreviation for *Direction Generale de la Securite Exterieure*, a principal intelligence agency in France connected with military and strategic intelligence, electronic intercepts, and foreign intelligence. The DGSE is under the direction of the Prime Minister of France.

DIA [C3I] Abbreviation for Defense Intelligence Agency, an agency responsible for military and strategic intelligence.

DIAC [D] Abbreviation for Defense Industry Advisory Committee.

diacetylmorphine [LE] A controlled substance that is a narcotic. (*See* QUICK REFERENCE.)

Diane [C,G&PS] Slang for meperidine, a stimulant.

diaper change [LE] Slang term for replacing batteries in a hand-held transceiver or surveillance transmitter.

diazepam [LE] A controlled substance that is a minor tranquilizer. (*See* QUICK REFERENCE.)

dibber [LE] Name of a bomb specifically designed for use by law enforcement and/or the military to produce the maximum possible area of damage and upheaval to a road or concrete runway.

dibble & dabble [C,G&PS] Slang for the occasional use of narcotics.

DIC [I] Abbreviation for the Defense Intelligence Community. This includes the Defense Intelligence Agency (DIA), the National Security Agency (NSA), and the military services' intelligence offices including the Department of Defense (DOD), and its related agencies within the United States government.

dick 1. [LE] Slang term for a police detective. 2. [C,G&PS] Slang term for a small amount of some narcotic.

Didrex [LE] Brand name for a controlled substance that is a stimulant. (*See* QUICK REFERENCE.)

DIDS [US] Abbreviation for Defense Integrated Data System.

DIE [I] Abbreviation for *Departamentul de Informatii Externe*, the foreign intelligence service for the Romanian government. The DIE is responsible for certain training programs (*See* PFLP-GC) and electronic surveillance in support of KGB operations in the Mediterranean.

digipeater [C] A repeater that is used for packet radio. (*See* PACKET RADIO.)

digital [C] Descriptive of communication signals that use characters or numbers.

digital receiver [C] A radio receiver that utilizes synthesized circuits.

dihedral [A] The upward inclination of an aircraft wing in front-view, used to create (generate) a rolling movement in sideslips.

DIL [C3I] Abbreviation for Diversity Interfacility Link.

Dilaudid [LE] Brand name for a controlled substance that is a narcotic. (*See* QUICK REFERENCE.)

dime [C,G&PS] *See* DIME BAG.

dime bag [C,G&PS] Slang for a packet of narcotics with a street value of $10.

dinosaur [LE] A derogatory term for a law enforcement officer who tends to want to do things the old way.

dinky dows [C,G&PS] Slang for marijuana. The term originated in the combat zones of Vietnam where marijuana was used by American troops as a get away from the reality of what was going on around them.

DIP 1. [M] Abbreviation for Digital Image Processing. 2. [US] Naval aviation voice brevity code meaning the lowering of sonar into the water.

DIPCO [D] Acronym for a diplomatic courier who is in the employ of a specific foreign government.

dipole antenna [C] A simple half-wavelength, center-fed antenna.

direct action [TRG] A blending of many terrorist/radical groups and created by merging the NAPAP, an ultraleft French terrorist group and the French Red Brigade. Other members come from the many radical anti-NATO groups in Europe.

dirt bag [C,G&PS] Slang for a low-life individual with a long history of criminal activities.

dirty 1. [C,G&PS] Slang for drugs in possession. 2. [LE] In law enforcement, of or referring to someone who is under suspicion or has on his/her person drugs or stolen property.

dirty dishes [LE] Slang for incriminating evidence, usually planted to make an individual appear guilty.

DIS 1. [I] Abbreviation for Defense Investigative Service. This agency of the Department of Defense conducts all the individual background security checks and issues security clearances to military personnel. **2.** [I] Abbreviation for Defense Intelligence Service of the United Kingdom. The DIS gathers military intelligence and reports its findings to MI6 for action.

DISCO [GOV] Abbreviation for Defense Industrial Security Clearance Office, an agency of the Department of Defense responsible for individual, industrial, and facility security clearances.

Discoverer [US] Code name for the United States satellite program that provided the cover for the CIA Corona satellite project. (*See* CORONA.)

disinformation [I] False or misleading information developed to confuse and/or discredit the opposition. (*See* DECEPTION MATERIAL.)

disposable load [A] The payload/warload of a vehicle or aircraft, plus the fuel and operating crew.

DISTAN [US] Designation for Distributed Interactive Secure Telecoms.

ditty bops [LE] Slang for young thugs, usually gang members in a group.

DIV [B] Designation for Diversified programming.

DLA [US] Abbreviation for Defense Logistics Agency.

DLA(CAS)HQ [US] Designation for Defense contract administration services headquarters.

DLB [I] Abbreviation for Dead-Letter Box (*See* DEAD DROP).

DM **1.** [CW] Designation for nausea gas (Adamsite). This chemical agent is used by the military and law enforcement and causes sneezing, nausea, and depression. **2.** [I] Abbreviation for Deception Material, material that is passed along (usually by an undercover agent) to the criminal elements, foreign governments, or someone suspected of "working for the other side." DM has every appearance of being the real thing, but is, in fact, false. Its purpose is to mislead. **3.** [C3I] Abbreviation for Digital Multiplex.

DMD [US] Abbreviation for Digital Message Device.

DME [M] Abbreviation for Distance Measuring Equipment (navaid).

DMS [C3I] Abbreviation for Defense Meteorological Satellite.

DMSP [C3I] Abbreviation for Defense Meteorological Satellite Program.

DMT [LE] Designation for a controlled substance that is a hallucinogen. (*See* QUICK REFERENCE.)

DMV [D] Abbreviation for Department of Motor Vehicles.

DNA [LE] Abbreviation for deoxyribonucleic acid. Laboratory experts can use samples of hair, blood, semen, or skin left by a criminal to find his unique genetic code. Scientists find the code, which looks like the bar code found on supermarket merchandise when processed by DNA technicians, by unraveling the compound of DNA, which is in every cell of the human body. Once a code is found at a crime scene, investigators can compare it with the genetic code of a suspect. DNA analysis is the strongest form of evidence there is for identifying criminals—especially in cases of sexual assault. Theoretically, the odds against two people having the same DNA structure are 30 billion to 1.

DNI **1.** [C3I] Abbreviation for Digital Non-Interpolated. **2.** [M] Abbreviation for Director of Naval Intelligence.

DNR [LE] Abbreviation for Do Not Resuscitate, a medical term meaning not to restore breathing or revive a person who has had a failure of all other vital signs or who apparently is dead.

DNVT [C3I] Abbreviation for Digital Nonsecure Voice Terminal.

DOA **1.** [LE] Abbreviation for Dead on arrival. **2.** [C,G&PS] Designation for PCP. (*See* QUICK REFERENCE.) **3.** [I] Abbreviation for Direction of Arrival.

DOB [D] Abbreviation for Date of Birth.

DOC Specialty code for document examination, photographic.

docket numbers [LE] Slang for active criminals or individuals caught in a criminal activity.

documentation [I] Any item of hardware, document, photographs, or related personal effects that will lend some authenticity to a story. A false background that has good documentation makes it believable and accepted.

DOD [US] Abbreviation for Department of Defense.

Doe [LE] Slang for methamphetamines. (*See* QUICK REFERENCE.)

dog house radar [I] An intermediate-range Soviet radar system that is in place on the outskirts of Moscow. Its primary mission is to detect low-flying stealth aircraft. (*See* TRY ADD RADAR.)

DOJ [LE] Abbreviation for Department of Justice.

dollies [LE] Slang term for a commercial version of methadone (dolophine).

dolly [US] Naval aviation voice brevity code meaning airborne data link equipment.

dolophine [LE] Name of a controlled substance that is a narcotic. (*See* QUICK REFERENCE.)

DOM 1. Specialty code for domestic. 2. [LE] Designation for a controlled substance that is a hallucinogen, also known as STP. (*See* QUICK REFERENCE.)

domestic [C,G&PS] Slang for home-grown, not smuggled, marijuana.

do meth [C,G&PS] Slang for injecting methedrine (speed).

domino [C,G&PS] Slang term for an individual wanting narcotics.

donut dollies [LE] Slang term for female Red Cross workers.

doobie [C,G&PS] Slang for a marijuana cigarette.

doo jee [C,G&PS] Slang for heroin. (*See* QUICK REFERENCE.)

dope [C,G&PS] Slang term for any and all narcotics, but usually heroin.

doper [C,G&PS] Slang for a drug user.

dope run [C,G&PS] Slang term for a trip to obtain marijuana or drugs.

doppler [A] Of or referring to radar that exploits the frequency shift that is produced by the relative speed of the target, especially used in detecting low-flying aircraft.

doppler effect [C] The change in frequency of a sound or radio/radar signal.

do-rag [C,G&PS] Slang for a blue (Crips) or red (Bloods) bandanna worn by street gang members showing their gang affiliation.

doriden [LE] Name of a controlled substance that is a sedative. (*See* QUICK REFERENCE.)

dosaaf [USSR] Abbreviation for *Dobrovol'noye Obshchestvo Sodeystviya Armii, Aviatsii, Flotu* (Russian Volunteer Society for Cooperation with the Army, Aviation, and the Fleet).

DOT 1. [GOV] Abbreviation for Department of Transportation. 2. [C3I] Abbreviation for Designated Optical Tracker.

double agent [I] An individual who is cooperating with a foreign intelligence group while at the same time working for, and under the direction of, another country. A double agent works for two different organizations, is loyal to one, and betrays the other.

double L [LE] Acronym for a land-line station-to-station telephone.

double trigger [TRG] A process used by terrorist groups to explode a bomb in a high-flying aircraft. Attached to the bomb is a barometric device set to start a sequence of events as the aircraft reaches a certain altitude. At that altitude, the barometric device activates a second trigger, an electronic timer, to make the bomb explode at a later time. (*See* BAROMETRIC CHAMBER.)

double trouble [LE] Slang for the consumption of liquor and barbiturates at the same time.

DOV [LE] Abbreviation for Discreet Operations Vehicle.

down converter [C] An electronic device (converter) whose output is a lower frequency.

downers [C,G&PS] Slang for a narcotic or drug that also is a sedative or depressant.

down habit [C,G&PS] A slang term meaning that an individual has a major and chronic addiction to narcotics or drugs.

down link [C] The rebroadcast signal from a satellite.

down with someone [C,G&PS] Slang term meaning to share drugs.

downs [C,G&PS] Slang for barbiturates. (*See* QUICK REFERENCE.)

downers [C,G&PS] Slang for depressants, usually a barbiturate.

DPCM [C3I] Abbreviation for Differential Pulse Code Modulation.

DRAMA [US] Abbreviation for Digital Radio and Multiplex Acquisition.

DRB [GOV] Abbreviation for Defense Review Board.

dreamer [C,G&PS] Slang term for a larger than usual injection of morphine.

DRG Specialty code for drugs referring to criminal dependency.

DRH [TRG] Abbreviation for Dutch Red Help. This left-wing terrorist group has conducted a number of training exercises with the Palestinians. The DRH has also given funds and weapons to the IRA.

dripper [C,G&PS] Slang term for the syringe and needle used for drug injections.

Drop 1. [I] Slang term for a location to leave a message or item for later pickup in a clandestine operation. (*See* DEAD DROP.) 2. [C,G&PS] Slang term meaning to inject or swallow a narcotic or drug.

drop a dime [C,G&PS] Slang term meaning to be an informer, to provide information to a law enforcement agency about a specific crime or individual criminal act.

drop gun [C,G&PS] Slang for a handgun, most often found by a law enforcement officer at a crime scene. The found gun is later "dropped" by that officer at another crime scene to justify a shooting of dubious nature.

dropped [C,G&PS] Slang term meaning to be arrested.

dropper [C,G&PS] Slang term meaning a dripper with a needle that is reused over and over and a medicine dropper that is used as the syringe. This outfit usually is a last resort drug kit.

drug manufacturing chemicals [LE] Methamphetamines can be made from a number of differ-ent chemicals, many of which can be purchased legitimately from chemical supply companies or hardware stores. Some of the common chemicals, and their dangers, include the following:

- Red phosphorous: if overheated, it can easily convert to yellow or white phosphorous, which can set off flash fires without warning and causes serious and deep skin burns
- Hydriodic acid: can convert to hydrogen iodide gas, which is fatal if inhaled
- Thionyl chloride: as it vaporizes, it can produce sulphuric and hydrochloric acid, which can cause respiratory problems and burns the skin
- Phenylacetic acid: a precursor to benzyl cyanide, which is fatal if inhaled
- Alcohol and sodium metal: the two can react in water, causing explosions and fire

Some methods used to manufacture methamphetamines use heavy metals, such as lead acetate, as catalysts. Those can build up in a person's body, causing lead poisoning.

dry cleaning [I] A technique used by covert operators to detect surveillance of their operation. Dry cleaning involves electronic sweeps of rooms to detect recording equipment, and protection methods to stop outside penetration by photographic or electronic means.

dry out [LE] To detoxify from narcotics or drugs.

dry run [I] The rehearsal of a covert operation, or a plan that has not resulted in successful intelligence gathering.

D.S. [LE] *See* DUMP SITE.

DSARC [C3I] Abbreviation for Defense System Acquisition Review Council.

DSAT [I] Acronym for Defensive SATellite, a satellite that is in orbit solely to protect other satellites.

DSCS 1. [C3I] Abbreviation for Defense Satellite Communication System. 2. [GOV] Abbreviation for Defense Satellite Communication System.

DSI [C3I] Abbreviation for Digital Speech Interpolation.

DSMP [GOV] Abbreviation for Defense Satellite Meteorological Program.

DSN [C3I] Abbreviation for Defense Switching(ed) Network.

DSP [C3I] Abbreviation for Defense Support Program.

DST [I] Abbreviation for the Bureau for Defence and Surveillance of the Territory is the domestic counter-intelligence of France. It is directed by the French Minister of the Interior.

DSVT [C3I] Abbreviation for Digital Secure Voice Terminal.

DTE [C3I] Abbreviation for Data Terminating Equipment.

DTH [C3I] Abbreviation for Down The Hill Radio communications.

DTMF [C] Abbreviation for Dual-Tone Multi-Frequency pad. This is the specific circuit that permits telephone dial tones to be generated. DTMF is widely used in VHF and UHF transceivers for scanner usage.

DTS [C3I] Abbreviation for Digital Terminal System.

DTSC [C3I] Abbreviation for Defense Telecommunication System Center.

DTU [USSR] Abbreviation for Dorozhno-Transportnyy Upravleniye (Road and Transportation Directorate).

DU Abbreviation for depleted uranium, a material used to manufacture high sectional density armor-piercing projectiles. High sectional density means a flatter trajectory, less effect by environmental elements, and greater retained kinetic energy. (*See* A-10.)

dubok [USSR] Russian for "drop dead."

DUI [LE] Abbreviation for Driving Under the Influence. DUI also is defined as drunk driving or driving under the influence of drugs or narcotics.

duige [C,G&PS] Slang for heroin. (*See* QUICK REFERENCE.)

duke [LE] Slang for a black member of a white gang. A duke usually is a strongarm type and collector of bad debts. (*See* BLOODS and CRIPS.)

dummy **1.** Slang for someone who isn't very smart. **2.** [LE] A container filled with a fake (nonnarcotic) material but sold, or offered, as the genuine article. It usually is a packet prepared by a law enforcement agency.

dump site [LE] Slang term for a common gravesite, usually used in criminal cases involving a serial killer. The killer tends to take victims to various locations and often dumps bodies at a site he believes "safe" or with some special meaning. An example is the Green River murders.

dust [C,G&PS] Slang for cocaine. (*See* QUICK REFERENCE.)

duster [C,G&PS] Slang for a marijuana cigarette made with heroin or PCP.

DVP [C] Abbreviation for Digital Voice Protection, an electronic voice/data scrambling system.

DWI **1.** [LE] Abbreviation for Driving While Intoxicated. **2.** [LE] Abbreviation for Driving While Impaired, usually by narcotics/drugs.

DX [C] The communications (radio) abbreviation for distance.

DXer [C] Slang for a ham radio operator and/or shortwave listener who make attempts to hear or communicate with distant broadcasting stations.

dyke [LE] Slang for a female homosexual who plays the part of a male in a relationship; also called a lesbian.

dynamite **1.** [C,G&PS] Slang for very pure heroin. **2.** [C,G&PS] Slang for a very powerful blend of morphine and cocaine. **3.** [C,G&PS] Slang for a very powerful blend of marijuana.

dynamiter [C,G&PS] Slang for a cocaine addict.

DZ [M] Abbreviation for Drop Zone. A drop zone is for parachute and/or combat troops and related ground support hardware.

E

E [E] Designation for electric field intensity.

EA-6B *See* A-6.

EAA [US] Abbreviation for Experimental Aircraft Association.

E-Bird [E] Designation for electronic beam ionization of a semi-conductor device.

EAM **1.** [C3I] Abbreviation for Emergency Action Message. **2.** [GOV] Abbreviation for Electronic Accounting Machine. **3.** [D] Designation for The Greek National Liberation Front.

earthquake [D] The sudden shifting of two blocks of the Earth's crust along a crack called a *fault*. The motion originates at an underground point called the focus. The epicenter is the point on the earth's surface directly above the focus. Shockwaves travel outward from the focus, becoming fainter over distance. (*See* SEISMOGRAPH.) The following are steps to take after an earthquake:

- Stay as calm as you can.

- Check for fire or safety hazards. Shut off the main gas valve and notify the gas company if there is a leak.

- Make sure water is clean and free of sediments. Avoid drinking contaminated water. Notify the water company if you spot any unusual odors or contaminants.

- Shut off the power at the control box if there is any damage to electric wiring. Check your chimney for cracks and damage but approach it cautiously. Chimneys can topple during an aftershock.

- If you are a ham radio operator or scanner fan, check your outside antenna using the same rules of safety as for a chimney.

- Open closets and storage areas cautiously. Beware of objects falling off shelves.

- Have a flashlight ready to use at your home and place of business.

- Take refuge under something sturdy. Stay away from mirrors, windows or glass doors. If you are in an automobile and an earthquake or some other disaster happens, don't stop near something that could collapse, explode, or in some other way harm you.

- Tune in to local radio stations that have emergency broadcast frequencies. Watch television to stay informed.

- Gather together nonperishable food.

- Gather several days' supply of drinking water. Water is all around you—in water heaters, ice trays, canned vegetables. Fill up your bathtub. To get water from the heater, shut off the water inflow.

- Inspect your house or apartment for cracks in the walls or the foundation. Cracks in the foundation wider than $1/8$ inch indicate a potential weakness.

- Keep on hand in your home some emergency gear: bottled water, blankets, a fire extinguisher, a wind-up or battery clock, a manual can opener, flashlight, pet food, as well as playing cards and books, functional clothing. While such a collection would be difficult to maintain at your place of work, keep in mind that in a disaster you could be cut off from a variety of things you might need to survive. A few items kept in a small box under your desk might save your life someday.

- Do not use your kitchen stove; it might not be working for lack of gas or electricity. Use barbecues or camp stoves for cooking. Use up food that will spoil.

- Do not search for a gas leak with a match.

- Do not turn on the gas or operate electrical switches or appliances. Sparks can ignite gas from broken lines.

- Do not touch downed power lines or electrical wiring of any kind.

- Do not eat or drink anything from open containers near shattered glass.

- Do not try to go downstairs during an earthquake. Stairways can collapse.

- Do not walk through your house or workplace without shoes.

- Do not drive or walk to a disaster area. Let the emergency rescue teams, police, and fire fighters do the jobs they have been trained to do.

Easter eggs   [C,G&PS] Slang for rock cocaine.

EBS   [G] Abbreviation for Emergency Broadcast System. The EBS in the United States is designed to get essential information from government agencies to the public. Once or more each week since it was established in 1964, radio listeners have been subjected to an occasional announcement advising them "This is a test of the Emergency Broadcasting System. If this had been a real emergency, you should stay tuned to your local radio station until given further instructions"—followed by an annoying tone. EBS was a by-product of the Cold War, when government officials were concerned mostly about an atomic bomb or missile attack from the Soviet Union. EBS was intended as a warning system. As the Cold War cooled, EBS has more and more become a system for use after a disaster hits. In a real emergency, local civil defense or public safety officers prepare text for a message they wish the public to hear. That message is delivered by hand or telephone to what's called a primary EBS station. If that station is unable to transmit, the assignment moves on to a secondary EBS station.

EC   [EW] Abbreviation for Electronic Combat.

eccentricity   [NASA] The configuration (shape) of the orbit of a satellite in flight. The eccentricity of a satellite's orbit is based on its apogee (the farthest point it is away from the earth's atmosphere) and its perigee (the nearest point it is into the earth's atmosphere). The eccentricity is computed mathematically prior to launch.

ECCM   [EW] Abbreviation for Electronic Counter-countermeasures.

Echo   [A,LE,MIL] Designation for the letter *E*.

ECM   **1.** [EW] Abbreviation for Electronic Countermeasures—usually some form of jamming. **2.** [C3I] Abbreviation for Electronic Combat Measures.

ECOM   [C3I] Abbreviation for Electronic Computer Originated Mail.

ECPA   [GOV] Abbreviation for The Electronics Communication Privacy Act of 1986.

ECS   [C3I] Abbreviation for European Communications Satellite.

ecstasy   [LE] Slang term for a mind-altering drug. (*See* MDMA.)

ED   Specialty code for Electronic Detection.

ED   [CW] Designation for a blister agent (Ethyldichlorarsine). This chemical warfare agent was developed for use by the military. It can be dispersed in a variety of ways including the application by low-flying aircraft. When ED comes into contact with the skin of humans or animals, it causes painful blisters.

eden   [I] Slang for an individual hired from outside because of unique qualifications by a government agency, such as the FBI or CIA, to work as a covert agent on a special project or mission.

edge work   [LE] Slang for the marking of playing cards that are used in gambling.

EDP   [LE] Abbreviation for Emotionally Disturbed Person.

EDU   [LE] Background code for education.

Edward   [A,LE,MIL] Designation for the letter *E*.

EE   [D] Designation for English.

E and E   [M] Abbreviation for Evade and Escape.

EEI   [I] Abbreviation for Essential Elements of Information. In an intelligence operation, this must include the specific and detailed information regarding the hostile individual or agency. That information then is assessed carefully for methods that suggest the best ways of penetration.

egg   [LE] Slang for a naive person who tends to gamble over their skill level.

EHF   [C3I] Abbreviation for Extremely High Frequency, such as 25 GHz−300 GHz on microwaves.

EIA   [C3I] Abbreviation for Electronic Industries Association.

eight   [C,G&PS] *See* EIGHTH.

eight-ball   [C,G&PS] Slang for $1/8$ ounce of cocaine.

eighth   [C,G&PS] Slang for $1/8$ ounce of heroin.

eighty-sixed   [M] An old military term, sometimes used by law enforcement officers meaning "removed" or "canceled out" and used in the context of a person, place, or thing.

EIRP   [C3I] Abbreviation for Equivalent Isotropic Radiated Power.

EJ   [EW] Abbreviation for Expendable Jammer.

EJS   [M] Designation for Enhanced Joint Tactical Information Distribution System. (*See* JTIDS.)

EL   [C3I] Abbreviation for Elevation.

ELAS   [D] Designation for The Greek National Popular Liberation Army.

elephant dust   [C,G&PS] Slang for PCP. (*See* QUICK REFERENCE.)

ELC   Specialty code for electronic surveillance.

elevator   [A] A movable surface on the trailing edge of the horizontal tail (or tailplane) of an airplane that provides pitch control on low-speed aircraft.

elevon   [A] A trailing edge surface on the wing of a tailless delta aircraft (such-as the B-2) that provides both pitch and roll control. Stealth aircraft being used by the U.S. military are designed with elevon control surfaces.

ELF   **1.** [C3I] Abbreviation for Extremely Low Frequency, which are frequencies in the range of 30 to 300 Hz. **2.** [TRG] Eritrean Liberation Front, a terrorist/radical group.

elicitation   [I] The acquisition of intelligence from a person or group that does not disclose the intent of the interview or conversation. Both the intelligence community and law enforcement agencies use this technique to gather information about an adversary.

ELINT   [C3I] Abbreviation for ELectronic INTelligence, information that is derived by the interception and study of electromagnetic radiation generated from noncommunication sources. Radar transmissions are one source of ELINT. The reception of enemy radio transmissions is another. The data received that concerns a Soviet jamming system would be considered ELINT. ELINT does not include communications intelligence.

ELN   **1.** [TRG] Designation for the Bolivian terrorist "liberation" movement. The ELN reflects a frustration within Bolivia for a better form of government. The method employed against the government is to kill the officials. This has created a police state rather than bring about real change toward something better. **2.** [TRG] Abbreviation for Ejercito de Liberacion National, a radical/terrorist group headquartered in Peru.

ELP   [I] Abbreviation for Exercito de Libertacao Portugues.

ELS   [TRG] Designation for the Southern Liberation Army, headquartered in Mexico. This group of radicals conduct acts of terror against local government officials.

ELSIG   [M] Designation for electronic security.

ELT   [C3I] Abbreviation for Emergency Locator Transmitter.

ELV   [C3I] Abbreviation for Expendable Launch Vehicle.

EM   Specialty code for Embezzlement.

EMC [EW] Abbreviation for Electromagnetic Compatibility.

EMCON [EW] Acronym for Emission Control.

EMD [M] Abbreviation for Each Military Department.

Emergency Frequencies—Cellular Frequency Groups The Federal Communications Commission (FCC) has allocated specific frequencies that apply nationwide to the cellular telephone frequency network. Because any of these frequencies can be assigned to any cell nationwide, it is difficult to determine, using the usual methods, what frequencies, usage, and specific channels have been assigned to your listening areas.

TABLE E-1 is the most comprehensive cellular telephone frequency listing ever prepared. The listing will be especially helpful to law enforcement agencies wanting to track criminal elements and drug dealers who use the cellular telephone system.

It is very unique in that it allows scanner users to identify specific channels they hear and not only target a particular set of frequencies in a bandwidth, but also to target a particular area as well. This gives the law enforcement agency or scanner users the capability of monitoring every single cellular transmission made in a specific geographical area by channel, and also know the mode of operation (voice, control, or signaling) for a given frequency.

Knowing the area that a call is made from can usually fill in most of the "gaps" cellular

Table E-1. Emergency Cellular Telephone Frequencies

Channel Number	Base Transmit Frequency (MHz)	Mobile Transmit Frequency (MHz)	Channel Usage Type	Channel Number	Base Transmit Frequency (MHz)	Mobile Transmit Frequency (MHz)	Channel Usage Type
1	870.0300	825.0300	Voice	30	870.9000	825.9000	Voice
2	870.0600	825.0600	Voice	31	870.9300	825.9300	Voice
3	870.0900	825.0900	Voice	32	870.9600	825.9600	Voice
4	870.1200	825.1200	Voice	33	870.9900	825.9900	Voice
5	870.1500	825.1500	Voice	34	871.0200	826.0200	Voice
6	870.1800	825.1800	Voice	35	871.0500	826.0500	Voice
7	870.2100	825.2100	Voice	36	871.0800	826.0800	Voice
8	870.2400	825.2400	Voice	37	871.1100	826.1100	Voice
9	870.2700	825.2700	Voice	38	871.1400	826.1400	Voice
10	870.3000	825.3000	Voice	39	871.1700	826.1700	Voice
11	870.3300	825.3300	Voice	40	871.2000	826.2000	Voice
12	870.3600	825.3600	Voice	41	871.2300	826.2300	Voice
13	870.3900	825.3900	Voice	42	871.2600	826.2600	Voice
14	870.4200	825.4200	Voice	43	871.2900	826.2900	Voice
15	870.4500	825.4500	Voice	44	871.3200	826.3200	Voice
16	870.4800	825.4800	Voice	45	871.3500	826.3500	Voice
17	870.5100	825.5100	Voice	46	871.3800	826.3800	Voice
18	870.5400	825.5400	Voice	47	871.4100	826.4100	Voice
19	870.5700	825.5700	Voice	48	871.4400	826.4400	Voice
20	870.6000	825.6000	Voice	49	871.4700	826.4700	Voice
21	870.6300	825.6300	Voice	50	871.5000	826.5000	Voice
22	870.6600	825.6600	Voice	51	871.5300	826.5300	Voice
23	870.6900	825.6900	Voice	52	871.5600	826.5600	Voice
24	870.7200	825.7200	Voice	53	871.5900	826.5900	Voice
25	870.7500	825.7500	Voice	54	871.6200	826.6200	Voice
26	870.7800	825.7800	Voice	55	871.6500	826.6500	Voice
27	870.8100	825.8100	Voice	56	871.6800	826.6800	Voice
28	870.8400	825.8400	Voice	57	871.7100	826.7100	Voice
29	870.8700	825.8700	Voice	58	871.7400	826.7400	Voice

Table E-1. Continued

Channel Number	Base Transmit Frequency (MHz)	Mobile Transmit Frequency (MHz)	Channel Usage Type	Channel Number	Base Transmit Frequency (MHz)	Mobile Transmit Frequency (MHz)	Channel Usage Type
59	871.7700	826.7700	Voice	111	873.3300	828.3300	Voice
60	871.8000	826.8000	Voice	112	873.3600	828.3600	Voice
61	871.8300	826.8300	Voice	113	873.3900	828.3900	Voice
62	871.8600	826.8600	Voice	114	873.4200	828.4200	Voice
63	871.8900	826.8900	Voice	115	873.4500	828.4500	Voice
64	871.9200	826.9200	Voice	116	873.4800	828.4800	Voice
65	871.9500	826.9500	Voice	117	873.5100	828.5100	Voice
66	871.9800	826.9800	Voice	118	873.5400	828.5400	Voice
67	872.0100	827.0100	Voice	119	873.5700	828.5700	Voice
68	872.0400	827.0400	Voice	120	873.6000	828.6000	Voice
69	872.0700	827.0700	Voice	121	873.6300	828.6300	Voice
70	872.1000	827.1000	Voice	122	873.6600	828.6600	Voice
71	872.1300	827.1300	Voice	123	873.6900	828.6900	Voice
72	872.1600	827.1600	Voice	124	873.7200	828.7200	Voice
73	872.1900	827.1900	Voice	125	873.7500	828.7500	Voice
74	872.2200	827.2200	Voice	126	873.7800	828.7800	Voice
75	872.2500	827.2500	Voice	127	873.8100	828.8100	Voice
76	872.2800	827.2800	Voice	128	873.8400	828.8400	Voice
77	872.3100	827.3100	Voice	129	873.8700	828.8700	Voice
78	872.3400	827.3400	Voice	130	873.9000	828.9000	Voice
79	872.3700	827.3700	Voice	131	873.9300	828.9300	Voice
80	872.4000	827.4000	Voice	132	873.9600	828.9600	Voice
81	872.4300	827.4300	Voice	133	873.9900	828.9900	Voice
82	872.4600	827.4600	Voice	134	874.0200	829.0200	Voice
83	872.4900	827.4900	Voice	135	874.0500	829.0500	Voice
84	872.5200	827.5200	Voice	136	874.0800	829.0800	Voice
85	872.5500	827.5500	Voice	137	874.1100	829.1100	Voice
86	872.5800	827.5800	Voice	138	874.1400	829.1400	Voice
87	872.6100	827.6100	Voice	139	874.1700	829.1700	Voice
88	872.6400	827.6400	Voice	140	874.2000	829.2000	Voice
89	872.6700	827.6700	Voice	141	874.2300	829.2300	Voice
90	872.7000	827.7000	Voice	142	874.2600	829.2600	Voice
91	872.7300	827.7300	Voice	143	874.2900	829.2900	Voice
92	872.7600	827.7600	Voice	144	874.3200	829.3200	Voice
93	872.7900	827.7900	Voice	145	874.3500	829.3500	Voice
94	872.8200	827.8200	Voice	146	874.3800	829.3800	Voice
95	872.8500	827.8500	Voice	147	874.4100	829.4100	Voice
96	872.8800	827.8800	Voice	148	874.4400	829.4400	Voice
97	872.9100	827.9100	Voice	149	874.4700	829.4700	Voice
98	872.9400	827.9400	Voice	150	874.5000	829.5000	Voice
99	872.9700	827.9700	Voice	151	874.5300	829.5300	Voice
100	873.0000	828.0000	Voice	152	874.5600	829.5600	Voice
101	873.0300	828.0300	Voice	153	874.5900	829.5900	Voice
102	873.0600	828.0600	Voice	154	874.6200	829.6200	Voice
103	873.0900	828.0900	Voice	155	874.6500	829.6500	Voice
104	873.1200	828.1200	Voice	156	874.6800	829.6800	Voice
105	873.1500	828.1500	Voice	157	874.7100	829.7100	Voice
106	873.1800	828.1800	Voice	158	874.7400	829.7400	Voice
107	873.2100	828.2100	Voice	159	874.7700	829.7700	Voice
108	873.2400	828.2400	Voice	160	874.8000	829.8000	Voice
109	873.2700	828.2700	Voice	161	874.8300	829.8300	Voice
110	873.3000	828.3000	Voice	162	874.8600	829.8600	Voice

Table E-1. Continued

Channel Number	Base Transmit Frequency (MHz)	Mobile Transmit Frequency (MHz)	Channel Usage Type	Channel Number	Base Transmit Frequency (MHz)	Mobile Transmit Frequency (MHz)	Channel Usage Type
163	874.8900	829.8900	Voice	215	876.4500	831.4500	Voice
164	874.9200	829.9200	Voice	216	876.4800	831.4800	Voice
165	874.9500	829.9500	Voice	217	876.5100	831.5100	Voice
166	874.9800	829.9800	Voice	218	876.5400	831.5400	Voice
167	875.0100	830.0100	Voice	219	876.5700	831.5700	Voice
168	875.0400	830.0400	Voice	220	876.6000	831.6000	Voice
169	875.0700	830.0700	Voice	221	876.6300	831.6300	Voice
170	875.1000	830.1000	Voice	222	876.6600	831.6600	Voice
171	875.1300	830.1300	Voice	223	876.6900	831.6900	Voice
172	875.1600	830.1600	Voice	224	876.7200	831.7200	Voice
173	875.1900	830.1900	Voice	225	876.7500	831.7500	Voice
174	875.2200	830.2200	Voice	226	876.7800	831.7800	Voice
175	875.2500	830.2500	Voice	227	876.8100	831.8100	Voice
176	875.2800	830.2800	Voice	228	876.8400	831.8400	Voice
177	875.3100	830.3100	Voice	229	876.8700	831.8700	Voice
178	875.3400	830.3400	Voice	230	876.9000	831.9000	Voice
179	875.3700	830.3700	Voice	231	876.9300	831.9300	Voice
180	875.4000	830.4000	Voice	232	876.9600	831.9600	Voice
181	875.4300	830.4300	Voice	233	876.9900	831.9900	Voice
182	875.4600	830.4600	Voice	234	877.0200	832.0200	Voice
183	875.4900	830.4900	Voice	235	877.0500	832.0500	Voice
184	875.5200	830.5200	Voice	236	877.0800	832.0800	Voice
185	875.5500	830.5500	Voice	237	877.1100	832.1100	Voice
186	875.5800	830.5800	Voice	238	877.1400	832.1400	Voice
187	875.6100	830.6100	Voice	239	877.1700	832.1700	Voice
188	875.6400	830.6400	Voice	240	877.2000	832.2000	Voice
189	875.6700	830.6700	Voice	241	877.2300	832.2300	Voice
190	875.7000	830.7000	Voice	242	877.2600	832.2600	Voice
191	875.7300	830.7300	Voice	243	877.2900	832.2900	Voice
192	875.7600	830.7600	Voice	244	877.3200	832.3200	Voice
193	875.7900	830.7900	Voice	245	877.3500	832.3500	Voice
194	875.8200	830.8200	Voice	246	877.3800	832.3800	Voice
195	875.8500	830.8500	Voice	247	877.4100	832.4100	Voice
196	875.8800	830.8800	Voice	248	877.4400	832.4400	Voice
197	875.9100	830.9100	Voice	249	877.4700	832.4700	Voice
198	875.9400	830.9400	Voice	250	877.5000	832.5000	Voice
199	875.9700	830.9700	Voice	251	877.5300	832.5300	Voice
200	876.0000	831.0000	Voice	252	877.5600	832.5600	Voice
201	876.0300	831.0300	Voice	253	877.5900	832.5900	Voice
202	876.0600	831.0600	Voice	254	877.6200	832.6200	Voice
203	876.0900	831.0900	Voice	255	877.6500	832.6500	Voice
204	876.1200	831.1200	Voice	256	877.6800	832.6800	Voice
205	876.1500	831.1500	Voice	257	877.7100	832.7100	Voice
206	876.1800	831.1800	Voice	258	877.7400	832.7400	Voice
207	876.2100	831.2100	Voice	259	877.7700	832.7700	Voice
208	876.2400	831.2400	Voice	260	877.8000	832.8000	Voice
209	876.2700	831.2700	Voice	261	877.8300	832.8300	Voice
210	876.3000	831.3000	Voice	262	877.8600	832.8600	Voice
211	876.3300	831.3300	Voice	263	877.8900	832.8900	Voice
212	876.3600	831.3600	Voice	264	877.9200	832.9200	Voice
213	876.3900	831.3900	Voice	265	877.9500	832.9500	Voice
214	876.4200	831.4200	Voice	266	877.9800	832.9800	Voice

Table E-1. Continued

Channel Number	Base Transmit Frequency (MHz)	Mobile Transmit Frequency (MHz)	Channel Usage Type	Channel Number	Base Transmit Frequency (MHz)	Mobile Transmit Frequency (MHz)	Channel Usage Type
267	878.0100	833.0100	Voice	319	879.5700	834.5700	Signaling
268	878.0400	833.0400	Voice	320	879.6000	834.6000	Signaling
269	878.0700	833.0700	Voice	321	879.6300	834.6300	Signaling
270	878.1000	833.1000	Voice	322	879.6600	834.6600	Signaling
271	878.1300	833.1300	Voice	323	879.6900	834.6900	Signaling
272	878.1600	833.1600	Voice	324	879.7200	834.7200	Signaling
273	878.1900	833.1900	Voice	325	879.7500	834.7500	Signaling
274	878.2200	833.2200	Voice	326	879.7800	834.7800	Signaling
275	878.2500	833.2500	Voice	327	879.8100	834.8100	Signaling
276	878.2800	833.2800	Voice	328	879.8400	834.8400	Signaling
277	878.3100	833.3100	Voice	329	879.8700	834.8700	Signaling
278	878.3400	833.3400	Voice	330	879.9000	834.9000	Signaling
279	878.3700	833.3700	Voice	331	879.9300	834.9300	Signaling
280	878.4000	833.4000	Voice	332	879.9600	834.9600	Signaling
281	878.4300	833.4300	Voice	333	879.9900	834.9900	Signaling
282	878.4600	833.4600	Voice	334	880.0200	835.0200	Control
283	878.4900	833.4900	Voice	335	880.0500	835.0500	Control
284	878.5200	833.5200	Voice	336	880.0800	835.0800	Control
285	878.5500	833.5500	Voice	337	880.1100	835.1100	Control
286	878.5800	833.5800	Voice	338	880.1400	835.1400	Control
287	878.6100	833.6100	Voice	339	880.1700	835.1700	Control
288	878.6400	833.6400	Voice	340	880.2000	835.2000	Control
289	878.6700	833.6700	Voice	341	880.2300	835.2300	Control
290	878.7000	833.7000	Voice	342	880.2600	835.2600	Control
291	878.7300	833.7300	Voice	343	880.2900	835.2900	Control
292	878.7600	833.7600	Voice	344	880.3200	835.3200	Control
293	878.7900	833.7900	Voice	345	880.3500	835.3500	Control
294	878.8200	833.8200	Voice	346	880.3800	835.3800	Control
295	878.8500	833.8500	Voice	347	880.4100	835.4100	Control
296	878.8800	833.8800	Voice	348	880.4400	835.4400	Control
297	878.9100	833.9100	Voice	349	880.4700	835.4700	Control
298	878.9400	833.9400	Voice	350	880.5000	835.5000	Control
299	878.9700	833.9700	Voice	351	880.5300	835.5300	Control
300	879.0000	834.0000	Voice	352	880.5600	835.5600	Control
301	879.0300	834.0300	Voice	353	880.5900	835.5900	Control
302	879.0600	834.0600	Voice	354	880.6200	853.6200	Control
303	879.0900	834.0900	Voice	355	880.6500	835.6500	Voice
304	879.1200	834.1200	Voice	356	880.6800	835.6800	Voice
305	879.1500	834.1500	Voice	357	880.7100	835.7100	Voice
306	879.1800	834.1800	Voice	358	880.7400	835.7400	Voice
307	879.2100	834.2100	Voice	359	880.7700	835.7700	Voice
308	879.2400	834.2400	Voice	360	880.8000	835.8000	Voice
309	879.2700	834.2700	Voice	361	880.8300	835.8300	Voice
310	879.3000	834.3000	Voice	362	880.8600	835.8600	Voice
311	879.3300	834.3300	Voice	363	880.8900	835.8900	Voice
312	879.3600	834.3600	Voice	364	880.9200	835.9200	Voice
313	879.3900	834.3900	Signaling	365	880.9500	835.9500	Voice
314	879.4200	834.4200	Signaling	366	880.9800	835.9800	Voice
315	879.4500	834.4500	Signaling	367	881.0100	836.0100	Voice
316	879.4800	834.4800	Signaling	368	881.0400	836.0400	Voice
317	879.5100	834.5100	Signaling	369	881.0700	836.0700	Voice
318	879.5400	834.5400	Signaling	370	881.1000	836.1000	Voice

Table E-1. Continued

Channel Number	Base Transmit Frequency (MHz)	Mobile Transmit Frequency (MHz)	Channel Usage Type	Channel Number	Base Transmit Frequency (MHz)	Mobile Transmit Frequency (MHz)	Channel Usage Type
371	881.1300	836.1300	Voice	423	882.6900	837.6900	Voice
372	881.1600	836.1600	Voice	424	882.7200	837.7200	Voice
373	881.1900	836.1900	Voice	425	882.7500	837.7500	Voice
374	881.2200	836.2200	Voice	426	882.7800	837.7800	Voice
375	881.2500	836.2500	Voice	427	882.8100	837.8100	Voice
376	881.2800	836.2800	Voice	428	882.8400	837.8400	Voice
377	881.3100	836.3100	Voice	429	882.8700	837.8700	Voice
378	881.3400	836.3400	Voice	430	882.9000	837.9000	Voice
379	881.3700	836.3700	Voice	431	882.9300	837.9300	Voice
380	881.4000	836.4000	Voice	432	882.9600	837.9600	Voice
381	881.4300	836.4300	Voice	433	882.9900	837.9900	Voice
382	881.4600	836.4600	Voice	434	883.0200	838.0200	Voice
383	881.4900	836.4900	Voice	435	883.0500	838.0500	Voice
384	881.5200	836.5200	Voice	436	883.0800	838.0800	Voice
385	881.5500	836.5500	Voice	437	883.1100	838.1100	Voice
386	881.5800	836.5800	Voice	438	883.1400	838.1400	Voice
387	881.6100	836.6100	Voice	439	883.1700	838.1700	Voice
388	881.6400	836.6400	Voice	440	883.2000	838.2000	Voice
389	881.6700	836.6700	Voice	441	883.2300	838.2300	Voice
390	881.7000	836.7000	Voice	442	883.2600	838.2600	Voice
391	881.7300	836.7300	Voice	443	883.2900	838.2900	Voice
392	881.7600	836.7600	Voice	444	883.3200	838.3200	Voice
393	881.7900	836.7900	Voice	445	883.3500	838.3500	Voice
394	881.8200	836.8200	Voice	446	883.3800	838.3800	Voice
395	881.8500	836.8500	Voice	447	883.4100	838.4100	Voice
396	881.8800	836.8800	Voice	448	883.4400	838.4400	Voice
397	881.9100	836.9100	Voice	449	883.4700	838.4700	Voice
398	881.9400	836.9400	Voice	450	883.5000	838.5000	Voice
399	881.9700	836.9700	Voice	451	883.5300	838.5300	Voice
400	882.0000	837.0000	Voice	452	883.5600	838.5600	Voice
401	882.0300	837.0300	Voice	453	883.5900	838.5900	Voice
402	882.0600	837.0600	Voice	454	883.6200	838.6200	Voice
403	882.0900	837.0900	Voice	455	883.6500	838.6500	Voice
404	882.1200	837.1200	Voice	456	883.6800	838.6800	Voice
405	882.1500	837.1500	Voice	457	883.7100	838.7100	Voice
406	882.1800	837.1800	Voice	458	883.7400	838.7400	Voice
407	882.2100	837.2100	Voice	459	883.7700	838.7700	Voice
408	882.2400	837.2400	Voice	460	883.8000	838.8000	Voice
409	882.2700	837.2700	Voice	461	883.8300	838.8300	Voice
410	882.3000	837.3000	Voice	462	883.8600	838.8600	Voice
411	882.3300	837.3300	Voice	463	883.8900	838.8900	Voice
412	882.3600	837.3600	Voice	464	883.9200	838.9200	Voice
413	882.3900	837.3900	Voice	465	883.9500	838.9500	Voice
414	882.4200	837.4200	Voice	466	883.9800	838.9800	Voice
415	882.4500	837.4500	Voice	467	884.0100	839.0100	Voice
416	882.4800	837.4800	Voice	468	884.0400	839.0400	Voice
417	882.5100	837.5100	Voice	469	884.0700	839.0700	Voice
418	882.5400	837.5400	Voice	470	884.1000	839.1000	Voice
419	882.5700	837.5700	Voice	471	884.1300	839.1300	Voice
420	882.6000	837.6000	Voice	472	884.1600	839.1600	Voice
421	882.6300	837.6300	Voice	473	884.1900	839.1900	Voice
422	882.6600	837.6600	Voice	474	884.2200	839.2200	Voice

Table E-1. Continued

Channel Number	Base Transmit Frequency (MHz)	Mobile Transmit Frequency (MHz)	Channel Usage Type	Channel Number	Base Transmit Frequency (MHz)	Mobile Transmit Frequency (MHz)	Channel Usage Type
475	884.2500	839.2500	Voice	527	885.8100	840.8100	Voice
476	884.2800	839.2800	Voice	528	885.8400	840.8400	Voice
477	884.3100	839.3100	Voice	529	885.8700	840.8700	Voice
478	884.3400	839.3400	Voice	530	885.9000	840.9000	Voice
479	884.3700	839.3700	Voice	531	885.9300	840.9300	Voice
480	884.4000	839.4000	Voice	532	885.9600	840.9600	Voice
481	884.4300	839.4300	Voice	533	885.9900	840.9900	Voice
482	884.4600	839.4600	Voice	534	886.0200	841.0200	Voice
483	884.4900	839.4900	Voice	535	886.0500	841.0500	Voice
484	884.5200	839.5200	Voice	536	886.0800	841.0800	Voice
485	884.5500	839.5500	Voice	537	886.1100	841.1100	Voice
486	884.5800	839.5800	Voice	538	886.1400	841.1400	Voice
487	884.6100	839.6100	Voice	539	886.1700	841.1700	Voice
488	884.6400	839.6400	Voice	540	886.2000	841.2000	Voice
489	884.6700	839.6700	Voice	541	886.2300	841.2300	Voice
490	884.7000	839.7000	Voice	542	886.2600	841.2600	Voice
491	884.7300	839.7300	Voice	543	886.2900	841.2900	Voice
492	884.7600	839.7600	Voice	544	886.3200	841.3200	Voice
493	884.7900	839.7900	Voice	545	886.3500	841.3500	Voice
494	884.8200	839.8200	Voice	546	886.3800	841.3800	Voice
495	884.8500	839.8500	Voice	547	886.4100	841.4100	Voice
496	884.8800	839.8800	Voice	548	886.4400	841.4400	Voice
497	884.9100	839.9100	Voice	549	886.4700	841.4700	Voice
498	884.9400	839.9400	Voice	550	886.5000	841.5000	Voice
499	884.9700	839.9700	Voice	551	886.5300	841.5300	Voice
500	885.0000	840.0000	Voice	552	886.5600	841.5600	Voice
501	885.0300	840.0300	Voice	553	886.5900	841.5900	Voice
502	885.0600	840.0600	Voice	554	886.6200	841.6200	Voice
503	885.0900	840.0900	Voice	555	886.6500	841.6500	Voice
504	885.1200	840.1200	Voice	556	886.6800	841.6800	Voice
505	885.1500	840.1500	Voice	557	886.7100	841.7100	Voice
506	885.1800	840.1800	Voice	558	886.7400	841.7400	Voice
507	885.2100	840.2100	Voice	559	886.7700	841.7700	Voice
508	885.2400	840.2400	Voice	560	886.8000	841.8000	Voice
509	885.2700	840.2700	Voice	561	886.8300	841.8300	Voice
510	885.3000	840.3000	Voice	562	886.8600	841.8600	Voice
511	885.3300	840.3300	Voice	563	886.8900	841.8900	Voice
512	885.3600	840.3600	Voice	564	886.9200	841.9200	Voice
513	885.3900	840.3900	Voice	565	886.9500	841.9500	Voice
514	885.4200	840.4200	Voice	566	886.9800	841.9800	Voice
515	885.4500	840.4500	Voice	567	887.0100	842.0100	Voice
516	885.4800	840.4800	Voice	568	887.0400	842.0400	Voice
517	885.5100	840.5100	Voice	569	887.0700	842.0700	Voice
518	885.5400	840.5400	Voice	570	887.1000	842.1000	Voice
519	885.5700	840.5700	Voice	571	887.1300	842.1300	Voice
520	885.6000	840.6000	Voice	572	887.1600	842.1600	Voice
521	885.6300	840.6300	Voice	573	887.1900	842.1900	Voice
522	885.6600	840.6600	Voice	574	887.2200	842.2200	Voice
523	885.6900	840.6900	Voice	575	887.2500	842.2500	Voice
524	885.7200	840.7200	Voice	576	887.2800	842.2800	Voice
525	885.7500	840.7500	Voice	577	887.3100	842.3100	Voice
526	885.7800	840.7800	Voice	578	887.3400	842.3400	Voice

Table E-1. Continued

Channel Number	Base Transmit Frequency (MHz)	Mobile Transmit Frequency (MHz)	Channel Usage Type	Channel Number	Base Transmit Frequency (MHz)	Mobile Transmit Frequency (MHz)	Channel Usage Type
579	887.3700	842.3700	Voice	623	888.6900	843.6900	Voice
580	887.4000	842.4000	Voice	624	888.7200	843.7200	Voice
581	887.4300	842.4300	Voice	625	888.7500	843.7500	Voice
582	887.4600	842.4600	Voice	626	888.7800	843.7800	Voice
583	887.4900	842.4900	Voice	627	888.8100	843.8100	Voice
584	887.5200	842.5200	Voice	628	888.8400	843.8400	Voice
585	887.5500	842.5500	Voice	629	888.8700	843.8700	Voice
586	887.5800	842.5800	Voice	630	888.9000	843.9000	Voice
587	887.6100	842.6100	Voice	631	888.9300	843.9300	Voice
588	887.6400	842.6400	Voice	632	888.9600	843.9600	Voice
589	887.6700	842.6700	Voice	633	888.9900	843.9900	Voice
590	887.7000	842.7000	Voice	634	889.0200	844.0200	Voice
591	887.7300	842.7300	Voice	635	889.0500	844.0500	Voice
592	887.7600	842.7600	Voice	636	889.0800	844.0800	Voice
593	887.7900	842.7900	Voice	637	889.1100	844.1100	Voice
594	887.8200	842.8200	Voice	638	889.1400	844.1400	Voice
595	887.8500	842.8500	Voice	639	889.1700	844.1700	Voice
596	887.8800	842.8800	Voice	640	889.2000	844.2000	Voice
597	887.9100	842.9100	Voice	641	889.2300	844.2300	Voice
598	887.9400	842.9400	Voice	642	889.2600	844.2600	Voice
599	887.9700	842.9700	Voice	643	889.2900	844.2900	Voice
600	888.0000	843.0000	Voice	644	889.3200	844.3200	Voice
601	888.0300	843.0300	Voice	645	889.3500	844.3500	Voice
602	888.0600	843.0600	Voice	646	889.3800	844.3800	Voice
603	888.0900	843.0900	Voice	647	889.4100	844.4100	Voice
604	888.1200	843.1200	Voice	648	889.4400	844.4400	Voice
605	888.1500	843.1500	Voice	649	889.4700	884.4700	Voice
606	888.1800	843.1800	Voice	650	889.5000	844.5000	Voice
607	888.2100	843.2100	Voice	651	889.5300	844.5300	Voice
608	888.2400	843.2400	Voice	652	889.5600	844.5600	Voice
609	888.2700	843.2700	Voice	653	889.5900	844.5900	Voice
610	888.3000	843.3000	Voice	654	889.6200	844.6200	Voice
611	888.3300	843.3300	Voice	655	889.6500	844.6500	Voice
612	888.3600	843.3600	Voice	656	889.6800	844.6800	Voice
613	888.3900	843.3900	Voice	657	889.7100	844.7100	Voice
614	888.4200	843.4200	Voice	658	889.7400	844.7400	Voice
615	888.4500	843.4500	Voice	659	889.7700	844.7700	Voice
616	888.4800	843.4800	Voice	660	889.8000	844.8000	Voice
617	888.5100	843.5100	Voice	661	889.8300	844.8300	Voice
618	888.5400	843.5400	Voice	662	889.8600	844.8600	Voice
619	888.5700	843.5700	Voice	663	889.8900	844.8900	Voice
620	888.6000	843.6000	Voice	664	889.9200	844.9200	Voice
621	888.6300	843.6300	Voice	665	889.9500	844.9500	Voice
622	888.6600	843.6600	Voice	666	889.9800	844.9800	Voice

users leave out of their conversations. It is important to keep in mind, however, that within each cellular area the frequencies can change occasionally. To meet user needs, frequencies can be added or assigned elsewhere. As channels change, it will be necessary to update your listening records accordingly.

The major problem for many law enforcement agencies tracking criminal elements and others monitoring cellular transmissions is a method of channel/frequency detection. With every passing day, cellular telephone usage is becoming a more common adjunct to the radio communication networks used by business, law enforcement, and government agencies—and criminals. An inexpensive Frequency Capture Device has recently been developed by the Key Research Company.

The FCD operates effectively with popular scanners. The module is simple to install using standard hand-tool and the easy-to-follow instructions. The FCD automatically stores frequencies detected over a long term (such as overnight) and retains them in a memory bank of the scanner for later recall and evaluation. For further details about this Key Research device, contact them directly at P.O. Box 5054, Cary, NC 27511.

Emergency Response Plan   In addition to the frequencies you have found in this and other sections of this book, various city departments in your area, in conjunction with county, state, federal, and private agencies, will work together to bring relief to the devastated areas. Most cities follow detailed plans of action devised for such emergencies. Here are some of the key players and their primary responsibilities as found in many of those local emergency relief plans. You should have the various frequencies they use as a part of your scanning files:

City

- City manager's office—public information, supply and procurement
- City planning—situation analysis
- Fire—fire and rescue
- General city services—utilities
- Police—alerting and warning, access control, law enforcement, evacuation
- Parks and recreation—care and shelter
- Personnel resource management—personnel
- Public works—construction and engineering, transportation, utilities

- Schools—care and shelter, transportation

County

- Emergency services—coordination of relief agencies
- General County Services—logistics
- Sheriff/Constable—alerting and warning, law enforcement
- Fire District—fire and rescue
- Social Services—Shelter, health
- Health Department—medical, mental health, toxic hazards
- Coroner—Identification of victims
- Water and Sanitation—Utilities

Private

- American Red Cross—care and shelter
- Hospitals—medical
- Telephone Company—communications
- Electric Company/Gas Company—power and gas
- Water Company—water
- Salvation Army—care and shelter, supplies
- Ham Radio Operators—communications
- Radio & Television Stations—communications
- Churches and Schools—care and shelter
- Citizen Band (CB) Local Radio Network—reports from the scene of the emergency, information on what immediate assistance is needed

(*See* CITIZENS BANDS CHANNELS AND FREQUENCIES.)

State

- Emergency Services Offices—public information, disaster assessment, fire and rescue
- Employment Development—volunteer coordination
- General State Services—supplies, procurement
- State Police/Highway Patrol—law enforcement
- Architect—engineering services
- Social Services—mass care and shelter
- Highway Department—Transportation, highways, rescue, engineering reconstruction

Federal

- Federal Emergency Management Agency (FEMA)—coordination, damage information, reconstruction loans, and federal grant programs
- General Services Administration—resources support
- Army Corps of Engineers—construction
- U.S. Coast Guard—rescue, transportation
- U.S. Marines—rescue, transportation, law enforcement
- U.S. Army—rescue, transportation, law enforcement
- U.S. Air Force—medical evacuation, supply and support
- National Guard—law enforcement, transportation, construction, medical evacuation
- Department of Agriculture—food procurement
- Department of Defense—urban search and rescue
- Department of Health and Human Services—crisis counseling
- National Communications System (NCS)—communications

emergency/distress frequencies worldwide The following frequencies have been designated as distress or emergency frequencies:

- 500 KHz—international CW/MCW distress and calling
- 2182 kHz—international voice distress, safety, and calling; particularly useful for communications between aircraft and ships
- 8364 kHz—international CW/MCW lifeboat, life raft, and survival craft
- 40.5 MHz—U.S. Army FM distress (most Army aircraft have the capability to home on FM frequencies)
- 121.5 MHz—international voice aeronautical emergency
- 156.8 MHz—FM U.S. voice distress and international voice safety and calling

- 243.0 MHz—joint/combined military voice aeronautical emergency and international survival craft

search and rescue dedicated frequencies Certain frequencies have been specified for use during a search and rescue (SAR) mission. These are:

- 3023.5 kHz—international voice SAR on scene
- 5680 kHz—international voice SAR on scene
- 123.1 MHz—international voice SAR on scene
- 138.78 MHz—U.S. military voice SAR on scene, and direction finder (DF)
- 155.16 MHz—FM frequency used by some states and local agencies for coordinating SAR operations
- 282.8 MHz—joint/combined on-scene and DF

EMI [C3I] Abbreviation for Electromagnetic Interference.

EMIAT [I] Abbreviation for Etat-Major Inter-Armees Terrestres.

EMMPS [US] Designation for Enhanced Minimum Essential Emergency Communications Network (MEECN) Message Processing System.

EMP [C3I] Abbreviation for Electromagnetic Pulse.

employee [I] In an intelligence operation, an employee is an individual, other than an intelligence agent, employed by an intelligence service.

empty suit [LE] A fellow officer who is disliked. The term sometimes is used to refer to a female police officer.

emrel [C,G&PS] Slang for morphine.

EMS [LE] Abbreviation for Emergency Medical Service.

endoscope [LE] Originally a medical instrument to look into the human body, this tool also is used in law enforcement surveillance operations to view and photograph individuals in another room. A tiny hole drilled through a wall gives the user a wide-angle view of whatever is going on.

ENG [B] Abbreviation for Electronic News Gathering (television).

ENSCE [C3I] Abbreviation for Enemy Situation Correlations Element.

entacannon [LE] An air-powered device favored by antiterrorist units and law enforcement agencies that uses a projectile to breech brick walls or heavy doors with a single shot. The device is sometimes referred to as a breecher.

enterprise [I] A covert operation supplied with off-the-shelf hardware and specifics by the CIA.

EOC [LE] Abbreviation for Emergency Operations Center.

EOD [M] Abbreviation for Explosive Ordnance Disposal (unit).

EOKA [TRG] Abbreviation for *Ethniki Organosis Kypriakou Agonistov*, the major Cypriot terrorist group. This group has supporters in the U.S. and is also known as the *Ethniki Organosis Kyprion Agoniston*, the National Organization of Cypriot Fighters.

EOR [M] Abbreviation for Explosive Ordnance Reconnaissance.

EORSAT [US] Acronym for Electronic Ocean Reconnaissance Satellite.

EPIRB [C3I] Abbreviation for Emergency Position Indicating Radio Beacon. The EPIRB is a VHF positioning indicator used in emergencies.

EPL [TRG] Abbreviation for *Ejercito Popular de Liberacion*, a radical/terrorist group operating in Colombia.

E.P.L.A. [I] Abbreviation for Eritrean Peoples Liberation Army (*See* ERITREA.)

E.P.L.F. [I] Abbreviation for Eritrean Peoples Liberation Front. (*See* ERITREA.)

EPROM [C3I] Abbreviation for Electronically Programmable Read Only Memory.

EQU Specialty code for equine (horse) injury.

equanil [LE] Name of a controlled substance, a sedative. (*See* QUICK REFERENCE.)

ER-2 [I] Designation for the latest version of a high-altitude research aircraft derived from the Air Force U-2 spy plane. The ER-2 carries forward-looking infrared (FLIR) and sensors developed for forest fire research. These instruments measure thermal energy at infrared wavelengths and other wavelength bands that vividly show the location of an advancing fire front. The ER-2 is equipped to show the conditions on the ground and beam data directly to firefighters in that area.

E.R.A. [I] Abbreviation for Eritrean Relief Association. (*See* ERITREA.)

ERADCOM [C3I] Acronym for Army Electronics Research and Development Command.

ERAPS [C3I] Abbreviation for Expendable Reliable Acoustic Path Sonnobuoy.

ERCS [US] Abbreviation for Emergency Rocket Communications System.

ERIS [C3I] Designation for Exo-atmospheric Reentry Vehicle Interception System, satellite recovery by aircraft.

Eritrea [GOV] Name given by the Italians to the rugged land-mass stretching northward from Ethiopia to the Sudan. (*See* E.P.L.F.; E.P.L.A.; E.R.A.; DERG.)

EROS 1. [C3I] Abbreviation for Earth Resource Observation System. EROS is a high-altitude, long-term satellite. **2.** [TRG] Abbreviation for Eelam Revolutionary Organization of Students, a well-educated group of students active against the government policies of Sri Lanka.

ERP 1. [C] Abbreviation for Effective Radiated Power, the transmitter power that actually is radiated by the antenna array. **2.** [TRG] A small left-wing Argentine terrorist group that conducted many activities in the late 1970s. On rare occasion, members have been known to work with the Tupamaros and other left-wing groups. The ERP is known to have been responsible for the destruction of three government-owned broadcasting stations in Latin America since 1984. The group is also known as the Ejercito Revolucionario del Pueblo Argentina, they are active in Argentina and El Salvador.

ERT [HRU] Abbreviation for Emergency Response Team(s), the antiterrorist and hostage rescue units of the Royal Canadian Mounted Police.

ERTS [C3I] Abbreviation for Earth Resources Technology Satellite.

ES Specialty code for Escort Service.

ESA [C3I] Abbreviation for European Space Agency.

ESC [C3I] Abbreviation for Engineering Service Channel.

ESD [C3I] Abbreviation for Electronic Systems Division.

ESF [US] Abbreviation for Economic Support Fund.

ESI 1. [LE] Abbreviation for Extremely Sensitive Information. 2. [HRU] Abbreviation for Escadron Special d'Intervention, the Belgian hostage rescue and antiterrorist unit of the Gendarmerie Royale.

ESM [C3I] Abbreviation for Electronic Support Measures, usually in the form of a radar warning receiver.

espionage [I] In an intelligence/military operation, the intelligence activity aimed at the acquiring of classified information. In most cases, information comes from an agent inside a hostile intelligence organization.

ESU [LE] Abbreviation for Emergency Services Unit.

ETA 1. [TRG] Abbreviation for *Euzakadi Ta Askatasuma*, a Basque separatist movement. They have conducted assassinations, sabotage, and kidnappings. The ETA is responsible for the murder of Carrero Blanco, the Spanish Prime Minister. Some of their operations have been carried out in France, but the majority have been conducted in Spain. The group is also known as the *Euzkadi ta Azkatazuna*. 2. [LE] Abbreviation for Estimated Time of Arrival.

ETDL [US] Abbreviation for Electronics Technology and Devices Laboratory.

ETSS [US] Abbreviation for Electronic Telecommunications Switching System.

EUCOM [NATO] Acronym for European Command.

EUROCOM [C] Acronym for European Communications.

Every mother's blood [C,G&PS] A vodka-based drink laced with a variety of hallucinogens.

EVS [C3I] Abbreviation for Enhanced Videotex Services.

EW [C3I] Abbreviation for Electronic Warfare.

EWL [US] Abbreviation for Electronics Warfare Laboratory.

EXCOM [US] Acronym for Executive Committee.

executive action [I] Generally a euphemism for assassination, used in covert operations to describe a program aimed at the overthrow of a certain foreign leader or specific adversary by some method of assassination. Such decisions usually are made by an 'executive group' and therein lies the term.

EXP Specialty code for explosives and firearms ordnance.

experimental aircraft flight test frequencies (Lockheed Aircraft) *See* TABLE E-2.

Exploited Children National Hotline The number for the hotline is 1−800−843−5678.

Table E-2. Lockheed Aircraft Experimental Aircraft Flight Test Frequencies

VHF (MHz)		
121.7000	123.2000	123.4500
121.9000	123.3250	123.5200
122.9000	123.3500	123.5500
122.9500	123.4250	123.9000

UHF (MHz)			
275.2000	314.6000	345.4000	382.6000

HF (kHz)		
3281	6550	13312
3443	8822	17964
5469	11306	21931

explorers club [C,G&PS] Slang term for a group of individuals who use LSD together.

extra class [C] Of or referring to the highest class of radio amateur as far as privileges to the license holder is concerned.

eyeball [LE] A subject under surveillance who is being observed directly by a field agent or is under visual surveillance by a team.

eye dropper [C,G&PS] The medicine dropper attached to a hypodermic needle used to inject drugs.

eye openers [C,G&PS] Slang for amphetamines. (*See* QUICK REFERENCE.)

eyes [LE] Slang term for night vision viewing equipment or binoculars.

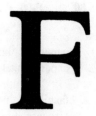

F-1 [LE] Designation for primary frequency 1, or Channel 1.

F-2 [LE] Secondary frequency 2, or Channel 2.

F-3 Designation for the narrow-band National Security Agency (NSA) ASCII code receiving antenna. When used with a portable receiver, the F-3 systems allows an intelligence agent or CIA case officer to listen in (and record) ASCII code commands as they are entered on a computer keyboard. The F-3 receiver/recorder is hand held and can detect ASCII transmissions at some distance through a ten-inch-thick concrete wall. To protect against this kind of reception from U.S. computers by a foreign country, the United States Department of Defense has developed the Tempest (shielding) program that is mandated on certain computer hardware used in government and by the military. (*See* TEMPEST.)

F-4 Designation for U.S. military jet fighter aircraft produced by McDonnell Aircraft Company. It is also known as the F-4 Phantom II.

F-5 Designation for U.S. military jet fighter aircraft produced by the Northrop Corporation. It is also known as the F-5 Freedom.

F-14 Designation for U.S. military jet fighter aircraft produced by Grumman Aircraft. It is known as the F-14 Tomcat.

F-15 Designation for U.S. military jet fighter aircraft produced by McDonnell Aircraft Company. It is also known as the F-15 Eagle.

F-16 Designation for U.S. military jet fighter aircraft produced by General Dynamics. It is known as the F-16 Fighting Falcon.

F-18 Designation for U.S. military jet fighter aircraft produced by the McDonnell Douglas Corporation in association with Northrop Aircraft. It is also known as the F/A-18 Hornet.

F-19 Designation for a stealth aircraft. As in many defense programs, underlying purposes are to conceal the actual motive. The F-19 stealth aircraft concept was actually a decoy program conceived by the United States Defense Intelligence Agency to deceive "stealth watchers" into believing that a certain design concept was under development by the Lockheed-California Company. Minor bits of information came out of program that gave those with any interest a mental conception of how the F-19 might appear in reality. The end result was that the Testors model company developed a model based upon those minor bits of data.

On the model packaging the builder was advised: "Stealth is in the news, but so little is known about the plane that its mystique has now reached grand proportions. In fact, Stealth has been newsworthy for years. As early as the mid-1930s German engineers had designed Stealth systems to 'hide' their submarine's conning towers and periscopes. By 1945, the United States had developed an airborne Stealth material known as MX-410. It was effective to a degree, but it was a primitive technology. Some Lockheed U-2s were equipped with Stealth materials but the airplanes did not fly well. Work continued.

"Design criteria were established. Stealth aircraft required 'low observables' in six disciplines: radar, infrared, noise, smoke, contrails, and optical visibility. Simply stated, Stealth should be undetectable. Quiet. Virtually invisible. Several manufacturers proceeded with Stealth research in the 1970s and developed prototypes. Lockheed and Northrop both built aircraft to fulfill Stealth objectives, and it is generally known that others have produced experimental planes or nonflying test models.

"Stealth fighters, after which the kit was fashioned, now operate from remote top-secret airbases. Laser technology is employed to locate select targets and guide its AGM-65D Maverick missiles and 'smart' bombs. With outer wing panels folded, F-19s fit inside Lockheed's C-5 Galaxy for air transport.

"This authentic 1/48-scale F-19 Stealth fighter is based upon years of extensive research. All specifications were obtained by The Testor Corporation from unrestricted public sources. Because it is a model, and critical full-scale internal components are not depicted, it does not expose any classified systems."

Much of what was said about the F-19 was based on the realities of stealth technology but the aircraft itself was pure fiction according to a well-placed source in the Air Force. The purpose, of course, was to divert attention from the development of the F-117 and other stealth designs. It is interesting to note that when the Testor model appeared, the press and media took the "bait" and government officials, as well as Lockheed and Northrop aircraft designers, were quick to acknowledge that the model was "close" to the real thing. One other interesting note is the various scale-model versions of the B-2 and F-117 aircraft available in hobby stores.

F-90 Designation for a stealth fighter produced by the Lockheed-California Company. It is also known as the RF-90A Specter. This is just one of Lockheed's stealth fighter concepts. The F-90 is a clandestine reconnaissance/strike aircraft. The first version was produced in the late 1970s under the XST (Experimental Stealth Technology) program and designated the YE-20. Five prototype aircraft were manufactured for test purposes. Since then, approximately 60 of the RF-90A Spector aircraft have been produced. Officially they are known as COSIRS, from Covert Survivable In-weather Reconnaissance Strike aircraft. These aircraft take off and land at secure military installations away from the public eye. Their flight-path takes them to high altitude to accomplish their mission.

F-90G Designation for an updated limited-production version of the F-90. The F-90G does not have a conventional cockpit and relies instead on a closed-circuit television system and forward looking infrared sensors (FLIR) for the pilot to 'see' outside the aircraft. This craft is also known as the F-90G Ghost.

F-111 Designation for the U.S. military variable-sweep swing wing fighter/bomber aircraft produced by General Dynamics Corporation.

F-117A Designation for Lockheed's Nighthawk, an advanced version of its stealth reconnaissance/strike aircraft. In flight testing of the F-117A, it has been referred to as "Vapor" in radio communications with ground stations. The F-117A is based on technology developed between Lockheed and Northrop. The original testbed was designed by Northrop and designated the X-4. Best available information indicates the weapons bay is loaded with 2-3 BLU-109/B Paveway III laser-guided penetration bombs with nuclear warheads. The BLU-109 is designed to penetrate 15-20 ft. of reinforced concrete before detonation.

F-117B Designation for the most advanced version of the Vapor. It has been refined to carry nuclear weapons in a bay below the pilot compartment. The external surface of the F-117B is covered with a "smart skin" that detects incoming radar signals. The material, as well as the design configuration, can absorb any such signal, making the aircraft invisible to electronic inspection. Modifications in the airframe have allowed for the installation of long-range fuel tanks and additional surveillance hardware when used for deep target penetration.

FAA [US] Abbreviation for Federal Aviation Administration. TABLE F-1 lists the most-used radio frequencies for the FAA.

FAAD [C3I] Abbreviation for Forward Area Air Defense.

Table F-1. FAA Frequencies

FAA Nationwide Civil Frequencies Network

Frequency	Purpose
121.500	Emergency
122.000	Enroute Flight Advisory
122.050	Enroute Flight Advisory
122.100	Flight Service Stations (receive only)
122.150	Flight Service Stations (receive only)
122.200	Common Enroute Service
122.300	Flight Service Stations (see FSS)
122.400	Flight Service Stations (see FSS)
122.600	Flight Service Stations (see FSS)
123.600	Airport Advisory Channel
135.975	Enroute Flight Advisory (high altitude)

FAA Nationwide VHF Radio Systems Network

Frequency	Purpose
172.925	Facilities 1
172.950	Facilities 2
172.975	Facilities 3
172.850	Facilities 4
172.875	Facilities 5
172.900	Facilities 6
172.825	Facilities 7
172.125	Facilities 8
172.150	Facilities 9
172.175	Facilities 10
166.175	Facilities 11

FAASV [M] Abbreviation for Field Artillery Ammunition Support Vehicle.

fabricator [I] An intelligence operative or law enforcement agent who provides false information to an adversary or the news media.

FAC [M] Abbreviation for Forward Air Controller, that is, the control of aircraft providing close air support for friendly troops.

FACE [UK] Code name for Field Artillery Computer Equipment.

FACH [HRU] Designation for the anti-hijacking unit of the Chilean Air Force.

facsimile [fax] [C] A method of encoding data, transmitting it over the telephone lines, and receiving hard (text) copy, line drawings, or photographs.

factory [C,G&PS] Slang term for the equipment used for the injection of drugs.

fade [LE] Slang term that is used in gambling with dice meaning to cover a wager made by someone else playing the game.

fading dice [LE] A slang term for the loading of dice to make them come up with certain numbers.

FAI [A] Abbreviation for Federation Aeronautique Internationale, the worldwide organization responsible for the supervision of international aviation record attempts.

Fairbanks Highway Research Station [I] On a highway in Langley, Virginia, is a roadside sign reading "Fairbanks Highway Research Station." This is the only signpost that indicates the road leading into the Headquarters of the CIA. The Fairbanks Highway Research Station has never existed at that location.

fair dice [LE] Dice that are honest, not loaded.

fall [C,G&PS] Slang term meaning to be arrested.

falling in love [I] One failing of an intelligence agent that makes them most vulnerable to blackmail is to develop an emotional attachment for someone who "works for the other side." When such a situation is recognized as a threat to the security of an operation or other agents, it is described as falling in love.

FALN [TRG] Abbreviation for *Fuerzos Armados de (la) Liberacion Nacional*, a Puerto Rican terrorist group. They are known to have conducted many bombings and in 1981 were the major players in a plot to kidnap the son of President Reagan. This group has an active following in Venezuela.

false flag [I] A law enforcement agent or intelligence operative involved in the recruitment into a group that makes a deliberate misrepresentation of their employer to achieve acceptance into that group.

famine [C,G&PS] The term used to express the absence of drugs or narcotics available for sale on the street.

fantasy factory [I] The nickname at the United States Secret Service's Intelligence Division for the special group of agents that piece together plots and counterplots, hoping to beat to the punch an assassin who is trying to kill the President or others who are under Secret Service protection.

FAR **1.** [TRG] Designation for the Armed Revolutionary Force, a Guatemalan-based terrorist group trained and funded by the Cuban military, and supplied weapons by the KGB. The FAR assassinated the United States ambassador to Guatemala in 1968. The group is also known as the Fuerzas Armadas Rebeldes. **2.** [US] Abbreviation for Federal Aviation Regulations. **3.** [US] Abbreviation for Federal Acquisition Regulation.

FARC [TRG] Abbreviation for Fuerzas Armadas Revolucionarias de Colombia, an active terrorist/radical group in Colombia. The group is known to have killed government officials. The main body of the organization is made up of young students who have gone into hiding.

FARL [TRG] Designation for the Lebanese Armed Revolutionary Faction, a small but active terrorist organization that tends to specialize in bombings.

farm, The [I] Slang for the CIA training center located in Virginia. This is where new agents are trained and evaluated for a third of a year, then assigned to duty.

FARN [TRG] Designation for Armed Forces of National Resistance, an underground group considered radical to the government of El Salvador and dangerous to the military. Members of the FARN bomb and attack troop operations and conduct sabotage whenever possible as a gesture of their dislike for the military.

FAS [C3I] Abbreviation for Frame Acquisition and Synchronization.

fast movers [US] A naval aviation voice brevity code meaning jet aircraft.

fast roping [M] Slang term referring to a law enforcement and military rapid insertion method used in hostage and antiterrorist operations. A fast roper exits a hovering helicopter and descends quickly toward the ground on a rope. The method also is used to rappel down the face of a building.

fast-scan TV [C] Abbreviation for Fast-Scan Television, normal television that has been adapted by amateur television and radio operators.

FATAH [TRG] Designation for *Harakat Tahrir Falistin*, a terrorist and radical group headquartered in Palestine.

father [US] Naval aviation voice brevity code meaning tacan, an ultrahigh frequency electronic air navigation system. (*See* TACAN.)

FATT [US] Abbreviation for Forward Area Tactical Teletype.

fax [C] *See* FACSIMILE.

FBI [US Department of Justice] Abbreviation for Federal Bureau of Investigation. Responsible for domestic counterintelligence, counterespionage, surveillance, intrastate crimes, and foreign intelligence collection in the United States and all of its territories. (*See* FEDERAL LAW ENFORCEMENT NATIONWIDE COMMUNICATIONS FREQUENCIES.)

FBM [US] Abbreviation for Fleet Ballistic Missile.

FBW [A] Abbreviation for Fly-By-Wire, that is, electrically signalled computerized controls.

FC Specialty code for Fire Cause.

FCC [C3I] [US] Abbreviation for Federal Communications Commission.

FCC microfiche A listing that contains the current frequency allocations to government agencies, police, and commercial/private users. Most of the microfiche that would be useful to communications and scanner buffs have been discontinued and classified by the government. A listing of the microfiche that are available can be obtained by written request from: National Technical Information Service (NTIS), United States Department of Commerce, Springfield, Virginia, 22161 or by calling 1−800−336−4700. The NTIS catalog for microfiche contains a price list. (*See also* RESOURCES.)

FCD **1.** [USSR] Abbreviation for First Chief Directorate of the KGB, the Soviet intelligence service. **2.** [M] Abbreviation for Field Control Division. **3.** [G] Abbreviation for Frequency Capture Device. The PS-90 and S-45 search and store modules are manufactured by the Key Research Company (P.O. Box 5054, Cary, NC 27511) for the Radio Shack PRO-2004 and PRO-2005 scanning receivers. Installation of either module in these receivers automates the storage of frequencies found so that searches can be conducted over long periods of time without operator involvement. When the FCD module is activated using the standard keyboard controls, the unit automatically stores in the scanner's memory up to 255 of those radio frequencies picked up during a frequency search. When the $2^3/4$-inch by $3^1/2$-inch by $3/8$-inch module is deactivated, using keyboard controls, all frequencies stored in the memory of the scanner can be reviewed in the same manner as preprogrammed frequencies. For further information, write Key Research, enclosing a self-addressed, stamped envelope. Because two versions of the FCD exist, ask for information and pricing on the S-45 and PS-90.

FD [GOV] Abbreviation for Fire Department.

FDCS [C3I] Abbreviation for Flight Deck Communications System.

FDM [C3I] Designation for Frequency Division Multiplex/Frequency Modulation.

FDMA [C3I] Abbreviation for Frequency Division Multiple Access.

F.D.N. [US] Abbreviation for *Fuerza Democratica Nicaraguense,* the Nicaraguan Democratic Force, the U.S.-supported political organization of the Contras in Nicaragua.

FDX [C3I] Abbreviation for Full Duplex.

FEBA [M] Abbreviation for Forward Edge of the Battle Area.

FED 1. Background code for Federal Bureau of Investigation, CIA, etc. **2.** [GOV] Slang for a federal agent, usually referring to a narcotics agent.

Fedaj Khalq [TRG] A radical group headquartered in Iran. English translation: Fedaj Struggle.

federal law enforcement communications radio frequencies *See* TABLE F-2.

feed material [I] Information that is usually true—and therefore can be verified—but in reality is unimportant. When feed material is supplied to an individual, the hope is that he/she will pass it along to another intelligence agency, thereby enhancing the status of the operator. This method is applied in intelligence and law enforcement operations to firmly establish the creditability of an undercover agent.

feet dry [US] Naval aviation voice brevity code meaning flying over land.

feet wet [US] Naval aviation voice brevity code meaning flying over water.

FEL [C3I] Abbreviation for Free Electron Laser.

FEMA [G] Abbreviation for the Federal Emergency Management Agency. FEMA coordinates financial aid and relief to people made homeless by disasters such as an earthquake or flood. To speed the processing of a FEMA application, it is best to have the following facts ready to present to the claims officer or field agent. This information, if you contact any relief organization for personal assistance, will also speed along the processing of your claim and get you resettled sooner.

- The address where you were living when the disaster struck
- Your Social Security number
- Your present address—exactly where you are staying now that the actual disaster has passed
- The total household gross income before taxes
- The monthly living expenses for each individual living in the household
- Insurance policy information if any items destroyed were insured
- A dollar estimate of damages to both real and personal property
- If your claim is for real property you also should have:

    o Names of the property owners and an address and/or telephone number where they can be contacted
    o If rental property, the renters' names
    o The mortgage-holder's name, if applicable
    o Directions on how a FEMA agent can find the property (residence) address

Table F-2. Federal Law Enforcement Communications Frequencies

Alcohol Tobacco and Firearms

Operation	Purpose	F	Input	Output	Tone
Nationwide	Operations direct	A1		165.2875	167.9
Nationwide	Operations tactical	A2		166.5375	167.9
Nationwide	Operations repeaters	A3	166.5375	165.2875	167.9
Nationwide	Treasury common	A4		166.4625	167.9
Nationwide	Tactical 1	A5		165.9125	167.9
Nationwide	Tactical 2 AID	A6		173.8875	167.9
Nationwide	Tactical 3	A7		168.0000	167.9
Nationwide	Arson Investigations	A8	166.5375	173.8875	167.9
Nationwide	Surveillance			166.2875	none
Nationwide	Surveillance			170.4125	none
Nationwide	ATF Internal Affairs			407.150	none
Nationwide	Treasury Internal Affairs			409.150	none

Drug Enforcement Administration

Operation	Purpose	F	Input	Output	Tone
Nationwide	Operational repeaters	1	416.050	418.625	156.7
Nationwide	Operational repeaters	2	416.325	418.900	156.7
Nationwide	Operations direct	3		418.750	156.7
Nationwide	Operations direct	4		418.675	156.7
Nationwide	Operations repeaters	5	415.600	418.825	156.7
Nationwide	Operations repeaters	6	416.200	418.950	156.7
Nationwide	Operations repeaters	7	417.025	418.975	156.7
Nationwide	Operations tactical	8		418.175	156.7
Coast Guard coordination				418.575	
Government coordination				418.050	
Air-ground tactical				418.500	
Tactical				418.700	
Tactical				418.800	

Federal Bureau of Investigation

Operation	Purpose	F	Input	Output	Tone
Nationwide	Nationwide common	A4		167.5625	167.7
Nationwide	FBI-SWAT	A7	167.5375	163.8625	167.9
Nationwide	Nationwide common	B4		167.5625	167.9
Nationwide	FBI-SWAT	B7	167.5375	163.8625	167.9

(Note: Local frequencies are available elsewhere (*see* PUBLICATIONS; RESOURCES)

United States Marshal Service

Operation	Purpose	F	Input	Output	Tone
Nationwide	Operations repeaters	1	163.8125	163.200	none
Nationwide	Operations direct	2		163.200	none
US Borders	Canadian/Mexico	3	163.8125	164.600	none
Nationwide	Operations direct	4		164.600	none
Nationwide	Metro repeaters	5	170.850	162.7875	none
Nationwide	Metro direct	6		162.7875	none
Nationwide	Intercity repeaters	7	170.850	162.7875	none
Nationwide	Intercity station-car	8		162.7875	none
Nationwide	Bureau of Prisons 1	9		170.875	none
Nationwide	Bureau of Prisons 2	10		170.925	none
Nationwide	Operations repeaters	11	163.8125	163.200	none
Nationwide	Operations repeaters	12	163.8125	163.200	none
Nationwide	Operations repeaters	13	163.8125	163.200	none
Nationwide	Federal Court security			170.750	none
Nationwide	Federal Court security			170.850	none

fence [LE] Slang for a criminal receiver of stolen property who tends to buy low when obtaining the property, and sells at a less than market value when disposing of it.

fentanyl analogs [LE] A chemical composition that is residue from the use of China White, a synthetic heroin compound. If medical tests on a dead body discover residue of fentanyl analogs, the likelihood is that the person died from a drug overdose. (*See* CHINA WHITE.)

ferret 1. [I] Designation for a class of U.S. satellite that measures radar signals from foreign ground stations. The orbit of Ferret class satellites is as low as a few hundred miles, to approximately 35,000 miles. 2. [I] An aircraft, foreign or domestic, that gives the impression it is about to penetrate an unauthorized zone or cross a border, which tricks ground radar operators into turning on their system. 3. [LE] A barricade-penetrating 12-gauge shotgun round that will deliver CS or CN tear gas.

ferry dust [C,G&PS] Slang for heroin. (*See* QUICK REFERENCE.)

FEST [M] Abbreviation for Field Epidemiological Survey Team, a special medical unit of U.S. Army Special Forces. Members are sent into zones to search out infectious diseases that might affect the results of a field operation.

FET [C3I] Abbreviation for Field Effect Transistor.

FF 1. [LE] Abbreviation for Field File. 2. [D] Designation for French.

FFD [C3I] Abbreviation for Formal Functional Description.

FFG [M] Designation for Guided missile frigate.

FFR [I] Abbreviation for False-Flag Recruitment, an intelligence operation in which an individual is recruited into believing he/she is cooperating with a specific intelligence organization of a particular country. The truth is, the person has been deceived and, unknowingly, actually is working for and cooperating with agents of an intelligence agency from another country. FFR is used in the same way in many areas of law enforcement where the recruited person is given to believe one thing while his/her involvement actually relates to something else.

FI Specialty code for Fingerprinting (ID) Identification.

field-strength meter [C] Of or referring to a device that is able to measure the signal strength of radio waves.

field man [I] An intelligence agent or police officer who is in place and working in an undercover capacity.

field mouse [I] The code name involving the installation of electronic intelligence surveillance hardware on Auxiliary General Environmental Research (AGER) ships.

fiend [C,G&PS] A drug addict who is addicted to morphine.

filtering [C] In a radio receiver, filtering is the process of removal or attenuation of unwanted signals by radio-frequency and/or audio-frequency filters.

fine stuff [C,G&PS] Slang for top-grade marijuana.

finger [C,G&PS] Slang term meaning to incriminate someone in a criminal act.

fink [C,G&PS] Slang term for an informer, a criminal-type who shares what information he/she has with law enforcement officials in return for certain favors.

fire ant [M] A super-secret military/federal law enforcement remote weapons system designed to blast through armor. The Fire Ant consists of a four-wheel all-terrain vehicle, operated by remote-control. Fire Ant shoots a 15-in., 22-lb copper slug at a velocity of 6,600 ft/s. It has an effective range of up to one-third of a mile. The copper lens-shaped slug is mounted in a launcher that looks like a small spotlight. A detonator sets off a high explosive that deforms the lens-shaped disk into a ball. The projectile travels down a path toward the lens' focal point. Dispersion at 550 yd ($1/3$ mile) is less than 3 ft. Intelligence indicates that the Fire Ant was developed as a small transportable device for use against terrorists.

Fire 10-Codes   TABLE F-3 is a list of Fire 10-Codes in the order most often used nationwide.

fire mousetrap [LE] The Fire Mousetrap system uses an infrared camera mounted on board a helicopter to cut through the smoke of a forest fire. Using a computer, the Fire Mousetrap gives the exact latitude and longitude of hot spots in the fire zone and then transmits that information to ground crews that direct other helicopters carrying water. The Fire Mousetrap systems makes it possible for pilots to pinpoint an air drop of fire retardant without ever seeing the blaze.

firestorm [LE] Slang for multiple fires set in close proximity by the same person or persons.

FISINT [C3I] Abbreviation for Foreign Instrumentation and Signals Intelligence.

Fit [C,G&PS] Slang for the hardware used for the injection of drugs.

Five-O [C,G&PS] Slang term used by criminal elements who believe the individual referred to as a Five-O is an undercover police officer. The term is derived from the television series "Hawaii Five-O."

fix [C,G&PS] Slang for an injection of narcotics, that is, someone needing a fix.

F&S man [I] Slang term that refers to the flaps & seals man.

flake [C,G&PS] Slang for cocaine. (*See* QUICK REFERENCE.)

flap [LE] Slang for the commotion, bad publicity, or controversy that results from a bungled law enforcement or intelligence operation.

flaps & seals man [I] The expert who opens and closes mail for the purpose of examination in an intelligence operation.

flash [C,G&PS] Street slang describing the sensation across the chest or abdomen from an injection of heroin.

flashing **1.** [C,G&PS] Slang for the sniffing of glue or chemical solvents. **2.** [C,G&PS] Slang for an individual who is wearing a load of gold jewelry. A few heavy gold chains worn around the neck are sometimes referred to by the police as the "Mr. T starter kit."

flash paper [C,G&PS] A product made for use in magic shows that also is used by drug dealers and gamblers to write their illegal business transactions on. Should they be approached by the police, a quick touch by a cigarette to a corner of a sheet of flash paper makes everything disappear "in a flash." That is one reason a suspect is commanded to keep his hands in sight.

flashing tin [LE] Slang for a law enforcement officer to show his badge of authority.

FLB [TRG] Abbreviation for *Front de Liberation de la Bretagne*, a radical/terrorist group operating out of headquarters in Paris, France. Associated with the Breton Liberation Front, they support the ideals of the IRA with funding. The FLB is a Marxist separatist movement much like the BLF.

flea powder [C,G&PS] Slang term for narcotics of very poor quality.

flicks [LE] Surveillance films or videotape.

flimflam [LE] Any type of confidence game.

flip [C,G&PS] Slang term meaning to be on an acid trip.

flipped [C,G&PS] Slang term meaning to be acting just a little crazy—usually caused by drugs.

FLIR [C3I] Abbreviation for Forward-Looking Infrared (Radar). *See* GREEN MERCHANT and HYDROPONICS for applications of this military device by the Drug Enforcement Administration.

FLN [TRG] Designation for Algerian National Liberation Front. This terrorist group has kept a low profile for a number of years following a raid gone wrong in Algeria where three of their leaders were killed by a bomb they were preparing to set.

FLNC [TRG] Designation for Corsican National Liberation Front.

Table F-3. Fire 10-Codes.

Code	Meaning
10−1	Call by telephone to *(usually headquarters)*
10−1	Receiving poorly
10−2	Involved in accident
10−2	Report/or return to headquarters
10−2	Receiving well
10−3	Police needed at scene
10−3	Fire investigator needed at *(location)*
10−3	Contact fire dispatcher by telephone
10−3	Use when police are needed to disperse a crowd
10−3	Use when violence occurs or crowd becomes hostile
10−3	Testing alerting system
10−4	Message received OK
10−5	Need ambulance or emergency unit
10−5	Repeat message
10−6	In service, in quarters
10−6	Send utility technician *(gas, water, electric)*
10−6	Stand by
10−7	Out of service
10−7	Verify address
10−8	In service, on radio:
	Code 1—Leaving quarters other than own
	Code 2—On air, not in own response unit/area
10−9	Bomb threat
10−9	Civilian fatality at scene
10−9	Location
10−9	Off the air
10−10	Public service unit needed *(gas, water, electric)*
10−10	Emergency—clear this channel/frequency
10−10	What is your location?
10−11	Arson
10−11	Request radio check—or test count
10−12	Repeat message
10−12	Assisting unit *(location)*
10−12	First arriving unit give preliminary
10−13	Request fire prevention inspector at scene
10−13	Unit *(number)* cover the following location at *(place)*
10−13	Request arson inspector immediately at *(location)*
10−14	Fire company/response unit on scene
10−14	Unit *(number)* is located at *(location)*
10−14	There has been a breakdown of firefighting apparatus

Table F-3. Continued

Code	Meaning
10−15	Photographer needed at *(location)*
10−15	Police requested for traffic control at *(location)*
10−15	Chief *(person)* report to *(location)*
10−16	State fire marshal needed at *(location)*
10−16	Urgent police matter
10−16	False alarm
10−17	Building inspector needed at *(location)*
10−17	Responding to alarm at *(location)*
10−18	Police tow truck needed at *(location)*
10−18	Returning from alarm at *(location)*
10−18	Return all units except engine/squad and ladder company required at the scene
10−19	Mechanic needed at *(location)* for *(specific reason)*
10−19	Return all units except company required at the scene
10−20	What is your location or destination?
10−20	Proceed with caution
10−20	Proceed to call box location at reduced speed
10−21	1st alarm—company *(name)* responding
10−21	Stand by for additional information
10−21	Contact *(person)* by telephone at *(location)*
10−21	Multiple dwelling fire
10−21	Brush fire
10−22	2nd alarm—companies *(name)* responding
10−22	Determine origin of call
10−22	House fire
10−22	Outside rubbish fire
10−23	3rd alarm—companies *(number)* responding
10−23	Holding all companies for investigation
10−23	Abandoned/derelict vehicle fire
10−23	Need additional assistance
10−23	Highrise building fire
10−24	4th alarm—companies *(number)* responding
10−24	Holding specific companies
10−24	Automobile/truck fire
10−25	5th alarm—companies *(number)* responding
10−25	False alarm
10−25	Manhole or transformer vault fire:
	Code 1—Manhole fire extends to building(s)
	Code 2—Blown manhole cover(s) or smoke under pressure
	Code 3—Smoke seeping from manhole—condition is not as severe as Code 1 or 2
10−25	Unnecessary alarm
10−25	Brush fire
10−25	Explosive mixture in sewer system

Table F-3. Continued

Code	Meaning
10−26	Working fire *(give nature of fire)*
10−26	Emergency—give details:
	A—Washdown
	B—Drowning
	C—Rescue
10−26	Food on stove (burning)
10−27	Can handle situation *(specific nature of incident)*
10−27	Send police to scene
10−27	Trash compactor fire *(inside/outside)* building
10−28	Return to quarters
10−28	Subway and/or railroad fire:
	Code 1—Underground—in tunnel
	Code 2—Surface—above ground or out in the open
10−29	Possible explosive device
10−29	Situation under control
10−30	Explosion
10−30	Fire out, cancel response
10−31	Train or subway accident at *(location)* with fire
10−31	Clogged incinerator *(inside/outside)* building
10−31	Fatality at scene—notify police & coroner
10−32	Major automobile, bus, or ship accident
10−32	Defective furnace or electric heater
10−32	District chiefs on duty—report in person to HQ
10−33	Odor of smoke reported *(most specific location)*
10−33	District chiefs needed at *(location)* for *(specific reason)*
10−33	Fire inspector needed at *(location)* for *(specific reason)*
10−33	Building collapse at *(location)*
10−34	Construction site collapse
10−34	Sprinkler system emergency—or failure
10−34	Company *(number)* report to district chief at *(location)*
10−35	Unit dispatched to fire scene awaiting instructions
10−35	People trapped
10−35	Automatic alarm system emergency/failure
10−36	People overcome by smoke or gas
10−36	Vehicle emergency—person trapped
	Code 1—Accident and/or washdown—gasoline spillage
	Code 2—Accident—no gasoline spillage
	Code 3—Accident-electrical/explosion hazard
10−37	Assist civilian [applies whether or not F.D.-related]
10−38	Steam leak—possible explosion hazard
10−38	Natural gas leak—possible explosion hazard

Table F-3. Continued

Code	Meaning
10−39	Airport standby
10−39	Water conditions:
	Code 1—Water leak inside structure
	Code 2—Broken water main in street
10−40	Aircraft crash
10−40	Utility emergency:
	Code 1—Gas emergency *(gas main leak/uncontrollable gas leak*)
	Code 2—Electrical emergency (wires down, sparking fixture, short circuit)
10−41	Incendiary or suspicious fire—notify Fire Marshal:
	Code 1—Occupied structure. Definite indications of incendiarism. Fire Marshal to respond.
	Code 2—Occupied structure. While no definite indications of incendiarism, witnesses and/or other civilians have information that might be of value. Fire Marshal to respond.
	Code 3—Vacant building. Heavy volume of fire indicates definite incendiarism. Fire Marshal to respond as other priorities permit.
	Code 4—Vacant building. Obviously incendiary and it appears that there is very little chance for apprehension or obtaining information leading to the individual or individual(s) responsible. Notification for Fire Marshal's evaluation as priorities permit.
10−42	Civil disturbance with fire involved
10−43	Hostage situation
10−44	Request for ambulance
10−45	Dead on arrival, or possible dead body:
	Code 1—Victim is deceased
	Code 2—Victim is probably deceased
	Code 3—Victim is seriously injured and near death
10−46	Request for Emergency Medical Services (EMS) dispatch
10−47	Request police assistance
10−48	Hazardous chemical spill
10−48	Request for police assistance [shots fired]
10−49	Contact/locate *(person)*
10−50	Operation Foamite
10−51	Cancel all activities and report for duty
10−55	Fire injury—civilian
10−56	Fire injury—fireman
10−59	Water pressure alert, phase 1
10−60	Dangerous chemicals/spill—use caution
10−60	Water pressure alert, phase 2
10−63	Units responding to assignment
10−70	In-line plumbing
10−75	Request for additional fire units *(specific need)*
10−76	Request for additional fire personnel *(specific need)*
10−77	Fire vehicle accident at *(location)*
10−77	Request for additional supervisory fire personnel
10−80	Hazardous materials
10−82	Ambulance/rescue unit leaving scene with patient
10−83	Dead body found at scene

Table F-3. Continued

Code	Meaning
10–84	Report your arrival at scene or fire call box
10–88	Ambulance/rescue unit arriving on scene
10–90	Information supplied is not correct
10–92	False alarm
10–93A	Person has refused medical aid and signed release form
10–93B	Refused medical aid—authority of *(physician, police agency)*
10–94	Patient treated but not transported to medical facility
10–94A	Patient treated by *(person)* and transported to *(facility)*
10–95	On scene treatment
10–98	Ambulance/rescue unit available by radio
10–99	Ambulance on stand by at station
10–99	Fatality—fireman
10–99	Fire unit(s) will remain on scene
10–100	High-rise structure fire
10–500	Emergency!
10–600	Civil disaster, operation alert, three tones on radio, then repeated
10–700	Civil disaster, operation activated, four tones on radio, then repeat
10–800	Natural disaster, operation alert, three tones on radio, then repeat
10–900	Natural disaster, operation activated, four tones on radio, then repeated

FLO [TRG] Abbreviation for French Liberation Organization, a Canada-based terrorism group headquartered in Quebec. This group has been responsible for many assassinations and bombings in Canada. The group is also known as the *Front de Liberation du Quebec.*

floating [C,G&PS] Slang term for being under the influence of narcotics.

flower [C,G&PS] Name of the top of the marijuana plant, the Colas de zorras, or foxtails. This is where the most of the cannabinol resin resides.

FLTSATCOM [US] Acronym for FLeeT SATellite COMmunications (system).

flushing [C,G&PS] Slang for the procedure of drawing blood into a syringe before injecting a drug to ensure that the vein is open and the needle has properly penetrated. Usually only long-time users adopt this procedure.

flutter [C,G&PS] Slang term meaning to conduct a polygraph or lie detector test.

fly-by-night [C,G&PS] Slang term for a young (10- to 15-year-old) prostitute.

flyer [LE] Name for a pilot of surveillance aircraft or helicopter.

FM 1. [M] Abbreviation for Field Manual. 2. [B] Abbreviation for Frequency Modulation.

FM band [C] Name of the broadcast band from 88 to 108 MHz.

FMC [M] Abbreviation for Fully Mission Capable.

FMLN [TRG] Designation for *Frente Farabundo Marti*, a terrorist group with headquarters in San Salvador.

FMPR [TRG] Designation for Manuel Rodriguez Patriotic Front, a radical group based in the jungles of Chile that lives off the land and makes occasional strikes against government facilities. The FMPR is known to be well armed and equipped.

FMS [US] Abbreviation for Foreign Military Sales.

foamex [LE] An explosive product supplied in an aerosol container similar to that of a shaving cream can. Foamex is safe to handle and has a number of applications including use by law enforcement SWAT units to spray into keyholes, around entry doors and hinges, and on vertical surfaces such as steel roll-up doors. Foamex is produced by the British firm, Explosive Developments LTD. (*See* PRIMAFOAM.) Although these products are still in the early stages of development, they are expected to improve greatly in the next few years.

FOBS   [M] Abbreviation for Fractional Orbiting Bombardment System.

FOCAS   [US] Abbreviation for Fiber Optical Communications for Aerospace Systems.

FOG   [I] Abbreviation for Foreign Operating Group (DIA).

FOGM   [C3I] Abbreviation for Fiber-Optic Guided Missile.

FOI   [GOV] Abbreviation for Freedom Of Information (act).

fold up   [C,G&PS] Slang term meaning to withdraw from the use of drugs.

footballs   [C,G&PS] Slang term for amphetamines. (*See* QUICK REFERENCE.)

Force 777   [HRU] The antiterrorist and hostage rescue unit of the Egyptian Army Commandos.

FORSCOM   [M] Acronym for FORceS COMmand.
DMT. (*See* QUICK REFERENCE.)

FOTE   [C3I] Acronym for Follow-On Test and Evaluation.

FOUO   [GOV] Abbreviation for For Official Use Only.

fourth of July   [LE] Slang term for an excessive amount of explosives—either used or found at a specific location by law enforcement officers at the scene of a crime.

fox   [US] Naval aviation voice brevity code meaning a missile firing.

Foxtrot   [A,LE,MIL] Designation for the letter *F*.

FP-25   [TRG] Designation for one of many anti-NATO groups located throughout Europe. FP-25 is a Portuguese group that surfaces from time to time to conduct a radical act against a NATO installation. The groups main efforts have been directed toward acts of arson. The group is also known as the *Forcas Populares do 25 Abril*.

FR   Specialty code for fraud.

frame   **1.** [C,G&PS] Slang term meaning to blame someone for something he/she did not do. **2.** [C,G&PS] Slang for a handgun.

Frank   [A,LE,MIL] Designation for the letter *F*.

FRAP   [TRG] The *Fuerzas Revolucionarias Armadas del Pueblo*, a Leninist group headquartered in Spain. The group's acts of terrorism have surfaced as an occasional killing of some (unprotected) government official. The group has supporters in Mexico. An active arm of this organization with a more radical membership than the norm is known as *Frente Revolucionario Anti Fascista y Patriotico*.

freak   [C,G&PS] Slang for a promiscuous woman who gives away her sexual favors. She usually is a dope user.

freebase   [C,G&PS] A method used to ingest a purer form of cocaine. The cocaine is contained in an extraction pipe and heated. The heat burns away the excess hydrochloride salts, then the remaining cocaine is inhaled.

French blues   [C,G&PS] Slang for a blending of amphetamines and barbiturates.

French Red Brigade   [TRG] A French terrorist group that is almost an exact copy of the Italian Red Brigade as far as motivation of terrorist purpose is concerned. The FRB certainly is not as well organized as the Italian Red Brigade, lacks a large membership, and is nowhere as effective in its terrorist operations. Nevertheless, its terrorist acts have been most effective.

FREPALINA   [TRG] Designation for Paraguayan National Liberation Front, a terrorist group that is part of the Junta de Coordinacion Revolucionaria—various terrorist groups located throughout South America.

frequency calibrator   [C] An electronic device that transmits marker frequencies for the purpose of calibrating radio receiving equipment.

frequency crystal   [C] A quartz crystal that specifically determines the receiving or transmitting frequency in certain radio receivers, radio transmitters, or transceivers.

frequency database and filing program Elsewhere in this book you will find information on how to obtain a very sophisticated computer database program for use on an MS-DOS computer system. The program in FIG. F-1 is more simple in nature, is written in a BASIC computer language that will work on most computers in a straightforward manner, or with very slight modifications to fit the BASIC commands used by your computer system. It is included here with appreciation to the United States Customs Service. On line 30 between the quote characters, enter your name as you input the commands into your computer using the BASIC programming language.

frequency and wavelength computer program You might need to convert a frequency to a specific wavelength in the design of an antenna system. The following computer program written in BASIC creates a quick and accurate mathematical method of calculation and conversion of frequency to wavelength, or wavelength to frequency. *See* Fig. F-2.

Fromandskorpset [HRU] Name of members of the Danish military who are also combat swimmers. These individuals are part of the antiterrorist unit responsible for the protection of offshore oil rigs and Danish ports.

front man [LE] Slang for an individual, usually with no criminal record, who acts as a go-between in an illegal activity.

front money [LE] Payment made in advance, most likely involving an illegal act.

froth [I] Code name indicating signal intelligence (SIGINT) information regarding the movement of Soviet aircraft in United States airspace. The Soviet Union conducts surveillance flights into U.S. airspace almost daily.

fruit [C,G&PS] Slang for homosexual.

fruit salad [C,G&PS] Slang for a mixture of drugs in pill form.

FSC [US] Abbreviation for Federal Supply Classification.

FSD [C3I] Abbreviation for Full-Scale Development.

FSED [C3I] Abbreviation for Full-Scale Engineering Development.

FSK [C] Abbreviation for Frequency Shift Key, the modulation method for RTTY and other means of radio frequency transmission.

F.S.L.N. [TRG] Abbreviation for *Frente Sandinista de Liberacion Nacional* (National Liberation Front), a terrorist organization headquartered in Nicaragua.

FSS **1.** [A] Abbreviation for Flight Service Station, which provides specific information to aircraft pilots on airport conditions, weather, radio aids, and processes flight plans from pilots/aircraft in transit. **2.** [M] Abbreviation for Fast Sealift Ships.

FSVS [C3I] Abbreviation for Future Secure Voice System.

FSX [M] Designation for Fighter Support Experimental, is a proposed joint effort between Japan and the United States to convert the U.S. F-16 fighter aircraft for Japanese use. Modifications include advanced material usage in the fuselage and tail, radar-absorbing material on the leading-edge flaps, the addition of a drag chute, improvements in the engine performance, increased wing size, a longer nose, advanced avionic systems added, including improved radar, a vertical stabilizer installed under the pilot compartment on the belly of the aircraft, and the ability to carry four Mitsubishi Type 80 antiship missiles.

FTC [M] Abbreviation for Fast Time Constant.

FTS [M] Abbreviation for Full-Time Support.

FTT [M] Designation for an Army Special Forces Training Team sent to assist friendly countries. Such a team is usually identified as an "A-Detachment, FTT."

fully [C,G&PS] Slang for an automatic weapon, usually a machine gun.

fuzz [C,G&PS] Slang for a law enforcement officer.

FY **1.** Specialty code for Feasibility. **2.** [US] Abbreviation for Fiscal Year.

```
 10    CLS
 15    FOR X=1 TO 3;PRINT:NEXT X
 20    PRINT "FREQUENCY DATABASE"
 25    PRINT "FOR"
 30    PRINT "your name here in upper case"
 35    PRINT "AGENCY OR SERVICE WANTED:"
 40    PRINT "(1)POLICE"
 45    PRINT "(2)FIRE"
 50    PRINT "(3)MEDICAL EMERGENCY"
 55    PRINT "(4)FEDERAL AGENCIES"
 60    PRINT "(5)MILITARY"
 65    PRINT "(6)OTHER"
 70    INPUT A$
 75    IF A$="1" THEN 120
 80    IF A$="2" THEN 205
 90    IF A$="3" THEN 310
 95    IF A$="4" THEN 410
100    IF A$="5" THEN 510
105    IF A$="6" THEN 610
110    IF A$=" " THEN 20
115    GOTO 9999
120    FOR X=1 TO 3;PRINT:NEXT X
125    PRINT "POLICE"
130    PRINT "(YOUR FREQUENCIES)"
200    GOSUB 1000
205    FOR X=1 TO;PRINT:NEXT X
210    PRINT "FIRE"
215    PRINT "(YOUR FREQUENCIES)"
300    GOSUB 1000
310    FOR X=1 TO 3;PRINT:NEXT X
315    PRINT "MEDICAL EMERGENCY"
320    PRINT "(YOUR FREQUENCIES)"
400    GOSUB 1000
410    FOR X=1 TO 3;PRINT:NEXT X
415    PRINT "FEDERAL AGENCIES"
420    PRINT "(YOUR FREQUENCIES)"
500    GOSUB 1000
510    FOR X=1 TO 3;PRINT:NEXT X
515    PRINT "MILITARY"
520    PRINT "(YOUR FREQUENCIES)"
600    GOSUB 1000
610    FOR X=1 TO 3;PRINT:NEXT X
615    PRINT "OTHER"
620    PRINT "(YOUR FREQUENCIES)"
700    GOSUB 1000
1000   PRINT "DO YOU WANT OTHER AGENCIES <Y> OR <N>"
1010   INPUT B$
1020   IF B$="Y" THEN 1-6
1030   IF B$="N" THEN 9999
1040   IF B$ "Y" PRINT (Y) OR (N)
1050   IF B$ "N" PRINT (Y) OR (N)
1060   GOTO 1010
1070   RETURN
9999   END
```

Fig. F-1. Frequency database and filing program.

```
10   "F" CLEAR
20   PAUSE"FREQUENCY OR WAVELENGTH"
30   INPUT"WANT F OR W ?" ,A$
40   IF A$="F" THEN 90
50   INPUT"FREQUENCY (MHZ) = ";F
60   W=300/F
70   PRINT F;" MHZ = ";W;" METERS"
80   GOTO 10
90   INPUT"WAVELENGTH (METERS) = ";W
100  F=300/1
110  PRINT W;" METERS = ";F;" MHZ"
120  GOTO 10
```

Fig. F-2. Frequency and wavelength computer program.

G

g [D] The acceleration due to gravity. A fighter aircraft turning at a 6g ratio is producing a lift equal to six times its actual gross weight.

GA [CW] Designation for a nerve agent (Tabun). This chemical warfare agent was developed for use by the military. It is a cholinesterase inhibitor, attacking the human nervous system. It can be dispersed into an area using a variety of methods. It acts quickly and kills moments after contact.

GaAs FET [C3I] Designation for GAllium ArSenide Field-Effect Transistor.

gadget [US] Naval aviation voice brevity code meaning radar equipment.

Gaes [HRU] The Colombian Army antikidnapping unit.

gage [C,G&PS] Slang for marijuana. (*See* QUICK REFERENCE.)

Gajda [HRU] The Colombian Air Force antihijacking unit.

galosh [I] The operational missile system surrounding Moscow. The system is also known as ABM-1b.

gambit [US] Code name for the KH-8 surveillance satellite system.

gamma guppy [US] Code name for a microwave intelligence intercept program to collect electronic and communication transmissions generated by members of the Soviet Politburo. Gamma guppy data was mostly gathered by satellite or low-flying border surveillance aircraft.

gangbanging **1.** [C,G&PS] Slang for gang activity, almost always violent. **2.** [C,G&PS] Slang for gangs fighting to protect their turf.

gangster [C,G&PS] Slang for a criminal element in the community.

gangster-type [C,G&PS] Slang for an individual, without a criminal record, who tends to act out the mannerisms or have the attitudes of a criminal or gangster-type.

gangster-type piece [C,G&PS] Slang for a sawed-off shotgun.

gang warden [C,G&PS] Slang for a police officer or sheriff's deputy.

ganja [C,G&PS] Slang for marijuana. (*See* QUICK REFERENCE.)

Gap [TRG] A group of former Italian military men turned terrorist trainers. Members get together occasionally to train new members in the tactics used by commandos. The Gap seems to have a gripe about many things that support the communication system of Italy. Acts they take to demonstrate their dislike tend to make the system even worse. Certain skills they have developed have been passed along to the Palestinians.

garbage [C,G&PS] A catchall term referring to all types of low-quality drugs, narcotics, or marijuana.

Garda Siochana [HRU] The Special Branch of the Irish National Police that has the responsibility for hostage rescue operations in Ireland.

gasoline dope [C,G&PS] Slang for a powerful synthetic heroin—its chemical name is 3-methyl-fentanyl—also known as China White. (*See* CHINA WHITE.)

gate [US] Naval aviation voice brevity code meaning flying at a maximum speed for a limited time.

GAU [USSR] Abbreviation for *Glavnoye Arkhivnoye Upravleniye*, the Main Archive Administration.

gauge [C,G&PS] Slang for marijuana. (*See* QUICK REFERENCE.)

GB [CW] Designation for the nerve agent Sarin. This chemical warfare agent is designed for quick kills over a large area. It is a cholinesterase inhibitor much like the chemical agent GA, and can be dispersed into an area using a variety of methods.

GBs [C,G&PS] Slang for barbiturates, defined in street slang as goofballs.

GB2 [CW] Designation for a two-component nerve agent (Sarin) that remains dangerous for only a few hours after release. A tiny bit of this agent disrupts the human nervous system and prevents the body from working. It makes the victim lose control of body functions, and causes breathing and the heart to stop.

GCE [C3I] Abbreviation for Ground Communications Equipment, or Ground Control Equipment.

GCGN [HRU] Abbreviation for Groupement de Commando of the Garde Nationale. This commando unit is patterned after the British SAS. The responsibilities of these Tunisian Gendarmeries is hostage rescue and antiterrorist operations.

GCHQ [UK] Abbreviation for Government Communications Headquarters for the United Kingdom, which is responsible for all electronic intercepts.

GCI [M] Abbreviation for Ground-Control Interception.

GCWR [LE] Abbreviation used by law enforcement agencies nationwide, usually in trucking accidents, to indicate a violation of the Gross Combination Weight Rating.

GD 1. Specialty code for Guard Dogs. 2. [M] Abbreviation for Group Delay Distortion. 3. [CW] Designation for the nerve agent soman. This chemical warfare agent has many of the same characteristics as the chemical nerve agents GA and GB. Although it is a cholinesterase inhibitor, GD acts much more quickly and has long-lasting residual effects on human beings entering the area unprotected at a much later time.

GD [CW] Designation for the nerve agent soman. This chemical warfare agent was developed by the Soviet Union. Thickened soman is used as the basic cholinesterase inhibitor. In field operations, this Soviet nerve agent has been referred to as VR-55. *See* VX for an American nerve agent of parallel design. The characteristics are the same as GA and GB.

GDCR [TRG] Abbreviation for *Guerrilleros Del Cristo Rey*, Warriors of Christ the King, a right-wing Spanish neo-Nazi group involved in bombings and an occasional killing in Spain.

gear 1. [C,G&PS] Slang for the hardware used for injecting narcotics. 2. [C,G&PS] Slang for various kinds of narcotics.

gebist [USSR] Slang for KGB members; used by many Soviet citizens.

geed-up [C,G&PS] Slang term meaning to be under the influence of some narcotic.

geezer [C,G&PS] Slang for a very small quantity of some drug or narcotic; i.e., "He has a geezer of gauge."

gelignite [TRG] An explosive, stick or block form, often used by terrorist groups when constructing car bombs.

GEM [M] Abbreviation for Ground Effects Machine (hovercraft).

gemonil [LE] Name of a controlled substance, a barbiturate. (*See* QUICK REFERENCE.)

general class [C] Of or referring to the most common class of amateur radio license.

generated keys [I] The numerical key sequences derived through a complicated cryptographic manipulation of key phrases or numbers, or a combination of phrases and numbers.

Genetrix [US] One of the code names for the Air Force's high-altitude, long-range reconnaissance/surveillance balloon project. (*See* GOPHER, GRANDSON, GREYBACK.)

Genyosha [LE] Name of the Dark Ocean Society of Japan, a secret organization made up of members of the *yakuza* (Japan's gangsters) and the rightist element of local government. (*See* YAKUZA.)

GEO [HRU] Abbreviation for *Grupo Especial de Operaciones*, the Spanish Police National antiterrorism and hostage rescue unit.

GEODSS [C3I] Abbreviation for Ground-based Electro-Optical Deep Space (sensors) Surveillance System.

George [A,LE,MIL] Designation for the letter *G*.

GEOS [HRU] Designation for the Colombian Police National Special Operations Group. Responsibilities include antiterrorism activities and hostage rescue. The GEOS are especially well trained.

geosynchronous [NASA] Of or referring to a synchronous orbit 22,300 miles above the equator of the earth. A satellite positioned in geosynchronous orbit does not move relative to the spot on earth over which it orbits.

Gertrude [US] Naval aviation voice brevity code for an underwater telephone system, or sonar.

get high [C,G&PS] Slang for the feeling expressed from smoking marijuana.

get off [C,G&PS] Slang for the feeling an individual expresses from the effect of a drug or narcotic.

getting off [C,G&PS] *See* GET OFF.

GFAE [US] Abbreviation for Government Finished Aerospace Equipment.

GFE [US] Abbreviation for Government Furnished Equipment.

GG [D] Designation for German.

ghana [C,G&PS] Slang for marijuana. (*See* QUICK REFERENCE.)

GHQ [M] Abbreviation for General HeadQuarters.

GHz [C] Abbreviation for Gigahertz, 1 billion Hz.

giant talk [US] Code name for the early warning airborne high-frequency communications system.

gig [D] Slang for a job. The term comes from musicians who used the word to represent a playing engagement.

GIGN [HRU] Abbreviation for *Groupement d'Intervention de la Gendarmerie Nationale*, a French Police counterterrorist unit. The hostage rescue unit members of the GIGN are drawn from the militarized *gendarmerie*.

GIGH [HRU] Designation for the hostage rescue unit of the government of Morocco, the *Groupement d'Intervention de la Gendarmerie Nationale*.

gimmicks [C,G&PS] Slang for the hardware that is used for the injection of heroin.

giri [LE] The closest English translation is "obligation," or "debt." It is often used with the word *ninjo*—meaning empathy or compassion—to describe the "honorable" traditions of the *yakuza*, the gangsters of Japan. (*See* YAKUZA.)

girl [C,G&PS] Slang for cocaine. There are a wide variety of acronyms and abbreviations for cocaine. Girl or girls is one of the terms that carries on in the narcotics trade because it leaves open the opportunity of a more definable description i.e., "Brown on their outside skins" meaning not the best of quality.

GIS [HRU] Abbreviation for *Groupe Interventional Speciale*, the hostage rescue and antiterrorism unit of the *carabinieri*, the Italian police.

giving head [C,G&PS] Slang for a sex act performed in exchange for drugs.

GKES [USSR] Abbreviation for *Gosudarstvennyy Komitet po Vneshnim Ekonomicheskim Svyazyam*, the State Committee for Foreign Economic Relations.

GKNT [USSR] Abbreviation for *Gosudarstvennyy Komitet po Nauki i Teknologii*, the State Committee for Science and Technology.

GKO [USSR] Abbreviation for *Gosudarstvennyy Komitet Oborony*, the State Committee of Defense.

GLA [C,G&PS] Abbreviation for Grand larceny.

glass 1. [C,G&PS] Slang for stolen jewelry. 2. [C,G&PS] Slang for a smokeable methamphetamine. (*See* ICE.)

GLCM [C3I] Abbreviation for Ground-Launched Cruise Missile.

glom [LE] Slang meaning to arrest an individual.

glom on [C,G&PS] Slang meaning to be arrested.

glued [C,G&PS] Slang meaning to be arrested.

GMA [C3I] Abbreviation for Gated Mode Acquisition.

GND CON [A] Abbreviation for GrouND CONtrol.

Go [C,G&PS] Slang meaning to make a deal.

GOA [LE] Abbreviation for Gone On Arrival.

goblin [US] Naval aviation voice brevity code meaning an electronic warfare problem exists.

GOE [HRU] Abbreviation for *Grupo de Operacoes Especiais*, the antiterrorism and hostage rescue unit of the Portuguese *Policia de Seguranca Publica*.

GOES [C3I] Abbreviation for Geostationary Operational Environmental Satellite.

go fast [C,G&PS] A trucker's slang for a methamphetamine he will use to stay awake behind the wheel for hours. A call for this drug will be quickly answered by a citizens band (CB) drug dealer anywhere in the nation. Go fast could mean methamphetamine, cocaine, and other drugs. The use of narcotics by long-haul drivers is a growing problem for law enforcement because state police lack field-testing abilities.

going down [C,G&PS] Fighting alongside your set, that is, neighborhood gang members. Also called going down with the set.

going up [C,G&PS] Slang for an individual under the influence of narcotics.

gold 1. [C,G&PS] Slang for money. 2. [C,G&PS] Slang for marijuana. (*See* QUICK REFERENCE.) 3. [C,G&PS] Catchall term for all types of high-quality drugs, narcotics, or marijuana.

gold dust [C,G&PS] Slang for cocaine. (*See* QUICK REFERENCE.)

golden arches [LE] Slang for a McDonald's restaurant; sometimes used by law enforcement to indicate a place to meet.

Golf [A,LE,MIL] Designation for the letter *G*.

gomme L [TRG] Name of an explosive that is favored by many of the terrorist/radical groups in Italy and France.

gong [C,G&PS] Slang for an opium pipe.

gong-beater [C,G&PS] Slang for an individual who smokes opium.

good fellow [LE] Slang for an executioner, a hit man, or an individual who has killed someone on orders from a criminal group.

good go [C,G&PS] Slang for a purchase of narcotics at a price lower than that usually offered from other sources.

goods [C,G&PS] Slang for drugs or narcotics.

Goodyear Tire and Rubber Co. blimp communication frequencies. *See* TABLE G-1.

goofballs [C,G&PS] Slang for barbiturates. (*See* QUICK REFERENCE.)

goofing [C,G&PS] Slang for an individual on drugs who acts as if he is drunk.

Table G-1. Goodyear Co. Blimp Communication Frequencies

Frequency	Purpose
123.0500	Airport/landing site
123.2000	Airport/landing site
123.2500	Airport/landing site
132.0000	Goodyear Public Relations
151.6200	Blimp & ground crew
151.6250	Blimp & ground crew
153.3200	Goodyear Aerospace network
167.5625	Remote to law enforcement
460.0250	Remote to law enforcement
462.0500	Goodyear Aerospace network
462.2250	Goodyear Aerospace network
465.0250	Remote to law enforcement
465.9125	Operations/sports event
465.9375	Operations/sports event
465.9625	Operations/sports event

goofing around [C,G&PS] Slang meaning to act in an aggressive way, usually caused by the taking of some barbiturate.

GOPE [HRU] Abbreviation for *Grupo de Operaciones Especiales*, the police emergency response team (bomb and terrorist operations) and the hostage rescue unit of the Chilean Caribineros.

Gopher [M] *See* GENETRIX.

gouching [C,G&PS] Slang for the euphoric feeling connected with heroin.

GOV Background code for state government.

gow head [LE] Slang for an individual who is addicted to narcotics.

GP 1. [CW] Designation for a nerve agent. GP is a nerve agent composed of an unknown (secret) chemical compound. Each generation of nerve agent in the "G" series appears to be a modification of the last—usually easier to handle, quicker acting, and with less side effects. GP is believed to be a cholinesterase inhibitive nerve agent. 2. [TRG] Abbreviation for *Gauche Proletariene*, a French terrorist group. The GP appears to have a variety of motives for their terrorist acts, generally having to do with NATO operations in Europe and the various military forces.

GPMG [M] Abbreviation for General Purpose Machine Gun.

GPS [C3I] Abbreviation for Global Positioning System.

GPU **1.** [M] Abbreviation for Ground Power Unit. **2.** [USSR] Abbreviation for *Gosudarstvennoye Politicheskoye Upraveniye*, the State Political Directorate.

GPWS [M] Ground Proximity Warning System.

gramoxone [GOV] A paraquat-based herbicide used for eradication of marijuana and opium.

grand slam [US] Naval aviation voice brevity code meaning all enemy aircraft are destroyed.

grandson [N] *See* GENETRIX.

GRAPO [TRG] Abbreviation for *Grupo de Resistencia Antifascista Primo de Octubre* (the First of October Anti-Fascist Resistance Group), a Spanish terrorist group that was very active in the late 1970s. Since then membership has dropped off, but those remaining have carried out bank robberies, the assassination of police officers and public officials in Spain, and kidnappings and bombings. The group's motives appear to be in support of the Marxist movement.

grass [C,G&PS] Slang for marijuana. (*See* QUICK REFERENCE.)

graymail [I] An attempt on the part of an individual or agency to coerce another individual or agency to do something that is within his power but that he really doesn't want to do. The initiating individual or agency might threaten to expose certain details about the individual or agency that could be shared legally. Blackmail is illegal, while graymail is forced revelation.

grayswirl [C,G&PS] Slang for LSD. (*See* QUICK REFERENCE.)

GRC [TRG] Abbreviation for German Revolutionary Cell, a West German terrorist group that wants to have its society much as it was in the Nazi era. The GRC is an anti-NATO organization.

green [C,G&PS] Slang for money.

green deck [US] Naval aviation voice brevity code meaning the flight deck on an aircraft carrier is clear for launch and recovery.

green hornets [C,G&PS] Slang for the drug Dexamyl, a barbiturate.

green merchant [LE] The Drug Enforcement Administration code name for the on-going intelligence operation that seeks to locate, arrest, and prosecute those individuals and/or commercial business operations who knowingly sell equipment allegedly used to grow marijuana indoors. (*See* FLIR; HYDROPONICS.)

green pine [US] Slang for an early warning airborne ultrahigh frequency communications system.

greenies [C,G&PS] Slang for amphetamines. (*See* QUICK REFERENCE.)

greta [C,G&PS] Slang for marijuana. (*See* QUICK REFERENCE.)

Greyback [M] *See* GENETRIX.

grey wolves [TRG] The militant arm of the National Action Party of Turkey. The Grey Wolves are a right-wing terrorist group, also known as the *Bozkurtlar*.

G-ride [C,G&PS] Slang for a stolen automobile.

griefo [C,G&PS] Slang for marijuana. (*See* QUICK REFERENCE.)

grifa [C,G&PS] Mexican for marijuana.

grooving [C,G&PS] Slang for the feeling of an individual who is under the influence of a narcotic or drug.

ground control [C,G&PS] Slang for the individual who gives out LSD at a drug party.

groundsat [UK] Code name for tactical radio system.

ground track [NASA] The path on earth over which a satellite in orbit will travel.

ground wave [C] That part of a radio transmission that follows the curvature of the earth.

GRP **1.** [C3I] Abbreviation for group. **2.** [M] Abbreviation for Glass Reinforced Plastic.

GRU [USSR] Abbreviation for *Glavnoye Razvedyvatel'noye Upravleniye*, the Main Intelligence Directorate of the General Staff. The GRU is responsible for military intelligence and electronic intercepts.

gryphon [US] Code name for secure shore-to-ship communications system.

GSA [C3I] Abbreviation for General Services Administration.

GSE [M] Abbreviation for Ground Support Equipment.

GSG-9 [HRU] Abbreviation for *Grenzschutzgruppe 9*, Border Patrol Unit 9, a West German counterterrorist unit. Members of this group are Federal Border Police.

GSRU [HRU] Abbreviation for General Staff Recon Unit, the hostage rescue unit of the Israeli military.

GSTS [C3I] Abbreviation for Ground-based Surveillance and Tracking System.

GSU [HRU] Abbreviation for the General Services Unit of the Kenya Police. Within the GSU is the Recce Unit that provides the national antiterrorism and hostage rescue strike force.

GTS [M] Abbreviation for Gas Turbine Starter.

GU Specialty code for guards.

Guadalajara green [C,G&PS] A type of marijuana that is grown in Jalisco, Mexico. Guadalajara green has a reputation of being a good-quality marijuana.

Guardians of the Islamic Revolution [TRG] A terrorist group headquartered in Frankfurt, West Germany. It is a Palestinian cell of Ahmed Jibril's hard-line Popular Front for the Liberation of Palestine-General Command. It is suspected of some involvement in the bombing of Pan American World Airways Flight 103 over Scotland in December 1988, where approximately 280 people died.

GUKR [USSR] Abbreviation for *Glavnoye Upravleniye Kontrrazvedki*, the Main Administration for Counterintelligence.

GULAG [USSR] Designation for *Glavnoye Upravleniye LAGerey*, the Main Administration of Corrective Labor Camps.

Gum 1. [C,G&PS] Slang for opium. (*See* QUICK REFERENCE.) **2.** [USSR] Abbreviation for *Glavnoye Upravleniye Militsii*, the Main Administration of Militia.

gumi [LE] Term used by members of the Japanese *yakuza* (Japan's criminal element) to describe their gang, company, or association. (*See* YAKUZA.)

GUMZ [USSR] Abbreviation for *Glavnoye Upravleniye Mestami Zaklyucheniya*, the Main Administration of Places of Detention.

Gun 1. [C,G&PS] A firearm. **2.** [C,G&PS] Slang for the needle used in injecting heroin.

guns [C,G&PS] Slang for strong-arm tactics.

GUPO [USSR] Abbreviation for *Glavnoye Upravleniye Pozharnoi Okhrany*, the Main Administration of Fire Protection.

Gurentai [LE] One of the three major gangster organizations involved in blackmarket operations in Japan. Other groups are the *Tekiya* and the *Bakuto*.

guru [C,G&PS] An individual—sometimes imaginary—who has been with the drug-addicted person on a drug trip.

GVWR [LE] Abbreviation used usually in trucking accidents to indicate a violation of the Gross Vehicle Weight Rating.

GW [M] Abbreviation for Guided Weapon.

GWEN [C3I] Abbreviation for Ground Wave Emergency Network, a communications system designed to link government and U.S. military operations in the event of a nuclear war.

H

H **1.** [C,G&PS] Slang for heroin. (*See* QUICK REFERENCE.) **2.** [CW] Designation for the blister agent, Mustard Gas. This chemical warfare agent attacks human membranes such as the lungs and eyes. It can cause severe skin inflammation, shortness of breath, and blindness.

habit [C,G&PS] Addiction to drugs.

HAHO [M] Abbreviation for High Altitude, High Opening, a military parachute technique in which the parachute is opened almost immediately upon exiting the aircraft at high altitude. This technique has been applied by antiterrorist troops wishing to enter a zone undetected, using controllable parachutes.

hair [LE] Law enforcement forensic scientists at the FBI laboratory can tell a great deal about the owner when human hair is found at a crime scene. Apart from its vulnerability to fire, human hair is almost impossible to destroy. It decays at such a slow rate that it is practically nondisintegrative. Human hair cannot be destroyed by cold, change of climate, water, or other natural forces, and it is resistant to many kinds of acids and corrosive chemicals. This is why it clogs sinks and drainpipes. A single strand of human hair in the hands of a forensic scientist can tell the age and sex of the owner, drugs and narcotics the owner has taken, and through DNA evaluation and sample comparison from whose head the hair came. (*See* DNA.)

hairy [C,G&PS] Slang for heroin. (*See* QUICK REFERENCE.)

Halcon 8 [HRU] The Argentinian Special Counter-Terrorism Team of the Army Commandos.

haldol [LE] A controlled substance, a major tranquilizer. (*See* QUICK REFERENCE.)

half-load [C,G&PS] Slang for fifteen decks of heroin.

half-pint [LE] Slang for the minor child of a law enforcement officer.

half-signal [LE] Slang for the wife of a law enforcement officer.

half-wave dipole [C] *See* DIPOLE ANTENNA.

HALO [M] Abbreviation for High Altitude, Low Opening, a military free-fall parachuting technique.

ham [C] Slang for a licensed amateur radio operator.

ham band [C] Radio-frequency bandwidths allocated or used in part by amateur radio operators.

hammer [C,G&PS] Slang for a converted flare gun or 22-caliber pen gun.

hand held [C] Of or referring to any small radio transceiver, receiver, or transmitter that is operated by holding in the hand.

hand-to-hand go [LE] Slang for the delivery time that is scheduled for a payoff.

hang up [C,G&PS] Slang for the withdrawal from narcotics.

happy dust [C,G&PS] Slang for cocaine. (*See* QUICK REFERENCE.)

happy stick [C,G&PS] Slang for a marijuana cigarette that has been laced with PCP.

hard stuff [C,G&PS] Slang for drugs and narcotics that are very potent.

hard target [I] An enemy country that intelligence agents find difficult to penetrate at worthwhile levels. The term also is used in law enforcement indicating the difficulty of getting inside a gang or specific group of individuals.

hardening [I] Methods and techniques developed to enhance the ability of a satellite to survive attack. Laser-resistant coated camera lenses is one example. Shielded electronic circuits and protective external shielding are other ways of hardening a satellite.

hardness [C,G&PS] Slang for a law enforcement officer.

hardness bull [C,G&PS] Slang for a law enforcement officer, usually a detective, who works on the street.

HARM [C3I] Abbreviation for High-speed Anti-Radiation Missile.

Harry [C,G&PS] Slang for heroin. (*See* QUICK REFERENCE.)

hash [C,G&PS] Slang for hashish. (*See* QUICK REFERENCE.)

hashish 1. [LE] The resin from the tops and leaves of the marijuana (cannabis sativa) plant. It can be found in liquid or solid form and often is dried and baked into small bricks or round, flat cakes. The color of hashish in one of these forms ranges from dark green to black and from light tan to dark brown. Hashish is smoked by inserting some of the dried material into a cigarette or in liquid form by adding it to marijuana in a pipe. Hashish is much more potent than marijuana. 2. [LE] A controlled substance, cannabis. (*See* QUICK REFERENCE.)

hash oil [LE] Name of a controlled substance, cannabis. (*See* QUICK REFERENCE.)

haven dust [C,G&PS] Slang for cocaine. (*See* QUICK REFERENCE.)

have quick [US] Code name for antijam radio system.

HAW [I] Abbreviation for Homing All the Way.

Hawaiian sunshine [C,G&PS] Slang for LSD. (*See* QUICK REFERENCE.)

hawk [C,G&PS] Slang for LSD. (*See* QUICK REFERENCE.)

hawkin' hubba [C,G&PS] Slang for selling rock cocaine.

hay [C,G&PS] Slang for marijuana and/or hashish.

hay head [C,G&PS] Slang for a marijuana smoker.

H&C [C,G&PS] Slang for heroin and cocaine dependence.

HD [CW] Designation for a blister agent, mustard gas. This chemical warfare agent causes blindness, and attacks the lungs and surface of exposed skin.

HDLC [C3I] Abbreviation for High Level Data Link Control.

HDTV [C3I] Abbreviation for High Definition TV.

HDX [C3I] Abbreviation for Half Duplex.

head 1. [C,G&PS] Slang for a drug addict. 2. [C,G&PS] Slang for a marijuana user. 3. [C,G&PS] Used by marijuana smokers to indicate that an individual is not only a marijuana smoker, but is attuned to the reaction he/she receives from the narcotic effect of marijuana. Marijuana gives each user a different level of head.

headphone [C] A miniature audio speaker that fits over or into the human ear for better hearing.

head shop [C,G&PS] A shop where drug and narcotic paraphernalia is sold. These shops have generally gone underground because of individual state legislation. A thrift shop in northern California sold marijuana pipes as bird feeders.

heads up [C,G&PS] Slang for LSD. (*See* QUICK REFERENCE.)

HEAR [LE] Abbreviation for Hospital Emergency Ambulance Radio.

hearts [C,G&PS] Slang for amphetamines. (*See* QUICK REFERENCE.)

heat 1. [C,G&PS] Slang for a law enforcement officer. 2. [C,G&PS] Slang for pressure put upon an individual by a police officer.

heavenly blue [C,G&PS] Slang for LSD. (*See* QUICK REFERENCE.)

heavy [C,G&PS] In the drugs/narcotic trade, referring to a person who is considered important or one to be reckoned with. (*See* LIGHTWEIGHT.)

HEDS [C3I] Abbreviation for High Endoatmospheric Defense System.

heeled [LE] Slang for an individual who is stopped by police and found to have on his person either a weapon or narcotics.

hep [C,G&PS] Slang term meaning to understand.

Helen [C,G&PS] Slang for heroin. (*See* QUICK REFERENCE.)

hemp 1. [C,G&PS] Slang for marijuana. (*See* QUICK REFERENCE.) **2.** [US] Abbreviation for High Altitude Electromagnetic Pulse.

HEMTT [M] Abbreviation for Heavy Expanded Mobility Tactical Truck.

hen house radar [I] Slang for the Soviet early-warning, long-range radar that the USSR depends on to detect incoming ballistic missiles.

Henry 1. [C,G&PS] Slang for heroin. (*See* QUICK REFERENCE.) **2.** [A,LE,MIL] Designation for the letter *H*.

Herb [C,G&PS] Slang for marijuana. (*See* QUICK REFERENCE.)

HERO [M] Abbreviation for Hazards of Electromagnetic Radiation to Ordnance.

heroin 1. [C,G&PS] Name of an alkaloid that is derived from morphine. The chemical name for heroin is diacetylmorphine. Heroin usually is in powder form, but also can be found as a pill. The color in either form ranges from tan to brown, and in more refined examples is white or slightly off-white. Heroin is injected, but can be smoked and snorted through the nose. **2.** [LE] Name of a controlled substance, a narcotic. (*See* QUICK REFERENCE.)

hertz [Hz] [C] The unit of frequency; one hertz equals one cycle per second.

heterodyne [C] The audio beat note that is created from combining two close frequency signals.

hexagon [US] Code name for the KH-9 surveillance satellite system.

HF [C3I] Abbreviation for High Frequency, 3 MHz to 30 MHz.

HFCRSP [C3I] Abbreviation for High-Frequency Communications Replacement System Program.

HFDM [C3I] Abbreviation for High-Frequency Digital Modem.

HFIC [US] Abbreviation for High-Frequency Intra-task force Communications.

HFIP [C3I] Abbreviation for High-Frequency Improvement Program.

hiding place [I] *See* DEAD DROP.

high [C,G&PS] Slang for someone feeling the effect of a narcotic.

high roller [C,G&PS] Slang for an individual who gambles for high stakes.

high as a kite [C,G&PS] Slang term referring to an individual who is under the influence of a narcotic.

hikori [C,G&PS] Another name for peyote. (*See* QUICK REFERENCE.)

hip [C,G&PS] Slang term referring to an individual who is in tune with whatever is going on around him, usually someone in the drug/narcotics community.

his stick [C,G&PS] Slang for an individual who has taken up life on the street.

hit 1. [C,G&PS] Slang term meaning to kill. **2.** [C,G&PS] Slang meaning to purchase narcotics. **3.** [C,G&PS] Slang meaning to win at gambling.

hit the pit [C,G&PS] Slang for a narcotics injection into the inner elbow.

hit the street [LE] Slang for a law enforcement officer acknowledging that he is going on patrol.

hitting [C,G&PS] Slang for drugs or narcotics that have been adulterated.

hitting the stuff 1. [C,G&PS] Slang for an individual who is under the influence of liquor. **2.** [C,G&PS] Slang for an individual who is under the influence of a narcotic.

hittin' up [C,G&PS] Slang for painting graffiti.

Hizb Allah [TRG] A Shiite underground terrorist group that is headquartered in Lebanon.

HLLV [C3I] Abbreviation for Heavy Lift Launch Vehicle.

HML [C3I] Abbreviation for Hard Mobile Launcher.

HMMWV [C3I] Abbreviation for High-Mobility Multipurpose Wheeled Vehicle.

HMS [M] Abbreviation for Helmet-Mounted Sight (weapon).

HNT [LE] Abbreviation for Hostage Negotiating Team.

hocus [C,G&PS] Slang for morphine. (*See* QUICK REFERENCE.)

HOE [C3I] Abbreviation for Homing Overlay Experiment.

hog 1. [C,G&PS] Slang for a drug addict who

takes large amounts of drugs. **2.** [C,G&PS] Slang for PCP. (*See* QUICK REFERENCE.) **3.** [C,G&PS] Slang for benactyzine. (*See* QUICK REFERENCE.)

Hogan's Alley [LE] A fictitious but strikingly realistic town built on a wooded, 20-acre site at the FBI Academy, about 40 miles south of Washington, D.C., where students practice nabbing criminals, interrogating witnesses, and gathering evidence.

HOIS [I] Abbreviation for Hostile Intelligence Service (DIA).

HOJ [M] Abbreviation for Home on Jam.

holding [LE] Slang meaning to have narcotics in possession.

holding hands [US] Naval aviation voice brevity code meaning flying in formation.

home base [US] Naval aviation voice brevity code meaning home base.

home front [LE] Slang for headquarters of law enforcement officers.

homegrown [C,G&PS] Referring to domestic marijuana, marijuana that is grown in the United States, not smuggled across the border from Mexico.

home on jam Slang for electronic jamming.

homes [C,G&PS] Slang for homeboys or home-girls who are the neighborhood residents and often gang members.

honey trap [I] An operation that is designed to compromise an opponent sexually. This is a common practice in many intelligence operations.

honkte [LE] Slang meaning to be suspect of an individual.

hooch [C,G&PS] Slang for marijuana. (*See* QUICK REFERENCE.)

hood [C,G&PS] Slang for neighborhood people, often gang members.

hookah [C,G&PS] Slang for a pipe used for smoking hashish.

hooked [C,G&PS] Slang for someone addicted to narcotics i.e., "He's hooked."

hooked up [C,G&PS] Slang for describing an individual who is somehow connected to organized crime.

hooker [US] Naval aviation voice brevity code meaning a fishing vessel.

hop head [C,G&PS] Slang for an individual addicted to drugs.

hop joint [C,G&PS] Slang for a location where opium is smoked.

hoppy [C,G&PS] Slang for a drug addict.

horn [C,G&PS] Slang meaning to snort heroin or cocaine.

horning [C,G&PS] Slang meaning to sniff cocaine into the nose.

horse [C,G&PS] Slang for heroin. (*See* QUICK REFERENCE.)

hot **1.** [C,G&PS] Of or referring to stolen property. **2.** [US] Naval aviation voice brevity code meaning active antisubmarine electronic warfare contact and/or the use of live ordnance.

hot bust [LE] Slang for an arrest that has been set up by the police or federal agents based on hard evidence in hand or by long-term surveillance.

Hotel [A,LE,MIL] Designation for the letter *H*.

hot paper [LE] Slang for stolen money or stocks and securities.

hot stuff [C,G&PS] Slang for stolen property.

hot heroin [C,G&PS] Slang for heroin that has somehow been poisoned and then sold to an individual who is suspected of informing to the police. Note: This is a common practice with drug dealers with the intent sometimes to supply "the competition" with bad drugs. This approach tends to get a lot of people killed.

hot load [C,G&PS] Slang for a drug overdose that has resulted in death.

HOW [LE] Abbreviation for House of Worship, when referring to crime against a church or synagogue.

HP **1.** [M] Abbreviation for High Pressure. **2.** [M] Abbreviation for Horsepower.

HPA [C3I] Abbreviation for High Power Amplifier.

HQ [M] Abbreviation for Headquarters.

HRB [TRG] Abbreviation for *Hrvatsko Revolucionarno Bratstvo*, also known as the Croatian Revolutionary Brotherhood (CRB), this terrorist group has carried out hijackings and bombings against the Yugoslav government because it is dominated by Serb factions.

HRT (FBI) [HRU] Abbreviation for Hostage Response Team of the Federal Bureau of Investigation, United States Department of Justice. At the national and local level, HRT "Hurt" units exist to handle terrorist incidents. HRT units are located in most major cities of the United States.

HRU [LE] Abbreviation for Hostage Rescue Unit, a term used to describe either a law enforcement, military, or government operated antiterrorism, antihijacking, or hostage rescue specialist team.

HS [CW] Designation for the blister agent, mustard gas. This is a chemical warfare agent that blisters and burns the eyes, skin, and membranes of human beings. It can cause severe lung problems that result in death. HS also can cause blindness.

HT [C] Designation for Hand-held Radio Transceiver, the abbreviation for walkie-talkie.

HUD [M] Abbreviation for Heads-Up Display, a weapon system.

huff [LE] Slang meaning to sniff glue.

HUMINT [I] Abbreviation for Human Intelligence, intelligence information collected by an individual, especially someone in the business of spying.

hungry croaker [C,G&PS] Slang for a physician who offers narcotics and drugs for sale. This type of individual is usually addicted.

hustle [C,G&PS] Slang meaning to seek money, usually to purchase drugs, by some devious method.

hustling [C,G&PS] The means by which an individual supports a drug or narcotic habit.

HVIT [US] Abbreviation for High-Volume Information Transfer.

hydromorphone [LE] A controlled substance that is a narcotic. (*See* QUICK REFERENCE.)

hydroponics [LE] The science of growing plants in soil-free, mineral-rich solutions. It is commonly used for cucumbers and tomatoes but marijuana growers also have used the technique for years. One marijuana plant uses only 1 square foot of space, so a compact, 400-square-foot greenhouse turning out marijuana year round could generate from $4 million to $5 million in sales each year simply by using hydroponics. A greenhouse operation is obviously less detectable, so law enforcement agencies are using Forward-Looking Infrared (FLIR) as a means of detecting the rooftop heat at night created by the marijuana growing lights. Once a "hot spot" shows up, it becomes a simple matter for foot patrol investigations and surveillance. (*See* FLIR; GREEN MERCHANT.)

hydrus [US] Code name for secure ship-to-shore communications systems.

hype [C,G&PS] Slang for a narcotics addict.

I

I or the I [LE] Designation for an interstate highway.

IA Specialty code for Investigation Accountant.

IAD **1.** [M] Abbreviation for Immediate Action Drill. Drills called under this command stress all aspects of counterinsurgency and counterterrorist training. The drill itself emphasizes a readiness for any eventuality. **2.** [LE] Abbreviation for Internal Affairs Division. **3.** [A] Abbreviation for International Air Distress, a frequency signal.

I.A.D.B. Abbreviation for Inter American Development Bank, a branch of World Bank.

IAGC [C] Abbreviation for Instantaneous Automatic Gain Control.

IAMP [M] Abbreviation for Imagery Acquisition and Management Program (System).

IAP [M] Abbreviation for Improved Accuracy Program.

IAS [A] Abbreviation for Indicated Airspeed.

IATA [A] Abbreviation for International Air Transport Association.

IC **1.** [I] Abbreviation for Intelligence Cycle, the steps by which intelligence information is assembled, assessed, and made available to the end user. The cycle is comprised of four basic phases:

- Direction, a determination of the intelligence requirements, the preparation of a collection plan, the specific task of collection agencies and their resources, and an on-going evaluation of the productivity of the project;

- Collection, the exploitation of information sources and the delivery of the collected information to the proper intelligence processing unit for use in the production of hard intelligence data;

- Process, those steps whereby the information gathered becomes good and useful intelligence through the process of evaluation, analysis, integration, and interpretation; and

- Dissemination, the distribution of information or intelligence products that results in oral, written, or graphic form. All intelligence and law enforcement agencies worldwide tend to use these same steps.

2. [I] Abbreviation for Intelligence Community, that part of government consisting of all agencies that produce intelligence and counterintelligence material. This includes the Central Intelligence Agency, the National Security Agency, the Defense Intelligence Agency, and certain groups within the United States Department of Defense. **3.** [C3I] Abbreviation for Integrated Circuit.

ICAO [A] Abbreviation for International Civil Aviation Organization.

ICBM [C3I] Abbreviation for Intercontinental Ballistic Missile. The CIA says 15 Third World Countries are developing their own ballistic missiles and could have them in place by the end of the century. The missiles could carry conventional explosives, chemical weapons, or even nuclear weapons to other countries. The range of the missiles varies from 30 miles to more than 1,500 miles. Many countries already have bought ballistic missiles from abroad or developed their own small fleets of them. These include Afghanistan, Argentina, Brazil, India, Iran, Iraq, Israel, Kuwait, Libya, North Korea, Pakistan, Saudi Arabia, South Korea, Syria, and South Yemen.

ice **1.** [C,G&PS] Slang for stolen jewelry. **2.** [C,G&PS] Slang for cocaine. **3.** [C,G&PS] Slang for a smokable, colorless, odorless form of methamphetamine (speed) also known by the names snot, glass, quartz, and rice. It acts on the brain in less than 15 seconds, providing a long high. Ice does not cause the rapid twitching and jerking usually related to crack and cocaine users. Originally developed in Hawaii, ice can be produced easily by a local drug chemist in an uncomplicated cooking process. Ice stimulates dopamine production in the brain. This, in turn, stimulates pleasure centers, unleashing vast amounts of energy giving the user the impression that he is almost superhuman. Problems can arise for the long-term ice user because brain cells get greedy and demand additional dopamine. When the high from smoking ice wears off in 12 to 24 hours, withdrawal symptoms are very similar to crack and cocaine addiction.

- A puff of crack cocaine buoys its user for approximately 20 minutes, but the high from smoking ice endures for 12 to 24 hours.

- Ice can be manufactured in a clandestine speed laboratory, whereas cocaine must be extracted from the leaf of the coca plant and then refined.

- Because it is odorless, ice can be smoked in public virtually without detection. In its solid form, the drug resembles rock candy or a chip of ice. When lighted in a glass pipe, the crystals turn to liquid and produce a potent vapor that enters the bloodstream directly through the lungs. Ice reverts to its solid state when it cools, thus becoming reusable and highly transportable.

(*See* GLASS; QUARTZ; RICE; SNOT.)

ice cream habit   [C,G&PS] Slang for an irregular habit of drug usage.

ice cream man   [C,G&PS] Slang for an individual selling opium.

Ichiwa-kai   [LE] An offshoot of the *Yamaguchi-gumi*, Japan's largest *yakuza* crime syndicate. The *Ickiwa-kai* is the fifth-largest *yakuza* organization in Japan. (*See* YAKUZA.)

ICPO   [LE] Abbreviation for International Criminal Police Organization. (*See* INTERPOL.)

I.C.R.C.   Abbreviation for International Committee of the Red Cross.

ICS   [I] Abbreviation for The Intelligence Community Staff, which is supervised by the director of the CIA. The ICS is the coordinating nerve center for intelligence operations of the United States.

ICS 3   [UK] Abbreviation for Integrated Communications System.

ID   1. [LE] Abbreviation for Identification. 2. [LE] Abbreviation for Intelligence Division.

IDA   1. [C3I] Abbreviation for Institute of Defense Analysis. 2. [A,LE,MIL] Designation for the letter *I*.

Idealist   [US] Code name for high-altitude surveillance aircraft that conduct electronic and photographic reconnaissance missions along the borders of the Soviet Union.

IDHS   [C3I] Abbreviation for Intelligent Data Handling System.

idiot pills   [C,G&PS] Slang for barbiturates.

IDTU   [C,G&PS] Abbreviation for Intoxicated Driver Testing Unit.

IE   [I] Abbreviation for Intelligence Estimate, an appraisal of the intelligence elements as they relate to a specific situation or condition and the determination of the courses of action that will be followed.

IED   [LE] Abbreviation for Improvised Explosive Device.

IEEE   [C3I] Abbreviation for Institute of Electrical and Electronics Engineers.

IEMATS   [US] Abbreviation for Improved Emergency Message Automation Transmission System.

IF   [C3I] Abbreviation for Intermediate Frequency.

IFB   [US] Abbreviation for Invitation For Bid.

IFF   [M] Abbreviation for Identification, Friend or Foe, a system using electromagnetic transmissions to which equipment carried by friendly forces automatically responds, for example, by emitting pulses, thereby distinguishing themselves from enemy forces. IFF also is the discrete Identification, Friend or Foe code assigned to a particular aircraft, ship, or other vehicle for identification by electronic means. (*See* STRANGLE and STRANGLE PARROT.)

IFL   [C3I] Abbreviation for Interfacility Link.

IFLP   [TRG] Abbreviation for Italian Front for the Liberation of the Proletariat, an Italian anti-NATO terrorist group.

IFM   [C] Abbreviation for Instantaneous Frequency Measurement.

IFR   [A] Abbreviation for Instrument Flight Rules.

IGE   [M] Abbreviation for In-Ground Effect, which refers to helicopter performance.

II   **1.** Specialty code for insurance investigation. **2.** [M] Abbreviation for Image Intensification.

IIP   [G] Abbreviation for Incredibly Important Person. This term has been used between communication agencies to clearly describe an individual ranked as the highest of stature without divulging the name or military rank for security reasons.

IIR   [M] Abbreviation for Imaging Infrared.

ill   [C,G&PS] Term for the description of an individual sick from the symptoms of a drug or narcotic withdrawal.

illegal   **1.** [I] Of or referring to an act not approved under the law. **2.** In an intelligence operation, an agent or employee of an intelligence agency who is sent into a situation where he knowingly is representing his employer. In law enforcement, an individual might be encouraged to join a gang in the hope that at some later time that individual will become an informer.

illegals & legals   [USSR] The terms used by the Soviet intelligence community that distinguishes between the field agents they have outside their country who are on official diplomatic missions (legal) and those (illegals) who are operating outside the protection offered a diplomat. The illegals are usually intelligence agents working with false credentials.

illness   [USSR] Soviet slang for being placed under arrest.

ILS   **1.** [A] Abbreviation for Instrument Landing System. **2.** [M] Abbreviation for Integrated Logistic Support.

IMA   [M] Abbreviation for Individual Mobilization Augmentees.

IMC   [A] Abbreviation for Instrument Meteorological Conditions.

IMET   [US] Abbreviation for International Military Education and Training Program.

I'm flush   [C,G&PS] The statement someone might make to a drug dealer indicating that he has money to make a purchase.

IMINT   [C3I] Acronym for Imagery Intelligence.

Immigration, U.S.   [GOV] The agency of the U.S. government that stops and searches individuals and automobiles at U.S. borders looking for people trying to enter the United States by less than legal means. Their radio frequencies are listed in TABLE I-1.

I'm looking   [C,G&PS] The statement someone might make to a drug dealer indicating he is looking for drugs, as in "I'm looking for some H."

IMO   [C3I] Abbreviation for International Maritime Organization.

IMP   [C3I] Abbreviation for Interplanetary Monitoring Platform.

impulse radar   [I] A technological radar breakthrough in the United States that illuminates low-flying Stealth aircraft crossing the borders of the U.S. It is capable of providing accurate three-dimensional pictures of almost any flying machine, from jet fighters to commercial airliners. Typical Stealth aircraft are coated with porous materials dotted with cavities designed to absorb certain radar frequencies. Impulse radar will defeat such a design with radar energy microwaves that are 50,000 times as powerful as existing radars. At the heart of impulse radar is a key component called a Bulk Avalanche Semiconductor Switch (BASS), which creates thousands of high-speed, high-energy microwave pulses every second. Much of the funding on this classified project has come from Boeing Incorporated. A unique feature of impulse radar is that when an aircraft or missile is detected, the operator can then zoom in on the target on his viewing screen for positive identification.

Table I-1. Immigration—Border Patrol Nationwide Frequency Plan

Group 1	Border Patrol	F	Input	Output	Tone
	Border Patrol repeaters	1	162.825	163.625	100.0
	Border Patrol repeaters	2	162.925	163.625	100.0
	Border Patrol direct	3		163.625	100.0
	Border Patrol direct	4		163.675	123.0
	Border Patrol repeaters	5	162.825	163.675	123.0
	Border Patrol repeaters	6	162.925	163.675	123.0
	Border Patrol repeaters	7	162.825	163.725	151.4
	Border Patrol repeaters	8	162.925	163.725	151.4
	Border Patrol repeaters	9	162.825	163.775	206.6
	Border Patrol repeaters	10	162.925	163.775	206.6
	Border Patrol direct	11		168.8625	100.0
	Border Patrol repeaters	12	165.925	168.8625	100.0
	Border Patrol direct	13		165.925	100.0
	Border Intrusion Alarm			170.625	
	Border Intrusion Alarm			170.650	
	Border Intrusion Alarm			170.700	
	Border Intrusion Alarm			170.775	
Group 2	**Border Patrol**				
	Border Patrol repeaters	1	162.875	163.725	100.0
	Border Patrol repeaters	2	162.975	163.725	100.0
	Border Patrol direct	3		163.725	100.0
	Border Patrol direct	4		163.775	123.0
	Border Patrol repeaters	5	162.875	163.775	123.0
	Border Patrol repeaters	6	162.975	163.775	123.0
	Border Patrol repeaters	7	162.825	163.625	151.4
	Border Patrol repeaters	8	162.850	163.725	151.4
	Border Patrol repeaters	9	162.900	163.625	206.6
	Border Patrol repeaters	10	162.975	163.675	206.6
	Border Intrusion Alarm			170.625	
	Border Intrusion Alarm			170.650	
	Border Intrusion Alarm			170.700	
	Border Intrusion Alarm			170.775	
Group 3	**Immigration Service**				
	Immigration repeaters	1	162.850	163.650	100.0
	Immigration repeaters	2	162.950	163.650	100.0
	Immigration direct	3		163.650	100.0
	Immigration direct	4		163.750	123.0
	Immigration repeaters	5	162.850	163.750	123.0
	Immigration repeaters	6	162.950	163.750	123.0
	Immigration repeaters	7	162.850	163.625	151.4
	Customs Service direct	8		165.2375	
	INS-BP tactical 1	9		162.900	206.6
	INS-BP tactical 2	10		163.700	206.6
	INS-BP tactical repeater	11	162.900	163.700	107.2
	Border Intrusion Alarm			170.625	
	Border Intrusion Alarm			170.650	
	Border Intrusion Alarm			170.700	
	Border Intrusion Alarm			170.775	
Group 4	**Allied Agencies**				
	OCDETF	1	163.665	165.925	100.0
	Border Patrol repeaters	2	162.900	163.775	100.0

Table I-1. Continued

Group	Border Patrol	F	Input	Output	Tone
	Immigration direct	3		162.850	100.0
	ATF Bureau repeaters	4	166.5375	165.2875	
	Customs Service repeaters	5	166.4375	165.2375	
	Border Patrol repeaters	6	162.825	163.625	123.0
	Border Patrol repeaters	7	162.875	163.625	151.4
	Border Patrol repeaters	8	162.975	163.625	151.4
	Border Patrol repeaters	9	162.875	163.675	206.6
	Immigration repeaters	10	162.950	163.750	206.6
	Anti-Smuggling direct	11		165.875	103.5
	Anti-Smuggling repeater	12	168.975	165.875	103.5
	Anti-Smuggling direct	13		168.975	103.5
	Anti-Smuggling repeater	14	168.975	165.875	100.0
	Unassigned	15			
	FBI Nationwide common	16		167.5625	167.9
	Border Intrusion Alarm			170.625	
	Border Intrusion Alarm			170.650	
	Border Intrusion Alarm			170.700	
	Border Intrusion Alarm			170.775	
Group 5	**Border Patrol**				
	Border Patrol repeaters	1	162.825	163.625	none
	Border Patrol repeaters	2	162.925	163.625	none
	Border Patrol direct	3		163.625	none
	Border Patrol direct	4		163.675	none
	Border Patrol repeaters	5	162.825	163.675	none
	Border Patrol repeaters	6	162.925	163.675	none
	Border Patrol repeaters	7	162.825	163.725	none
	Border Patrol repeaters	8	162.925	163.725	none
	Border Patrol repeaters	9	162.825	163.775	none
	Border Patrol repeaters	10	162.925	163.775	none
	Border Patrol direct	11		168.8625	none
	Border Patrol repeaters	12	165.925	168.8625	none
	Border Patrol direct	13		165.925	none
	Unassigned	14			
	Unassigned	15			
	Coast Guard & Rescue	16		157.050	none
	Border Intrusion Alarm			170.625	
	Border Intrusion Alarm			170.650	
	Border Intrusion Alarm			170.700	
	Border Intrusion Alarm			170.775	
Group 6	**Border Patrol**				
	Border Patrol repeaters	1	162.875	163.725	none
	Border Patrol repeaters	2	162.975	163.725	none
	Border Patrol direct	3		163.725	none
	Border Patrol direct	4		163.775	none
	Border Patrol repeaters	5	162.875	163.775	none
	Border Patrol repeaters	6	162.975	163.775	none
	Border Patrol repeaters	7	162.825	163.625	none
	Border Patrol repeaters	8	162.850	163.725	none
	Border Patrol repeaters	9	162.900	163.625	none
	Border Patrol repeaters	10	162.975	163.675	none
	Treasury common	11		166.4625	none
	Wide area ininerant	12		163.100	none

Table I-1. Continued

Group	Border Patrol	F	Input	Output	Tone
	Interagency common	13		168.350	none
	Law Enforcement common	14		155.370	none
	National Law Enforcement	15		155.475	none
	Law Mutual Aid	16		154.920	none
	Border Intrusion Alarm			170.625	
	Border Intrusion Alarm			170.650	
	Border Intrusion Alarm			170.700	
	Border Intrusion Alarm			170.775	
Group 7	**Immigration Service**				
	Immigration repeaters	1	162.850	163.650	none
	Immigration repeaters	2	162.950	163.650	none
	Immigration direct	3		163.650	none
	Immigration direct	4		163.750	none
	Immigration repeaters	5	162.850	163.750	none
	Immigration repeaters	6	162.950	163.750	none
	Immigration repeaters	7	162.850	163.625	none
	Customs Service direct	8		165.2375	none
	INS-BP tactical 1	9		162.900	none
	INS-BP tactical 2	10		163.700	none
	INS-BP tactical repeaters	11	162.900	163.700	none
	Undetermined	12		163.370	none
	Undetermined	13		163.050	none
	Undetermined	14	163.050	163.9625	none
	Undetermined	15		163.9625	none
	Marshal Service direct	16		163.200	none
	Border Intrusion Alarm			170.625	
	Border Intrusion Alarm			170.650	
	Border Intrusion Alarm			170.700	
	Border Intrusion Alarm			170.775	
Group 8	**Allied Agencies**				
	OCDETF	1	163.665	165.925	none
	Border Patrol repeaters	2	162.900	163.775	none
	Immigration direct	3		162.850	none
	ATF Bureau repeaters	4	166.5375	165.2875	none
	Customs Service repeaters	5	166.4375	165.2375	none
	Border Patrol repeaters	6	162.825	163.625	none
	Border Patrol repeaters	7	162.875	163.625	none
	Border Patrol repeaters	8	162.975	163.625	none
	Border Patrol repeaters	9	162.875	163.675	none
	Immigration repeaters	10	162.950	163.750	none
	Anti-Smuggling direct	11		165.875	none
	Anti-Smuggling repeater	12	168.975	165.875	none
	Anti-Smuggling direct	13		168.975	none
	Unassigned	14			
	Unassigned	15			
	Mutual Aid	16		154.920	none
	Border Intrusion Alarm			170.625	
	Border Intrusion Alarm			170.650	
	Border Intrusion Alarm			170.700	
	Border Intrusion Alarm			170.775	

IMRO [TRG] Abbreviation for Inner Macedonian Revolutionary Organization.

I'm way down [C,G&PS] The statement someone might make indicating he needs a drug or narcotic, as in "I'm way down this week."

IN Specialty code for interpreting language.

INA [TRG] Abbreviation for Irish Northern Aid, known to U.S. antiterrorism authorities as the major support and funding group of the Irish Republican Army (IRA) headquartered in the United States. Headed by Dan McCormick, this organization is heavily involved with "terrorist activities and the supplying of weapons and explosives to the IRA" according to an intelligence report prepared by the U.S. State Department.

Inagawa-Kai [LE] The first Japanese branch of the *yakuza* to operate in the United States. Headquartered in Tokyo, it is the fourth largest criminal syndicate in Japan. It conducts extensive criminal activities in the port city of Yokohama. (*See* YAKUZA.)

INCA 1. [C3I] Abbreviation for Intelligence Communications Architecture. 2. [US] Abbreviation for Integrated Nuclear Communications Assessment.

incentive [C,G&PS] Slang for cocaine.

IND 1. Specialty code for industrial accident. 2. [M] Abbreviation for Improvised Nuclear Device.

India [A,LE,MIL] Designation for the letter *I*.

Indian Black [LE] Slang for a type of especially potent marijuana, also known as Indian Black Gungeon, that originally came from Africa.

Indian hay [C,G&PS] Slang for marijuana grown in the United States from the seeds of Indian Black marijuana. (*See* INDIAN BLACK.)

INEWS [C3I] Abbreviation for Integrated Electronic Warfare System.

INF [C3I] Abbreviation for Intermediate Range Nuclear Forces.

infiltration [I] Term for placing an intelligence operative, law enforcement officer, or other person, in a target area or within a targeted group or organization to gather information.

informant [I] An individual who wittingly or unwittingly provides information to an intelligence agent, a clandestine group, or law enforcement. In reporting such information, this individual is often cited as the source. In the intelligence profession, an informant also is referred to as an access agent, who is paid for the data he/she supplies.

informer [LE] An individual who intentionally discloses personal facts or information about groups or activities to law enforcement officers.

INLA [TRG] Abbreviation for Irish National Liberation Army, a group of very radical individuals who are much more militant than members of the Irish Republican Army (IRA). The INLA has been responsible for more killings and bombings in Ireland than any other organization.

in place [I] A term used in law enforcement and the covert operations of intelligence agents indicating an operative (undercover operator) is in place and working on a specific assignment.

INO/INU [USSR] Abbreviation for *Inostrannyy Otdel/Inostrannoye Upravleniye*, the Foreign Department/Foreign Directorate of the Cheka, GPU, and OGPU.

INR [US] Designation for Bureau of Intelligence and Research, the intelligence service of the United States Department of State.

INS 1. Background code for insurance adjuster, claims examiner, or insurance investigator. 2. Specialty code for insurance investigation. 3. [A] Designation for Inertial Navigation System.

INSCOM [I] Designation for The United States Army's Intelligence and Security Command. INSCOM is responsible for all U.S. Army intelligence units, data gathering, and covert operations.

instant zen [C,G&PS] Slang for LSD. (*See* QUICK REFERENCE.)

in shape [C,G&PS] Slang for in possession of narcotics.

INT Background code for military investigator, that is, Criminal Investigation Division, (CID) CIC, OSI, and so on.

INTACS [US] Acronym for Integrated Tactical Communications Study.

Interception [I] Generally, the collection of electromagnetic signals such as radio communications without the knowledge of the communicants.

International Morse Code TABLE I-2 lists the Morse Code.

Interpol Acronym for INTERnational criminal POLice organization headquartered in Paris. The member countries of INTERPOL/ICPO are: Algeria, Argentina, Australia, Austria, Bahamas, Bahrain, Bangladesh, Belgium, Benin, Bolivia, Brazil, Burma, Burundi, Cameroon, Canada, Central Africa Republic, Chad, Chile, Republic of China, Colombia, Congo, Costa Rica, Cuba, Cyprus, Denmark, Dominican Republic, Ecuador, Egypt, El Salvador, Ethiopia, Fiji, Finland, France, Gabon, Germany (Federal Republic), Ghana, Greece, Guatemala, Guinea, Guyana, Haiti, Honduras, Iceland, India, Indonesia, Iran, Iraq, Ireland, Israel, Italy, Ivory Coast, Jamaica, Japan, Jordan, Kenya, Khmer Republic, Korea (Republic), Kuwait, Laos, Lebanon, Lesotho, Liberia, Libya, Liechtenstein, Luxembourg, Madagascar, Malawi, Malaysia, Mali, Malta, Mauritania, Mauritius, Mexico, Monaco, Morocco, Nauru, Nepal, Netherlands, Netherlands Antilles, New Zealand, Nicaragua, Niger, Norway, Oman, Pakistan, Panama, Papua New Guinea, Paraguay, Peru, Philippines, Portugal, Qatar, Romania, Rwanda, Saudi Arabia, Senegal, Sierra Leone, Singapore, Somalia, Spain, Sri Lanka, Sudan, Surinam, Swaziland, Sweden, Switzerland, Syria, Tanzania, Thailand, Togo, Trinidad and Tobago, Tunisia, Uganda, United Arab Emirates, United States of America, United Kingdom, Upper Volta, Uruguay, Venezuela, Yemen (Arab Republic), Yugoslavia, Zaire, and Zambia. INTERPOL has no worldwide investigators or special agents. It serves as a clearing house for information on international criminal activities and specific individuals suspected of crimes and terrorism. The INTERPOL network of tracking tourists and international travelers is a quick means of sharing information and contacting counterparts in other law enforcement agencies, as well as keeping track of criminals on the move. (*See* IPA.) Interpol Frequencies: 2593, 2840, 3593, 3705, 3714, 4444, 4632.5, 4837.5, 4855.5, 5104, 5208, 5300, 5305.5, 5895, 6700, 6792, 6900, 6905, 7401, 7532, 7832, 7906, 8038, 8045, 8080, 9105, 9200, 9250, 9285, 9821, 10200, 10295, 10390, 11538, 13500,

Table I-2. International Morse Code

Letters

A	.-	N	-.
B	-...	O	---
C	-.-.	P	.--.
D	-..	Q	--.-
E	.	R	.-.
F	..-.	S	...
G	--.	T	-
H	....	U	..-
I	..	V	...-
J	.---	W	.--
K	-.-	X	-..-
L	.-..	Y	-.--
M	--	Z	--..

Digits

0	-----	5	.....
1	.----	6	-....
2	..---	7	--...
3	...--	8	---..
4	....-	9	----.

Special Characters

period	.-.-.-
comma	--..--
question mark	..--..
dash	-....-
slash	-..-.

Operating Characters

error	....
wait	.-...
end of message	.-.-.
go ahead	-.-
end of session	...-.-

13520, 13747, 13820, 14607.5, 14707, 14,808.5, 14817.5, 14827, 15502.5, 15555.5, 15592, 15864, 15738, 18190, 18380, 18505.5, 19130, 19360, 19405, 19560.5, 21785, 21807.5, 24072, 24110, 24210.5, 27360.5, 27505.5, 27845.

interrogation   [LE] The systematic effort to gather information and certain facts by the process of direct questioning of an individual. The process is used by law enforcement, intelligence agencies, and the military in a similar manner.

in the bag   [LE] Slang for a law enforcement officer in uniform.

in the clear   [C] Term meaning being able to transmit or receive radio transmissions without scrambling.

in the dark   [US] Naval aviation voice brevity code meaning not visible on my radar.

in the pocket   [LE] Slang for an individual's whereabouts known by enforcement officer.

into   [C,G&PS] Slang for an individual involved in some activity, i.e., "She's into narcotics."

Intruder   [M] *See* A-6.

IO   **1.** [I] Abbreviation for Intelligence Officer, a professional employee of an intelligence-gathering organization. **2.** [I] Abbreviation for Illegal Operation. In intelligence-gathering operations, such activities are conducted by a senior intelligence agent who takes his orders from a superior somewhere else in the world.

IOB   [I] Abbreviation for Intelligence Oversight Board.

IOC   [A] Abbreviation for Initial Operational Capability i.e., aircraft flight testing assessment.

IONDS   [C3I] Abbreviation for Integrated Operational Nuclear Detonation and Detection System.

ionosphere   [NASA] The reflecting layer of ionized particles that surround the earth.

IP   [M] Abbreviation for Initial Point, a navigational reference point used in a ground attack.

IPA   [LE] Abbreviation for the International Police Association (not to be confused with the International Criminal Police Organization (INTERPOL). It is a banding together of law enforcement agencies for the express purpose of exchanging information, methods, techniques, and specific approaches to certain criminal/civil problems. In each of the following countries, factions of the IPA exist: Antigua, Argentina, Australia, Austria, Barbados, Belgium, Bermuda, Brazil, Canada, Denmark, Eire, Finland, France, Germany, Ghana, Gibralter, Greece, Guyana, Holland, Hong Kong, Iceland, Israel, Italy, Jamaica, Japan, Kenya, Luxembourg, Malta, Mauritius, Netherlands Antilles, New Zealand, Nigeria, Norway, Philippines, Rhodesia, St. Lucia, San Marino, Seychelles, Spain, Sri Lanka, Surinam, Sweden, Switzerland, Turkey, Uganda, United Kingdom, United States of America, and Zambia. (*See* INTERPOL.)

IPF   [C3I] Abbreviation for Initial Production Facility.

IPS   [C3I] Abbreviation for Information Processing System.

IR   **1.** [I] Designation of Illegal Residency, an intelligence apparatus established in a foreign country and composed of one or more intelligence officers, and which has no apparent connection with the sponsoring intelligence organization or with the government of the country operating the intelligence organization. **2.** [EW] Abbreviation for Infrared. **3.** [I] Abbreviation for Intelligence Report.

IRA   [TRG] Abbreviation for Irish Republican Army. There are a number of factions with the IRA organization. The original purpose of the Irish nationalist group was to unite Ireland. That purpose quickly became religion against religion—the Protestants fighting the Catholics. One splinter group of the IRA is the PIRA, the Provisional Irish Republican Army, which is a Marxist faction of the IRA and has carried out many terrorist operations in England and Northern Ireland. The IRA is also known as the Irish Revolutionary Army.

IRMB   [C3I] Abbreviation for Intermediate-Range Ballistic Missile.

IRC   [D] Abbreviation for International Reply

Coupon, a coupon available at any United States Post Office for sending return postage internationally.

IRCM [EW] Abbreviation for Infrared Countermeasure.

IR&D [C3I] Abbreviation for Independent Research & Development.

IRG [TRG] Abbreviation for Iranian Revolutionary Guards, also known as Pasdaran.

irgun [TRG] Name of a terrorist group headquartered in Palestine also known as *Irgun Zvai Leumi*.

IRLS [EW] Abbreviation for Infra-Red Linescan.

IRR [US] Abbreviation for Integrated Radio (communications) Room.

IS 1. Specialty code for Industrial Survey. 2. [I] Abbreviation for Internal Security. 3. [I] Abbreviation for Interval Signal, which is used in the staging process of a raid.

ISA 1. [I] Abbreviation for Intelligence Support Activity, the U.S. Army's supersecret intelligence unit of the Joint Special Operations Command. Members are trained as counterterrorism commandos and undercover agents for special field operations. 2. [NASA] Abbreviation for International Standard Atmosphere.

ISC [I] Abbreviation for the U.S. Army's Intelligence and Security Command. This group conducts background checks on individual military personnel and issues security clearances.

ISDN [C3I] Abbreviation for Integrated Services Digital Network.

Islamic Holy War in Hejaz [TRG] A Lebanese underground terrorist organization headquartered in West Beirut that has mounted a growing campaign of terror against Saudi diplomats abroad.

Islamic Jihad [TRG] A terrorist group descended from a half-dozen medieval cults of assassins. Members of this group have been responsible for the death of hundreds in their part of the world, the most infamous being the bombing of the Marine compound and United States embassy in Beirut. The Islamic Jihad is most likely the greatest terrorist threat to American facilities located in Europe.

ISO 1. [I] Abbreviation for Illegal Support Officer, an intelligence officer assigned to an agency whose primary function is to support illegals (*See* ILLEGAL) by supplying them with items required to carry on their daily activities. Another responsibility of the ISO is to gather data that will serve as feed material. (*See* FEED MATERIAL.) 2. [C3I] Abbreviation for International Standards Organization.

ITU [C3I] Abbreviation for International Telecommunication Union.

IUS [NASA] Abbreviation for Inertial Upper Stage.

IV Specialty code for Investigation.

IVCS [US] Abbreviation for Integrated Vehicle Communications System.

IVS [C3I] Abbreviation for Interactive Video Service.

IVSN [NATO] Abbreviation for Initial Voice Switched Network.

Ivy Bells [US] Code name for the electronic induction devices installed near undersea cables to intercept communications transmitted on those circuits.

IZL [TRG] Abbreviation for *Ingun Zvai Leumi*, a terrorist group active in Palestine. IZL is also known as *Ingun*.

J

J 1. [C,G&PS] Slang for a marijuana cigarette. 2. [EW] Abbreviation for Jamming. 3. [NASA] Abbreviation for Joule (SI Unit).

J-2 [US] Designation for assistant chief of staff for military intelligence.

jab [C,G&PS] Slang for the intravenous injection of heroin.

jack up [C,G&PS] Slang for the injection of a narcotic into the vein.

jacking off [C,G&PS] Slang term for slowly depressing the plunger of a hypodermic needle to prolong the effect of an injection.

JACWA [NATO] Abbreviation for Joint Allied Command Western Approaches.

JAEIC [NASA] Abbreviation for Joint Atomic Energy Intelligence Committee.

JAG [US] Abbreviation for Judge Advocate General.

jaguar-V [UK] Code name for jamming guarded radio, very high frequency hopping radio system.

jail bait [C,G&PS] Slang term for an underaged juvenile, usually female.

jail plant [C,G&PS] Slang for narcotics, usually concealed on a free person, smuggled into a jail or prison complex for transfer to an inmate. Prison and jail systems tend to be lax concerning what contraband civilian staff and guards can bring into an institution.

jam [C,G&PS] The process of a law enforcement officer patting down an individual for weapons or dope.

JAMAC [US] Abbreviation for Joint Aeronautical Materials Activity.

Jamaica black [C,G&PS] Slang term for marijuana. (*See* QUICK REFERENCE.)

JAN [NASA] Abbreviation for Joint Army-Navy.

JANAP 1. [US] Abbreviation for Joint Army-Navy-Air Force Publication. 2. [NATO] Abbreviation for Joint Army-Navy-Air Force Procedure.

JAN GRID [NATO] Acronym for Joint Army-Navy Grid System.

JAN STD [NATO] Abbreviation for Joint Army-Navy Standard.

JAPC [NATO] Abbreviation for Joint Air Photo Center.

JARC [NATO] Abbreviation for Joint Air Reconnaissance Center.

JAS [NASA] Abbreviation for Journal of Aerospace Science.

JASDF [M] Abbreviation for Japan Air Self-Defense Force.

JATCCCS [US] Abbreviation for Joint Advanced Tactical C3 System.

JATO [A] Abbreviation for Jet-Assisted Take-Off.

JB [NASA] Abbreviation for Junction Box.

JCAG [TRG] Abbreviation for Justice Commandos of Armenian Genocide. This terrorist group has conducted kidnappings and killings worldwide, mostly directed toward members of the Turkish diplomatic corps. The JCAG has active members in the United States.

JCL [NASA] Abbreviation for Job Control Language.

JCMP [US] Abbreviation for Joint Cruise Missile Project.

J-CODE [NATO] Acronym for Justification Code.

JCP [NASA] Abbreviation for Joint Power Conditions.

JCS [C3I] Abbreviation for Joint Chiefs of Staff.

JCT [NASA] Abbreviation for Junction (connection).

JDL 1. [TRG] Abbreviation for Jewish Defense League. The JDL is active on the east coast of the United States. It is a very militant group, and carry out attacks on individuals and organizations it perceives as an enemy. It is most active in and around the New York City area. **2.** [US] Abbreviation for Joint Directors of Laboratories.

JDS [NATO] Abbreviation for Joint Defense Staff.

JED [NASA] Abbreviation for Julian Ephemeris Data.

jee gee [C,G&PS] Slang for heroin. (*See* QUICK REFERENCE.)

jefe [C,G&PS] Slang for a boss, the top man, or chief in a Mexican drug or narcotic operation.

jelly babies [C,G&PS] Abbreviation for amphetamines. (*See* QUICK REFERENCE.)

jet fuel [C,G&PS] Abbreviation for PCP. (*See* QUICK REFERENCE.)

JETS [NASA] Abbreviation for Joint Electronic Type (Designation) System.

JETT [NASA] Acronym for Jettison.

JFK Center [M] Designation for the United States Army Center for Military Assistance. It was formerly known as the Special Warfare Center (SWC).

JG [US] Abbreviation for Junior Grade (military officer).

Jim [C,G&PS] Slang for stolen jewelry, usually stones.

Jim Jones [C,G&PS] Slang for a marijuana cigarette laced with cocaine and dipped in PCP.

JINTACCS [C3I] Designation for Joint Interoperability of Tactical Command and Control Systems.

JIR [NASA] Abbreviation for Job Improvement Request.

JIS [NASA] Abbreviation for Joint Integrated Simulation.

jive [C,G&PS] Slang for marijuana. (*See* QUICK REFERENCE.)

jive sticks [C,G&PS] Slang term for marijuana cigarettes.

JJ [D] Designation for Japanese.

JLC [US] Abbreviation for Joint Logistics Commanders.

JLCAT [US] Abbreviation for Joint Logistics Commander's Action Team.

J/M [NASA] Abbreviation for Jettison Motor.

JMSDF [M] Abbreviation for Japan Maritime Self-Defense Force.

JMSNS [US] Abbreviation for Justification of Major Systems New Start.

JO **1.** [US] Abbreviation for Journalist (civil/military). **2.** [NASA] Abbreviation for Job Order.

JOC [NASA] Abbreviation for Joint Operations Center.

JOD **1.** [NASA] Abbreviation for Joint Occupancy Data. **2.** [NASA] Abbreviation for Joint Occupancy Date.

joe [C,G&PS] A white member of a black gang. (*See* CRIPS and BLOODS.)

John [A,LE,MIL] Designation for the letter *J*.

john [C,G&PS] Slang for the client of a prostitute.

Johnson [C,G&PS] Slang for a stolen vehicle.

Johnson grass [C,G&PS] Term used by Mexican marijuana smugglers to indicate a low quality of weed (marijuana). The term indicates it is so bad it tastes like hay grown in Johnson County, Texas.

joint **1.** [C,G&PS] Slang for a prison or jail facility. **2.** [C,G&PS] Slang for a marijuana cigarette.

JOIP [NASA] Abbreviation for Joint Operations Interface Procedure.

JOP **1.** [NASA] Abbreviation for Joint Operating Procedure. **2.** [NASA] Abbreviation for the Jupiter (mission) Orbiter Probe—Galileo.

jojee [C,G&PS] Slang for heroin. (*See* QUICK REFERENCE.)

jolly beans [C,G&PS] Slang for pep pills—uppers.

jolt [C,G&PS] Slang for an intravenous injection of heroin.

Jones **1.** [C,G&PS] Slang for an individual with a heroin habit. **2.** [C,G&PS] Slang for heroin. (*See* QUICK REFERENCE.)

JOPES [C3I] Abbreviation for Joint Operation Planning & Execution System.

JOPS [C3I] Abbreviation for Joint Operational Planning System.

JOTS [C3I] Abbreviation for Joint Operational Tactical System.

JOU Background code for investigative journalist.

JOVIAL [NASA] Abbreviation for Joules Own Version International Algebraic Language.

joy pop [C,G&PS] Slang for the occasional injection or use of heroin or to inject heroin on the job to get a level of euphoria to reduce work stress.

joy powder [C,G&PS] Slang for heroin. (*See* QUICK REFERENCE.)

JP-4 [US] Designation for jet fuel, used mostly for USAF aircraft.

JP-5 [US] Designation for jet fuel (Navy aircraft).

JP **1.** [NASA] Abbreviation for Jet Propellant. **2.** [NASA] Abbreviation for Jet Propulsion.

JPC [NASA] Abbreviation for Joint Power Condition.

JPL [C3I] Abbreviation for Jet Propulsion Laboratory, located in southern California.

JPP [NASA] Abbreviation for Joint Program Plan.

JPWC [M] Abbreviation for Joint Psychological Warfare Committee.

JRA [TRG] Abbreviation for Japanese Red Army. Members of the JRA are also known as Sekigun. The JRA is closely associated with the Popular Front for the Liberation of Palestine (PFLP). The JRA has been responsible for hijackings, killings, embassy seizures, and bombings.

JRC **1.** [TRG] Abbreviation for Junta for Revolutionary Coordination. This group is an off-shoot of the Tupamaros, also known as the Movimiento de Liberation National (MLN), which is no longer active. They sometimes surface as a multinational group with limited membership activity in Uruguay. **2.** [I] Abbreviation for Joint Reconnaissance Center.

JRDOD [US] Abbreviation for Research & Development Objective Document.

J/S [EW] Abbreviation for Jamming to Signal Ratio.

JSC [NASA] Abbreviation for Johnson Space Center.

JSCP [US] Abbreviation for Joint Strategic Capability Plan.

JSDF [M] Abbreviation for Japanese Self-Defense Force.

JSLWG [NASA] Abbreviation for Joint Spacelab Working Group.

JSOC [M] Abbreviation for Joint Special Operations Command. JSOC is in charge of every military counterterrorist force in the world connected with the United States government. Headquartered in a classified area of Fort Bragg in Fayetteville, N.C., the JSOC directs the activities of five primary military counterterrorist units, including the Army's Intelligence Support Activity, the Air Force's Special Operations Wing, and the Army Task Force 160. (Task Force 160 is the transportation arm of these units. Based at Fort Campbell in Kentucky, it is made up of more than 900 specialists flying helicopter gunships and fixed-wing aircraft.) These three units have the sole purpose of supporting the two government groups created to carry out counterterrorist and hostage-rescue missions. One of these units is SEAL (Sea-Air-Land) Team Six, a 175-frogman Navy unit headquartered at the Little Creek Naval Amphibious Base outside of Norfolk, VA. Hand-to-hand combat, scuba diving using special 'closed-circuit' breathing apparatus, underwater demolition, wilderness survival in hostile areas, and clandestine infiltrations are the specialties of SEAL Team Six. Delta Force is the other U.S. commando unit supported by of the JSOC. Delta Force also is headquartered in a classified (off-limits) zone at Fort Bragg.

JSOP [US] Abbreviation for Joint Strategic Objectives Plan.

JSPS [US] Abbreviation for Joint Strategic Planning System.

JSS [US] Abbreviation for Joint Surveillance System.

JST [NASA] Abbreviation for Joint Systems Test.

JSTARS [C3I] Abbreviation for Joint Surveillance Targeting Acquisition Radar System.

J-STARS [US] Abbreviation for Joint Surveillance, Tracking, and Attack Radar System. J-STARS is a joint program between the Air Force and the Army to develop airborne radar systems that can find, track, classify, and identify ground targets. What the Airborne Warning/Control System (AWACS) airborne radar did for air battles, J-STARS will do for the ground.

JT-7 [I] Designation for fuel unique to the SR-71. (*See* SR-71.)

JTA [NASA] Abbreviation for Job Task Analysis.

JTACMS [M] Abbreviation for Joint Tactical Missile System.

JTC3A [C3I] Abbreviation for Joint Tactical Command, Control, and Communications Agency.

JTCG [US] Abbreviation for Joint Technical Coordinating Group.

JTDE [US] Abbreviation for Joint Technology Demonstrator Engine.

JT&E [US] Abbreviation for Joint Test & Evaluation.

JTF [M] Abbreviation for Joint Task Force, a group of military specialists that plan operations in certain crisis situations worldwide that concern U.S. policy and/or affairs of state. They determine the best game plan and mission leaders.

JTFP [GOV] Abbreviation for Joint Tactical Fusion Program.

JTFS [C3I] Abbreviation for Joint Tactical Fusion System.

JTG [NASA] Abbreviation for Joint Training Group.

JTIDS [C3I] Abbreviation for Joint Tactical Information Distribution System.

Judy [US] Air intercept voice brevity code meaning "I have contact and am taking over intercept."

jugged [C,G&PS] Slang term meaning to be arrested and jailed.

juggle [C,G&PS] Slang term meaning to stay just one step ahead of law enforcement officials.

juggler [C,G&PS] Slang term for an addict who also sells narcotics.

juice [C,G&PS] In the drug/narcotic trade, slang for power, connections, or money.

Juliet [A,LE,MIL] Designation for the letter *J*.

jump 1. [US] Abbreviation for Joint Uhf Modernization Project. 2. [US] Naval aviation voice brevity code meaning to disengage combat.

jumped in [C,G&PS] Referring to a ritual beating that is used to initiate a new member into a street gang.

jumpseat [US] Code name for an elliptically orbiting signal intelligence (SIGINT) satellite that conducts surveillance missions over the Soviet Union.

jungle [LE] Slang for a gang-infested turf, often in and around a housing project.

junk [C,G&PS] Slang for narcotics. (*See* QUICK REFERENCE.)

junker [C,G&PS] Slang for a narcotic/drug addict.

junkie [C,G&PS] Slang for a drug addict.

JURG [NASA] Abbreviation for Joint Users (computer) Requirements Group.

JVX [US] Designation for Joint Service Advanced Vertical Lift Aircraft Development Program (Experimental).

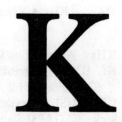

K [C] Abbreviation for Kilocycle.

KA-60 [M] (*See* A-6.)

K agent [CW] Designation for Soviet incapacitating agent (nerve gas).

kai [LE] Japanese for "society," or "association." Often used as part of a gang (criminal element) name.

Karen [US] Code name for Drug Enforcement Administration (DEA) identification operation.

Kathryn [US] Code name for digital data communications system.

Kawa group [TRG] A Kurdish nationalist terrorist group that receives training from the Turkish People's Liberation Army (TPLA). It is primarily an anti-Turkish, antigovernment group.

KBA [US] Abbreviation for Killed By Air.

K-band [NASA] Designation for 10,900 to 36,000 MCS.

KC [C] Abbreviation for Kilocycle.

kcal [NASA] Abbreviation for Kilocalorie.

KCAS [NASA] Abbreviation for Knots Calibrated Airspeed.

KC/S [C] Abbreviation for Kilocycles per second.

KE [NASA] Abbreviation for Kinetic Energy.

kee [C,G&PS] Designation for a kilogram, or 2.2 pounds of a narcotic. This term is most likely used in relationship to a quantity of heroin.

keef [C,G&PS] Slang for hashish. (*See* QUICK REFERENCE.)

Keesee [US] Slang for secure communications equipment.

keister plant [C,G&PS] Slang for narcotics that are hidden in the rectum, often used by international travelers.

keister stash [C,G&PS] (*See* KIESTER PLANT.)

kennan [I] Code name for the KH-11 surveillance satellite system. (*See* KH-11.)

kennel [LE] Slang for the headquarters of a police officer.

Kentucky blue [C,G&PS] Slang for marijuana grown in the "blue grass" state.

key [C,G&PS] Slang for one kilogram of any drug. A kilogram is also 2.2 pounds. A "key" of any drug is usually compressed into brick form for ease of transport and storage.

keyhole [I] Code name for the KH-12 surveillance satellite system. The KH-13 is being readied for flight and will carry a unique instrument package. (*See* KH-12.)

KEW [M] Abbreviation for Kinetic Energy Weapon.

kg [D] Abbreviation for kilogram.

KGB [USSR] Abbreviation for *Komitet Gosudarstvennoy Bezopasnosti*, Soviet Committee for State Security. The KGB is responsible for military and strategic intelligence, domestic and foreign counterintelligence, and electronic intercepts. The KGB has a long-established network of agents worldwide who conduct an aggressive intelligence collecting and special operations program.

KH Code name for Keyhole. (*See* KEYHOLE.)

KH-12 The KH-12 is a photo-reconnaissance surveillance satellite, code named "keyhole." The KH-12 was designed to help military and arms-control experts keep tabs on Soviet missile activities. Cameras ejected from the KH-12 dropped into the Pacific ocean areas and were snagged at low altitude by aircraft.

KH-13 Designation for an unmanned (US) space station, capable of radar imaging, sensor detection, and photography. Delayed from an earlier launch by the Space Shuttle Discovery accident, KH-13 will offer a much greater intelligence-gathering capability than any other satellite flown to date. Because of its secret military applications, it probably will be launched before the end of the century with little fanfare.

KHz   Abbreviation for Kilohertz, 1000 Hz.

KI   [USSR] Abbreviation for Komitet Informatsii (Committee of Information).

KIA   [US] Abbreviation for Killed In Action.

kick   [C,G&PS] Slang term for the euphoria experienced from drugs.

kick a habit   [C,G&PS] Slang term meaning to withdraw from the use of drugs.

kief   [C,G&PS] Slang for hashish. (*See* QUICK REFERENCE.)

kif   [C,G&PS] Slang for marijuana. (*See* QUICK REFERENCE.)

killing house   [HRU] Slang for an area of special rooms that are designed as a training center for close quarters battle situations. Hostage rescue units use these areas, which can simulate the interior of a building, ship, or aircraft so assault tactics can be practiced in as realistic an environment as it is possible to create. (*See* CQB.)

kilo   1. [C,G&PS] Abbreviation for a kilogram (kilo) is 2.2 pounds of a narcotic. 2. [US] Naval aviation voice brevity code meaning to change (radio) frequency. 3. [A,LE,MIL] Designation for the letter *K*.

King   [A,LE,MIL] Designation for the letter *K*.

kiss-off   1. [C,G&PS] Slang term meaning to kill someone. 2. [C,G&PS] Slang term meaning to betray an individual or for one criminal element to expose the activities of another individual or group to the police. 3. [C,G&PS] Slang for the last dose of medication given to a drug addict.

kit   [C,G&PS] The hardware used for the injection of drugs by an addict.

kite   [US] In naval mine warfare, a device which when towed, submerges and planes under the water at a predetermined depth without any sideways displacement. Underwater mines are snagged by the kite cable and explode.

KKE   Designation for The Greek Communist Party.

KKK   1. [D] Abbreviation for *Khymer Kampuchea Krom* (Cambodian). 2. Abbreviation for Ku Klux Klan, a white supremacy radical group founded and currently active in the United States. Intelligence estimates indicate that membership is small. The organization usually has a "kleagle" who heads a statewide group made up of "klaverns" representing local memberships.

KKKK   Abbreviation for Knights of the Ku Klux Klan, active members of the KKK.

km   [D] Abbreviation for kilometer.

KMODC   [C3I] Abbreviation for Key Material Ordering/Distribution Center.

KMR   [US] Abbreviation for Kwajalein Missile Range.

KMS   [C3I] Abbreviation for Key Management System.

KN   [D] Abbreviation for Kenya Navy.

knife rests   [US] Department of Defense code name for the long-wave Soviet early-warning radar designed to reduce the penetration of stealth aircraft across Soviet borders. (*See* BISTATIC RADAR.)

KNO   [NASA] Abbreviation for Kano, Nigeria, a remote NASA tracking site.

knocked in   [C,G&PS] Slang term referring to someone arrested for possession of narcotics.

knocked up   [C,G&PS] Slang term indicating an individual has a sure thing, such "He has that deal knocked up."

Kokuryu-Kai   [LE] Designation for the secret Amur River Society of Japan. The *Kokuryu-Kai* is also known as the Black Dragon Society. There are members of this ultranationalist group active in the United States. The *Kokuryu-Kai* is made up, in part, of some of the original descendants of the Dark Ocean Society. (*See* GENYOSHA.)

komissar   [LE] The computer system of the West German government that tracks the movement of individuals suspected of terrorism.

Kommando Jihid   [TRG] The Islamic terrorist group responsible for the hijacking of an Indonesian airliner flying to Thailand in 1981. The Kommando jihid leaders are Soviet trained.

Krasnaya Zvezda   [USSR] The Soviet Military journal, *Red Star*, the official unclassified publication of the Soviet Ministry of Defense. Universities in the United States with Russian Studies classes should have this publication in their library. *Krasnaya Zvezda* carries occasional articles on communications and electronic warfare.

KRU [USSR] Abbreviation for *Kontrrazvedyvatel-'noye Upravleniye*, the Counterintelligence Directorate.

KSC [NASA] Designation for John F. Kennedy Space Center.

KSCAP [NASA] Abbreviation for Kennedy Space Center Area Permit.

KU-band [NASA] Designation for 15.250 to 17.250 GHz.

KUSP [M] Abbreviation for Ku-Band Signal Processor.

kV Abbreviation for kilovolt.

KVA [C3I] Abbreviation for Kilovolt-Ampere.

kW Abbreviation for kilowatt, equal to $1^{3}/_{4}$ hp or to 1000 watts.

kWh Abbreviation for kilowatt hours.

KYBD [NASA] Abbreviation for keyboard.

L

L **1.** [NASA] Abbreviation for Launch. **2.** [CW] Designation for the blister agent Lewisite. This chemical warfare agent initially irritates the nasal passages. It then burns and causes blisters on the skin and in the membrane areas of the body, such as the lungs. Lewisite also is a deadly poison, and because it acts so slowly as related to other chemical warfare agents, death is slow and very painful.

LA [NASA] Abbreviation for Launch Abort.

LAAAS [US] Abbreviation for Low-Altitude Airfield Attack System.

la turnabouts [C,G&PS] Slang term for amphetamines. (*See* QUICK REFERENCE.)

lab **1.** [C,G&PS] A facility where heroin or morphine is converted. **2.** [US] Abbreviation for Low-Altitude bombing.

lacrosse [US] A surveillance satellite deployed by the space shuttle that uses radar to see through clouds. Lacrosse could be crucial for guiding stealth aircraft toward targets. Lacrosse also maintains round-the-clock surveillance on the current Soviet missile activities.

LAD [US] Abbreviation for Low-Altitude Dispenser.

LAGEOS [M] Acronym for Laser Geodynamic Satellite.

LAGS [NASA] Abbreviation for Launch Abort Guide Simulation.

LAH [US] Abbreviation for Light Attack Helicopter.

LAHS [M] Abbreviation for Low Altitude, High Speed, a parachuting technique developed by antiterrorist military groups in which the jumper is rapidly extracted from the aircraft at low altitude.

LAIR [NASA] Abbreviation for Liquid AIR.

LAMARS [US] Abbreviation for Large Amplitude Multimode Aerospace Research Simulator.

LAMPS [C3I] Abbreviation for Light Airborne MultiPurpose Systems.

LAN [C3I] Abbreviation for Local Area Network.

land [C,G&PS] Slang for the experience of coming off drugs.

LAN/PDL [C3I] Abbreviation for Local Area Network/Program Design Language.

LANTIRNS [C3I] Abbreviation for Low-Altitude Navigation/Targeting Infrared for Night System (usage).

lap [US] In naval mine warfare, that strip or section of an area assigned to a single mine sweeper, mine-sweeping helo or a formation of sweepers for a run through the area that might hold underwater mines.

lap track [US] In underwater naval mine warfare, the centerline of a lap. (*See* LAP.)

larceny [LE] A law enforcement term meaning the unlawful taking of property.

LARF [TRG] Abbreviation for Lebanese Armed Revolutionary Faction. One of many factions of the Lebanese terror organization. The LARF has been responsible for the death of more than 20 American citizens traveling in Europe.

LARS [C3I] Abbreviation for Learning and Recognition System.

LASA [US] Abbreviation for Laser Anti-Satellite Weapon.

LASER [C3I] Acronym for Light Amplification by Simulated Emission of Radiation.

LASERCOM [US] Acronym for Laser Communications (systems).

LASINT [I] Acronym for Laser Intelligence, the data that is collected about foreign laser technology and capabilities. The United States has a highly classified LASINT satellite currently in orbit.

LASS [M] Abbreviation for Local Area Sensor System.

LASV [A] Abbreviation for Low Altitude Supersonic Vehicle.

LATA [C3I] Abbreviation for Local Access and Transport Areas.

launch schedule for the U.S. space program Although other launches will occur in the window of this schedule, missions listed in TABLE L-1 are related in some way to military applications of the space program or surveillance technology.

LAV [C3I] Abbreviation for Light Armored Vehicle.

LAV-AF [M] Abbreviation for Light Armored Vehicle, Air Force.

LAW [M] Abbreviation for Light Antitank Weapon.

law enforcement agencies *See* APPENDIX A.

LAWS [M] Abbreviation for Light Antitank Weapon System.

lay down [C,G&PS] Slang for a location where opium is smoked.

lay on the hop [C,G&PS] Slang term meaning to smoke some opium.

layout [C,G&PS] Slang for the hardware used for the injection of drugs.

L-band [NASA] Designation for 390 to 1550 MHz.

L&C [NASA] Abbreviation for Laboratory and Checkout.

LC [NASA] Abbreviation for Launch Complex.

LCC **1.** [C3I] Abbreviation for Life Cycle Costs. **2.** [NASA] Abbreviation for Launch Control Center.

LCD **1.** Abbreviation for Liquid Crystal Display, a viewing screen usually seen on laptop computers. It is a low-powered display common on scanners and other radio receivers. **2.** [NASA] Abbreviation for Launch Countdown.

LCS [C3I] Abbreviation for Launch Control System.

LCT [C3I] Abbreviation for Low Cost Terminal.

L&D [NASA] Abbreviation for Landing and Deceleration.

LDEC [NASA] Abbreviation for Lunar Docking Events Controller.

LDEF [NASA] Abbreviation for Long Duration Exposure Facility where satellites are launched by the space shuttle to test various applications or systems that are recovered on a later flight. (*See* TDRS.)

LDP [D] Abbreviation for The Liberal-Democratic Party of Japan. Members of the LDP have dominated the politics of Japan since the mid-1950s.

leaf [C,G&PS] Slang for cocaine. (*See* QUICK REFERENCE.)

leaping [C,G&PS] Slang term for the description of an individual who is under the influence of a drug or narcotic.

LED [C] Abbreviation for Light-Emitting Diode, a light display common to scanners and communications receivers.

leg, a [I] Slang for an intelligence agent or law enforcement officer conducting surveillance on foot.

legal [I] Slang for an intelligence/espionage agent who enters a country using an official position as a cover.

legend [I] A plausible account of an individual's background. It might incorporate real facts, such as a city lived in, but a false identity. The purpose of an invented name and biography is to hide the actual identity of an intelligence agent.

LEHI [TRG] Abbreviation for *Lohame Herut Israel*, a terrorist organization also known as the Stern Gang, headquartered in Palestine.

LEHMIC [C3I] Abbreviation for Lumped Element Hybrid Microwave Integrated Circuit.

lemonade [C,G&PS] Slang for a very poor grade of heroin.

LEN [C3I] Abbreviation for Large Extension Node.

LEO [C3I] Abbreviation for Low Earth Orbit.

LES [NASA] Abbreviation for Launch Escape Subsystem.

LET [A] Abbreviation for Leading Edge Tracking.

lethal pellet A pellet the size of a pin-head that can be fired from a compressed gas operated

Table L-1. Launch Schedule for the U.S. Space Program

Year	Month		Mission
1990	Oct.	(*)	*Mission*: Ulysses *Purpose*: To study the environment of the Sun
1991	Jan.	(#)	*Mission*: Tethered Satellite System *Purpose*: The study of gas clouds and electrical fields in outer space
1991	Feb.	(#)	*Mission*: International Microgravity Laboratory *Purpose*: To establish the system for long-term life-in-space science studies
1991	May	(#)	*Mission*: Atmospheric Laboratory for Applications and Science Studies *Purpose*: Study variations in the solar spectrum and the Earth's atmosphere
1991	July	(#)	*Mission*: Spacelab *Purpose*: Low-gravity experiments
1991	Aug.	(+)	*Mission*: Extreme Ultraviolet Explorer *Purpose*: Catalog the ultraviolet spectrum of the stars and galaxies
1991	Oct.	(*)	*Mission*: Upper Atmosphere Research Satellite *Purpose*: The study of physical processes in the upper atmosphere
1991	Nov.	(#)	*Mission*: Doppler Imaging Interferometer *Purpose*: Study upper-atmosphere winds through the use of radar
1991	Nov.	(+)	*Mission*: Small Explorer-1 *Purpose*: The first of a series to study space physics and atmospheric science
1992	May	(#)	*Mission*: Space Radar Laboratory *Purpose*: Acquire radar images of the Earth's surface
1992	June	(+)	*Mission*: TOPEX/Poseidon *Purpose*: An extended study of the relationship of ocean systems to the climate of the Earth
1992	Sept.	(+)	*Mission*: Mars Observer *Purpose*: The study of the climate and surface of Mars
1992	Sept.	(#)	*Mission*: Space Shuttle High-energy Astrophysics Laboratory *Purpose*: The study and evaluation of x-ray sources and spectrums that exist in outer space
1993	June	(*)	*Mission*: Gravity Probe *Purpose*: The prototype of a space mission that is designed to test Einstein's theory of relativity
1993	June	(+)	*Mission*: Polar *Purpose*: To study the physical properties of the Aurora Borealis
1993	Nov.	(#)	*Mission*: Waves in Space Plasmas *Purpose*: To study the gaslike particles in space with radio-signal experiments
1994		(+)	*Mission*: X-ray Timing Explorer *Purpose*: The study of the compact x-ray sources. The program will evaluate black holes and neutron stars
1995		(*)	*Mission*: [PROPOSED] Advanced X-ray Astronomy Facility *Purpose*: A satellite observatory with a high-resolution telescope on board Current plans are to have the satellite in orbit for at least fifteen years
1996		(+)	*Mission*: [PROPOSED] Comet Rendezvous Asteroid Flyby *Purpose*: To study the origin and evolution of the solar system

Table L-1. Continued

Year	Month	Mission
1997		(+) *Mission*: [PROPOSED] Earth Observing System
		Purpose: Orbit and study the Earth in detail
1998		(+) *Mission*: [PROPOSED] Cassini
		Purpose: To study Saturn
1999		(*) *Mission*: [PROPOSED] Space Infrared Telescope Facility
		Purpose: Measure the infrared emissions from the Milky Way to obtain a clear picture of the galaxy
2000		(?) *Mission*: [PROPOSED] Mars Rover Sample Return
		Purpose: The collection of Martian-soil samples and their return to Earth for examination and evaluation

(+) Launched by expendable rocket
(*) Launched by the space shuttle
(#) Research programs that will be carried on-board the shuttle

umbrella. The first known use was in the killing of Georgi Markov, a Bulgarian who worked in London for the BBC World Service. His on-air comments were anything but complementary toward the regime running his native country. One day, while waiting for a bus to take him home, a sharp jab in his right thigh caused him to turn around and face a stranger carrying an umbrella who muttered an apology and disappeared into the crowd. Two days later Georgi Markov suddenly died. His death was sufficiently mysterious to warrant an investigation by London's Metropolitan Police Laboratory. As the body was autopsied, pathologist Rufus Crompton discovered a tiny pin-head size pellet in the thigh of the Bulgarian. An electron microscope was used to examine the pellet. It was made of a very hard metal and composed of 10% iridium and 90% platinum. Two holes that met had been drilled into the pellet and later scientific tests revealed a residue of ricin, a toxic as deadly as cobra venom in those holes. (*See* RICIN.)

LETN [LE] Abbreviation for The Law Enforcement Television (cable) Network, which is broadcast to 900 stations in 50 states. It is used to train police officers in law enforcement tactics ranging from suicide prevention of individuals in custody to how to use surveillance hardware. The cable network programs are received by satellite transmission from the Dallas-based Law Enforcement Television Network and are encoded so only police department subscribers can watch the programs. The network broadcasts cost subscribers between $288–$588 a month depending on the size of the police department. Markel Services, a liability insurer for many police departments across the United States, is offering a 10 percent discount on insurance rates to law enforcement agencies subscribing to LETN programming as a training tool for sworn police officers.

level [US] In an air intercept, a word meaning, "Contact designated is at your (altitude) angels."

Level 6/5/4/3/2/1 [US] The federal Bureau of Prisons rates its 53 institutions nationwide on a scale of 1 to 6, ranging from minimum security camps without fences to the supermaximum security facility at Marion, Illinois. Lewisburg, together with facilities at Leavenworth, Kansas, and Lompoc, California, are next down the security line from Marion and are rated as Level 5.

LF Abbreviation for Low Frequency (30–540 kHz).

LFC [NASA] Abbreviation for Large Format Camera.

LGW [US] Abbreviation for Laser Guided Weapon, a weapon that utilizes a seeker to detect laser energy that is reflected from a laser marked/designated target. A computer controller guides the LGW to the point from which the laser energy is being reflected.

LHe [NASA] Abbreviation for Liquid Helium.

librium [LE] Name of a controlled substance that is a minor tranquilizer. (*See* QUICK REFERENCE.)

lid [C,G&PS] Slang for an ounce (approximately) of marijuana.

LIDAR [M] Acronym for Laser-Radar.

lid poppers [C,G&PS] Slang for amphetamines. (*See* QUICK REFERENCE.)

lieutenant [LE] Slang for the intermediary in a criminal operation who represents the drug/narcotic supplier or importer and sells products to various drug dealers.

lifer [LE] Slang for a prison inmate serving a life sentence.

lift the plant [C,G&PS] Slang for the removal of narcotics from a hidden location.

light intensifier [I] An electronic viewing device that allows law enforcement officers, military intelligence, and antiterrorism units to see in very low-light conditions. As the name suggests, whatever light is available (stars, moonlight, man-made illumination) is intensified making it possible to see in an otherwise impossible situation.

lightning arrester [C] A protection device that guards against damage to communications equipment from lightning strikes to the antenna or electrical system.

lightweight [C,G&PS] A lightweight is a person in the drug/narcotic trade lacking great importance.

Lima [A,LE,MIL] Designation for the letter *L*.

Lincoln [A,LE,MIL] Designation for the letter *L*.

linear amplifier [C] A common radio transmitting device that will increase the signal output of a transmitter.

line-of-sight [C] The maximum distance traveled by UHF transmissions and to some VHF radio-frequency waves. (*See* UHF; VHF.)

line [C,G&PS] Slang for an individual dose of cocaine.

line-X [USSR] The field section of the KGB responsible for all technical and scientific espionage operations. This section of the KGB is headquartered at Number 2, Dzerzhinsky Square, Moscow, USSR.

linex [HRU] A flexible explosive favored by hostage rescue units because it can be adapted quickly to many situations and specific needs.

LiOH [NASA] Chemical designation for Lithium Hydroxide.

lippman [I] A special high-resolution photographic emulsion used in the preparation of microdots. Microdots are pin-size photographic reductions of documents, pictures, and intelligence data. Lippman emulsion also is used to prepare a mikrat. (*See* MIKRAT.)

Lipton tea [C,G&PS] Slang for poor-quality example of marijuana.

liquid sky [C,G&PS] Slang for heroin. (*See* QUICK REFERENCE.)

lit up [C,G&PS] Slang for someone who is under the influence of narcotics, i.e., "He's really lit up on those jelly babies."

little D [C,G&PS] Slang for dilaudid. (*See* QUICK REFERENCE.)

little double [C,G&PS] Slang for a very short barreled sawed-off shotgun, i.e., "He's hiding in the back room of the store with a little double."

LKA [LE] Abbreviation for Last Known Address.

L-L [NASA] Abbreviation for Line-to-Line.

L&L [NASA] Abbreviation for Launch and Landing.

LL [LE] Abbreviation for Land Line (telephone).

LLCF [NASA] Abbreviation for Launch and Landing Computational Facilities.

LLTV [LE] Abbreviation for Low-Light (level) Television.

LMSS [C3I] Abbreviation for Land Mobile Satellite Service.

LNA [C3I] Abbreviation for Low Noise Amplifier.

L/O [NASA] Abbreviation for Lift-Off.

LO [C] Abbreviation for Local Oscillator.

LOA [GOV] Abbreviation for Letter Of Agreement.

load **1.** [C,G&PS] Slang term describing a bulk sale of heroin. A load consists of thirty bags or balloons of heroin. **2.** [C,G&PS] Slang for a collection of drugs/narcotics that are hidden in a single location for sale or pick up.

loaded [LE] Slang for an individual who is under the influence of liquor or drugs.

locals [GOV] Slang for a reference to local police officers.

LOCAP [US] Acronym for LOw Combat Air Patrol.

LOCE [C3I] Abbreviation for Limited Operational Capability for Europe.

locoweed [C,G&PS] Slang for marijuana or hashish.

LODE [C3I] Abbreviation for Large Optics Demo Experiment.

LOFAR [NASA] Acronym for Low Frequency Acquisition and Ranging.

log [D] Abbreviation for logarithmic.

logic bomb A computer virus or worm triggered by a certain value or set of code commands appearing in a specific location of the computer's memory. A logic bomb operates at random in a computer program. It also can operate by some deliberate command that might be usual for a computer operator, such as calling up a program. (*See* VIRUS.)

LOI [NASA] Abbreviation for Lunar Orbit Insertion.

long run [C,G&PS] Slang for an individual who lives on the street and has used drugs over a long period.

long wave [B] Of or referring to the AM broadcast band used in Europe. It is below the United States AM broadcast band and operates between 148.5 and 183.5 MHz.

looking [C,G&PS] Slang meaning seeking narcotics.

LOR [NASA] Abbreviation for Lunar Orbit Rendezvous.

LORAN [A] Acronym for LOng RAnge Navigation.

lords [C,G&PS] Slang for hydromorphone, a dilaudid.

LORO [C] Abbreviation for Lobe On Receive Only.

LOS **1.** [C3I] Abbreviation for Line of Sight, a radio communications. **2.** [NASA] Abbreviation for Lift-Off Simulator.

lost and missing children: *See* CENTER FOR MISSING CHILDREN.

louie [LE] In a surveillance operation, a term indicating that a vehicle has just made a left turn.

love weed [C,G&PS] Slang for marijuana. (*See* QUICK REFERENCE.)

love wood [C,G&PS] Slang for hashish. (*See* QUICK REFERENCE.)

LP [M] Abbreviation for Low Pressure.

L-P [NASA] Abbreviation for Low Pressure.

LPC [C3I] Abbreviation for Linear Predictive Coding.

LPI [M] Abbreviation for Low Probability of Intercept.

LRE [C3I] Abbreviation for Low Rate Encoding.

LRF [HRU] Abbreviation for Light Reaction Forces, the antiterrorism and hostage rescue unit of the Philippine government.

LRINF [M] Abbreviation for Longer Range Intermediate-range Nuclear Forces.

LRP [M] Abbreviation for Long-Range Reconnaissance Patrol.

LRTNF [M] Abbreviation for Long-Range Theater Nuclear Forces.

L/S [NASA] Abbreviation for Landing Site.

L&S [NASA] Abbreviation for Logistics and Support.

LSAR [M] Abbreviation for Logistic Support Analysis Record.

LSB [NASA] Abbreviation for Lower Side Band.

LSD [C,G&PS,LE] Abbreviation for lysergic acid diethylamide, a synthetic drug derived from lysergic acid, an alkaloid found in ergot. Ergot is a tiny fungus that grows on rye and other grains. In its purest form, it is white and odorless. It usually is cut with powdered sugar before sale. LSD usually is taken orally and can be snorted or injected. Mixed with water, LSD tabs can be created by the drug dealer for small "hits." (*See* QUICK REFERENCE.)

LSD tabs [C,G&PS] Small squares or circles of blotter-type paper that usually are identified by various colors (strength) and are marked with patterns that indicate exactly where LSD has been applied. The number of "hits" (doses) marked on a tab is a further indicator of strength. LSD doses are ingested by placing all or part of the tab into the mouth.

LSI [C3I] Abbreviation for Large-Scale Integration.

LSR [NASA] Abbreviation for Land Sea Rescue.

LS/ST [NASA] Abbreviation for Light Shield/Star Tracker.

LSST [NASA] Abbreviation for Launch Site Support Team.

L&T [NASA] Abbreviation for Laboratory and Test.

LT [M] Abbreviation for Lookthrough.

LTBT [GOV] Abbreviation for Limited Test Ban Treaty.

LTM [C3I] Abbreviation for Laser Transfer Module.

LTTE [TRG] Abbreviation for Liberation Tigers of Tamil Eelam, a group of murdering terrorists based in Sri Lanka. The group robs and kills people of wealth in Sri Lanka to support its organization and political views.

ludes [C,G&PS] Slang for quaaludes, also known as the drug methaqualone. (*See* QUICK REFERENCE.)

luding [C,G&PS] Slang for the ingestion of methaqualone.

LUF [C] Abbreviation for Lowest Usable Frequency.

lumber [C,G&PS] Slang for sticks and stems that are mixed in with a load of marijuana to add bulk and weight.

lush [C,G&PS] Slang for one who uses alcohol to excess.

lusher [C,G&PS] Slang for an individual who drinks to excess.

LVT [M] Abbreviation for Assault Amphibian Vehicle.

LWIR [C3I] Abbreviation for Long Wavelength Infrared.

LWS [NASA] Abbreviation for Lightning Warning System.

LZ [M] Abbreviation for Landing Zone.

M

M 1. [C,G&PS] Designation for morphine. (*See* QUICK REFERENCE.) 2. [A] Designation for Mach (number). 3. [C] Designation for Mobile Units (mobile units only) used on this frequency/channel—no base station. This code is usually used in surveillance operations or in the course of a law enforcement raid. It is a clear indicator that officers are on foot, communicating with each other.

M-16 Designation for the standard assault weapon issued to the U.S. military. The M-16 has a firing rate of up to 950 rounds per minute when used in the fully automatic mode. The standard ammunition magazine issued with the weapon holds either 20 or 30 rounds. Magazines are often taped together side by side with the loading end facing in opposite directions so the user can quickly eject an empty magazine, flip it around, and reload in one swift movement.

M-19 [TRG] Designation for *Movimiento 19 Abril*, a terrorist group with headquarters in Colombia. This group is involved in drug traffic and kidnappings, as well as political terrorism, to raise money. Colombia criminal elements are the root of M-19, and payoff's to law enforcement officials who allow the practices of M-19 to continue are commonplace.

MAC [M] Abbreviation for Military Airlift Command.

MAC C2 [C3I] Abbreviation for Military Airlift Command and Control.

MACCS [US] Abbreviation for Marine Air Command Control System.

mace 1. [LE] Trademark for a type of tear gas (usually capitalized). 2. [LE] Any of a variety of hallucinogenic drugs.

machinery [C,G&PS] Slang for the hardware that is used in the injection of narcotics.

mack [C,G&PS] Slang for a hustler or pimp.

mackman [C,G&PS] Slang for a pimp.

MAD 1. [M] Frequency signal for Military Air Distress. 2. [M] Abbreviation for Magnetic Anomaly Detector, a device used for locating submerged submarines. 3. [I] Designation for West German military intelligence, which is responsible for military intelligence operations and electronic intercepts.

made guy [LE] Slang for an individual known to have killed for some group connected with organized crime. This person might have been arrested for the crime, but more likely is the prime suspect.

MAF [M] Abbreviation for Marine Amphibious Force.

magic mist [C,G&PS] Slang for PCP. (*See* QUICK REFERENCE.)

magic mushrooms [C,G&PS] The common name for the active ingredient in *psilocybe mexicana*. In its purest form, it is a white crystallike material. In raw form, it looks like a dried and chopped mushroom. In low doses, it creates a sense of detachment with reality in the user. (*See* PSILOCYBIN.)

magnum [US] A surveillance satellite for eavesdropping on worldwide communications from space. The Magnum program follows the rhyolite/aquacade satellite missions.

main man 1. [C,G&PS] Slang for a central figure in the drug/narcotic trade. A primary drug dealer or a producer or manufacturer of narcotics. 2. [LE] Slang for the primary individual who is under surveillance. 3. [C,G&PS] Slang for a partner in criminal activities.

mainline [C,G&PS] Slang for an intravenous injection of heroin.

mainliner [C,G&PS] Slang for a drug addict who intravenously injects narcotics.

maintaining [C,G&PS] Slang for the ability to appear to remain coherent while at the same time under the effect of drugs. An individual capable of maintaining has learned to focus his actions in such a way as to appear close to normal.

maintenance [LE] The process of maintaining a drug-free environment when treating an addiction to drugs or narcotics.

make [LE] Slang term meaning to identify or be identified, especially a police officer working undercover.

make a meet [LE] Slang term meaning to establish a time and location to buy or sell narcotics or stolen property.

make a turn [C,G&PS] Slang term meaning to make the effort to withdraw from the use of drugs.

MAL Specialty code for malpractice/medical or legal.

man [C,G&PS] Slang for an individual who is a source for drugs or narcotics.

manicure [C,G&PS] Slang for the process of preparing marijuana for sale or use.

manicured [C,G&PS] Slang for clean marijuana.

manicured tea [C,G&PS] Slang for machine-made, as opposed to hand-rolled, marijuana cigarettes.

MANO 1. [TRG] Abbreviation for *Movimiento Argentino Nacional Organisacion*, a terrorist/radical group operating in Argentina. 2. [TRG] Designation for *Mano Blanca*, a terrorist group headquartered in Guatemala.

MAP [US] Abbreviation for Military Assistance Program.

MAR 1. [TRG] Abbreviation for *Movimiento de Accion Revolucionaria*, a terrorist group based in Mexico. In very general terms, it is an intelligence-gathering group involved in the sabotage of commercial developments related to the government. Its funding comes from it and intelligence flows to the KGB. 2. Background code for maritime.

marijuana [LE] One of the hemp plant family of plants that is also known as the *cannabis sativa*. Marijuana has the general appearance of the cooking seasoning oregano. Depending on a variety of growing factors, the color of freshly cut marijuana ranges from greenish brown to grayish green. The mind altering ingredient in marijuana is tetrahydrocannabinol (THC). Marijuana usually is smoked in hand-rolled cigarettes or small pocket pipes. Hashish is made from the tops and leaves of marijuana plants. In some instances, marijuana prices have been as high as $300 an ounce—in part because of increased cultivation costs of sinsemilla, a semiseedless strain of the crop that is far more potent than traditional commercial grade marijuana. As law enforcement officials continue to close in on the growers, smugglers, sellers, and users of marijuana, the price will continue to increase. Studies in the U.S. educational system have revealed that daily marijuana users do poorer in school, miss more school, spend more evenings each week out of the home, are more likely to use other drugs, and are more likely to associate with other users. These same studies also show that marijuana causes an impairment in short-term memory, fragmented speech, disjointed thinking, and loss of train of thought. (*See* QUICK REFERENCE; THC.)

mark [LE] Slang for an individual who has been targeted by criminal elements as someone they can rob or steal from with little effort.

marked cards [LE] Slang for playing cards that can be identified from the backside.

maroon shield [US] Code name for terrestrial microwave encryption equipment.

marshal service [LE] Designation for the United States Marshal Service. (*See* FEDERAL LAW ENFORCEMENT NATIONWIDE COMMUNICATIONS FREQUENCIES.)

MARV [C3I] Designation for Maneuvering Reentry Vehicle.

Mary 1. [C,G&PS] Slang for marijuana. (*See* MARIJUANA.) 2. [A,LE,MIL] Designation for the letter *M*.

Mary good [C,G&PS] Slang for marijuana. (*See* MARIJUANA.)

Mary Jane [C,G&PS] Slang for marijuana. (*See* MARIJUANA.)

Mary Warner [C,G&PS] Slang for marijuana. (*See* MARIJUANA.)

maser [C3I] Acronym for Microwave Amplification by Stimulated Emission of Radiation.

MASST [US] Abbreviation for Major Ship Satellite Terminal.

maestro [LE] Term for the second in command in a Mafia family.

matchbox [C,G&PS] Slang for a small prepackaged container of marijuana.

MATS [D] Abbreviation for Mobile Automatic Telephone System.

MAW [M] Abbreviation for Marine Aircraft Wing.

Mayflower [US] Code name for ballistic submarine communications project.

maypole [US] Naval aviation voice brevity code meaning a sonobuoy.

MBC [TRG] Abbreviation for Mohamed Boudia Commando, a terrorist group also known as the Carlos Gang.

MBFN [M] Abbreviation for Multiple Beam Forming Network.

MBFR [GOV] Abbreviation for Mutual and Balanced Force Reductions.

MBS [B] Abbreviation for Mutual Broadcasting System.

MBTA [C3I] Abbreviation for Multiple Beam Torus Antenna.

MC-130 Designation for The Combat Talon aircraft, a low-flying transport/rescue plane that can evade radar detection and slip into enemy territory at a 200-foot altitude, even in zero visibility, dropping off men or supplies with pin-point accuracy. This aircraft is the backbone of Task Force-160 for troop and supply support.

MCC [C3I] Abbreviation for Mission Control Center or Mobile Command Center.

MCE [C3I] Abbreviation for Modular Control Equipment.

MCG [C3I] Abbreviation for Memory Controller Group.

MCS 1. [M] Abbreviation for Maneuver Control System. 2. [C3I] Abbreviation for Maritime Communications Subsystem. 3. [NASA] Abbreviation for Multichannel Communications Support.

MCU [C3I] Abbreviation for Monitor and Control Unit.

MDA [C,G&PS] Designation for a drug is chemically related to mescaline and amphetamines. The chemical name for MDA is methylenedioxamphetamine. It usually is found in powdered form and is off-white to light brown in color. As a liquid, MDA is dark red to light brown in color. It is usually ingested by mouth, but can be snorted or injected. The reaction to MDA is very similar to LSD.

MDMA [C,G&PS] Designation for the drug known as ecstasy. This mind-altering substance is used worldwide as an enhancement to the act of sex.

MDS [C] Abbreviation for Minimum Discernible Signal.

MDTS [US] Abbreviation for Megabit Digital Troposcatter Subsystem.

ME Specialty code to Medical Evidence.

Mebaral [LE] Designation for mephobarbital, a controlled substance that is a sedative. (*See* QUICK REFERENCE.)

mechanic 1. [LE] Slang for a hired killer. A mechanic usually is given a target and free hand in the method used to dispatch the person targeted. 2. [LE] Slang for an individual skilled in handling playing cards. 3. [LE] Slang for a skillful gambler.

MEDCOMM [LE] *See* MEDICAL RADIOCOMMUNICATION NETWORK.

MEDAX [US] Acronym for MEssage DAta eXchange terminal.

medical hype [C,G&PS] Slang for an individual who, for some medical reason, has been given a drug or narcotic as a part of his treatment and has become addicted.

medical radiocommunications nationwide frequency network (MEDCOMM) The frequencies in TABLE M-1 are authorized for the purpose of medical emergency units to conduct radio operations for delivering or rending medical services nationwide. These frequencies can be used

Table M-1. Medical Radiocommunications Nationwide Frequency Network

Base and Mobile MHz	Mobile Only MHz	Channel Name
463.000	468.000	MED-ONE
463.025	468.025	MED-TWO
463.050	468.050	MED-THREE
463.075	468.075	MED-FOUR
463.100	468.100	MED-FIVE
463.125	468.125	MED-SIX
463.150	468.150	MED-SEVEN
463.175	468.175	MED-EIGHT

Other medical activity frequencies:

33.0200	45.9600	155.1750
33.0400	46.0000	155.2050
33.0600	46.0400	155.2200
33.0800	47.4600	155.2350
33.1000	47.5000	155.2650
37.9000	47.5800	155.2800
37.9400	47.6200	155.2950
37.9800	47.6600	155.3550
45.9200	155.1600	168.1625
453.0125	458.1125	467.9375
458.0375	458.1875	468.0125
458.0625	465.5152	468.0375
458.0875	465.5375	468.0625
458.0125	465.5625	468.0875

exclusively or in conjunction with local emergency frequency assignments.

medical response codes Communications are often necessary within the medical community between an ambulance and hospital, or an ambulance and a law enforcement agency. The Medical Response Codes (MRC) listed in TABLE M-2 are the most common that are in use across the United States.

Table M-2. Medical Response Codes

Code	Meaning
Code 0	Nonmedical transport
Code 1	Route call
Code 2	Immediate response—private call
Code 3	Police/fire emergency
Code 4	Private emergency
Code 5	Immediate response—police/fire
Code 6	Round trip
Code 7	Dead person

MEECN [C3I] Abbreviation for Minimum Essential Emergency Communications Network.

meet [C,G&PS] Slang for an appointment between a drug seller and buyer.

Mellaril [LE] Brand name for thioridazine, a controlled substance. It is a major tranquilizer. (*See* QUICK REFERENCE.)

melter [C,G&PS] Slang for morphine. (*See* QUICK REFERENCE.)

melting [C,G&PS] Slang term for undergoing the process of withdrawal from drug or narcotics without the benefit of medical assistance.

meprobamate [LE] A controlled substance that is a sedative/hypnotic. (*See* QUICK REFERENCE.)

MERANDCOM [US] Designation for Army Mobility Equipment Research and Development Command.

MERC [D] Slang for mercenary, a soldier of fortune who offers his fighting skills and talent for a price.

merchandise [C,G&PS] Slang for narcotics or drugs.

merlin [US] Code name for ballistic submarine communications project.

mesc [C,G&PS] Slang for mescaline, the alkaloid in peyote.

mescal button [C,G&PS] Slang for peyote. (*See* QUICK REFERENCE.)

mescaline [LE] A controlled substance. It is an hallucinogen. The head of peyote cactus are cut off, dried, then chopped, ground, or sliced. When chopped or sliced, peyote heads are called buttons. Buttons are usually eaten. When ground into a fine powder, it is smoked, causing the user to hallucinate. (*See* QUICK REFERENCE.)

MESP [C3I] Abbreviation for Minuteman Extended Survivability Program.

meth [C,G&PS] Slang for methamphetamine. (*See* QUICK REFERENCE.)

methadone [LE] Name of a substitute drug used to treat people addicted to heroin. Methadone, over the long term, is equally addictive as heroin. Methadone is a controlled substance, a narcotic. (*See* QUICK REFERENCE.)

methamphetamine [LE] Name of a controlled substance that is a stimulant. (*See* QUICK REFERENCE.)

methamphetamine user symptoms and medical problems [LE] Methamphetamine users can become irritable, talkative, paranoid, or violent as the drug euphoria fades. Users were known as speed freaks as early as the 1960s. The drug suppresses the appetite and frequent use can lead to malnutrition. Prolonged use of speed can cause a psychosis, a serious mental disorder. It also can cause chorea, a neurological syndrome that produces continual jerky movements. Speed's effects can last for up to 10 hours. It is cheaper than cocaine. An ounce of cocaine has a street value of approximately $1,000; an ounce of speed goes for about $800.

methaqualone [LE] Name of a controlled substance. It is a sedative/hypnotic. (*See* QUICK REFERENCE.)

metharbitol [LE] A controlled substance that is a sedative/hypnotic. (*See* QUICK REFERENCE.)

methedrine [LE] A controlled substance, a stimulant. (*See* QUICK REFERENCE.)

meth head [C,G&PS] Slang for a regular user of methamphetamines.

MEWSG [C3I] Abbreviation for Multi-Service Electronic Warfare Support Group.

MEWSS [C3I] Abbreviation for Mobile Electronic Warfare Support System.

Mexican brown [C,G&PS] Slang for marijuana. (*See* MARIJUANA.)

Mexican blue [C,G&PS] Slang for LSD made in Mexico.

Mexican green [C,G&PS] Slang for marijuana. (*See* MARIJUANA.)

Mexican mud [C,G&PS] Slang for very crude opium.

Mexican red [C,G&PS] Slang for sodium capsules.

mezz [C,G&PS] Slang for hashish. (*See* QUICK REFERENCE.)

MF [C3I] Abbreviation for Medium Frequency, 300 kHz – 3.0 MHz.

MFTDMA [C3I] Abbreviation for Multiple Frequency Time Division Multiple Access.

MG [LE] Abbreviation for Machine Gun.

MGB [USSR] Abbreviation for Ministerstvo Gosudarstvennoy Bezopasnosti, Ministry of State Security.

MH Specialty code for Missing Heir.

MHV [M] Abbreviation for Miniature Homing Vehicle.

MI 1. Specialty code for Marine Investigation. 2. [I] Abbreviation for Military Intelligence, the basic, estimative, or current intelligence available regarding any foreign military group or military related situation or activity.

MI5 [I] Designation for the Security Service of the United Kingdom. MI5 reports directly to the Secret Service (MI6) and is responsible for domestic counterintelligence. Agents of MI5 are headquartered at every embassy of the U.K.

MI6 [I] Designation for the Secret Service of the United Kingdom. MI6 is responsible for all military, strategic, and foreign counterintelligence.

Michoacan [LE] Name of a state in Mexico. Also a type of marijuana grown in the state.

Mickey D's [LE] A nearby McDonald's that is a place where police officers can meet to exchange information.

mickey mouse [C,G&PS] Slang for the occasional use of heroin.

MICNS [US] Abbreviation for Modular Integrated Communications and Navigation System.

microdot [I] A photographically reduced document, reduced to the size of a period at the end of a sentence, then applied to the body of another letter or document. Microdot technology continues to be used in various areas of espionage activity. (*See* MIKRAT.)

micro-dot [C,G&PS] A small amount of lysergic acid diethylamide (LSD) on a slip of paper. The slip of paper is swallowed for a narcotic reaction.

MIDAS [M] Abbreviation for Missile Defense Alarm System.

MIDS [NATO] Abbreviation for Multifunction Information Distribution System.

MiG [USSR] Abbreviation for Mikoyan-Gurevich, an aircraft designer.

MiG-25 [USSR] Designation for military jet fighter aircraft, the Foxbat.

MiG-29 [USSR] Designation for military jet fighter aircraft, the Fulcrum.

MiG-31 [USSR] Designation for the most advanced military jet fighter aircraft of the Soviet Union, an upgraded version of the MiG-25.

Mike **1.** [D] Slang for one-millionth of a gram, a microgram. **2.** [D] Slang for microphone. **3.** [A,LE,MIL] Designation for the letter *M*.

Mike force [M] Designation for mobile strike force, military/government or law enforcement personnel, on a joint mission.

mikrat [I] A photographically reduced message. A mikrat is much smaller than a microdot. A mikrat can be attached to any solid object for transport. It is so tiny it is difficult to spot. It is a unique tool in the intelligence war. At the destination point, the mikrat is removed by someone knowing its exact location, and enlarged by another photographic process to a readable size. A mikrat can be projected onto a screen, or printed in a photographic darkroom on photo print paper.

MIL Background code for army, navy, air force, coast guard, and marines.

MILE [C3I] Abbreviation for Minuteman Integrated Life Extension.

Military Aircraft Aerial Refueling Frequencies Day and night, at hundreds of points above the earth, U.S. military aircraft are rendezvousing with aerial refueling tankers so missions can be extended by many hours. The linkup between a surveillance aircraft or SAC bomber can happen anywhere. Following the action on these frequencies, which are listed in TABLE M-3, can result in exciting listening.

MILSTAR [C3I] Designation for Military Strategic and Tactical Relay System.

military operations areas As military pilots crisscross the United States in various types of aircraft, they fly in zones under the control of specific government facilities. These are known as military operations areas (MOAs). Pilots often report the controlling zone they have departed from as a part of their communications process and may discuss their destination in air-to-air or air-to-ground conversations. TABLE M-4 includes code names and facilities nationwide. Many of the civilian facilities listed are used as points of embarkation for helicopter assault activities of U.S. Customs and Drug Enforcement Administration agents.

miltown [LE] Name of a controlled substance, a sedative. (*See* QUICK REFERENCE.)

MIR [TRG] Designation for a Chilean terrorist group that has maintained a very low profile since 1987. This group is active in Venezuela and Peru,

Table M-3. Military Aircraft Aerial Refueling Frequencies

228.0	290.9	344.7
233.7	291.2	348.3
235.1	291.9	348.9
238.9	292.3	350.0
239.8	293.0	352.6
242.3	295.4	352.9
242.5	295.8	353.0
242.7	298.3	354.2
254.6	301.6	358.2
255.4	305.5	359.1
255.6	305.7	360.5
259.3	311.0	361.6
259.4	314.2	363.1
260.2	315.9	364.2
261.9	318.0	366.3
266.5	319.4	372.2
267.8	319.5	372.3
273.5	319.8	381.3
276.1	320.9	384.6
276.4	321.0	385.8
279.8	321.2	388.4
283.8	322.8	391.0
283.9	324.2	391.8
286.2	324.3	391.9
286.3	336.1	394.9
286.9	339.2	395.9
288.8	340.8	396.2
288.9	343.1	396.5
289.4	343.5	396.9

Table M-4. Military Operations Areas

Code Name	Facility
ABEL	MCAS Yuma, AZ
ADA EAST/WEST	McConnell AFB, KS
AMES	NAS Mountain View, CA
ANCHOR BAY	NAS Alameda, CA
ANNE	Barksdale AFB, LA
AUSTIN 1, 2	NAS Fallon, NV
AVON-North-South-East	MacDill AFB, FL
BAGDAD 1	Luke AFB, AZ
BAKER	George AFB, CA
BASINGER	MacDill AFB, FL
BAY SIDE	San Francisco International, CA
BEAK A, B & C	Holloman AFB, NM
BEAUFORT 1, 2 & 3	MCAS Beaufort, SC
BEAVER	Duluth International Airport, MN
BENNING	Fort Benning, GA
BIG BEAR	Griffiss AFB, NY
BIRMINGHAM 1, 2	Birmingham Municipal Airport, AL
BISON	McConnell AFB, KS
BOONE	Des Moines Municipal Airport, IA
BRADY	Bergstrom AFB, TX
BRISTOL	Twentynine Palms Airport, CA
BRONSON	Grand Forks AFB, ND
BROWNWOOD 1 & 2	NAS Dallas, TX
BRUNEAU 1 & 2	Mountain Home AFB, ID
BRUSH CREEK	Rickenbacker ANGB, OH
BULLDOG A, B & D	Shaw AFB, SC
CALVERTON 1 & 2	Bethpage Municipal Airport, NY
CAMDEN RIDGE	Dannelly Field, AL
CAMPBELL 1 & 2	Fort Campbell, KY
CHASE 1, 2 & 3	NAS Chase Field, TX
CHINA	McClellan AFB, CA
CHINOOK A & B	Whidbey Island Airport, WA
CHIPPEWA	Muni Airport, Battle Creek, MI
COCOA	Patrick AFB, F
COLLINS	Phelps Collins ANGB, MI
COLUMBUS 1, 2, 3 & 4	Columbus AFB, MS
COMPLEX	Edwards AFB, CA
CONDOR 1 & 2	Pease AFB, NH
CROWNPOINT	Kirtland AFB, NM
CRYSTAL	Kelly AFB, TX
DEEPWOODS	Bangor Metropolitan Airport, ME
DELMAR	Patuxent River NAS, MD
DEMO 1, 2 & 3	Quantico MCAF, VA
DESERT	Nellis AFB, NV
DESOTO	NAS New Orleans, LA
DEVILS LAKE	McChord AFB, WA
DRUM 1 & 2	Hancock Field, NY
DUKE	University Park Airport, PA
EAGLE 1, 2 & 3	Eielson AFB, AK
EDGEMONT	Ellsworth AFB, SD
EGLIN A, B, C, D, E & F	Eglin AFB, FL
EUREKA	McConnell AFB, KS
EVERS	Langley AFB, VA
FAGUS	Blytheville AFB, AR
FALCON 1 & 3	Griffiss AFB, NY

Table M-4. Continued

Code Name	Facility
FALLS 1	Volk Field, WI
FARMVILLE	Langley AFB, VA
FLAGLER	Buckley ANGB, CO
FOOTHILL 1 & 2	NAS Lemoore, CA
FORT BRAGG NORTH A & B	Fort Bragg, NC
FORT BRAGG SOUTH A & B	Fort Bragg, NC
FORT STEWART A, B1, B2 & C	Fort Stewart, GA
FREMONT	Buckley ANGB, CO
FUZZY	Tucson Municipal Airport, AZ
GABBS NORTH, SOUTH	NAS Fallon, NV
GALENA	Elmendorf AFB, AK
GAMECOCK A, B, C & D	Myrtle Beach AFB, SC
GAMECOCK I	Shaw AFB, SC
GAMECOCK J	Shaw AFB, SC
GANDY	Hill AFB, UT
GATOR LOW	NAS Cecil Field, FL
GLADDEN 1	Luke AFB, AZ
GOOSE	Kingsley Field, OR
GUNTERSVILLE	Dobbins AFB, GA
HATTERAS F	MCAS Cherry Point, NC
HAYS	McChord AFB, WA
HIAWATHA	K.I. Metropolitan, Sawyer, MI
HILLTOP	Metro Airport, Fort Wayne, IN
HOG 1, 2 & 3	Fort Smith, AR
HOLLIS	Sheppard AFB, TX
HOOD	Fort Hood, TX
HOTROCK 1, 2 & 3	England AFB, LA
HOWARD EAST	Metro Airport Springfield, IL
HOWARD WEST	Metro Airport Springfield, IL
HUMMER 1, 2, 3, 4, 5, 6 & 7	Mather AFB, CA
HUNTER	NAS Lemoore, CA
HURON	Phelps Collins ANGB, MI
INDIA 1, 2, 3	England AFB, LA
JENA 1, 2	England AFB, LA
JONES	Barksdale AFB, LA
JUNIPER A & B	McChord AFB, WA
KANE	NAS Miramar, CA
KINGSVILLE 1 & 2	NAS Kingsville, TX
KIOWA	Fort Indiantown Gap, PA
KIT CARSON A & B	Buckley ANGB, CO
LADY	Barksdale AFB, LA
LAKE ANDES	Metro Airport, Sioux City, IA
LAKE PLACID	MacDill AFB, FL
LAUGHLIN 1, 2 & 3	Laughlin AFB, TX
LAVETA	Buckley ANGB, CO
LINCOLN	Metro Airport Lincoln, NE
LIVE OAK	NAS Cecil Field, FL
LORING	McChord AFB, WA
LUCIN A, B & C	Hill AFB, UT
MARIAN	Patrick AFB, FL
MAXWELL 1, 2, 3, 4, 5, 6	Mather AFB, CA
MERAMAC	Lambert Field, MO
MERIDIAN 1 EAST & WEST	NAS Meridian, MS
MINNOW	Metro Airport Milwaukee, WI
MISTY 1, 2 & 3	Griffiss AFB, NY

Table M-4. Continued

Code Name	Facility
MOODY 1, 2A, 2B & 3	Moody AFB, GA
MORENCI	Metro Airport Tucson, AZ
NAKNEK 1 & 2	Elmendorf AFB, AK
NEW RAYMER A & B	Metro Airport Greely, CO (TAC)
OKANOGAN	Whidbey Island Airport, WA
OLYMPIC	Whidbey Island Airport, WA
O'NEILL	Metro Airport Lincoln, NE
ONTONAGON	Griffiss AFB, NY
OWYHEE	Mountain Home AFB, ID
PALATKA 1, 2 & 3	NAS Jacksonville, FL
PAMLICO A & B	NAS Oceana, VA
PARADISE	Mountain Home AFB, ID
PECK	Selfridge ANGB, MI
PECOS EAST HIGH & LOW	Cannon AFB, NM
PECOS WEST HIGH & LOW	Cannon AFB, NM
PECOS SOUTH HIGH & LOW	Cannon AFB, NM
PENSACOLA NORTH, SOUTH	NAS Pensacola, FL
PICKETT 1, 2 & 3	Byrd IAP, VA
PINE HILL EAST & WEST	NAS Meridian, MS
PINON CANYON	Fort Carson, CO
POWERS	Minot AFB, ND
QUAIL	MCAS Yuma, AZ
QUICK THRUST E, F, G, H	Shaw AFB, SC
QUICK THRUST I, J, L, M & N	Shaw AFB, SC
RAINIER 1, 2 & 3	Fort Lewis, WA
RALPH	Phelps Collins ANGB, MI
RANCH	NAS Fallon, NV
RANDOLPH 1A, 1B, 1C, 2A, 2B	Randolph AFB, TX
RAPPA 1 & 2	NAS Patuxent River, MD
RED HILLS	Metro Airport Terre Haute, IN
REESE 1, 2, 3, 4 & 5	Reese AFB, TX
RENO	Reno International Airport, NV
RESERVE	Metro Airport Tucson, AZ
RIVERS	Tinker AFB, OK
ROBERTS	NAS Lemoore, CA
ROBY	Dyess AFB, TX
ROOSEVELT	Whidbey Island Airport, WA
ROSE HILL	Metro Airport Jacksonville, FL
RUBY 1	Metro Airport Tucson, AZ
RUCKER A, B & C	Fort Rucker, AL
SADDLE A & B	Metro Airport Boise, ID
SALEM	Lambert Field, MO
SAYLOR	Mountain Home AFB, ID
SAYLOR 4	Mountain Home AFB, ID
SELL 1, LOW	Luke AFB, AZ
SEVIER A & B	Hill AFB, UT
SEYMOUR JOHNSON ECHO	Seymour-Johnson AFB, NC
SHEEP CREEK 1 & 2	Mountain-Home AFB, ID
SHEPPARD 1, 2, 3, 4 & 5	Sheppard AFB, TX
SHILO	Patrick AFB, FL
SHIRLEY 1	NAS Memphis, TN
SMOKY	McConnell AFB, KS
SNAKE 1	Mountain Home AFB, ID
SNAKE 2	Mountain Home AFB, ID
SNOOPY	Duluth International Airport, MN

Table M-4. Continued

Code Name	Facility
SNOWBIRD 1	Dobbins AFB, GA
SNOWBIRD 2	Shaw AFB, SC
STONY A & B	Elmendorf AFB, AK
STUMPY POINT	NAS Oceana, VA
SUNDANCE	Twentynine Palms Airport, CA
SUNNY	Luke AFB, AZ
SUSITNA	Elmendorf AFB, AK
SYRACUSE 1, 2, 3 & 4	Hancock Field, NY
TALON	Holloman AFB, NM
TEXON 1	Bergstrom AFB, TX
TIGER NORTH, SOUTH	McChord AFB, WA
TILFORD	Ellsworth AFB, SD
TOMBSTONE A, B & C	Davis-Monthan AFB, AZ
TRACY 1 & 2	McConnell AFB, KS
TRUMAN A, B & C	Richards-Gebaur AFB, MO
TURTLE	MCAS Yuma, AZ
TWELVE MILE	Metro Airport Fort Wayne, IN
TYNDALL A	Tyndall AFB, FL
TYNDALL B, C, D, E, F & G	Tyndall AFB, FL
VALENTINE	Holloman AFB, NM
VANCE 1A & 1B	Vance AFB, OK
VOLK, EAST A & B WEST	Volk Field, WI
VOLK A, B & C	Volk Field, WI
WAITTS	Fairchild AFB, WA
WASHITA	Sheppard AFB, TX
WHITMORE 1, 2, & 3	Beale AFB, CA
WILLIAMS 1, 2, 3 & 4	Williams AFB, AZ
WILLIAMS 3A	Davis-Monthan AFB, AZ
WILLISTON	McChord AFB, WA
YANKEE ONE	Bradley IAP, CT
YANKEE TWO	Bradley International, CT
YUKON 1 & 2	Eielson AFB, AK

as well as Chile, and is also known as the *Movimiento Independista Revolucionario Armada.*

miracle [US] Code name for ballistic submarine communications project.

MIRACL/SLBD [US] Abbreviation for Mid-Infrared Advanced Chemical Laser/Sea Lite Beam Director, an experimental high-energy laser system designed for the Navy to track and shoot down supersonic targets. The current model of MIRACL/SLBD is small enough to be installed in a military fighter aircraft in place of the conventional weapon system. Although it is still in the early stages of development, successful tests against subsonic targets were conducted in the fall of 1987 at the White Sands Missile Range in New Mexico when the device was "bigger than a house" by all reports.

MIRADCOM [US] Designation for Army MIssile Research And Development Command.

Miranda warning [LE] The warning that informs a person who is under arrest of his constitutional rights to have a lawyer present during questioning and to not incriminate himself. The warning must be given or the arrest is invalid.

MIRCOM [US] Designation for Army Missile Materiel Readiness Command.

MIRV [C3I] Abbreviation for Multiple Independently targetable Reentry Vehicle.

MIS Specialty code for missing persons, including children.

miss [C,G&PS] The failure to enter the vein during an attempt to inject drugs.

Miss Emma [C,G&PS] Slang for morphine. (*See* QUICK REFERENCE.)

missing children [LE] *See* CENTER FOR MISSING CHILDREN.

MLN [TRG] Abbreviation for *Movimiento de Liberacion Nacional* (*Tupamaros*), an active terrorist organization in Uruguay, Guatemala, and Chile.

MLRP [C3I] Abbreviation for Minuteman Long Range Plan.

MLRS [C3I] Abbreviation for Multiple-Launch Rocket System.

MM **1.** Specialty code for Medical Malpractice. **2.** [C3I] Abbreviation for Magic Mast, an antenna system.

MMIC [C3I] Abbreviation for Monolithic Microwave Integrated Circuits.

MMS [M] Abbreviation for Mast-Mounted Sight, a helicopter weapon-sight that is mounted above the main rotor blade.

MNLF [TRG] Abbreviation for Moro National Liberation Front, a radical group of terrorists based in the Philippines. The Moros are Moslem, and receive support and funds from Muammar el-Qaddafi.

M.O. [LE] Abbreviation for *Modus Operandi*, that is, method of operation. Criminals have a pattern of some type that relates to their activities. A burglar, for example, might only break into homes on Friday nights when residents are most likely to be away. The thief might gain entry by first ringing the doorbell and if it goes unanswered, trying a side or rear door. If the doors are locked, he will shatter the glass by applying tape in a cross-hatch pattern to muffle the sound. Upon entry, the thief takes only money or weapons. This pattern is his M.O. Generally, a criminal's M.O. changes with experience, and as the criminal gets older (in or out of prison) the M.O. is usually modified into whatever works the best. For example, the criminal might change the way he enters a building. The M.O. becomes a part of the police files; and with computer technology, they are easy to cross-reference.

MOA [GOV] Abbreviation for Memorandum Of Agreement.

mob **1.** [C,G&PS] Slang for a criminal group of individuals. **2.** [C3I] Abbreviation for Main Operating Base.

MoD [UK] Abbreviation for British Ministry of Defense.

MOD [C3I] Abbreviation for Modulator.

MOD C&W [B] Abbreviation for Modern Country & Western.

mode 1 [A] Designation for an international transponder signal used by military aircraft that are being used in a rescue operation of civilians.

mode 2 [A] Designation for an international transponder signal used by military aircraft for identification purposes.

mode 3 [A] Designation for an international transponder signal used by civilian aircraft for identification purposes.

mode 4 [A] Designation for international transponder signal used by civilian aircraft for identification purposes in a military operation.

MODEM [C3I] Designation for Modulator/Demodulator (communications).

MOF [LE] Abbreviation for Member Of the Force.

mokrei dela [USSR] Soviet term for a wet job. (*See* WET JOB.)

MOL [M] Designation for Manned Orbiting Laboratory—KH-10 satellite.

mole [I] Slang for an individual, considered hostile, who burrows into an organization or group for the purpose of gathering intelligence information.

moll buzzer [LE] Slang for a pickpocket who selects women as targets.

Molniya [USSR] Name of Soviet satellites. In the spy vs. spy intelligence activities carried out by various world governments, the Soviet Union has established a network of satellites that look down on every major continent. This system includes photographic, radar imaging, and communications interception satellites. The exact mission of these satellites is generally understood by the U.S. Defense Intelligence Agency. Close examinations of the Soviet craft have been undertaken for intelligence evaluation on certain flights of the U.S. space shuttle. It is certain that Soviet flights of their spacecraft also have included monitoring and photographing United States satellites at very close range.

MOMCOMS [C3I] Acronym for Man-on-the-move Communications System.

moniker [LE] Slang for a nickname.

monitoring [I] Observing, listening to, or recording of foreign or domestic activities or communications for the purpose of intelligence data collection.

monkey [C,G&PS] Slang for an individual with a drug/narcotics habit.

monkey juice [C,G&PS] Slang for PCP. (*See* QUICK REFERENCE.)

monkey on his back [C,G&PS] Slang for an individual using large amounts of narcotics; someone with a serious drug habit.

monster [C,G&PS] Slang for methedrine. (*See* QUICK REFERENCE.)

Montoneros [TRG] An organization that was active in the late 1970s and carried out kidnappings, bombings, and assassinations. It is a left-wing pro-Peron Argentinian group with supporters in Mexico and the United States. It is named after Juan Jose Valle Montoneros.

moon [C,G&PS] Slang for hashish that is obtained from peyote and cut into a flat button-like piece.

MOOP [USSR] Designation for *Ministerstvo Okhrany Obshchestvennogo Poryadka,* the Ministry for Maintenance of Public Order.

mooter [C,G&PS] Slang for a cigarette made from marijuana.

mope [LE] A derogatory term used in law enforcement that describes an individual who has a lengthy criminal history.

MOR [GOV] Abbreviation for Middle Of the Road.

mordida [C,G&PS] A Mexican term meaning a piece of the deal, the money, or the marijuana.

morph [C,G&PS] Slang for morphine. (*See* QUICK REFERENCE.)

morphie [C,G&PS] Slang for morphine. (*See* QUICK REFERENCE.)

morphine [LE] Name of a controlled substance, a narcotic. (*See* QUICK REFERENCE.)

morpho [C,G&PS] Slang for morphine. (*See* QUICK REFERENCE.)

MOS [M] Abbreviation for Military Occupation Specialty.

Moscow Centre [USSR] The headquarters for the Soviet KGB. The physical address of this facility is Number 2, Dzerzhinsky Square, Moscow, USSR. Moscow Centre has a code name in the CIA of Glass House.

Mossad [I] The Israeli Office of Intelligence and Special Missions. The Mossad is responsible for all foreign counterintelligence and strategic intelligence gathering.

MOT Specialty code for motorcycle accident.

mota [C,G&PS] A Mexican slang term for marijuana.

mother [C,G&PS] Slang for a drug or narcotics dealer.

mother's day [C,G&PS] Slang for the day monthly welfare checks come in the mail, among the hottest days for crack street sales.

Moukafaha [HRU] The antiterrorism and hostage rescue unit of the Lebanese Army.

MOU [GOV] Abbreviation for Memorandum Of Understanding.

mouse [C,G&PS] Slang for an individual who acts as an informer to a law enforcement agency. A mouse is often paid for his information by the police, and unlike some informers (who are simply street-wise) is a member of a gang or active with others in organized crime.

move [C,G&PS] Slang meaning to sell, transport, or deal in marijuana.

MP Specialty code for Missing Person.

MPCM [M] Abbreviation for Multi-Purpose Central Mount/Module.

MPDS [M] Abbreviation for Message Processing and Distribution System. It is used by the U.S. military complex to disseminate the same information to various agencies of the government and military installations.

MPH [LE] Abbreviation for Miles Per Hour.

MPL [TRG] Abbreviation for a small left-wing Honduran guerrilla group, the Cincheneros Popular Liberation Movement. The group carries out acts of terrorism and murder. In early 1989, they murdered General Gustavo Alvarez Martinez, a former head of the Honduran military who helped establish the Nicaraguan Contras and was once the United States staunchest ally in Central America. His "execution" was carried out in the name of the "Martyrs of the Honduran Revolution." As head of the national police, Alvarez became the godfather of the Contras by telling the CIA that anti-Sandinista forces could operate from Honduran territory. The CIA and Alvarez worked closely together to build the Contra rebel force to fight Nicaragua's leftist government.

MPS [M] Abbreviation for Maritime Positioning Ship.

MR [M] Abbreviation for milliradian, one thousandth of a radian. A radian is a unit of angular measurement equal to the angle at the center of a circle.

MR-8 [TRG] Designation for *Movimiento Revolucionario do Octobre, 8*, a terrorist group headquartered in Brazil.

MR-13 [TRG] Designation for *Movimiento Revolucionario Alejandro de Leon 13 Noviembre*, a terrorist group headquartered in Guatemala.

MRAAM [C3I] Abbreviation for Medium Range Air-to-Air Missile.

MRASM [C3I] Abbreviation for Medium Range Air-to-Surface Missile.

MRBM [C3I] Abbreviation for Medium-Range Ballistic Missile.

MRC [USSR] Abbreviation for Military Revolutionary Committee.

MRLA [TRG] Abbreviation for The Malayan Races Liberation Party, a terrorist/radical communist faction with a small splinter organization active in the United States. The majority of the MRLA thrust and energy is the placement of subversive wall posters and the painting of graffiti.

Mrs. White [C,G&PS] Slang for heroin. (*See* QUICK REFERENCE.)

MRT 1. Specialty code for maritime and cargo handling. 2. [C3I] Abbreviation for Miniature Receiver Terminal.

MRTA [TRG] Abbreviation for Tupac Amaru Revolutionary Movement, an active terrorist group operating in Peru.

MRVT [C3I] Abbreviation for Multiple Rate Voice Terminal.

MSAM [C3I] Abbreviation for Medium Surface-to-Air Missile.

MSC [US] Abbreviation for Military Sealift Command.

MSE [C3I] Abbreviation for Mobile Subscriber Equipment.

MSI [C3I] Abbreviation for Medium Scale Integration.

MSM [C3I] Abbreviation for Microwave Switch Matrix.

MSRT [C3I] Abbreviation for Mobile Subscriber Radio Terminal.

MSS [C3I] Abbreviation for Multi-Spectral Scanner.

MST [C3I] Abbreviation for Missile Surveillance Technology.

MTBF [A] Abbreviation for Mean Time Between Failures, a reliability measurement in hours used extensively in the electronic and aviation field.

MTCC [C3I] Abbreviation for Modular Tactical Communications Center.

MTI [M] Abbreviation for Moving Target Indication, a radar facility.

MTTR [C3I] Abbreviation for Mean Time To Repair.

MU [C,G&PS] Designation for marijuana. (*See* QUICK REFERENCE.)

mud [C,G&PS] Slang for very crude opium.

MUF [C] Abbreviation for Maximum Usable Frequency.

muffler [C,G&PS] A handgun sound-silencer.

mugger [LE] A strong-armed robber.

muggles [C,G&PS] Slang for hashish. (*See* QUICK REFERENCE.)

mula [C,G&PS] Mexican slang for a prostitute.

mule 1. [C,G&PS] Slang for an individual who carries narcotics from one point to another, usually for payment in money or drugs. 2. [C,G &PS] Slang for an individual who supplies drugs. 3. [M] Abbreviation for Modular Universal Laser Equipment.

MULTOTS [US] Abbreviation for MUltiple unit Test and Operational Training System.

MUN Background code for peace officer, county sheriff.

murphy game [C,G&PS] Slang for a scam using sex and drugs.

mushroom **1.** [C,G&PS] Slang for an innocent bystander who "popped up" in the wrong place at the wrong time and got wounded or killed in gangland crossfire. **2.** [US] Naval aviation voice brevity code meaning a special weapon system, that is, nuclear. **3.** [C,G&PS] Slang for psilocybin, a Mexican mushroom eaten as is or dried and ground into a powder.

music [US] Naval aviation voice brevity code meaning electronic jamming.

music box [I] Slang for Radio Transmitter.

musician [I] Slang for a clandestine radio operator.

mutt [LE] A derogatory term created by police officers describing an individual with a long history of violent crimes.

MUX [C3I] Abbreviation for Multiplex.

MVD [USSR] Abbreviation for *Ministerstvo Vnutrennikh Del*, the Ministry of Internal Affairs.

MWS [C3I] Abbreviation for Missile Weapon System.

MX **1.** [B] Designation for music. **2.** [M] Designation for missile (experimental).

mystic link [US] Code name for digital information distribution system.

Mystic Star frequencies The radio frequencies used by high-ranking military and government officials when traveling to stay in touch with their offices. *See* TABLE M-5; VIP.

Table M-5. Mystic Star Frequencies

3032.0	3046.0	3067.0	3071.0	11055.0				
3116.0				11118.0	11176.0	11180.0	11210.0	11226.0
3144.0	4721.0	4731.0	4742.0	11249.0	11407.0	11413.0		11441.0
4760.0				11460.0				
5688.0	5700.0	5710.0	5760.0	11466.0	11484.0	11488.0		11498.0
5800.0				11545.0				
5820.0	6683.0	6715.0	6738.0	11596.0	11615.0	11627.0		12324.0
6756.0				12317.0				
6757.0	6760.0	6790.0	6812.0	13201.0	13204.0	13214.0	13215.0	13241.0
6817.0				13247.0	13412.0	13440.0		13455.0
6830.0	6918.0	6927.0	6993.0	13457.0				
7316.0				13485.0	13585.0	13710.0		13823.0
7690.0	7735.0	7765.0	7813.0	13960.0				
7858.0				14715.0	14902.0	14913.0		15015.0
7997.0	8040.0	8060.0	8162.0	15036.0				
8170.0				15048.0	15091.0	15687.0		16080.0
8967.0	8992.0	8993.0	9007.0	16117.0				
9014.0				16320.0	16407.0	17385.0		17480.0
9017.0	9018.0	9020.0	9023.0	17972.0				
9026.0				17993.0	18027.0	18218.0		19047.0
9043.0	9120.0	9158.0	9180.0	20016.0				
9270.0				20053.0	20154.0	20313.0		22723.0
9320.0	9958.0	9991.0	10112.0	23265.0				
10427.0				25578.0	26471.0			
10530.0	10583.0	10881.0	11035.0					

N

NA [D] Abbreviation for North America or North American.

NAC [I] Abbreviation for National Agency Check, that part of a background investigation consisting of a cross-reference of all personnel files against the name of the individual in question. The investigator is looking for derogatory details and factors that might make the individual a security risk.

NACA [A] Abbreviation for The National Advisory Committee on Aeronautics.

NACK [C3I] Acronym for Negative Acknowledgement (repeat requested).

NADC [US] Abbreviation for Naval Air Development Center.

nail [C,G&PS] Slang for a hypodermic needle used by drug addicts.

nailed [C,G&PS] Slang for someone who is placed under arrest.

naked [I] Slang for an intelligence agent, law enforcement officer, or surveillance team operating without the benefit of backup or cover.

NAP [TRG] Designation for Armed Proletarian Nuclei, a very dangerous radical/terrorist group that has targeted a number of politicians for assassination in Italy.

NAPAP [TRG] An ultraleft French terrorist group based in Paris. The NAPAP is small in numbers, radical in attitude, and limited in activities because the majority of their funds come from within. The French DST (Bureau for Defense and Surveillance of the Territory) have kept the members of this organizations membership under close observation since 1985. Because of this the NAPAP has kept a low profile. English translation: Armed Nuclei for Popular Autonomy.

NAR [TRG] Abbreviation for *Nuclei Armati Revoluzionari*, a right-wing Italian group known to have been responsible for assassinations in Italy, and the 1980 bombing of the Bologna Railway Station.

NARADCOM [US] Designation for Army NAtick Research And Development COMmand.

narc [LE] Slang for a narcotics (police) officer.

narco [LE] Slang for a police detective involved with narcotic investigations.

narco bucks [C,G&PS] Slang for money derived from drug/narcotics trafficking.

NASA [C3I] Abbreviation for National Aeronautics and Space Administration.

NASCOM [US] Abbreviation for the NASA Communications Network.

nash [USSR] Soviet term meaning "one of our own."

national intelligence [I] Referring to any intelligence information produced by the Central Intelligence Agency that bears on the broad aspects of national policy and the national security of the United States.

NATO [C3I] Acronym for North Atlantic Treaty Organization.

NAVAID [M] Acronym for NAVigational AID.

NAVAIR [US] Acronym for NAVal AIR Systems Command.

naval aviation squadron nomenclature In communications scanning, it is important to know the type of aircraft involved in a mission. TABLE N-1 will aid that process as it relates to United States Navy helicopters and support aircraft involved in electronic warfare, rescue, and aerial refueling.

Navane [LE] Brand name of thiothixene, a controlled substance that is a major tranquilizer. (*See* QUICK REFERENCE.)

NAVCOMPARS [US] Acronym for the NAVal COMmunications Processing And Routing System.

Table N-1. Naval Aviation Squadron Nomenclature

Identifier	Type	Assignment
HAL	Helicopter	Attack light
HC	Helicopter	Combat support
HMH	Helicopter	Antisubmarine heavy (ASW)
HS	Helicopter	Antisubmarine (ASW)
HSL	Helicopter	Antisubmarine light (ASW)
HM/VOD	Helicopter	Mine countermeasures (Vertical on-board delivery)
HMM	Helicopter	Marine (main fighting force)
HMS	Helicopter	Marine (fire support)
HM	Helicopter	Marine (medical)
VA	Fixed wing	Attack aircraft
VAH	Fixed wing	Attack aircraft heavy
VAK	Fixed wing	Air-to-air refueling
VAQ		Tactical electronic warfare aircraft (ECM)
VAW		Carrier airborne early warning (AEW)
VC	Fixed wing—Composite	
VF	Fixed wing	Fighter
VFA	Fixed wing	Fighter strike
VFP	Fixed-wing Fighter	Photo intelligence
VMA	Fixed wing	Marine attack
VMAT	Fixed wing	Marine attack (training)
VP	Fixed wing	Patrol
VR	Fixed wing	Fleet logistics support
VS	Fixed wing	Antisubmarine
VX	Fixed wing	Experimental

NAVELEX [US] Acronym for NAVal ELEctronic Systems Command.

NAVFAC [US] Acronym for FACilities Engineering Command.

NAVFAC's [US] Designation for Naval Engineering Facilities worldwide.

NAVMACS [US] Acronym for NAVal Modular Automated Communications System.

NAVSEA [C3I] Acronym for NAVal SEA Systems Command.

NAVSTAR [M] Acronym for NAVigation Satellite Timing And Range.

NAVSUP [US] Acronym for NAVal SUPply Systems Command.

NAYLP [TRG] Abbreviation for National Arab Youth for the Liberation of Palestine, created in 1972 by Muammar el-Qaddafi. The purpose then was the hijacking of a Pan American airplane that resulted in the death of 32 people. Members of the NAYLP have gone on to other things. As an example, Abu Nidal (*See* ABU NIDAL) was a lead-er of the NAYLP and now leads his own terrorist organization.

NBC [B] Designation for NBC radio network.

NBC-S [B] Designation for NBC 'The Source' network.

NBC-T [B] Designation for NBC Talknet.

NBDVS [C3I] Abbreviation for Narrow Band Digital Voice System.

NBN [B] Abbreviation for National Black Network.

NCA [C3I] Abbreviation for National Command Authorities.

NCC [C3I] Abbreviation for Network Control Center.

NCIC [LE] Abbreviation for National Crime Information Center.

NCIC 2000 [LE] Designation for National (FBI) Criminal Information Computer. The database in this system contains a mass of information on almost every human being (foreign and domestic) who resides anywhere in the continental United

States. Background histories (including all known relationships with U.S. citizens) are maintained on many individuals who reside in another country. Data is continually gathered from a variety of sources including banks and business records, school and credit files; even public utilities and postal deliveries. This data is broken down into various categories for cross-reference and individual files are developed and maintained.

NCMC [C3I] Abbreviation for NORAD Cheyenne Mountain Complex.

NCS 1. [GOV] Abbreviation for National Communications System. **2.** [C3I] Abbreviation for Node Center Switch.

NDB [M] Abbreviation for Non-Directional Beacon, a navigational aid.

NDI [C3I] Abbreviation for Non-Developmental item.

NDS [C3I] Abbreviation for Nuclear Detection System.

NDDS [M] Abbreviation for Nuclear Detonation Detection System.

NEACP [US] Abbreviation for National Emergency Airborne Command Post.

need some work [C,G&PS] Slang meaning do you need some cocaine?

needle [C,G&PS] Slang for a hypodermic needle used for drug injection.

needleman [C,G&PS] Slang for a drug addict.

needler 1. [C,G&PS] Slang for an occasional drug user. **2.** [C,G&PS] An expression indicating satisfaction by the use of a needle for drug injections.

neighbor [I] Another branch of an intelligence operation.

Nellis Air Force Base [M] The headquarters for the 4450th Tactical Group assigned to fly the F-117A stealth aircraft. The F-117A's have been observed in flight across the United States. The following frequencies have been associated with F-117A overflights out of Nellis: 124.950 (approach), 279.700 (approach), 126.200 (tower), 324.300 (tower), and 289.400 (departure). Over-

flights of the United States have included the following frequency usage: 142.925, 149.505, 163.5125, 165.0125, 173.4125, 173.4375, 173.5625, 407.4000, 407.5000, and 409.0250.

Nembutal [LE] Brand name of pentobarbital, a controlled substance, a sedative. (*See* QUICK REFERENCE.)

nemmies [C,G&PS] Slang for the barbiturate Nembutal.

NEP [USSR] Abbreviation for New Economic Policy.

NEST 1. [I] Abbreviation for Nuclear Emergency Search Team. NEST is a special technical unit in the U.S. Department of Energy. Its mandate is to respond to any terrorist threat involving nuclear material or the loss of a nuclear device. **2.** [LE] Slang meaning subject's home or office is under surveillance.

network [I] Collectively, the agents making up an intelligence operation.

neutron recorder [A] A device designed to detect plastic explosives in aircraft luggage. (*See* THERMAL NEUTRON RECORDER and TNA.)

NF [C3I] Abbreviation for Noise Figure or Noise Factor.

NFIB [I] Abbreviation for National Foreign Intelligence Board, a group formed to provide the director of the CIA with advice concerning production, review, and coordination of national foreign intelligence.

NFIP [C3I] Abbreviation for National Foreign Intelligence Program.

NIA [I] Abbreviation for National Intelligence Authority, a group that has authority over the CIA.

nickel bag [C,G&PS] Slang for a five-dollar bag of narcotics.

NICP [GOV] Abbreviation for National Inventory Control Point.

NICS [NATO] Abbreviation for The NATO Integrated Communication System.

NICSMA [NATO] Abbreviation for NATO Integrated Communication System Management Agency.

NIE [I] Abbreviation for National Intelligence Estimate, an estimate that has been authorized by the DCI of the capabilities, vulnerabilities, and the probable courses of action of foreign nations, specifically as they relate to their intelligence community and the activities of those groups within and outside a certain country.

nimby [C,G&PS] Slang for barbiturates. (*See* QUICK REFERENCE.)

nines [C,G&PS] In the ongoing street/drug wars, nines are the 9mm handguns popular with the drug dealers because of the heavy fire power these weapons offer. Nines can carry up to 20 bullets.

NIS **1.** [US] Abbreviation for Naval Investigative Service. **2.** [NATO] Abbreviation for NATO Identification System.

NISC [I] Abbreviation for Naval Intelligence Support Center, the agency of the U.S. Navy responsible for creating all levels of technical intelligence. The NISC also operates many related research in highly classified private industry programs that involve scientific and technical intelligence methods, techniques, and systems as well as development programs for new hardware.

nitromite [LE] An easy-to-handle explosive, favored by terrorist and radical groups.

nitrotex [LE] An explosive sometimes used by terrorist and radical groups.

NKGB [USSR] Abbreviation for *Narodnyy Komissariat Gosudarstvennoy Bezopasnosti*, the People's Commissariat of State Security.

NKID [USSR] Abbreviation for *Narodnyy Komissariat Inostrannykh Del*, the People's Commissariat of Foreign Affairs.

NKO [USSR] Abbreviation for *Narodnyy Komissariat Oborony*, the People's Commissariat of Defense.

NKVMF [USSR] Abbreviation for *Narodnyy Komissariat Voyenno-Morskogo Flota*, the People's Commissariat of the Navy.

NKYu [USSR] Abbreviation for *Narodnyy Komissariat Yustitsii*, the People's Commissariat of Justice.

NLEEF [LE] Abbreviation for National Law Enforcement Emergency Frequency. In a national emergency, law enforcement agencies have agreed to coordinate their activities on the 155.475 frequency.

NM [M] Abbreviation for Nautical-Mile; 1 NM = 6080 ft or 1,854 m.

NMCC [C3I] Abbreviation for National Military Command Center or Network Management Command and Control.

NMCS [US] Abbreviation for National Military Command System.

NMP [US] Abbreviation for National Maintenance Point.

NOA [I] Abbreviation for *Nueva Organisacion Anticommunista*. With headquarters in Guatemala, not even the law enforcement agencies of this country know much about this underground organization and its membership except that it appears wide spread and gets some support/assistance from the CIA.

NOAA [GOV] Abbreviation for National Oceanic and Atmospheric Administration. NOAA has a standard broadcasting network across the United States. It supplies weather information on a 24-hour basis. Those weather reports can be found on one of the following broadcast channels:

Channel	Frequency
Channel 1	162.550 MHz
Channel 2	162.400 MHz
Channel 3	162.475 MHz
Channel 4	162.425 MHz
Channel 5	162.450 MHz
Channel 6	162.500 MHz
Channel 7	162.525 MHz
Channel 8	161.650 MHz
Channel 9	161.775 MHz
Channel 10	161.400 MHz
Military	163.275 MHz
Military	167.905 MHz
Military	173.025 MHz

NOCS [HRU] Abbreviation for *Nucleo Operativo Centrale di Sicurezza*, the Italian night assault hostage rescue unit that has specialized in antiterrorism acts against the Red Brigade. The NOCS trains and is headquartered at the Abbosanta Police Training Center on the island of Sardinia.

Noctec [LE] Brand name of chloral hydrate, a controlled substance that is a sedative. (*See* QUICK REFERENCE.)

NOD **1.** [M] Abbreviation for Night Observation Device. **2.** [C,G&PS] Slang meaning to sleep after an injection of heroin.

nod, on the [C,G&PS] Slang for the sleeplike condition that results from heroin usage.

NOI [C3I] Abbreviation for Notice of Inquiry.

NOIC [M] Abbreviation for Navy Operational Intelligence Center.

noisemaker [I] A transmitter used for mobile trailing of a subject or vehicle. It is a "bumber beeper" or an inside-the-vehicle surveillance radio.

no joy [US] Naval aviation voice brevity code meaning "I am unsuccessful."

Noludar Brand name of a controlled substance that is a sedative. (*See* QUICK REFERENCE.)

NORAD [C3I] Shortened form of NORth American Aerospace Defense Command. Its headquarters are located in Colorado.

NORSAR [GOV] Acronym for NORwegian Seismic ARray, which is used for the detection of earthquakes and nuclear explosions in Europe.

norteamericano [D] A person born and raised in the United States but living and working in Mexico while retaining his U.S. citizenship.

nose [C,G&PS] Slang for a handgun silencer.

nose candy [C,G&PS] Slang for cocaine. (*See* QUICK REFERENCE.)

notional [I] Fictitious, as applied to fictitious individuals, a false source of information, or an organization that simply does not exist beyond the name. A notional is often the basis for a police sting operation and a business (front) created by and for the police or intelligence agency as an illusion representing what is expected to be seen. The term also can relate to a (real) business that works with the police.

November [A,LE,MIL] Designation for the letter *N*.

NPA [LE] Abbreviation for The National Police Agency of Japan. The NPA is responsible for the administration and control of all Japanese police officers and law enforcement agencies.

NPG [GOV] Abbreviation for Nuclear Planning Group.

NPIC Abbreviation for National Photographic Interpretation Center.

NPR [B] Abbreviation for National Public Radio.

NREC Abbreviation for National Reconnaissance Executive Committee.

NRL [M] Abbreviation for Naval Research Laboratory.

NRO Abbreviation for National Reconnaissance Office.

NRPCs Abbreviation for Naval Regional (computer) Processing Centers.

NRZ [C3I] Abbreviation for Non-Return to Zero.

NSA [C3I] Abbreviation for National Security Agency, the most secret U.S. intelligence agency. The NSA is responsible for all U.S. communications security activities, including the development of codes and ciphers, all U.S. cryptographic and signal (electronic) intercepts, as well as computer security known as Tempest. (*See* TEMPEST.)

NSC [GOV] Abbreviation for National Security Council. The NSC advises the President of the United States on all matters that relate to national security with respect to the integration of domestic, foreign, and military policies.

NSCID [GOV] Abbreviation for National Security Council Intelligence Directive. Intelligence guidelines are developed and issued by the NSC to all U.S. intelligence agencies. NSCID's usually are augmented by more specific director of central intelligence directives and/or implemented by executive orders issued by the President of the United States.

NSFO [US] Abbreviation for Navy Special Fuel Oil.

NSIA [C3I] Abbreviation for National Security Industrial Association.

NSP [NASA] Abbreviation for Navy Space Project.

NSU   [LE] Abbreviation for Neighborhood Stabilization Unit.

NTDS   [US] Abbreviation for Naval Tactical Data System.

NTIA   [C3I] Abbreviation for National Telecommunications and Information Administration.

NTM   [GOV] Abbreviation for National Technical Means.

NTPF   [M] Abbreviation for Near-Term Prepositioning Forces.

NTS   [USSR] Designation for Narodno-Trudovoy Soyuz Rossiyskikh Solidaristov, the Popular Labor Alliance of Russian Solidarists.

number   **1.** [C,G&PS] Slang for a marijuana cigarette. **2.** [C,G&PS] Slang for a drug/narcotics run; to buy or sell. **3.** [C,G&PS] Slang for a unique experience from the use of narcotics or drugs.

number one   [LE] Slang for the prime individual, usually in a group of people, who is under surveillance.

number two   [LE] Slang for the second person in company with a prime suspect.

number three   [LE] Slang for a person set apart by some distance from a prime suspect.

number four   [LE] Slang for an innocent person at a scene under surveillance.

number five   [LE] Slang for referring to the No. 5 capsules containing five milligrams of some illegal substance.

Numorphan   [LE] Brand name of a controlled substance that is a narcotic analgesic. (*See* QUICK REFERENCE.)

NUSC   [US] Abbreviation for Naval Underwater Systems Center.

NVEOL   [US] Abbreviation for Night Vision and Electro-Optics Laboratories.

NX   Abbreviation for the news media.

O [C,G&PS] Abbreviation for opium. (*See* QUICK REFERENCE.)

O or the O [LE] Slang for the office of a (law) enforcement officer or an individual who is a criminal suspect.

OARS [NATO] Designation for Ocean Reconnaissance Submarine.

OAS **1.** [US] Abbreviation for Offensive Avionics Systems. **2.** [TRG] Abbreviation for *Organisation de l'Armee Secrete*, a group of terrorists active in Europe in the late 1960s. While it is believed the main body is defunct, the DGSE (Direction Generale de la Securite Exterieure) and Interpol maintain the names of known former members on a watch list, and they are occasionally put under some level of surveillance.

O.A.S. [GOV] Abbreviation for Organization of American States.

OASD [US] Abbreviation for Office of Assistant Secretary of Defense.

OASIS **1.** [US] Acronym for Operational Applications of Special Intelligence Systems. **2.** [NASA] Acronym for Oceanic and Atmospheric Scientific Information System.

OAST [NASA] Abbreviation for Office of Aeronautics and Space Technology.

OAU Abbreviation for Organization for African Unity.

OB [US] Abbreviation for Operations Base.

OBC [NASA] Abbreviation for Optical Bar Camera, a camera used in satellites for side-to-side (horizon-to-horizon) panoramic photography.

OBE [US] Abbreviation for Overcome, or Overtaken, By Events.

oblique [NASA] Of or referring to photographic or radar imagery that is taken at an angle. In satellite surveillance, such imagery could be ahead or behind the flight path, or to the left or right.

OBS [NASA] Abbreviation for Operational Bioinstrumentation System.

Ocean [A,LE,MIL] Designation for the letter *O*.

OCCB [LE] Abbreviation for Organized Crime Control Bureau.

OCCIS [US] Abbreviation for Operations Control and Command Information System.

OCCULT [US] Acronym for Optical Covert Communications Using Laser Transceivers.

OCE **1.** [US] Abbreviation for Office Chief of Engineers. **2.** [NASA] Abbreviation for Ocean Color Experiment.

OCPW [M] Abbreviation for Office of Chief of Psychological Warfare.

OCS [US] Abbreviation for Officer Candidate School.

OCU [M] Abbreviation for Operational Conversion Unit. This is where a military pilot learns to fly the type of aircraft he/she is to operate. One interesting note is that only about 1,600 pilots are qualified in the U.S. to fly the B-52's of the Strategic Air Command (SAC).

OD **1.** [C,G&PS] Abbreviation meaning to overdose. **2.** [C,G&PS] Designation for an overdose of some narcotic, usually heroin. **3.** [US] Abbreviation for Officer of the Day (Army/Air Force). **4.** [US] Abbreviation for Officer of the Deck (Navy/Marines/Coast Guard). **5.** [NASA] Abbreviation for Operational (communications) Downlink.

ODA [M] Abbreviation for Operational Detachment A, the basis Army Special Forces operational unit.

ODD [M] Abbreviation for Operational Detachment Delta, also known as Delta Force, the primary antiterrorist unit in the U.S. military.

OEAS [NASA] Abbreviation for Outboard Engine Cutoff.

OEM [GOV] Abbreviation for Office of Emergency Management.

OEP [GOV] Abbreviation for Office of Emergency Preparedness.

OES [NASA] Abbreviation for Orbiter Emergency Site.

OF [US] Designation for operations evaluation group.

O/F [NASA] Abbreviation for Oxidizer-to-Fuel ratio.

OFCO [I] Shortened form of the United States Army's OFfensive COunterintelligence Unit for covert operations. The unit usually is used against some activity of the Soviet Union.

off 1. [C,G&PS] Slang meaning to dispose of; get rid of someone or something. 2. [US] Slang for a group of officers.

offed [C,G&PS] A slang term in the drug/narcotic trade meaning to be killed or gotten rid of.

OFP [US] Abbreviation for Operational Flight Program.

OFT 1. [US] Abbreviation for Operational Flight Trainer. 2. [NASA] Abbreviation for Orbital Flight Test.

OG [M] Abbreviation for Operational Group (Command).

OGE [M] Abbreviation for Out-of-Ground Effect. This refers to the performance of a helicopter.

OGMT [NASA] Abbreviation for Orbiter Greenwich Mean Time.

OGPU [USSR] Abbreviation for *Obyedinennoye Gosudarstvennoye Politicheskoye Upravleiye*, the United State Political Directorate.

OGs [C,G&PS] Abbreviation for the Old Gangsters, leaders of gangs, sometimes the founders of a gang.

OHC [NASA] Abbreviation for Onboard Hard Copier, a FAX copier.

OIKB [HRU] Abbreviation for *Ozel Intihar Kommando Boluga*, also known as the Jandara Suicide Commandos of Turkey. The responsibility of these Turkish hostage rescuers is to give everything—even their lives—to stop terrorist activities in Turkey.

OIL Specialty code for oil field accident.

OJCS [C3I] Abbreviation for Organization of the Joint Chiefs of Staff.

OJE Background code for On-the-Job Experience, referring to an independent investigator or law office investigator.

old gangsters [LE] Slang for the leaders of a gang, often its founders as well. Law enforcement agencies have discovered that old gangsters sometimes change their ways and want to assist the police and community in reducing the criminal activities of younger criminal elements.

OM [D] Designation for adult male.

O&M [M] Abbreviation for Operations and Maintenance.

OMB [C3I] Abbreviation for Office of Management and Budget.

Omega 7 [TRG] An anti-Castro group that has more than a dozen bases of operations in southern and eastern states including Florida and New York. Although the group is anti-Castro in make-up, it is not considered by terrorism experts to be pro-American. This terrorist group has been very active in the New York area and has carried out bombings at pro-Cuban facilities.

omen [US] Code name for ballistic submarine communications project.

OMET [NASA] Abbreviation for Orbiter Mission Elapsed Time.

OMI [LE] Abbreviation for Our Main Interest.

OMJ [C3I] Abbreviation for Ortho-Mode Junction.

OMT [C3I] Abbreviation for Ortho-Mode Transducer.

O-NAV [NASA] Acronym for Onboard NAVigation.

one-time [C,G&PS] Slang term for a warning to police to "stay away" or "don't bother us" given by a gang.

onetime pad [I] A simple encoding method using five-letter groups (used only once) for encryption.

ONI [US] Abbreviation for Office of Naval Intelligence.

on ice [C,G&PS] Of or referring to someone who is in jail or prison.

Onkruit [TRG] A Dutch terrorist group headquartered in Amsterdam and involved in anti-NATO activities that include the sabotage of NATO aircraft. The group tends to try to subvert military personnel into assisting them in return for sexual favors. This has failed in the majority of instances because sex is so open (and available) in Holland. This group gives every appearance of having an internal conflict with leadership and limited funds from the membership to support the cause.

on target [US] In an air intercept, on target is a code meaning, "My fire control director(s) and/or system(s) have acquired the indicated contact and is (are) tracking successfully."

on the beam [C,G&PS] Slang for someone on drugs expressing that he feels very good.

on the block [C,G&PS] Slang for on the street.

on the bricks [C,G&PS] Slang meaning out of jail or prison.

on the job [LE] Of or referring to a police officer who is out of uniform but is working on an assignment.

on the nod [C,G&PS] Slang meaning sleepy from the effects of drugs.

on the perch [C,G&PS] Slang for being very high on some narcotic.

on the scene [LE] Slang meaning to be at a specific location.

on the set [LE] Slang for the location of a business or activity.

one-armed bandit [LE] Slang for a slot machine.

ONMM [C3I] Abbreviation for On-Board Microwave Modem.

ONR [US] Abbreviation for Office of Naval Research.

ONUC [GOV] Designation for United Nations Operations in the Congo.

ONUCA [GOV] Designation for United Nations Observer Groups in Central America.

ONUVEN [GOV] Designation for United Nations Observers for the Verification of the Elections in Nicaragua.

OO [USSR] Abbreviation for *Osobye Otdely*, the Special Department of the KGB—Military Counterintelligence; *Okhra nnoye Otdeleniye Otdeleniye* (tsarist security divisions).

OOD [US] Abbreviation for Officer Of the Deck (Navy).

OOL [NASA] Abbreviation for Out of Orbit (satellite) Launch.

OOS [NASA] Abbreviation for On-Orbit Station.

ooze [C,G&PS] Slang for any automatic weapon. The term originates from uzi.

OP [US] Abbreviation for Observation Post.

OPC [GOV] Abbreviation for Office of Policy Coordination.

open code [I] A seemingly innocuous message that, by some prearrangement or signal, actually will convey a different message. An open code might be: "We expect the weather along the coast to be very cold after midnight." That precise statement could actually mean: "Our submarine will be on the lookout for your signal at 1:00 P.M. sharp off the North Coast Point." Open codes are all types of communication where the esoteric references are only known to those who are involved.

open up [C,G&PS] The term used to indicate gambling activities are increasing.

Operation Cooperation [LE] Name of a cooperative venture of the drug authorities of Mexico and agencies of the U.S. government designed to stop illegal narcotic traffic between the two countries. The initial plan for operation cooperation was called operation intercept, which was a miserable failure. U.S. officials agreed in operation cooperation to provide the Mexican government with airplanes, money, men, and materials to fight drug dealers and marijuana growers in its own country. Much of the money, weapons, and hardware for the project disappeared in Mexico. (*See* OPERATION INTERCEPT.)

Operation Intercept [LE] Name of a border program between the United States and Mexico designed to stop illegal narcotics and drugs flowing into the U.S. The planned method for the success of Operation Intercept was to stop and inspect every individual and vehicle crossing into the U.S. at authorized border stations. On the first weekend that the plan was operated, traffic was backed up for more than six hours at the San Isidro border station located between San Diego, and Tijuana. Hardly any drugs were found and the operation was dropped after one month. (*See* OPERATION COOPERATION.)

OPF   [NASA] Abbreviation for Orbiter Processing Facility.

opium   [LE] Name of a controlled substance that is a narcotic. (*See* QUICK REFERENCE.)

OPP   [C3I] Abbreviation for Office of Plans and Policy.

OPSEC   [I] Abbreviation for OPerations SECurity, the term that is used to indicate the use of some form of deception to protect the secrecy of an operation.

OPTINT   [I] Abbreviation for Optical Intelligence.

OR   [US] Abbreviation for Operations Research.

Orange   [C,G&PS] Slang for amphetamines. (*See* QUICK REFERENCE.)

orange forces   [NATO] Designation for those forces that are used in the role of the enemy during NATO exercises.

orange sour   [US] A code in an air intercept meaning, "The weather is unsuitable for aircraft mission."

orange sunshine   [C,G&PS] Slang for LSD. (*See* QUICK REFERENCE.)

orange sweet   [US] A code in an air intercept meaning, "The weather is suitable for an aircraft mission."

order of battle   [M] Specific information regarding strength, command structure, identity, and disposition of personnel units, and equipment of any military force.

ORG   Specialty code for organized crime.

O&S   [US] Abbreviation for Operations & Support.

OSA   [US] Abbreviation for Operational Support Airlift.

Osasto Karhu   [HRU] The Finnish antiterrorist and hostage rescue unit of the Helsinki Mobile Police.

OSCAR   [US] Acronym for Optical Submarine Communications by Aerospace Relay.

Oscar   [A,LE,MIL] Designation for the letter *O*.

OSD   [C3I] Abbreviation for Office of the Secretary of Defense.

OSHA   [C3I] Abbreviation for Occupational Safety and Health Administration.

OSIS   [M] Abbreviation for Ocean Surveillance Information System.

OSO   [US] Abbreviation for Office of Sigint Operations.

OSSA   [NASA] Abbreviation for Office of Space Science and Applications.

OST   [C3I] Abbreviation for Office of Science and Technology.

OSTA   [NASA] Abbreviation for Office of Space and Terrestrial Application(s).

OSTDS   [NASA] Abbreviation for Office of Space Tracking and Data Systems.

OSTS   [NASA] Abbreviation for Office of Space Transportation Systems.

OT   [NASA] Abbreviation for Optical Tracker.

OTA   [C3I] Abbreviation for Office of Technology Assessment.

OT&E   [US] Abbreviation for Operational Test & Evaluation.

OTH   [US] Abbreviation for Over-The-Horizon radar system.

OTH-B   [C3I] Abbreviation for Over-The-Horizon Backscatter (radar).

OTH-R   [C3I] Abbreviation for Over-The-Horizon Radar.

OU   [LE] Abbreviation for Operations Unit.

ounce   [C,G&PS] Slang for an ounce of cocaine or marijuana.

our boy   **1.** [LE] Slang for an individual who is under primary surveillance. **2.** [LE] Slang for an individual, usually an informant, who is involved in an activity that is under surveillance.

our friend   [LE] Slang for an individual, usually an informant, who is somehow involved in an activity that is under surveillance.

our guy   [LE] Slang for a criminal informant.

our interest   [LE] Slang for a primary individual under surveillance.

our main interest   [LE] Slang for a subject who is under surveillance.

our man   1. [LE] Slang for a law enforcement officer. 2. [LE] Slang for an individual under surveillance. 3. [LE] Slang for an individual who works with law enforcement but who is not a police officer.

OUSD   [M] Abbreviation for Office of the Under Secretary of Defense.

OUSDRE   [C3I] Abbreviation for Office of Under Secretary of Defense for Research and Engineering.

out of it   1. [LE] Slang for an individual who is not a drug addict. 2. [LE] Slang for an individual who is strung out on drugs.

out of pocket   [LE] Slang term referring to someone who is no longer being kept under surveillance.

out of this world   [LE] Slang for someone who is under the influence of drugs or narcotics.

outfit   [LE] Slang for the hardware used by an individual for the injection of narcotics.

outside agency   Slang for the news media.

over-driving headlights   [LE] A term used by law enforcement traffic investigators meaning that a driver at the scene of an accident was traveling so fast that it was impossible to stop within the distance reached by the headlight beams.

oversalt   [US] The code name used to identify the peripheral electronic intelligence missions of the Air Force in the Far East.

overt   [I] Of or referring to the legal gathering of information by any means available.

OVS   [NASA] Abbreviation for Operational Voice System.

OW   [NASA] Abbreviation for Optical (photographic) Window.

OWD   [NASA] Abbreviation for One-Way Doppler.

OWDE   [NASA] Abbreviation for One-Way Doppler Extraction.

OWRL   [I] Abbreviation for One-Way Radio Link. The purpose of a OWRL is so an intelligence agent—at a scheduled time—can receive a radio transmission without the need for bulky equipment. This type of hardware usually is used in a surveillance operation where the need to respond or talkback is not necessary.

oxcart   [I] Code name for the SR-71 surveillance aircraft flying parallel to the borders of the Soviet Union. (*See* BLACKBIRD and SR-71.) Intelligence sources indicate that the SR-71 overflight program will be phased out during the early 1990s. Military satellites will continue surveillance programs near Soviet borders and the use of covert aircraft operations will come into play whenever necessary, although the SR-71 program is formally ended. Conditions have always dictate that a high-speed, high-altitude surveillance aircraft can get better pictures than a high-flying satellite.

oz   [LE] Term for an ounce of any drug.

P

P 1. [M] Abbreviation for Power. 2. [LE] Abbreviation for Paging.

P3I [M] Designation for Pre-Planned Product Improvement.

PACCS [US] Abbreviation for Post Attack Command and Control System.

pack [C,G&PS] Slang for a container of marijuana cigarettes.

package 1. [LE] Slang for an object that is under surveillance. 2. [LE] Slang for a suspect that is in custody. 3. [C,G&PS] Slang for morphine. (*See* QUICK REFERENCE.)

PACOSS [C3I] Abbreviation for Passive and Active Control Of Space Structures.

pad [LE] Slang for a house, apartment, or residence.

pago pago [C,G&PS] Slang for marijuana grown in a city environment, rather than in Mexico or in mountain country.

paint [US] Naval aviation voice brevity code meaning radar indication.

PAL [C3I] Abbreviation for Phase Alternate Line.

PAMA [C3I] Abbreviation for Pre-assigned Multiple Access.

Panama cut [C,G&PS] Slang for very good quality or excellent grade or marijuana.

Panama red [C,G&PS] Slang for red marijuana imported from Panama. It often is referred to as "red" and is known for its high quality.

Panama reed [C,G&PS] Slang for red marijuana imported from Panama.

panic [C,G&PS] Slang for a shortage of narcotics.

papa [M] Slang for scrambled communications.

Papa/Paul [A,LE,MIL] Designation for the letter *P*.

papaver somniferum [LE] Scientific name for the opium poppy, sometimes called "PS" by drug enforcement agents.

paper [LE] Slang for narcotics or drugs with a high street value hidden in a container and discovered by drug enforcement agents.

paper bag [C,G&PS] Slang for a paper bag or package of narcotics.

paper hanger [LE] Slang for an individual who write bank checks with no money in his bank account.

paper mill [I] Slang for a fabricator (*See* FABRICATOR) who provides false information on a consistent basis and in some volume to a law enforcement or intelligence group.

papers [C,G&PS] Slang for the paper used to roll a marijuana cigarette.

paradise [C,G&PS] Slang for cocaine. (*See* QUICK REFERENCE.)

PARAMP [C3I] Acronym for PARametric AMPlifier.

PARCS [C3I] Shortened form of Perimeter Acquisition Radar Attack Characterization System.

Parest [LE] Brand name of methaqaulone, a controlled substance, a sedative. (*See* QUICK REFERENCE.)

parkhill [US] Code name for portable secure speech equipment.

paroles [I] Key word intelligence agents use for mutual identification among themselves.

parrot [US] Naval aviation voice brevity code meaning a transponder.

Pasdaran [TRG] Iranian Revolutionary Guards (IRG).

pass [C,G&PS] To transfer money or narcotics.

passers [LE] Slang for shaved dice that favor the shooter.

PAT [M] Abbreviation for Passive Angle Track.

pat down [LE] The body search of a suspect conducted by a police officer during the arrest process.

PATS [C3I] Abbreviation for Precision Automatic Tracking System.

pathfinder [M] Name of a computer-generated night-vision system designed to mount in aircraft (presently only military configuration) that uses Forward-Looking Infrared (*See* FLIR) to create an image of the ground that appears on the wind screen display as if it were daylight. With the raster of the system turned off, Pathfinder is able to produce an enhanced image of objects that reflect infrared heat, (such as a tank) lock in the weapon system of the aircraft and destroy the target. Pathfinder requires no special helmet or goggles and creates the image from a FLIR pod mounted on the aircraft in company with the weapon system. Pathfinder allows an aircraft like the F-16 to fly very fast and at very low altitude with a sharp, clear, computer-generated real-time black and white image directly in front of the pilot, who can clearly define something as small as the heat generated by ground troops hidden in the darkness. Pathfinder is also used by U.S. Customs and drug enforcement.

pavement artist [LE] Slang for smooth operator or con artist.

pave paws [M] Slang for phased-array radars.

p-band [NASA] Designation for 225 to 390 MCS.

PBW [C3I] Abbreviation for Particle Beam Weapon.

PC 1. Specialty code for photocopy service. 2. [LE] Abbreviation for Penal Code.

PCA [C3I] Abbreviation for Physical Configuration Audit.

PC evidence [LE] Shortened form of Penal Code Evidence against a suspect that supports the foundation for an arrest.

PCM [C3I] Abbreviation for Pulse Code Modulation.

PCP [LE] Abbreviation for PhenCycladine Phosphate, a tranquilizer used by professional veterinarians. It is best defined as an anesthesia. It has hallucinogenic properties when used by people. Produced by a home chemist as a synthetic, PCP is rocklike or crystalline in form. In its purest synthetic form, it is off-white, but with additives used to reduce its potency, it can appear in a variety of colors, ranging from yellow to dark brown. PCP can be smoked, but usually is taken orally or by injection. (*See* QUICK REFERENCE.)

PD [I] Abbreviation for Probability of Detection.

PDA [C3I] Abbreviation for Preliminary Design Activities.

PDF [M] Abbreviation for Probability Density Function.

PDFLP [TRG] Abbreviation for Popular Democratic Front for the Liberation of Palestine, a terrorist/radical group supported in great part by funds from friends in the United States.

PDL [C3I] Shortened form of Position Location and Reporting System.

PDN [C3I] Abbreviation for Power Dividing Network.

PDO Background code for Public Defender's Office.

PDSS [C3I] Abbreviation for Post Deployment Software Support.

PE Specialty code for psychological stress evaluation.

peace 1. [C,G&PS] Slang for a handgun (misspelled as it is sometimes written). 2. [C,G&PS] Slang for PCP. (*See* QUICK REFERENCE.)

peace pill [C,G&PS] Slang for PCP. (*See* QUICK REFERENCE.)

peaches [C,G&PS] Slang for benzedrine tablets.

peak [C,G&PS] The high point experienced in a drug trip.

peanut butter [C,G&PS] Slang for heroin. (*See* QUICK REFERENCE.)

peanuts [C,G&PS] Slang for barbiturates in pill form.

peddler [C,G&PS] A supplier of narcotics.

peel & punch [LE] Slang for an entry technique used to open a safe. The facing side of the safe is penetrated using a chisel and hammer. The face of the safe is peeled back exposing the concrete liner. The liner is punched out allowing the contents inside the safe to be removed. More modern safes have an inner steel door making further entry even more difficult.

peg   [LE] Slang for a law enforcement officer.

pen   [LE] A small modified flare gun or 22/25 caliber pen gun. This type of weapon is used for quick close-in killing and usually is fired into the brain of the target by placing the tip of the barrel at the base of the skull next to the ear lobe and pointed upward. The kill is quick and almost bloodless.

penetration   **1.** [I] The recruitment of intelligence agents or the planting of agents within a targeted organization. **2.** [I] The methods used in the installation of electronic or technical monitoring devices.

pen yuen   [C,G&PS] Slang for opium. (*See* QUICK REFERENCE.)

pep pills   [C,G&PS] Slang for amphetamines. (*See* QUICK REFERENCE.)

peps   [C,G&PS] Slang for amphetamines. (*See* QUICK REFERENCE.)

per   [LE] Slang for a medical prescription.

Percodan   [LE] Brand name of a controlled substance, a narcotic. (*See* QUICK REFERENCE.)

perimeter surveillance   The placement of personnel who are conducting surveillance at a variety of locations that encircle the area being watched.

Persian heroin   [LE] A powerful synthetic heroin, its chemical name is 3-methylfentanyl and is several times more powerful than heroin. Also known as China White. (*See* CHINA WHITE.)

PET   [LE] Abbreviation for *Politiets Efterretningstjeneste*, the Danish State Police Intelligence Service.

peyote   [LE] Mescaline, a controlled substance, that is an hallucinogen. (*See* QUICK REFERENCE.)

PFA   [LE] Abbreviation for Probability of False Alarm.

PFIAB   [US] Abbreviation for President's Foreign Intelligence Advisory Board.

PFLP   [TRG] Abbreviation for The Popular Front for the Liberation of Palestine, a terrorist group formed in 1967 and almost as busy today as then. The PFLP has many close associations with terrorist groups in the Western world, has the support of Libya and receives funding and weapons from the Soviet Union. The PFLP is directed by Dr. G. Habash.

PFLP-GC   [TRG] Abbreviation for Popular Front for the Liberation of Palestine—General Command, Ahmed Jibril's Syrian controlled extremist terrorist group connected to aircraft bombings in Europe. According to intelligence sources, this group has received complex bomb-building instructions from agents of the Rumanian foreign intelligence service, known as the DIE from its name in Rumanian, Departmentul de Informatii Externe. DIE is the Rumanian arm of the Soviet KGB.

p-funk   [LE] Slang for a synthetic form of heroin produced in South America, also known as bosco.

PG   Specialty code for polygraph.

PGM   **1.** [GOV] Abbreviation for Program. **2.** [M] Abbreviation for Precision-Guided Munitions.

PH   **1.** Specialty code for photography. **2.** [M] Abbreviation for Probability of Hit.

phennies   [C,G&PS] Slang for barbiturates.

PHO   Specialty code for photography, forensic.

phonetic alphabet and numerals   Use the standard phonetic alphabet when it is necessary to identify any letter of the alphabet. This alphabet is listed in TABLE P-1. To distinguish numerals from words similarly pronounced, the proword figures usually is used preceding such numbers. When numerals are transmitted, the rules in TABLE P-1 for their pronunciation are always observed. Numbers are transmitted digit by digit except that exact multiples of thousands are spoken as such. However, there are special cases, such as Anti-Air Warfare reporting procedures when normal pronunciation of numerals is prescribed and this rule does not apply. For example, 17 would be seventeen. The decimal point is spoken as "DAY-SEE-MAL." *Example:* 123.4 is

Table P-1. Phonetic Alphabet and Numerals

Alphabet

Letter	Phonetic	Spoken As
A	Alfa	AL FAH
B	Bravo	BRAH VOH
C	Charlie	CHAR LEE or SHAR LEE
D	Delta	DELL TAH
E	Echo	ECK OH
F	Foxtrot	FOKS TROT
G	Golf	GOLF
H	Hotel	HOH TELL
I	India	IN DEE AH
J	Juliett	JEW LEE ETT
K	Kilo	KEY LOH
L	Lima	LEE MAH
M	Mike	MIKE
N	November	NO VEM BER
O	Oscar	OSS CAH
P	Papa	PAH PAH
Q	Quebec	KEH BECK
R	Romeo	ROW ME OH
S	Sierra	SEE AIR RAH
T	Tango	TANG GO
U	Uniform	YOU NEE FORM or OO NEE FORM
V	Victor	VIK TAH
W	Whiskey	WISS KEY
X	X-ray	ECKS RAY
Y	Yankee	YANG KEY
Z	Zulu	ZOO LOO

Numerals

Numeral	Spoken As
0	ZE-RO
1	WUN
2	TOO
3	TREE
4	FOW-ER
5	FIFE
6	SIX
7	SEV-EN
8	AIT
9	NIN-ER
44	FOW-ER FOW-ER
90	NIN-ER ZERO
136	WUN TREE SIX
500	FIFE ZE-RO ZE-RO
1478	WUN FOW-ER SEV-EN AIT
7000	SEV-EN TOU-SAND
16000	WUN SIX TOU-SAND
812681	AIT WUN TOO SIX AIT WUN

spoken as "WUN TOO TREE DAY-SEE-MAL FOW-ER." Dates are spoken with the months in full for example: "20 August" is spoken as "TOO ZE-RO AUGUST."

PHOTINT [I] Acronym for PHOTographic INTelligence, specific visual information or intelligence data that is developed and derived from photographs and their interpretation. PHOTINT is obtained from aircraft, satellites, and ground cameras.

PI 1. [M] Abbreviation for Photo Interpreter. 2. [I] Abbreviation for Positive Intelligence, intelligence data that has been interpreted and found to be true (positive). 3. Abbreviation for Private Investigator.

picked [LE] Slang meaning to be arrested.

pickle factory Insider name for the CIA.

pick up a case [LE] Slang meaning to develop a new informant.

piece 1.[C,G&PS] Slang for a firearm. 2. [C,G&PS] Slang for one ounce of heroin. 3. [C,G&PS] Slang for a young woman.

pig [C,G&PS] Slang for police/law enforcement officer.

pigeon 1. [LE] Slang for the subject who is under surveillance. 2. [LE] Slang for an individual who is the target of a criminal or criminal activity.

pigeons [US] Naval aviation voice brevity code meaning bearing and distance.

pigeon drop [LE] Slang for a confidence (con) game.

pilgrim [US] Code name for secure communications development program.

pill head [C,G&PS] Slang for an individual addicted to drugs in pill-form.

pin 1. [C,G&PS] Slang for a machine-made marijuana cigarette. 2. Specialty code for Personal Injury.

ping pong [US] Naval aviation voice brevity code meaning data exchange.

pin shot [C,G&PS] Slang for the injection of drugs into a vein without the benefit of a needle.

The skin is cut and the vein is punctured. A fountain-pen filler or medicine dropper is used to induce drugs.

pink chicks [C,G&PS] Slang for barbiturates.

pinks [C,G&PS] Slang for barbiturates.

pink ladies [C,G&PS] Slang for barbiturates.

PINS [M] Acronym for Palletized Inertial Navigation System.

pipe [C,G&PS] Slang for a large vein or artery in the human body.

PIRA [TRG] Abbreviation for Provisional Irish Republican Army. This Marxist faction of the Irish Republican Army (IRA) has conducted many hijackings, assassinations and bombings in England and Northern Ireland.

pirate tap [LE] Slang for an illegal telephone or line tap.

pitch [LE] To persuade a person to gather facts for a law enforcement or intelligence agency. If the individual is approached without prior cultivation, the process is known as a *cold pitch*.

PK [I] Abbreviation for Probability of Kill.

PL Specialty code for Product Liability.

Placidyl [LE] Brand name of ethchlorvynol, a sedative. (*See* QUICK REFERENCE.)

plain text [I] Unencrypted Communications.

plank [LE] A bridge or roadway overpass.

plant [LE] Slang for a hidden place where narcotics are kept.

play around [LE] Slang for an irregular narcotics habit. For example, "She tends to play around."

players [C,G&PS] Slang for dope dealers who are fancy dressers, have expensive cars, gold chains, women, and excessive amounts of pocket money.

play the point [C,G&PS] Slang meaning to act as a lookout for the police.

playmates [US] Naval aviation voice brevity code meaning aircraft involved in the same mission.

pleasure pebbles [C,G&PS] Slang for rock cocaine.

PLL [C3I] Abbreviation for Phase-Locked Loop.

PLM DELTA [G] Shortened form of Personnel Limited Movement Delta, the highest level of restriction placed on United States citizens (military, civilian, and all members of the U.S. government representing the needs of an embassy) located in a foreign country during a time of stress between the U.S. and that country, or when the government of a country is in a state of rebellion. PLM delta means stay inside your residence and be ready to evacuate immediately if so ordered.

PLO [I] Abbreviation for The Palestine Liberation Organization, the umbrella for at least eight Palestinian guerrilla/terrorist groups. It is governed by an executive committee made up of the factional leaders and other Palestinians. Policy decisions are put before the 450-member Palestine National Council for approval. Yasser Arafat, leader of the largest guerrilla group, Fatah, has been PLO chairman since 1969. He has said he cannot control all of the factions. Three major groups make up more than 80 percent of the PLO's strength:

- Fatah Founded by Arafat in 1959, it is politically moderate and has been based in Baghdad in recent years.

- The Popular Front for the Liberation of Palestine Formed in 1967 by Dr. George Habash, it follows a Marxist-Leninist ideology. It is headquartered in Damascus.

- Democratic Front for the Liberation of Palestine The leader, Nayef Hawatmeh, set up the group after he split with Habash's Popular Front in 1969. It has close ties to Moscow and is based in Damascus.

Other PLO Organizations follow:

- Popular Front for the Liberation of Palestine General Command Led by former Syrian army Captain Ahmed Jibril, it split with Habash's group to form a more radical group with

Syrian and Libyan backing. It operates out of Damascus.

- Palestine Liberation Front   Split from Jibril's group in 1977. One leader is Mohammed Abbas, also known as Abul Abbas, who was sentenced in absentia by an Italian court to life in prison for his role in plotting the 1985 hijacking of the Achille Lauro cruise ship during which a U.S. passenger was killed.

- Arab Liberation Front   Formed in 1969 by Abdel Rahim Ahmed and is controlled by Iraq. It is headquartered in Baghdad.

- Saiqa   This Syrian-controlled faction was formed in 1967. This group has kept very much to itself, and is suspected of a variety of terrorist acts.

- Popular Struggle Front   A small, radical group established in 1967 by Samir Goshen, a lawyer, and is headquartered in Damascus.

Groups Ostracized by the PLO are as follows:

- Fatah Revolutionary Council   A splinter terrorist group led by Abu Nidal, whose real name is Sabry al-Banna. He split with Arafat in 1972 and formed the group in 1976.

- Fatah Uprising   Led by Colonel Saeed Musa, or Abu Musa. These two individuals headed the Syrian-supported groups that rebelled against Arafat in 1983. The Fatah Uprising is based in Damascus.

- Fatah Corrective Movement   Based in Amman, Jordan. Atallah Atallah, the former Arafat security officer, leads the small group that seeks to oust Arafat as PLO chairman.

PLRS   [C3I] Abbreviation for Position, Location, and Reporting System.

PLSS   [C3I] Abbreviation for Precision Location Strike System.

Plug   [US] Naval aviation voice brevity code mean-

ing to make a connection with an aerial (tanker) refueler.

plumbing   [I] The assets or services used to support any clandestine operation. Plumbing could include surveillance teams, unaccountable funds, safe houses, and investigative research and work records for people who never existed.

PM   **1.** Specialty code for Professional Malpractice. **2.** [C3I] Abbreviation for Phase Modulation.

PMA   [C,G&PS] Designation for a chemical hallucinogen that is injected and available in capsule form. It is usually white, with the lower quality available in pink or light tan. PMA is an easily available street drug that increases heart rate and acts much like LSD. Excessive usage over a short term can cause convulsions, coma, and death without any physical warning. The chemical name for PMA is paramethoxyamphetamine.

PMD   [LE] Abbreviation for Public Morals Division.

PMR   [C3I] Abbreviation for Program Management Review.

PMRT   [C3I] Abbreviation for Preprogram Management Responsibility Transfer.

PNIE   [I] Abbreviation for Priority National Intelligence Estimate.

PNIO   [I] Abbreviation for Priority National Intelligence Objective.

pocket litter   [I] Slang for misleading material or documents carried by a law enforcement undercover or intelligence agent that offer a cover that will protect his background and identity. One law enforcement officer working undercover carried a false set of prison release and parole papers in his pocket as pocket litter to cover his professional status.

pogo   [US] Naval aviation voice brevity code meaning return to this frequency.

POI   [I] Abbreviation for Probability Of Intercept.

point   [C,G&PS] Slang for the needle used on an eye dropper or hypodermic syringe.

poison   [C,G&PS] Slang for cocaine or any other opiate.

poison act [LE] Slang for the Federal Narcotics Act.

poke [LE] Slang for smoking marijuana, usually in a pipe.

POL **1.** Background code for polygraph, voice stress analysis, and related areas of law enforcement or security. **2.** Specialty code for polygraph and PSE (voice stress).

POM [LE] Abbreviation for Program Objective Memorandum.

pop **1.** [C,G&PS] Slang term meaning to inject narcotics, usually just under the surface of the skin, rather than into a vein. This process prolongs the high experience. **2.** [LE] Slang for the injection of pills. **3.** [LE] Slang term meaning to arrest someone. (*See* POPPED.)

popeye [US] Naval aviation voice brevity code meaning in clouds or an area of reduced visibility.

popped [LE] Slang meaning to be arrested. (*See* POP.)

port [LE] A motel or hotel used by law enforcement, either for surveillance or a sting operation.

pot [C,G&PS] Slang for marijuana. (*See* QUICK REFERENCE.)

pot head [C,G&PS] Slang for a person who uses marijuana at a high rate.

POUM [USSR] Abbreviation for *Partido Obrero de Unificacion Marxista*, the Workers' Party of Marxist Unification.

PP **1.** [I] (*See* PSYCHOLOGICAL PROFILE.) **2.** Specialty code for Plant Protection. **3.** Designation for Portuguese.

PPI [M] Abbreviation for Plan Position Indicator.

PPS **1.** Specialty code for Personal Process Service. **2.** [C] Abbreviation for Pulses Per Second.

PPSE [C3I] Abbreviation for Programmer Support Environment.

PR [M] Abbreviation for Passive Ranging.

PRB Specialty code for probate and missing heirs.

PRD **1.** Specialty code for product liability. **2.** [TRG] Abbreviation for *Partido Revolucionario Dominican*, a terrorist group headquartered in the Dominican Republic.

Preludin [LE] Name of a controlled substance, a stimulant. (*See* QUICK REFERENCE.)

pressure fuse A mechanical device used to detonate a bomb, most often used under floorboards or a car seat. The weight of the victim releases a plunger that causes the bomb to explode.

PRE-TAXI CLNC [A] Designation for Pre-Taxi Clearance.

PRF [C] Abbreviation for Pulse Repetition Frequency.

PRI [C] Abbreviation for Pulse Repetition Interval.

prickly [C,G&PS] Slang for air entering into a vein during the careless injection of drugs.

Primafoam An explosive supplied in an aerosol container much like a shaving cream can. While inside the can, the explosive is insensitive to shock and cannot be detonated. Once dispersed from its container, the explosive can be detonated by using a blasting cap or detonating cord. (*See* FOAMEX.)

Prima Linea [TRG] An Italian terrorist group closely associated with the Red Brigades.

primary [I] Slang for the primary person under surveillance.

primo [C,G&PS] Term for first, best, and top qualify; usually used as a reference to marijuana.

principal agent **1.** [I] The undercover police officer or intelligence agent who recruits informants and then manages the resulting network. **2.** [I] In a foreign country, the agent who has recruited other agents, most likely a government employee or person working in sensitive area.

private [I] Of or referring to a conversation, over telephone or radio, that is switched to digital scrambling.

private side [I] Of or referring to a conversation, over telephone or radio, that is switched to a digital scrambling processor.

PRN [C3I] Abbreviation for Pseudo Random Noise.

product [I] A finished intelligence report. The product is disseminated by a law enforcement agency or intelligence group to the consumer.

product four [LE] Slang for a PCP and LSD combination, sometimes identified as Product IV.

production level [LE] Although most police departments have established no quota, parking control officers are expected to meet a production level of approximately 17 overtime or illegal parking tickets every day in most major cities of the United States. An aggressive San Francisco meter maid wrote 362 citations in a single day—a record that still stands. That worked out to about 48 citations every hour.

Projecto Talon [HRU] The antiterrorist and hostage rescue unit of the Brazilian Army Special Forces.

proprietaries [LE] Established commercial business organizations (operating) that are established and fully controlled by a law enforcement or intelligence agency. These front organizations serve a variety of purposes ranging from FBI sting operations to Drug Enforcement Administration (DEA) narcotic investigations.

prowler 1. [A] *See* A-6. 2. [LE] A sneak thief, an individual prowling around in an area where he has no legitimate purpose or business. Police agencies always consider an adult prowler as dangerous.

prowords Pronounceable words or phrases that have been assigned meanings for the purpose of expediting message handling on circuits where radiotelephone procedure is employed. In use by the U.S. government and military, no proword or combination of prowords is substituted for the textual content of a message. In communications between agencies or military units of different nationalities, the prowords can be replaced by their equivalent prosigns, where these exist, spelled out using the authorized phonetic equivalents. (*See* PHONETIC ALPHABET AND NUMERALS.) In the U.S. government and military the prowords and meanings in TABLE P-2 apply.

PRP [M] Abbreviation for Pulse Repetition Period.

PRT Specialty code for personal protection.

PS 1. Specialty code for Process Service. 2. [LE] Abbreviation for PERIMETER SURVEILLANCE, 3. [LE] To DEA agents abbreviation for picket surveillance. 4. [LE] *See* PAPAVER SOMNIFERUM.

PSAC [GOV] President's Science Advisory Committee.

PSAU [LE] Abbreviation for The Police Special Action Units of the Japanese police. These units specialize in counterterrorism and hostage rescue.

PSB [M] Abbreviation for Psychological Strategy Board.

PSE Specialty code for voice stress.

pseudonym [I] A false name that appears to be a true name.

psilocybin [LE] The active ingredient in psilocybe mexicana, more commonly known as *magic mushrooms* in a variety of forms. This drug in its purest form is an off-white crystallike material. Unprocessed, it looks like chopped mushrooms. Low doses give a sense of detachment from reality; higher doses cause reactions much like LSD. It is a controlled, hallucinogenic substance. (*See* QUICK REFERENCE.)

PSN [C3I] Abbreviation for Packet Switching Network.

PSTF [HRU] Abbreviation for Police Special Task Force, the South African antiterrorist unit directed by the Security Branch of the national African police.

psyched [C,G&PS] Referring to the excitement experienced on a drug trip.

psychological profile [I] Investigative agencies, using many past histories of criminals and their acts, can develop a profile of an individual based on the characteristics common to certain crimes. If the criminal is known, it is much more easy to determine what that individual might most likely do on the basis of his pre- and post-offense behavior. Information and specific details about an individual are the basis for the creation of a psychological profile.

PSY OPS [US] Abbreviation for PSYchological

Table P-2. Prowords and Their Explanations

Proword	Explanation
address group	The group that follows is an address group.
all after	The portion of the message to which I have reference is all that follows. The proword is equivalent to AA.
all before	The portion of the message to which I have reference is all that precedes. The proword is equivalent to AB.
authenticate	Station called is to reply to the challenge that follows.
authentication is	The transmission authentication of this message is ...
break	I hereby indicate the separation of the text from other portions of the message. The proword is equivalent to BT.
broadcast your net	Link the two nets under your control for automatic rebroadcast.
call sign	The group that follows is a call sign.
correct	You are correct or what you have transmitted is correct. The proword is equivalent to C.
correction	An error has been made in this transmission. Transmission will continue with the last word correctly transmitted. The proword is equivalent to EEEEEEEE.
correction	An error has been made in the transmission (or message indicated). The correct version is .... The proword is equivalent to C.
correction	That which follows is a corrected version in answer to your request for verification. The proword is equivalent to C.
disregard this	This transmission is in error. Disregard it.
transmission-out	This proword shall not be used to cancel any message that has been completely transmitted and for which receipt or acknowledgment has been received. The proword is equivalent to EEEEEEEE AR.
do not answer	Stations called are not to answer this call, receipt for this message, or otherwise to transmit in connection with this transmission. When this proword is employed, the transmission shall be ended with the proword out. The proword is equivalent to F.
execute	Carry out the intent of the message or signal to which this applies. To be used only with the Executive Method. The proword is equivalent to IX. This proword is followed by a five second dash signal.
execute to follow	Action on the following message or signal is to be carried out upon receipt of the proword execute. To be used only with the Delayed Executive Method. The proword is equivalent to IX.
exempt	The addresses immediately following are exempted from the collective call. The proword is equivalent to XMT.
figures	Numerals or numbers follow.
flash	Precedence flash. The proword is equivalent to Z.
from	The originator of this message is indicated by the address designator immediately following. The proword is equivalent to FM.
groups	This message contains the number of groups indicated by the numeral following. The proword is equivalent to GR.

Table P-2. Continued

Proword	Explanation
group no count	The groups in this message have not been counted. The proword is equivalent to GRNC.
I authenticate	The group that follows is the reply to your challenge to authenticate.
immediate	Precedence immediate. The proword is equivalent to O.
immediate execute	Action on the message or signal following is to be carried out on receipt of the word execute. To be used only with the Immediate Executive Method. The proword is equivalent to IX.
info	The addressees immediately following are addressed for information. The proword is equivalent to INFO.
I read back	The following is my response to your instruction to read back.
I say again	I am repeating transmission or portion indicated. The proword is equivalent to IMI.
I spell	I shall spell the next word phonetically.
I verify	That which follows has been verified at your request and is repeated. To be used only as a reply to verify.
message	A message that requires recording is about to follow. Transmitted immediately after the call. (This proword is not used on nets primarily employed for conveying messages. It is intended for use when messages are passed on tactical or reporting nets.)
more to follow	Transmitting station has additional traffic for the receiving station. This proword is equivalent to B.
number	Station serial number. The proword is equivalent to NR.
out	This is the end of my transmission to you and no answer is required or expected. The proword is equivalent to AR.
over	This is the end of my transmission to you and a response is necessary. Go ahead; transmit. The proword is equivalent to K.
priority	Precedence priority. The proword is equivalent to P.
read back	Repeat this entire transmission back to me exactly as received. The proword is equivalent to G.
relay (to)	Transmit this message to all addressees (or addressees immediately following this proword). The address component is mandatory when this proword is used. The proword is equivalent to T.
roger	I have received your last transmission satisfactorily.
routine	Precedence routine. The proword is equivalent to R.
say again	Repeat all of your last transmission. The proword is equivalent to IMI.
service	The message that follows is a service message. The proword is equivalent to SVC.
signals	The groups that follow are taken from a signal book. (This proword is not used on nets primarily employed for conveying signals. It is intended for use when tactical signals are passed on nontactical nets.) The proword is equivalent to HM HM HM.
silence	Cease transmission on this net immediately. (Repeated three or more times.) Silence will be maintained until lifted. (When an authentication system is in force, the transmission imposing silence is to be authenticated.)

Table P-2. Continued

Proword	Explanation
silence lifted	Silence is lifted. (When an authentication system is in force, the transmission lifting silence is to be authenticated.)
speak slower	Your transmission is too fast a speed. Reduce speed of transmission.
stop rebroadcasting	Cut the automatic link between the two nets that are being rebroadcast and revert to normal working.
this is	This transmission is from the station whose designator immediately follows. The proword is equivalent to DE.
time	That which immediately follows is the time or date-time group of the message.
to	The addressees immediately following are addressed for action. The proword is equivalent to TO.
unknown station	The identity of the station with whom I am attempting to establish communications is unknown. The proword is equivalent to AA.
verify	Verify entire message (or portion indicated) with the originator and send correct version. To be used only at the discretion of or by the addressee to which the questioned message was directed. The proword is equivalent to J.
wait	I must pause for a few seconds. The proword is equivalent to AS.
wait-out	I must pause longer than a few seconds. The proword is equivalent to AS AR.
wilco	I have received your signal, understand it, and will comply. To be used only by the addressee. Because the meaning of roger is included in that of wilco, the two prowords are never used together.
word after	The word of the message to which I have reference is that which follows _____. The proword is equivalent to WA.
word before	The word of the message to which I have reference is that which precedes _____. The proword is equivalent to WB.
words twice	Communication is difficult. Transmit(ting) each phrase (or each code group) twice. This proword can be used as an order, request, or as information.
wrong	Your last transmission was incorrect. The correct version is _____.

OPerationS, including all levels of propaganda and psychological techniques that will erode the opposition.

PSY WAR [I] Abbreviation for PSYchological WARfare.

PT Specialty code for patrol.

ptarmigan [UK] Code name for tactical mobile area communications system.

PTT [LE] Abbreviation for Police Tactical Team, the antiterrorist unit of the Singapore police.

PTU [C3I] Abbreviation for Program Track Unit.

publications *See* APPENDIX C.

puff [C,G&PS] Slang term meaning to smoke opium.

Puma Unit [HRU] The counterterrorist and hostage rescue unit of the Ecuadorian Army.

punk [LE] A term created within the prison system by inmates who wish to be identified by their manliness and refer to anyone who appears soft or a coward as a punk. In a prison homosexual relationship, the subservient (submissive) individual is known as a punk.

pure [C,G&PS] Slang for a narcotic of very high quality.

purple [C,G&PS] Term for Zacatecas purple, a high-quality marijuana grown in the mountainous state of Zacatecas in central Mexico. This marijuana is distinguished by seeds that turn purple, or a rich, reddish purple color when the weed is dry. Zacatecas purple is a very popular expensive weed.

purple haze [C,G&PS] Slang for LSD. (*See* QUICK REFERENCE.)

purple hearts [C,G&PS] Slang for phenobarbital. (*See* QUICK REFERENCE.)

push [C,G&PS] Slang meaning to offer narcotics for sale.

pusher [C,G&PS] Slang for an individual who sells drugs.

Pushkino Radar [I] The Soviet answer to the U.S. Cobra Dane radar system used to detect incoming ballistic missiles. Located outside Moscow, the Pushkino Radar installation is more than 120 feet high and 500 feet wide at the base. It offers the Soviet Union a long-range detection capability with 360 degrees of coverage.

put someone down [C,G&PS] A slang term meaning to treat someone as inferior. The term can have to do with the attitude, dress, or reference to a activity or relationship, i.e., 'His girlfriend dresses like a slut.'

PVR [C3I] Abbreviation for Personnel Vehicle Radar.

PW [C] Abbreviation for Pulsewidth.

Q **1.** [GOV] Designation for a high-level special security clearance that is assigned to individuals, entry into certain areas, and documents having to do with matters related to nuclear devices. It is assigned by the Department of Energy. **2.** [C,G&PS] Abbreviation for cocaine. (*See* QUICK REFERENCE.) **3.** [US] Designation for Designates Radar Countermeasure Equipped Aircraft.

Q-band [NASA] Designation for 36,000 to 46,000 MCS.

Q-codes [C] Q-Codes are used by ham radio operators—and on some occasions by law enforcement agencies, fire departments, and emergency services—as abbreviations or as a supplement to the 10-Code. Q-code questions and the proper response are:

QRG—What is my exact frequency?
Response: Your exact frequency is_____.

QRH—Does my frequency vary?
Response: Your frequency varies.

QRI—How is my tone?
Response: Your tone is (1-5; bad-good).

QRK—What is my readability?
Response: You are readable (1-5; bad-good).

QRL—Are you busy?
Response: I am busy.

QRM—Is there interference?
Response: There is interference.

QRN—Is there static?
Response: There is static.

QRO—Shall I increase power?
Response: Increase power.

QRP—Shall I decrease power?
Response: Decrease power.

QRQ—Shall I send (code) faster?
Response: Send faster at—(wpm).

QRS—Shall I send more slowly?
Response: Send more slowly at—(wpm).

QRT—Shall I stop sending?
Response: Stop sending.

QRU—Have you anything for me?
Response: I have nothing for you.

QRV—Are you ready?
Response: I am ready.

QRW—Shall I inform (person) that you are calling on (number) kHz?
Response: Please inform (person) that I am calling on (number) kHz.

QRX—When will you call again?
Response: At (number) hours on (number) frequency.

QRY—What is my turn?
Response: Your turn is numbered (number).

QRZ—Who is calling me?
Response: You are being called by (person) on (number) kHz.

QSA—What is my signal strength?
Response: Your strength is (1-5; bad-good).

QSB—Am I fading?
Response: You are fading.

QSD—Are my signals defective?
Response: Your signals are defective.

QSG—Shall I send (number) messages?
Response: Send (number) messages at one time.

QSK—Do you have break in?
Response: I have break in.

QSL—Will you acknowledge receipt?
Response: I acknowledge receipt.

QSM—Shall I repeat the message?
Response: Repeat the last (or (number)) message.

QSN—Did you hear me on (frequency)?
Response: I heard you on (frequency).

QSO—Can you communicate with (person)?
Response: I can communicate with (person).

QSP—Will you relay to (place)?
Response: I will relay to (place).

QST—General call to ARRL members.
Response: (individual) responding.

QSU—Shall I send on (frequency)?
Response: Send on (frequency).

QSV—Shall I send a series of Vs?
Response: Send a series of Vs.

QSW—Will you send on (frequency)?
Response: Send on (frequency).

QSX—Will you listen on (frequency)?
Response: I will listen on (frequency).

QSY—Shall I change to (frequency).
Response: Change to (frequency).

QSZ—Shall I send each word group more than once?
Response: Send each word group (number) times.

QTA—Shall I cancel message—?
Response: Cancel message—.

QTB—Do you agree with my word count?
Response: I agree with your word count.

QTC—How many messages do you have?
Response: I have (number) messages.

QTH—What is your location?
My location is (place).

QTR—What is the correct time?
The correct time is (time).

ARRL QN Signals for CW Net Use

(+)QNA—Answer in prearranged order.

(+)QNB—Act as relay between (person) and (person).

QNC—All net stations copy. I have a message for all net stations.

(+)QND—Net is directed (controlled by net control station).

(+)QNE—Entire net standby.

QNF—Net is free (not controlled).

QNG—Take over as net control station.

QNH—Your net frequency is high.

QNI—Net stations report in.
Response: I am reporting into the net. (Follow with a list of traffic or QRU).

QNJ—Can you copy me?

(+)QNK—Transmit messages for (person) to (place).

QNL—Your net frequency is low.

(+)QNM—You are QRMing the net. Standby.

QNN—Net control station is (name).
Response: What station has net control?

QNO—Station is leaving the net.

QNP—Unable to copy you.
Response: Unable to copy (person).

(+)QNQ—Move frequency to (frequency) and wait for (person) to finish handling traffic. Then send him traffic for _____.

(+)QNR—Answer (person) and receive traffic.

QNS—Following stations are in the net. This should follow with a list.
Response: Request list of stations in the net.

QNT—I request permission to leave the net for (number) minutes.

(+)QNU—The net has traffic for you. Standby.

(+)QNV—Establish contact with (person) on this frequency. If successful, move to (frequency) and send him traffic for _____.

QNW—How do I route messages for (person)?

QNX—You are excused from the net.

(+)QNY—Shift to another frequency (or to (number) kHz) to clear traffic with (person).

QNZ—Zero beat your signal with mine.

————

(+) For use only by the Net Control Station.

Q-course [M] Designation for the U.S. Army special forces qualification course.

Q-queen [C,G&PS] Slang for cocaine. (*See* QUICK REFERENCE.)

QD 1. Specialty code for examiner, questionable documents. 2. [US] Abbreviation for Quantity Distance, a term used in law enforcement and the military to equate a safe distance from a known explosive prior to detonation.

QEAM [E] Abbreviation for Quick Erecting Antenna Mast.

Q-message [NATO] Designation for classified navigational hazard message.

QOT&E [US] Abbreviation for Qualification Operational Test & Evaluation.

QRA [US] Abbreviation for Quick Reaction Alert.

QRC [US] Abbreviation for Quick Reaction Capability.

QRT [M] Abbreviation for Quick Reaction Team.

Q-SHIP [US] In military terms, a Q-ship is a decoy ship used to mislead the enemy.

Q-TECH [US] Abbreviation for Quality-TECHnology.

QUA [C3I] Abbreviation for Quadrature Amplitude Modulation.

Quaalude [LE] The prescription name for methaqualone. It is a controlled substance that is a sedative/hypnotic. (*See* QUICK REFERENCE.)

quail [US] An air-launched decoy missile carried internally in the B-52 and used to degrade the effectiveness of enemy radar, intercepter aircraft, air defense missiles, etc. Designated ADM-20.

quarter [C,G&PS] Slang for a one-quarter ounce of a narcotic.

quartz [C,G&PS] Slang for a smokable methamphetamine. (*See* ICE.)

Quebec/Queen [A,LE,MIL] Designation for the letter *Q*.

queen [C,G&PS] Slang for cocaine. (*See* QUICK REFERENCE.)

QUICK REFERENCES

ASSAULT-TYPE WEAPONS FAVORED BY STREET GANGS, DRUG DEALERS, SMUGGLERS, AND THE CRIMINAL UNDERWORLD

(With special appreciation to the FBI's National Center for the Analysis of Violent Crimes.)

Rifles/Long Guns

1. All models of Avtomat Kalashnikovs, such as the AK-47, manufactured by the Norinco, Mitchell and Poly Technologies companies
2. The Uzi and Galil made by Israeli Military Industries and imported into the United States by Action Arms Company
3. Beretta AR-70 and SC-70
4. CETME G3
5. Colt AR-15 and CAR-15

6. Baewoo K-1, K-2, Max 1 and Max 2
7. Fabrique Nationale FN/FAL, FN/LAR and FNC
8. FAMAS MAS223
9. Heckler & Koch HK-91, H-93, HK-94 and PSG-1
10. Ingram MAC 10 and MAC 11
11. SKS with detachable magazine
12. SIG AMT, SIG 500 series and SIG PE-57
13. Springfield Armory BM59 and SAR-48
14. Sterling MK-6 and SAR
15. Steyr AUG
16. Valmet M62, M71S, M78
17. Armalite AR-180 carbine
18. Bushmaster assault rifle (armgun)
19. Calico M-900 assault carbine
20. Mandall THE TAC-1 carbine
21. Plainfield Machine Co. carbine
22. PJK M-68 & M-69 carbine
23. Weaver Arms Nighthawk

Pistols

1. Action Arms UZI
2. Encom MP-9 and MP-45
3. MAC 10 and MAC 11
4. INTRATEC TEC-9
5. Mitchell Arms Spectre Auto
6. Sterling MK-7
7. Calico M-900
8. Colt .357 Python

Shotguns

1. Franchi SPAS 12 and LAW 12
2. Gilbert Equipment Co. Striker 12
3. Encome CM-55
4. SWD Streetsweeper

CONTROLLED SUBSTANCES MOST LIKELY TO BE INVOLVED IN A STREET ARREST OR DRUG RAID

(With appreciation to the U.S. Drug Enforcement Administration .)

Name	Qualifier	Name	Qualifier
Amphetamine	stimulant	Benzedrine	stimulant
Amytal	sedative	Biphetamine	stimulant
Angel Dust	hallucinogen	Cocaine	stimulant

Name	Qualifier	Name	Qualifier
Crack Cocaine	stimulant	Methamphetamine	stimulants
Crank	stimulant	Methaqualone	sedative/hypnotic
Codeine	narcotic	Methedrine	stimulant
Dalmane	sedative	Morphine	narcotic
Demerol	narcotic	Miltown	sedative
Desoxyn	stimulant	Navane	major tranquilizer
Dexedrine	stimulant	Nembutal	sedative
Dextroamphetamine	stimulant	Noctec	sedative
Diacetylmorphine	narcotic	Noludar	sedative
Diazepam	minor tranquilizer	Numorphan	narcotic
Didrex	stimulant	Opium	narcotic
Dilaudid	narcotic	Parest	sedative
DMT	hallucinogen	PCP	hallucinogen
Dolophine	narcotic	Percodan	narcotic
DOM	hallucinogen	Peyote	hallucinogen
Doriden	sedative	Placidyl	sedative
Equanil	sedative	Preludin	stimulant
Gemonil	barbiturate	Psilocybin	hallucinogen
Haldol	major tranquilizer	Qualliude	sedative/hypnotic
Hashish	cannabis	Ritalin	stimulant
Hash Oil	cannabis	Rock Cocaine	stimulant
Heroin	narcotic	Seconal	sedative
Hydromorphone	narcotic	Serax	minor tranquilizer
Librium	minor tranquilizer	Sommnafac	sedative
LSD	hallucinogen	Sopor	sedative
Marijuana	cannabis	Stelazine	major tranquilizer
Mebaral	sedative	STP	hallucinogen
Mellaril	major tranquilizer	Tenuate	stimulant
Meprobamate	sedative/hypnotic	Thorazine	major tranquilizer
Mescaline	hallucinogen	Tuinal	sedative
Methabarbitol	sedative/hypnotic	Valium	minor tranquilizer
Methadone	narcotic		

SECURITY CLEARANCE BASICS

Much of the foundation and philosophy behind data-sensitive and security classifications within the military/government/industrial complex is unclear to the unindoctrinated, and extends to many of those who have security authorizations. The following explanation has been prepared here with the assistance of the Computer Security Center of the United States Department of Defense (CSC/DOD).

Increasing levels of data sensitivity within the United States government, military, and civil contractors are defined as follows:

- *Unclassified (U)*—Data that is not sensitive or classified: publicly releasable information.

- *Not classified but sensitive (N)*—Unclassified but sensitive data. Much of this is For Official Use Only (FOUO) data, which is unclassified data that is exempt from release under the Freedom of Information Act. This includes data such as the following:
  ○ Manuals for DOD investigators or auditors
  ○ Examination questions and answers used in determination of the qualification of candidates for employment or promotion
  ○ Data that a statute specifically exempts from disclosure, such as Patent Secrecy data
  ○ Data containing trade secrets or commercial or financial information
  ○ Data containing internal advice or recommendations that reflect the decision-making process of an agency
  ○ Data in personnel, medical, or other files that, if disclosed, would result in an invasion of personal privacy
  ○ Investigative records

- *Confidential (C)*—The unauthorized disclosure of information that reasonably could be expected to cause damage to the national security.

- *Secret (S)*—The unauthorized disclosure of information that reasonably could be expected to cause serious damage to the national security.

- *Top secret (TS)*—The unauthorized disclosure of information that reasonably could be expected to cause exceptionally grave damage to the national security.

- *One category (1C)*—Top Secret Special Intelligence information e.g., Sensitive Compartmented Information (SCI) or operational information e.g., Single Integrated Operational Plan/Extremely Sensitive Information (SIOP/ESI) that requires special controls for restrictive handling.

- *Multiple categories (MC)*—Top Secret Special Intelligence or operational information that requires special controls for restrictive handling. This sensitivity level differs from the 1C level only in that there are multiple compartments involved.

Clearances

- *Uncleared (U)*—Personnel with no clearance or authorization. Permitted access to any information for which there are no specified controls, such as openly published information.

- *Unclassified information (N)*—Personnel who are authorized access to sensitive unclassified e.g., FOUO information, either by an explicit official authorization or by an implicit authorization derived from official assignments or responsibilities.

- *Confidential clearance (C)*—Requires United States citizenship and typically some limited records checking. In some cases, a National Agency Check (NAC) is required e.g., for U.S. citizens employed by colleges or universities.

- *Secret clearance (S)*—Typically requires a NAC, which consists of searching the FBI fingerprint and investigative files and the Defense Central Index of Investigations (CDII). In some cases, further investigation is required.

- *Top secret clearance based on a current background investigation [TS(BI)]*—Requires an investigation that consists of a NAC, personal contacts, record searches, and written inquiries. A BI typically includes an investigation extending back five years, often with a spot check investigation extending back 15 years.

- *Top secret clearance based on a current special background investigation [TS-(SBI)]*—Requires an investigation that, in addition to the investigation for a BI, includes additional checks on the subject's immediate family (if foreign born) and the spouse and neighborhood investigations to verify each of the subject's former residences in the United States where he resided six months or more. An SBI typically includes an investigation extending back 15 years.

- *One category (1C)*—In addition to a TS(SBI) clearance, written authorization for access to one category of information is required.

- *Multiple categories (MC)*—In addition to TS(SBI) clearance, written authorization for access to multiple categories of information is required.

The extent of investigation required for a particular clearance varies based both on the background of the individual under investigation and on derogatory or questionable information disclosed during the investigation. Individuals from non-DOD agencies might be issued DOD clearance if the clearance obtained in their agency can be equated to a DOD clearance. For example, the "Q" and "L" clearances granted by both the Department of Energy and the Nuclear Regulatory Commission are considered acceptable for issuance of a DOD industrial personnel security clearance. The "Q" clearance is considered an authoritative basis for a DOD Top Secret clearance (based on a BI) and the "L" clearance is considered an authoritative basis for DOD Secret clearance. U.S. government agencies that require employees and consultants on staff to have a security clearance include Department of Agriculture, Department of Commerce, Department of Interior, Department of Justice, Department of Labor, Department of State, Department of Transportation, Department of Treasury, Arms Control and Disarmament Agency, Environmental Protection Agency, Federal Emergency Management Agency, Federal Reserve System, General Accounting Office, General Services Administration, National Aeronautics and Space Administration, National Science Foundation, Small Business Administration, and the United States Information Agency. These are called user agencies (UA).

SERVICE CODES USED
WITH THE MASTER FILES OF GOVERNMENT MICROFICHE
(With permission of DataPort.)

Microfiche is available (*See* RESOURCES) containing the frequencies used by government agencies. Those (4×6 inch) fiche contain vast amounts of information, most of it pure guesswork to decipher unless you know the service codes. The bandwidths are listed in KHz/MHz while the types of modulation and other data is coded.

Communications technology at the government level has been wrapped in secrecy since the beginning of the cold war, but the need to understand it is greater than ever before for the policy makers who must turn that technology into practical intelligence tools as much as for ordinary people who pay for it with their taxes. Much of the microfiche information and service codes helpful in a microfiche search have disappeared from the scene. Sources for microfiche other than the FCC and NTIS are listed elsewhere in this reference book. Listed here are the service codes and other reference data found on the various set of microfiche that are in use and currently available:

Types of Modulation

Code	Type
A	Amplitude
F	Frequency (or Phase)
P	Pulse

Types of Transmission

Code	Type
0	Unmodulated carrier
1	Unmodulated telegraphy
2	Modulated telegraphy
3	Telephony
4	Facsimile
5	Television
6	Four-frequency telegraphy
7	Multichannel telegraphy
9	Other

Supplementary Characteristics

Code	Characteristic
A	Reduced carrier (single sideband)
H	Full carrier (single sideband)
J	Suppressed carrier (single sideband)
B	Two independent sidebands
C	Vestigial sideband
D	Amplitude-modulated pulse
E	Width-modulated pulse
F	Phase-modulated pulse
G	Code-modulated pulse

Frequencies

K	Kilohertz
M	Megahertz
G	Gigahertz
T	Terahertz

Frequencies are assigned to a number of government agencies. The service code for those individual agencies is listed alongside the frequency.

Code	Agency	Code	Agency
A	U.S. Department of Agriculture	FAA	Federal Aviation Administration
AF	U.S. Department of the Air Force	FCC	Federal Communications Commission
AGA	All Government Agencies	FEA	Federal Energy Administration
AOTC	Architect of the Capital	FRS	Federal Reserve System
AR	U.S. Department of the Army	G	Government
C	U.S. Department of Commerce	GPO	Government Printing Office
CG	U.S. Coast Guard	GSA	General Services Administration
CIA	Central Intelligence Agency	HHS	Health and Human Services
CPSC	Consumer Product Safety Commission	HR	House of Representatives
CSC	Civil Service Commission	HUD	Housing and Urban Development
DOE	U.S. Department of Energy	I	U.S. Department of the Interior
EPA	Environmental Protection Agency	IBWC	International Boundary & Water Comm.

Code	Agency	Code	Agency
ICC	Interstate Commerce Commission	OMB	Office of Management and Budget
J	U.S. Department of Justice	S	Department of State
	(United States Attorney)	SC	United States Supreme Court
	(U.S. Marshall Service)	SI	Smithsonian Institution
	(Federal Bureau of Investigation)	T	Department of the Treasury
L	U.S. Department of Labor	TRAN	U.S. Department of Transportation
LC	Library of Congress	TVA	Tennessee Valley Authority
N	U.S. Department of the Navy	USCP	U.S. Capitol Police
NASA	National Aeronautics & Space Admin.	USIA	U.S. Information Agency
NG	Nongovernment	USPS	U.S. Postal Service
NRC	Nuclear Regulatory Commission	USTC	U.S. Tax Court
NS	National Security Agency	VA	Veterans Administration
NSF	National Science Foundation		

Microfiche also can list the station class. With this added information, it is easy to determine exactly who is using what frequencies and for what reasons:

Class	Use	Class	Use
AX	Aeronautical Fixed Station	FAC	Airdrome Control Station
BC/BT	Broadcasting Station	FAT	Flight Test Station
BCI	International Broadcasting Station	FB	Base Station
EA	Mobile-satellite Space Station	FC	Coast Station
EC	Fixed-satellite space station	FCB	Marine Broadcast Station
ED	Space Telecommand Space Station	FL	Land Station
EE	Standard Freq-satellite Space Station	FLD	Telecommand Land Station
EG	Maritime Mobile-satellite Space Station	FLE	Telemetering Land Station
EH	Space Research Space Station	FLEA	Aeronautical Telemetering Land Station
EJ	Aeronautical Mobile Sat. Space Station	FLEB	Flight Telemetering Land Station
EK	Space Tracking Space Station	FLEC	Surface Telemetering Land Station
EM	Meteorological-Satellite Space Station	FLH	Hydrologic & Meteorological Land Station
EN	Radionavigation-Satellite Space Station		
EO	Aeronautical Radionavigation Satellite Space Station	FLU	Aeronautical Utility Land Station
		FX	Fixed Station
EQ	Maritime Radionavigation-Satellite Space Station	FXD	Telecommand Fixed Station
		FXE	Telemetering Fixed Station
ER	Space Telemetering Space Station	FXH	Hydrologic & Meteorological Fixed Station
ES	Inter-satellite Space Station		
ET	Space Operations Space Station	LR	Radiolocation Land Station
EU	Land Mobile-satellite Space Station	MA	Aircraft Station
EW	Earth Exploration-satellite Space Station	ME	Space Station
		ML	Land Mobile Station
EX	Experimental Station	MO	Mobile Station
EY	Time Signal-satellite Space Station	MOB	Radio Beacon Mobile Station
FA	Aeronautical Station	MOD	Telecommand Mobile Station
FAB	Aeronautical Broadcast Station	MOE	Telemetering Mobile Station

Class	Use
MOEA	Aeronautical Telemetering Mobile Station
MOEB	Flight Telemetering Mobile Station
MOEC	Surface Telemetering Mobile Station
MOH	Hydrologic & Meteorological Mobile Station
MOU	Aeronautic Utility Mobile Station
MR	Radiolocation Mobile Station
MS	Ship Station or Bridge-Bridge Station
OD	Oceanographic Data Interrogating Station
OE	Oceanographic Data Interrogating Station
RA	Radio Astronomy Station
RG	Radio Direction Finding Station
RL	Radionavigation Land Station
RLA	Aeronautical Marker Beacon Station
RLB	Aeronautical Radiobeacon Station
RLC	Radar Beacon (RACON) Station
RLG	Glide Path (Slope) Station
RLL	Localizer Station
RLM	Marine Radiobeacon Station
RLN	Loran Station
RLO	Omnidirectional Range Station
RLR	Radio Range Station
RLS	Surveillance Radar Station
RLTM	Radionavigation Land Test Station (Maintenance Test Facility)
RLTO	Radionavigation Land Test Station (Operational Test Facility)
RO	Radionavigation Mobile Station
ROA	Altimeter Station
SN	Sounder Network Station
SP	Sounder Prediction Station

Class	Use
SSS	Standard Frequency Station
TA	Mobile-satellite Earth Station
TB	Aeronautical Mobile-satellite Earth Station
TC	Fixed-satellite Earth Station
TD	Space Telecommand Earth Station
TE	Earth Station (Transmitting)
TG	Maritime Mobile-satellite Mobile Earth Station
TH	Space Research Earth Station
TK	Space Tracking Earth Station
TM	Meteorological-satellite Earth Station
TN	Radionavigation-satellite Earth Station
TP	Earth Station (Receiving)
TR	Space Telemetering Earth Station
TT	Space Operation Earth Station
TW	Earth Exploration-satellite Earth Station
TX	Maritime Radionavigation-satellite Earth Station
TY	Land Mobile-satellite Earth Station
TZ	Aeronautical Radionavigation-satellite Earth Station
WXB	Radar Beacon Precipitation Gauge Station
WXD	Meteorological Radar Station
WXR	Radiosonde Station
XC	Experimental Contract Developmental Station
XD	Experimental Developmental Station
XE	Experimental Export Station
XM	Experimental Composite Station
XR	Experimental Research Station
XT	Experimental Testing Station

AREA CODES USED WITH THE
MASTER FILES OF GOVERNMENT MICROFICHE

(With permission of DataPort.)

Area Code	Country
AFR	Africa
ANTR	Antarctica
ARCO	Arctic Ocean

Area Code	Country
ASIA	Asia
CAM	Central America
CBN	Caribbean

Area Code	Country	Area Code	Country
EUR	Europe	LONT	Lake Ontario
FE	Far East	LSUP	Lake Superior
GLM	Gulf of Mexico	MDE	Middle East
GTLK	Great Lakes	MED	Mediterranean Sea
INDO	Indian Ocean	OCNA	Oceania
LAM	Latin America	PAC	Pacific Ocean
LANT	Atlantic Ocean	SAS	South Asia
LERI	Lake Erie	SEA	South East Asia
LHUR	Lake Huron	SPCE	Space
LMIC	Lake Michigan		

COUNTRY CODES USED WITH THE
MASTER FILES OF GOVERNMENT MICROFICHE

(With permission of DataPort.)

Code	Country	Code	Country
ADL	Adelie Land	BLR	Byelo Russia
AFG	Afghanistan	BOL	Bolivia
AFI	French Territory of the Afars and Issas	BOT	Botswana
AFS	Republic of South Africa	BRB	Barbados
AGL	Angola	BRM	Burma
ALB	Albania	BRU	Brueni
ALG	Algeria	BUL	Bulgaria
AMS	St. Paul & Amsterdam Islands	CAF	Central Africa
AND	Andorra	CAN	Canada
AOE	Spanish Saharian Territory	CAR	Caroline Islands
ARG	Argentina	CBG	Khmer
ARS	Saudi Arabia	CHL	Chile
ASC	Ascension Island	CHN	China
ASO	South-West Africa	CHR	Christmas Island
ATN	Netherlands Antilles	CKH	Cook Island (South)
AUS	Australia	CKN	Cook Islands (North)
AUT	Austria	CLM	Colombia
AZR	Azores	CLN	Sri Lanka
B	Brazil	CME	Cameroon
BAH	Bahamas	CNR	Canaries (Islands)
BDI	Burundi	COG	Congo
BEL	Belgium	COM	Comoro
BER	Bermuda	CPV	Cape Verde
BGD	Bangladesh	CRO	Crozet Archipelago
BHR	Bahrain	CTI	Ivory Coast
BIO	British Indian Ocean Territory	CTR	Costa Rica

Code	Country	Code	Country
CUB	Cuba	INP	Portuguese India
CVA	Vatican City State	INS	Indonesia
CYP	Cyprus	IOB	British West Indies
D	Germany (Federal Republic)	IRL	Ireland
DAH	Benin	IRN	Iran
DDR	German Democratic Republic	IRQ	Iraq
DNK	Denmark	ISL	Iceland
DOM	Dominican Republic	ISR	Israel
E	Spain	IWA	Iwo Jima
EGY	Egypt	J	Japan
EQA	Ecuador	JAR	Jarvis Island
ETH	Ethiopia	JMC	Jamaica
F	France	JON	Johnson Island
FJI	Fiji Islands	JOR	Jordan
FLK	Falkland Islands	KEN	Kenya
G	United Kingdom	KER	Kerguelen Island
GAB	Gabon Republic	KOR	Republic of Korea
GC	United Kingdom Colonies	KRE	Democratic People's Republic of Korea
GDL	Guadeloupe	KWT	Kuwait
GHA	Ghana	LAO	Laos
GIB	Gibraltar	LBN	Lebanon
GIL	Gilbert Islands	LBR	Liberia
GMB	Gambia	LBY	Libya
GNE	Equatorial Guinea	LIE	Liechtenstein
GNP	Guinea-Bissau	LSO	Lesotho
GRC	Greece	LUX	Luxembourg
GRL	Greenland	MAC	Macao
GTM	Guatemala	MAU	Mauritius
GUB	Guyana	MCO	Monaco
GUF	Guyana (French)	MCS	Marcus Island
GUI	Guinea	MDG	Madagascar
GUM	Guam	MDR	Madeira
HGK	Hong Kong	MDW	Midway Islands
HNB	Belize	MEX	Mexico
HND	Honduras	MLA	Malasia
HNG	Hungary	MLD	Maldives
HOL	Netherlands	MLI	Mali
HTI	Haiti	MLT	Malta
HVO	Upper Volta (U.S.S.R.)	MNG	Mongolia
HWL	Howland Island	MOZ	Mozambique
I	Italy	MRA	Mariana Islands
ICO	Cocos Keeling Island	MRC	Morocco
IND	Republic of India	MRL	Marshall Islands

Code	Country	Code	Country
MRN	Marion Island	SHN	St. Helena
MRT	Martinique	SLM	Solomon Islands
MTN	Mauritania	SLV	El Salvador
MWI	Malawi	SMA	American Samoa
MYT	Mayotte Island	SMO	Western Samoa
NCG	Nicaragua	SMR	San Marino
NCL	New Caledonia	SNG	Singapore
NGR	Niger	SOM	Somali
NHB	New Hebrides	SPM	St. Pierre & Miquelon
NIG	Nigeria	SRL	Sierra Leone
NIU	Niue Island	STP	Sao Tome & Principe
NMB	Namibia	SUI	Switzerland
NOR	Norway	SUR	Surinam
NPL	Nepal	SWN	Swan Island
NRU	Nauru Island	SWZ	Swaziland
NZL	New Zealand	SYR	Syria
OCE	Polynesia	TAI	Taiwan
OMA	Oman	TCD	Chad
PAK	Pakistan	TCH	Czechoslovakia
PAQ	Easter Island	TGK	Tanzania
PHL	Phillipines	TGO	Togolese Republic
PHX	Phoenix Islands	THA	Thailand
PLM	Palmyra Island	TKL	Tokelau Islands
PNG	New Guinea	TMP	Timor
PNR	Panama	TON	Tonga
PNZ	Panama Canal Zone	TRC	Tristan de Cunha
POL	Poland	TRD	Trinidad & Tobago
POR	Portugal	TUN	Tunisia
PRG	Paraguay	TUR	Turkey
PRU	Peru	TUV	Tuvalu
PTC	Pitcairn Island	UAE	United Arab Emirates
PTR	Puerto Rico	UGA	Uganda
QAT	Qatar	UKR	Ekrain
REU	Reunion	URG	Uruguay
RHS	Rhodesia	URS	USSR
ROD	Rodriguez	US	50 United States
ROU	Romania	USA	48 Contiguous States
RRW	Rwanda	USP	The US and Possessions
RYU	Ryu Kyu Islands	VEN	Venezuela
S	Sweden	VIR	Virgin Islands
SDN	Sudan	VTN	Viet Nam
SEN	Senegal	WAK	Wake Island
SEY	Seychelles (Islands)	WAl	Wallis & Futuna Islands

Code	Country	Code	Country
YEM	Yemen Arab Republic	ZAI	Zaire
YMS	Yemen (People's Democratic Republic)	ZAN	Tanzania
YUG	Yugoslavia	ZMB	Zambia

SURPLUS COMMUNICATIONS EQUIPMENT
AND PROFESSIONAL RECORDING SYSTEMS FROM THE DOD

The Department of Defense retains only usable property for which there is a current or foreseeable requirement. Property is declared surplus when it becomes excess to military requirements because of changes in defense needs or unsuitable because of wear and tear or obsolescence and cannot be used by any other federal government activity. The surplus property is made available for donation to certain designated recipients authorized by law to obtain such property. Only that property that is not used or donated is offered for sale to the general public. Information included in this section is used with the specific permission of DataPort.

Department of Defense property is sold by Defense Reutilization and Marketing Region (DRMR) sales offices. Each sales office conducts sales of property held by those installations within its geographical area. This includes preparing sales catalogs, administering bid openings, making awards, and concluding all contractual arrangements. A sales office, upon request, will provide you with catalogs, at no charge, that list what they offer and describes the hardware in some detail. The catalogs also include information on how you should go about making a bid.

A prospective bidder is notified of the details of a sale by receiving a sales catalog. The catalog lists and describes the property offered for sale, identifies the place where the sale will be held, specifies the conditions under which the property is offered for sale, gives the location of the property, sets forth the inspection and sales dates, and designates the person to contact for further information. Catalogs are mailed well in advance of the date of sale to allow sufficient time for inspection of the property.

After your name has been placed on the mailing list for catalogs, you will be furnished copies of catalogs only when they include classes of property placed on sale in the geographical areas that you have specified on your application. To receive your application and have your name placed on the mailing list for catalogs you should write directly to a sales office of DRMR. You must request in writing to receive a bid application and for your name to be placed on the catalog list. Contact one of these offices:

Defense Reutilization and Marketing Region—Columbus
P.O. Box 500
Blacklick, OH 43004−0500
Telephone: 614−238−2114

Defense Reutilization and Marketing Region—Memphis
P.O. Box 14716
Memphis, TN 38114−0716
Telephone: 901−775−6417

Defense Reutilization and Marketing Region—Ogden
P.O. Box 53
Defense Depot Ogden
Ogden, UT 84407−5001
Telephone: 801−399−7257

Defense Reutilization and Marketing Region—Europe
APO NY 09633
Telephone: 06121−82−3505

Buyers located outside the United States should use the following address:

Defense Reutilization and Marketing Region—Europe
Postfach 2027
D6200 Wiesbaden, West Germany

Defense Reutilization and Marketing Sales Office—Hawaii
Post Office Box 211
Pearl City, HI 96782−0211
Telephone: 808−455−5158

Defense Reutilization and Marketing Office—Australia
FPO San Francisco 96680−2920
Telephone: 099−49−3214

Buyers interested specifically in communications equipment being offered in Australia should use the following address:

Defense Reutilization and Marketing Office
U.S. Naval Communications Station
Exmouth, Western Australia

Buyers in Canada should contact:

Crown Assets Disposal Corporation
P.O. Box 8451
Ottawa, Ontario, Canada K1G3J8
Telephone: 819−994−0074

The cover letter you receive with your application to the Defense Reutilization and Marketing Service will ask what specific property you are interested in purchasing. Following is a partial list of class numbers to assist you. A complete list is available when you request your name to be placed on the catalog mailing list:

Class No.	Description
5805	Telephone and Telegraph Equipment
5815	Teletype and Facsimile Equipment
5820	Radio and Television Communications Equipment, except Airborne
5821	Radio and Television Communications Equipment, Airborne

Class No.	Description
5825	Radio Navigation Equipment, except Airborne
5826	Radio Navigation Equipment, Airborne
5830	Intercommunication and Public Address Systems, except Airborne
5831	Intercommunication and Public Address Systems, Airborne
5835	Sound Recording and Reproduction Equipment
5845	Underwater (infrared) Communications Equipment

Contractor inventory is government-owned personal property that has been acquired by or in possession of a contractor, or subcontractor, which is in excess of the amount needed to complete performance of a contract. All sorts of communications hardware, photographic equipment, and even such unique devices as remote-control drone aircraft, safety and rescue equipment, and radar units are available. Information on the sale of contractor inventory by Department of Defense components can be obtained from the following offices:

Headquarters
Defense Logistic Agency
ATTN: DLA-AM
Cameron Station
Alexandria, VA 22304−6100
Telephone: 202−274−7707

Commander
Defense Contract Administration
  Services Region, Atlanta
805 Walker St.
Marietta, GA 30060−2789

Commander
Defense Contract Administration
  Services Region, Boston
495 Summer St.
Boston, MA 02210−2184

Commander
Defense Contract Administration
  Services Region, Chicago
O'Hare International Airport
P.O. Box 66475
Chicago, IL 60666−0475

Commander
Defense Contract Administration
  Services Region, Cleveland
Federal Office Building
1240 East Ninth St.
Cleveland, OH 44199−2036

Commander
Defense Contract Administration
  Services Region, Dallas
1200 Main St.
Dallas, TX 75202−4399

Commander
Defense Contract Administration
  Services Region, Los Angeles
11099 South LaCienega Blvd.
Los Angeles, CA 90045−6197

Commander
Defense Contract Administration
  Services Region, New York
201 Varick St.
New York, NY 10014−4811

Commander
Defense Contract Administration
  Services Region, Philadelphia
2800 South 20th St.
Philadelphia, PA 19101−7478

Commander
Defense Contract Administration
  Services Region, St. Louis
1136 Washington Ave.
St. Louis, MO 63101−1194

The General Services Administration (GSA) is responsible for the disposal of all U.S. government-owned surplus real property, including land, missile silos, and buildings; and for the disposal of surplus personal property generated by most of the civil agencies of the federal government. Sales are conducted by GSA regional offices located throughout the United States. For additional information on these sales, contact the Director, Personal Property Disposal, Federal Property Resources Service, at the following address:

GSA-FSS
Office of Property Management
Crystal Mall 4, Room 1019
Washington, D.C. 20406
Telephone: 703−557−0814

FREQUENCY GUIDE TO MILITARY DEMONSTRATION TEAMS

Frequency	Team Name	Frequency	Team Name
32.300	U.S.A. Golden Knights Parachute Team	143.600	U.S.N. Blue Angels
		148.550	U.S.A.F. Thunderbirds
34.350	U.S.N. Blue Angels	227.000	Canadian Snowbirds
42.350	U.S.A. Golden Knights Parachute Team	227.600	Canadian Snowbirds
		236.000	U.S.A.F. Thunderbirds
66.900	U.S.A.F. Thunderbirds	236.000	Canadian Snowbirds
114.950	U.S.A.F. Thunderbirds	236.550	U.S.A.F. Thunderbirds
118.100	U.S.N. Blue Angels	236.600	Canadian Snowbirds
118.100	U.S.A.F. Thunderbirds	236.600	U.S.A.F. Thunderbirds
118.200	U.S.N. Blue Angels	239.400	Canadian Snowbirds
120.450	U.S.A.F. Thunderbirds	239.800	Canadian Snowbirds
121.500	U.S.N. Blue Angels	240.500	Canadian Snowbirds
121.900	U.S.N. Blue Angels	241.400	U.S.A.F. Thunderbirds
123.400	U.S.A. Golden Knights Parachute Team	241.400	U.S.N. Blue Angels
		241.600	U.S.A.F. Thunderbirds
123.450	U.S.A.F. Thunderbirds	243.400	Canadian Snowbirds
123.600	U.S.A. Golden Knights Parachute Team	245.000	Canadian Snowbirds
		245.700	Canadian Snowbirds
123.400	U.S.A.F. Thunderbirds	250.400	U.S.N. Blue Angels
123.400	U.S.N. Blue Angels	250.500	U.S.N. Blue Angels
124.925	U.S.A.F. Thunderbirds	250.800	U.S.N. Blue Angels
140.400	U.S.A.F. Thunderbirds	250.850	U.S.A.F. Thunderbirds
141.450	U.S.A.F. Thunderbirds	251.400	U.S.N. Blue Angels
141.560	U.S.N. Blue Angels	251.600	U.S.N. Blue Angels
141.850	U.S.A.F. Thunderbirds	266.300	Canadian Snowbirds
142.000	U.S.N. Blue Angels	273.500	U.S.A.F. Thunderbirds
142.025	U.S.N. Blue Angels	275.350	U.S.N. Blue Angels
142.625	U.S.N. Blue Angels	275.800	Canadian Snowbirds
143.000	U.S.N. Blue Angels	283.500	U.S.A.F. Thunderbirds

Frequency	Team Name	Frequency	Team Name
283.900	Canadian Snowbirds	356.600	Canadian Snowbirds
289.400	Canadian Snowbirds	360.400	U.S.N. Blue Angels
294.500	Canadian Snowbirds	363.800	Canadian Snowbirds
294.700	U.S.A.F. Thunderbirds	378.500	Canadian Snowbirds
295.600	Canadian Snowbirds	382.900	U.S.A.F. Thunderbirds
295.700	U.S.A.F. Thunderbirds	384.400	U.S.N. Blue Angels
310.800	Canadian Snowbirds	391.900	U.S.N. Blue Angels
316.500	Canadian Snowbirds	394.000	U.S.A.F. Thunderbirds
322.300	U.S.A.F. Thunderbirds	394.400	U.S.N. Blue Angels
322.600	U.S.A.F. Thunderbirds	395.900	U.S.N. Blue Angels
322.800	Canadian Snowbirds	413.025	U.S.A.F. Thunderbirds
344.500	Canadian Snowbirds		

R **1.** [LE] Abbreviation for Residence (my R, or the suspect's R). **2.** [C] Designation for Repeater, a device rebroadcasting mobile radio transmissions, greatly extending the range of the signal. (*See* REPEATER.)

R.A. [LE] Abbreviation for Resident Agent, used in the F.B.I., etc.

rabbit [LE] Slang for an individual who might make an effort to escape, to run.

rabbit tracks [LE] Slang for an individual under surveillance who is moving around at a faster than normal pace. The person might believe he is being followed and making rabbit tracks in an effort to lose anyone that happens to be following.

RACES [C] Abbreviation for Radio Amateur Civil Emergency Services.

racket [US] Naval aviation voice brevity code meaning heavy rain or radar chaff. (*See* CHAFF.)

RADAR [M] Acronym for RAdio Detection And Ranging. (*See* BISTATIC RADAR; CARRIER-FREE RADAR; IMPULSE RADAR, RFR; RADIATION PISTOL; TRAFFIC RADAR.)

RADHAZ [M] Abbreviation for RADiation HAZard.

radiation pistol [I] Code named "Needle Point," this assassination weapon has been under development for a number of years by a variety of intelligence agencies. It must be used at very close range to be effective. It is a hand-held device that makes no noise. One model consists of a belt-mounted battery pack attached to a "pistol" about the size of a hand grinding tool. It directs a beam of high energy microwave radiation directly at the targeted victim. Microwave radiation has proven in laboratory tests to cause biological changes in cell structure that result in cancer. The first reported incidents of usage of the radiation pistol involved four senior editors in the Romanian section of Radio Free Europe who have died of cancer since 1981. In his debriefing following defection to the west, Lt. General Ion Mihai Pacepa discussed the development of this weapon with U.S. authorities. Other charges of microwave radiation usage as a method of secret liquidation are chronicled in Pacepa's book *Red Horizons* published in 1988. A series of radiation pistols has been developed by the United States CIA. (*See* RFR.)

RADINT [I] Abbreviation for Radar Intelligence.

radio frequencies [C] Radio frequencies are usually defined in kilohertz-per-second at and below 30,000 kHz, and in megahertz-per-second above this frequency. The frequency subdivisions are:

- Very low frequency (VLF), below 30 kHz
- Low frequency (LF), 30 to 300 kHz
- Medium frequency (MF), 300 to 3000 kHz
- High frequency (HF), 3000 to 30,000 kHz
- Very high frequency (VHF), 30 to 300 MHz
- Ultrahigh frequency (UHF), 300 to 3000 MHz
- Superhigh frequency (SHF), 3000 to 30,000 MHz
- Extremely high frequency (EHF), above 30,000 MHz.

Radiotekhnika The largest communications equipment, computer, and electronics store and showroom in the Soviet Union. Radiotekhnika is located in Moscow. Soviet products from this firm are available for export to the United States.

RAF [TRG] Abbreviation for Red Army Faction, also known as Baader-Meinhof Gang. This West German group has proven to be more resilient than terrorist experts ever suggested. They have survived and gone on to conduct one terrorist act after another although the original leaders have been killed or imprisoned. The RAF is named after Rote Armee Fraktion, a Western German terrorist.

RAG [LE] Abbreviation for Ring Airfoil Grenade. Less than two inches across, this grenade is launched from a rifle with a special adapter causing it to spin in flight. The RAG is designed for close-in riot control and has less impact on contact than the rubber bullets that are used mostly in Europe and Asia. Two versions are currently available to law enforcement and the military. The Sting RAG is made of soft rubber in the shape of a tube-like airfoil. The Soft RAG is identical in configuration to the Sting, but it contains a quantity of CS (teargas) in powdered form.

rag [LE] Slang for colored bandanna worn as gang insignia.

RAI Specialty code for railroad felony.

RAM [A] Abbreviation for Radar-Absorbent Material. Ram is crafted from iron compounds and other chemical substances whose molecules absorb radar energy and transform it into heat, rather than reflecting it. It is possible that a Soviet satellite system with very sensitive infrared sensors could detect the difference in heat ratio created by the flight of a U.S. stealth aircraft into Soviet airspace. (See STEALTH.)

rainbows [C,G&PS] Slang for Tuinal, a brand name of amobarbital, a barbiturate.

rap 1. [C,G&PS] Slang meaning to carry on a conversation. 2. [C,G&PS] Slang for a sentence in prison.

rappelling [HRU] The method of lowering a member of a hostage rescue team, snipers, and assault troops into an area quickly, either by helicopter or from the top of a building.

rare 1. [C,G&PS] Slang for the inhalation of cocaine. 2. [C,G&PS] Slang meaning to ingest heroin.

RAT [A] Abbreviation for Ram Air Turbine.

rat [C,G&PS] Slang for an informer.

ratboy 1. [C,G&PS] Slang for a person skilled in testing the strength of illegal drugs and narcotics. 2. [C,G&PS] Slang for an individual who offers the services of killing for hire, a hired assassin.

RAU [C3I] Abbreviation for Radio Access Unit.

raven 1. [LE] Slang for a male seducer used to lure a woman into a honey trap. (See HONEY TRAP.) 2. [I] An undercover agent who, against all odds, is somehow able to transmit information to his base of operation under the most difficult of circumstances.

raw intelligence [I] Collected intelligence information that has not been converted into a useful format.

RB [C3I] Abbreviation for Reference Burst.

RBC [C3I] Abbreviation for Remote Black Concentrator.

RBES [C3I] Abbreviation for Rule-Based Expert System.

RBID [C3I] Abbreviation for Reference Burst Identification.

RC-135 [EW] Designation for an electronic warfare surveillance aircraft used by the United States.

RCEID [LE] Abbreviation for Radio-Controlled Improvised Explosive Device.

RCO [C] Abbreviation for Remote Communications Outlet.

RCS 1. [I] Abbreviation for Radar Cross Section. 2. [C3I] Abbreviation for Reaction Control System.

RCVR [C3I] Abbreviation for Receiver.

RD [I] Abbreviation for Restricted Data, information that is classified by the very nature of the design or use. The term is most often used in relationship to nuclear devices, and in conjunction with other security classifications. The term RD also relates to restricted computer data.

R&D [M] Abbreviation for Research and Development.

RDF 1. [M] Abbreviation for Rapid Deployment Force. 2. [M] Abbreviation for Radio Direction Finding.

RDO [LE] Abbreviation for Regular Day Off.

RDTE [M] Abbreviation for Research, Development, Test, and Evaluation.

RDX [M] Designation for a military plastic explosive.

RE Specialty code for repossessing.

REA   Specialty code for real estate fraud.

REACT   [C] Acronym for Radio Emergency Associated Citizens Teams.

reader   [LE] Slang for a medical prescription for narcotics.

readers   [C,G&PS] Slang for playing cards that have been marked in some way so they can be read from the backside.

REC   Abbreviation for *Radioelektronnaya bor'ba*, a Soviet term meaning "radioelectronic combat." The Soviet term *bor'ba* is better defined as "struggle" because "combat" can give the impression that a state of military conflict exists. REC is one Soviet effort to make the enemy's radioelectronic equipment useless while maintaining a reliable communications operating system of their own. Radio Electronic Combat is considered by the Soviet military to also mean electromagnetic countermeasures.

red   *See* PANAMA RED.

redball   [LE] Slang for a red traffic light.

red balled   [LE] A term used by intelligence and law enforcement agents indicating that they were halted by a stop signal while following a suspect.

red bird   [C,G&PS] Slang for Seconal, a barbiturate.

redboarded   [LE] A term used in intelligence/surveillance indicating that an agent or police officer is stopped at a traffic light but the suspect is still moving.

Red Brigades   [TRG] An Italian left-wing terrorist group that first appeared in the 1970s. Since then, it has been responsible for assassinations, kidnappings, arson and bombing incidents throughout Europe. The Red Brigades members are on the Interpol most wanted list, and because of close associations with the Italian Prima Linea and the Azione Revoluzionaria terrorist groups, they easily blend into the shadows. The Red Brigades are known to receive funding from supporters in the United States.

red bullet   [C,G&PS] Slang for Seconal, a barbiturate.

red chicken   [C,G&PS] Slang for heroin imported from China.

REDCOM   [M] Abbreviation for Readiness Command.

Red Cross Emergency Communications in the U.S.   [G] The American Red Cross maintains its own continental communications network by means of telephone, amateur radio operations, and Western Union's Easylink system. This network is linked to all Red Cross chapters and field stations. It also links chapters and field stations overseas via military (MARS) communications. The options of telephone, Easylink Whisper Writer (which operates at 300 baud) are available to any continental facility. Western Union's computer assigns a number to every Easylink message, which provides message accountability. Overseas field stations are assigned a four-letter code, and they sequentially number every message they send. Emergency communications reverses the four-letter code. Every 24 hours, emergency communications units and the overseas field stations check the respective incoming logs and notify each other of the numbers of missing messages. These messages are then repeated under new message numbers. (*See* MARS.)

red deck   [US] Naval aviation voice brevity code meaning flight deck of aircraft carrier is not clear to launch or recover.

red devil   [C,G&PS] Slang for seconal, which is a barbiturate.

red door   [LE] A command (or signal) to stop an individual who is under surveillance or suspected of a crime at a red traffic light.

red flag   [C,G&PS] Slang for a procedure used to inject heroin. The needle is inserted into a vein and blood is drawn into the syringe. The heroin is then injected slowly to prolong the rush.

Red Army Faction   [TRG] The Red Army Faction has gained notoriety as one of Europe's deadliest leftist terrorist groups in two decades of bloody attacks on West German and American targets. The Red Army Faction began operating in the late 1960s. It was known then as the Baader-Meinhof gang, named after its founders Andreas Baader and Ulrike Meinhof. The Red Army Faction has a reputation as a brutal, well-organized group with a core of 20 to 30 members. Most of the original leaders of the group have been killed by police or have died in prison. The Red Army Faction remains an active terrorist group in Europe, singling out West German businessmen and American military personnel as prime targets. (*See* BAADER-MEINHOF.)

reds [C,G&PS] Slang for Gelatin capsules or spansules that contain Dexedrine.

reds and blues [C,G&PS] Slang for barbiturates. (*See* QUICK REFERENCE.)

reefer [C,G&PS] Slang for a marijuana cigarette.

reentry [C,G&PS] The process of returning to normalcy following the use of a drug or narcotic.

referentura [USSR] The rooms or electronic hardware located inside its facilities that are protected from electromagnetic interference (EMI) and radio frequency interference (RFI). In the United States government, this process is known by the Tempest codeword.

register [C,G&PS] To draw blood from a vein into a hypodermic syringe, ensuring that the vein has been penetrated and drugs can be injected.

REMBASS [US] Code name for unattended ground sensors and associated data communications equipment.

REP Abbreviation for *Radioelektronnoye podavleniye*, or radio electronic suppression, the process of disrupting and lessening the effectiveness of the enemy's radioelectronics systems by electronic means, especially in conjunction with all physical means, particularly with weapons that home in on enemy radiofrequency emissions.

repeater [C] A communications device that retransmits radio signals it receives from another source, often simultaneously. Many highway patrols across the United States use mobile extender radio transmitters in a repeater system for ease of communications. Radio repeaters are installed on hilltops or buildings for use by these low power transmitters. In some states like California, the Highway Patrol uses the Simplex system (*See* SIMPLEX) for statewide communication. Those highway patrols or state police, by state and fre-

quency, who use repeaters or the simplex system are listed in TABLE R-1.

requirement [I]A specific request for collection of intelligence information by a member of the law enforcement or intelligence community.

RER Abbreviation for *Radioelektronnaya razvedka*, or reconnaissance and intelligence, the process of gaining intelligence information from the enemy's radiofrequency emissions.

resident [I] The senior KGB officer who is in charge of an intelligence operation in a specific country or city anywhere in the world.

residentura All personnel and any intelligence operation located outside the Soviet Union.

restricted data *See* RD.

retinal pattern [LE] The blood vessel pattern at the back of the eye or retina. Retinal scans work

Table R-1. Repeater Frequencies Used by Highway Patrols

State	Frequency
Arizona	155.5050
Arkansas	154.7850
California	154.9050
Connecticut	154.8300, 154.1500
Delaware	465.4750
Florida	465.1625, 156.1800
Georgia	458.4875
Illinois	155.5050
Indiana	155.4450
Iowa	453.6250
Kentucky	154.6650
Louisiana	453.4500
Maryland	155.7300
Massachusetts	154.9200
Michigan	154.6950
Minnesota	458.2500, 453.2500
Missouri	154.9050
Nebraska	465.5250
Nevada	154.9200
North Carolina	159.2100
North Dakota	453.4500
Ohio	465.5500, 465.5250
Oklahoma	154.9050
Pennsylvania	154.7550
South Dakota	453.3750
Tennessee	154.9050
Virginia	453.3500
Washington	453.4750
Wisconsin	465.1250

by taking a picture of this blood vessel pattern. This picture then can be used to identify a particular person. The picture is taken using a computer and a special camera called a retinal scanner. The scanner uses a low-level light to take the picture. This light is the same light used on a remote control television or VCR. The process is simple and completely safe. (*See* BIOMETRICS.)

REZ   Abbreviation for *Radioelektronnaya zashchita*. This Soviet term means radioelectronic defense. The purpose is to ensure the continued operation of one's own radioelectronic system as an enemy conducts radioelectronic warfare, and to prevent the mutual interference of transmissions among the systems friendly to each other.

rezz   [LE] Slang for the residence of a criminal suspect.

RF   [C3I] Abbreviation for Radio Frequency.

RFI   [C3I] Abbreviation for Radio Frequency Interference.

RFP   [C3I] Abbreviation for Request For Proposal.

RFR   Abbreviation for Radio Frequency Radiation. In an effort to make the death of some political prisoners appear "natural" the Romanian secret service has reportedly installed microwave generators in certain confinement areas. This is according to Lt. General Ion Mihai Pacepa in his book *Red Horizons* published by Regnery Gateway Press. In *Red Horizons* Pacepa states that under the code name Radu radiation dosages over a short term generate lethal forms of cancer that kill and go undetected. (*See* RADIATION PISTOL.)

RFSM   [C3I] Abbreviation for Radio Frequency Spectrum Management.

RGD   [M] Abbreviation for Range Gate Deception.

RGWO   [M] Abbreviation for Range Gate Walk Off.

RH-53D   [M] Designation for a twin-turbine military helicopter, also known as the Sea Stallion.

RHAW   [M] Abbreviation for Radar Homing All the Way.

RHAWS   [M] Abbreviation for Radar Homing And Warning System.

RI   [M] Abbreviation for Radar Interference. Who would place a $90 million, high-powered radar station so close to an airport that it has to be shut down every time a plane lands? Someone, it turns out, who should know better: the United States Air Force Space Command. The problem exists at Warner Robins Air Force Base in Georgia, where a giant early-warning radar searches for missiles launched from submarines. But the apparatus is only 1.5 miles from the approach end of a runway, and Air Force electronic engineers fear that its emissions could trigger electromagnetic explosive devices on many military aircraft. Those devices are used mainly to discharge fuel tanks or fire air-to-air weapons. To guard against accidental explosions, the radar is manually shut down for up to 90 seconds whenever a plane approaches Robins Air Force Base. Although the Air Force insists that electronic flight-control circuits inside its aircraft are shielded against radar and radio emissions, it closed the radar station completely during a precision flying exhibition by the Air Force Thunderbirds. Several Army BlackHawk helicopters have crashed when its pilots flew too close to radio antennas elsewhere and lost control of their choppers. This problem has not been widely discussed outside of official Air Force circles. The Air Force has now compiled a list of 300 powerful radio and radar transmitters and receivers in the United States, and at 500 other locations elsewhere in the world that its pilots must avoid by a certain distance. The list has been classified as secret.

rice   1. [UK] Code name for internal communications equipment used between intelligence operations and military units. 2. [C,G&PS] Slang for a smokable methamphetamine. (*See* ICE.)

Richter   [D] Short for the Richter scale, a gauge of energy released by an earthquake or nuclear explosion as measured by the ground motion recorded on a seismograph. Every increase of one whole number, say from 4.2 to 5.2, represents a tenfold increase in ground motion. Based on the most current findings, some scientists say the amount of energy released under certain conditions might be as much as 30 times greater for each increase of one whole digit on the scale. (*See* EARTHQUAKE and SEISMOGRAPH.)

ricin A deadly poison, also known as ricinine, easily derived from the common castor oil plant. The beans of this plant are crushed to obtain castor oil. Rinin remains in the bean once the oil has been extracted. Efficiently extracted from the bean, ricin is twice as deadly as cobra venom and is known to have been used as a weapon of assassination. (*See* ROSARY BEAN.)

RICO [LE] Abbreviation for Racketeer Influenced and Corrupt Organizations Act. Under this statute, it is a federal crime to gain an interest in or control over any enterprise through a pattern of racketeering activity. The law defines such a pattern as the commission of two or more of at least 25 felonies—extortion, bribery, obstruction of justice, securities fraud, mail fraud, wire fraud, and so forth—over a 10-year period. On conviction, all income found to be from any racketeering enterprise is turned over to the government. This often can mean loss of the person's entire assets in addition to a fine of $25,000 per violation. Furthermore, a 1984 amendment to the law allows prosecutors to freeze suspected enterprise assets on court order at the time of indictment to preserve them from dissipation while the case is pending.

riff **1.** [C,G&PS] Slang meaning to carry on a conversation. **2.** [LE] Originally in the musical world of jazz, a particular solo instrument with the player showing off his skills. In the world of narcotics, a riff essentially means the same thing, usually by someone stealing drugs from another person.

rig [C,G&PS] The hardware used for injecting drugs.

rigor [LE] Short for rigor mortis, the hardening of muscles in a human body after death.

RIIS [C3I] Abbreviation for Route Integration Instrumentation System.

RINT [I] Abbreviation for Radiation INTelligence.

rip [C,G&PS] Slang meaning to steal.

rip off [LE] Slang meaning to steal something from an individual.

ripped [C,G&PS] Slang meaning to be high on drugs or narcotics.

Ritalin [LE] Brand name of methylphenidate, a controlled substance, a stimulant. (*See* QUICK REFERENCE.)

RKO [B] Abbreviation for RKO Radio Shows, special events.

RKO-1 [B] Designation for RKO One Network, youth programming.

RKO-2 [B] Designation for RKO Two Network, adult programming.

RMA [LE] Abbreviation for Refused Medical Assistance.

RMP [LE] Abbreviation for Radio Motor Patrol, patrol car.

RMS [TRG] Abbreviation for *Republik Malaku Selatan*, the South Moluccan Separatists, a terrorist group headquartered in Holland which has conducted hijackings and bombings throughout Holland.

RO [LE] Abbreviation for Registered Owner.

roach [C,G&PS] Slang for the butt of a marijuana cigarette.

roach clip [C,G&PS] Slang for a tweezerlike device or long pin for holding a marijuana (roach) cigarette so it can be smoked to its limit.

roach holder [C,G&PS] Slang for a tweezerlike or V-shaped device for holding a very short marijuana cigarette.

road condition codes *See* TABLE R-2.

rock [C,G&PS] Term for small crystals of cocaine.

rock cocaine [LE] Cocaine in the form of small crystals. (*See* QUICK REFERENCE.)

roll call [C,G&PS] A listing or roster of gang members.

roll over **1.** [C,G&PS] Slang for a defendant in a criminal case who becomes an informer. **2.** [LE] To give information to law enforcement agencies against others in return for special consideration. **3.** A person, usually more than an informant, who might be inside a gang.

Table R-2. Road Condition Codes

Code	Meaning
Code 1*(MCU)	No late report (also indicates clear weather)
Code 2*(MCU)	No oversize load (also indicates overcast weather)
Code 3*(MCU)	Weather conditions are restricted because of wind
Code 4*(MCU)	Weather conditions are restricted because of fog
Code 5*(MCU)	Weather conditions include blowing dust
Code 6*(MCU)	Visibility poor
Code 7*(MCU)	Rain
Code 8*(MCU)	Hail
Code 9*(MCU)	Snow
Code 10*(MCU)	Sleet (also indicates snowing very hard)
Code 11*(MCU)	Ground blizzard
Code 12*(MCU)	Snowslide
Code 13*(MCU)	Road(s) closed
Code 14*(MCU)	Road wet
Code 15*(MCU)	Road dry
Code 16*(MCU)	Road icy
Code 17*(MCU)	Road icy in spots
Code 18*(MCU)	Road snowpacked
Code 19*(MCU)	Road snowpacked in spots
Code 20*(MCU)	Chains required
Code 21*(MCU)	Road slushy
Code 22*(MCU)	Drifting snow
Code 23*(MCU)	Snow tires or chains are adequate

* Most Common Uses

Romeo/Robert [A,LE,MIL] Designation for the letter *R*.

root [C,G&PS] Slang for marijuana. (*See* QUICK REFERENCE.)

rope [C,G&PS] Slang for hashish that is made from hemp.

ropes [C,G&PS] Slang for large arteries or veins used for the injection of dope.

ROR [M] Abbreviation for Range Only Radar.

RO/RO [M] Abbreviation for Roll On/Roll Off.

RORSAT [US] Shortened form of Radar Ocean Reconnaissance SATellite.

rosary bean [I] The world's most common lethal source of vegetable poison. The beans are widely used in Europe to make religious rosaries and yield a toxin called abrin when soaked in water. These beans are being used by the Soviet Union and the United States to produce a deadly chemical weapons system. (*See* LETHAL PELLET.)

rosco [C,G&PS] Slang for a handgun.

rough stuff [C,G&PS] Term for the marijuana plant, in the rough, before it is dried and processed.

ROVS [USSR] Abbreviation for *Russkiy Obshche-Voyenskiy Soyuz*; also *Rossiyskiy Obshchevoinskiy Soyuz*, Russian Armed Forces Union; Russian General Military Union.

royal blue [C,G&PS] Slang for LSD. (*See* QUICK REFERENCE.)

RPV [M] Abbreviation for Remotely Piloted Vehicle (i.e., a radio controlled drone aircraft or missile).

RR [D] Designation for Russian.

R-R [B] Designation for the CBS 'Radio Radio' Network.

RRF [M] Abbreviation for Ready Reserve Force.

RS AS&I [C3I] Abbreviation for Re-entry System Aerial Surveillance and Intelligence.

RSDLP [USSR] Abbreviation for Russian Social Democratic Labor Party.

RSO 1. [C] Abbreviation for Receiver, Set-On. **2.** [US] Abbreviation for Reconnaissance Systems Officer.

RST [C] Abbreviation for The Readability/Signal Strength/Tone System used in communications. This system is based on:

Readability

1 Unreadable
2 Barely readable, an occasional word can be distinguished
3 Readable with considerable difficulty
4 Readable with practically no difficulty
5 Perfectly readable

Signal Strength

1 Faint signals, barely perceptible
2 Very weak signal
3 Weak signal
4 Fair signal
5 Fairly good signal
6 Good signal
7 Moderately strong signal
8 Strong signal
9 Extremely strong signal

Tone

1 Sixty-cycle ac or less, very rough and broad
2 Very rough ac, very harsh and broad
3 Rough ac tone, rectified but not filtered
4 Rough note, some trace of filtering
5 Filtered rectified ac but strongly ripple modulated
6 Filtered tone, definite trace of ripple modulation
7 Near pure tone, trace of ripple modulation
8 Near perfect tone, slight trace of modulation
9 Perfect tone, no trace of ripple or modulation of any kind

RTS [C3I] Abbreviation for Request To Send.

RU [USSR] Abbreviation for Razvedyvatel'noye Upravleniye, Intelligence Directorate.

rules [I] The guidelines established for any clandestine meeting. The rules can include place and time of contact, and clothing to be worn. Passwords are a part of the rules. If there are any variations to the prearranged rules, the meeting is called off.

rumble 1. [C,G&PS] A planned fight between two ganging factions. **2.** [LE] A shakedown against criminals by law enforcement officers. **3.** [C,G&PS] An ongoing program of searches as a form of harassment toward criminal elements, usually at a specific location, by law enforcement officials.

run 1. [C,G&PS] Slang for the sequence of time of an addiction to narcotics. **2.** [C,G&PS] Slang for a trip, usually meaning a trip to buy drugs.

runner [C,G&PS] Slang for an individual selling drugs on behalf of a dealer.

rush [C,G&PS] The feeling drug addicts claim to experience a few seconds after an intravenous injection of heroin.

RV 1. [I] Abbreviation for rendezvous. **2.** [NASA] Abbreviation for Reentry Vehicle.

RWR [M] Abbreviation for Radar Warning Receiver.

RX 1. [C] Designation for receiver (communications). **2.** [D] Designation for Religion or religious.

RZ 1. [TRG] Abbreviation for *Revolutionare Zellen*, a terrorist and radical group headquartered and very active in West Germany. **2.** [C3I] Abbreviation for Return to Zero.

S

SA **1.** Specialty code for safety services. **2.** [LE] Abbreviation for Small Arms (weapons). **3.** [D] Abbreviation for South America or South American.

S-BAND [NASA] A radio frequency band of 1550 to 5200 megahertz. Much of NASA's Space Shuttle in-flight communications are in this bandwidth.

S-BD [NASA] Abbreviation for S-band.

SA/BM [M] Abbreviation for Systems Analysis/ Battle Management.

Sabry Al-Banna *See* ABU NIDAL.

SAC [C3I] Acronym for Strategic Air Command (USAF).

SAACS [US] Abbreviation for Strategic Air Command Automated Command Control System.

SACDIN [C3I] Abbreviation for Strategic Air Command Digital Information Network.

sack [C,G&PS] Slang for heroin in a large quantity.

sacraments [C,G&PS] Slang for LSD. (*See* QUICK REFERENCE.)

sacred mushrooms [C,G&PS] Slang for psilocybin. (*See* QUICK REFERENCE.)

SACSA [US Military] Abbreviation for Special Assistant for Counterinsurgency and Special Activities.

SADE [C3I] Acronym for Solar Array Drive Electronics.

SAF [M] Abbreviation for Army Special Forces unit, consisting of a Special Forces Group skilled in unique elements of warfare (i.e., antiterrorism).

safe house [I] A location controlled by a law enforcement or intelligence agency that can provide a safe and secure facility to hide persons who are engaged in an intelligence (secret witness) operation. A safe house is often used for the debriefing process.

sagging [C,G&PS] Slang term for gang members wearing their pants or jeans two inches lower than their underwear as a showing of their machismo.

Saiqa [HRU] The Egyptian Army "Lightning Force" responsible for hostage rescue and antiterrorism operations.

SALT [C3I] Acronym for Strategic Arms Limitation Talks/Treaty.

salt shot [C,G&PS] Slang for an intravenous injection of salt and water into a narcotics addict who has overdosed using heroin. A salt shot has been known to revive an addict who otherwise might have died from the overdose.

SAM [C3I] Abbreviation for Surface-to-Air Missile.

Sam [A,LE,MIL] Designation for the letter *S*.

SAMOS [US] Abbreviation for Satellite and Missile Observation System.

SAMSARS [C3I] Abbreviation for Satellite Aided Maritime Search and Rescue System.

SAMT [US] Abbreviation for State-of-the-art Medium (computer) Terminals.

sandinismo [TRG] Term for the political ideology of Augusto Sandino and the F.S.L.N. (*See* SANDINISTA.)

Sandinista [TRG] This group, also known as Sandinist, was originally a supporter of Augusto Sandino. The political process in Nicaragua has resulted in the Sandinista Organization now supporting the goals of the F.S.L.N. (*See* F.S.L.N.)

sanguine [US] Code name for the ELF program. (*See* ELF.)

sanitize　[I] To delete or revise documents, photographs, reports, and other material to prevent the identification of an intelligence source or the detection of facts in a file that might prove to be embarrassing. Making sure that when meeting an informant you were not followed and your cover or that of your contact is not blown is to sanitize yourself.

Santeria, Cult of　[S] A cult imported into Mexico and the United States from Cuba. At its outset the cult combined Christianity with the religious traditions of West Africa. Santeria means "saint worship." More recently, the cult has changed direction and is known to include human cannibalism in its practices. Law enforcement reports indicate that victims are abducted off the streets. Victims are killed and their brains cut out and mixed with blood, herbs, rooster feet, goat heads, and turtles. During the cult ceremonies, the santero, or priest, offers this sacrifice to spirit gods known as the Seven African Powers. The mixture is then eaten by cult members in the belief that this process puts a magical shield around them that protects them from evil or harm, even bullets. The cult is currently very active (usually in populations made up of those with a Mexican heritage) and is known to be responsible for the disappearance of people in the United States and Mexico. An arrow tattooed on the shoulder of a member indicates that individual has been "authorized" to kill a human sacrifice. The cult is a blend of the satanic, voodoo, and black magick.

Santeria, religion of　Spanish for "worship of saints," *santeria*, is rooted in an ancient African religion. The Yoruba of Benin and western Nigeria were the original Santeros. When they were enslaved and brought to colonial Cuba they were forced to convert to Catholicism. The religion of Santeria is not a cult movement centered on the slaughter of animals, although the santeros sometimes sacrifice small animals. Santeros worship many humanlike gods, or *orishas*. The gods have powerful spirits and control what happens to people. The santeros believe that they can enlist the help of the gods through ritual white magic. Cuban, Mexican, Puerto Rican, and Dominican immigrants brought santeria with them to the east coast and southern border cities of the United States where a second generation is now practicing the faith. Law enforcement agencies estimate that there are at least 50,000 followers in the Miami area alone. The Santeria religion is practiced under many names, including Ifa, Sin Orisa, Vodun, Candomble, Umbanda, Lucumi, Regla Ocha, and The Religion.

SAOCS　[US] Abbreviation for Submarine/Aircraft Optical Communications System.

SAR　**1.** [M] Abbreviation for Search And Rescue. **2.** [M] Abbreviation for Specific Air Range, the distance that can be flown by an aircraft or missile per unit of fuel on board.

SARBE　[UK] Abbreviation for Search and Rescue Beacon Equipment.

sarin　[CW] Name of a nerve gas and chemical weapon produced by a number of countries. Sarin kills on contact when breathed into the lungs. The most common means of delivery is by artillery shell or bomb. The major disadvantage of chemical weapons like sarin is that it is carried by the wind and was best described in testimony before the United States Congress by Air Force General Charles L. Donnelly, Jr., who said of nonpersistent sarin bombs: "Two hundred feet away from impact, one could virtually hold his breath until it dissipates."

SARSAR　[C3I] Acronym for Search And Rescue Satellite-Aided Tracking System.

SAS　[M] Abbreviation for Special Air Service, the elite British military operations unit used in counterterrorist operations. New Zealand and Australia also have SAS units for hostage rescue and antiterrorism operations.

satch cotton　[C,G&PS] A small piece of cotton that has been saturated with heroin.

SATCOM　[C] Acronym for SATellite COMmunications—hardware and systems.

SATIN　[US] Shortened form of Strategic Air

Command Automated Total Information Network.

sativa [C,G&PS] Slang for marijuana. (*See* QUICK REFERENCE.)

SATKA [M] Abbreviation for Surveillance, Acquisition, Tracking, and Kill Assessment.

savama [LE] Iranian (revolutionary) secret police.

SAW [M] Acronym for Surface Acoustic Wave.

Sayaret Matkal [HRU] The Israeli antiterrorist and hostage rescue unit. Members of the Sayaret Matkal have designed and developed a number of entry tools that are used by other hostage rescue units worldwide.

SBA [US] Abbreviation for Small Business Administration.

SBI 1. Abbreviation for Special Background Investigation. The review of an individual's background, usually going back to high school with verification of jobs, travel, reputation, and finances over the previous fifteen years. An SBI is a major part of the security classification process for individuals involved in research projects for the United States government. 2. [C3I] Abbreviation for Space-Based Interceptor.

SBR [C3I] Abbreviation for Space-Based Radar.

SBS [M] Abbreviation for Special Boat Squadron, British Royal Marine Commandos who also are expert combat deep-water swimmers. SBS is responsible for counterterrorist operations in harbor facilities and around oil rigs in the North Sea, which are a prime target for terrorist groups.

SBSS [C3I] Abbreviation for Space-Based Space Surveillance.

scag [C,G&PS] Slang for heroin. (*See* QUICK REFERENCE.)

SCC [C3I] Abbreviation for System Control Center.

SCF [NASA] Abbreviation for Satellite Control Facility.

schmeck [C,G&PS] Slang for heroin. (*See* QUICK REFERENCE.)

school boy [C,G&PS] Slang for codeine in tablet form.

SCI [I] Abbreviation for Sensitive (or Special) Compartmented Information, specific information above the security classification of secret. SCI usually is a code word indicating a classified project.

SCIF [I] Abbreviation for Secure Compartmented Information Facility.

SCIP [D] Abbreviation for Society of Competitor Intelligence Professionals, a professional organization established to keep track of the methods used in the business community to gather competitor intelligence. The organization publishes a quarterly newsletter. (*See* PUBLICATIONS.)

SCN [C3I] Abbreviation for Strategic Communications Network.

scoff [C,G&PS] Slang term meaning to ingest (take by mouth) a narcotic.

scope 1. [M] A telescope attached to a firearm. 2. [M] Night-vision equipment. 3. [LE] Slang term meaning to look over an area, that is, "to scope the scene."

score 1. [C,G&PS] Slang term meaning to purchase narcotics. 2. [C,G&PS] Slang term meaning to find a drug dealer.

SCOT [UK] Shortened form of Shipborne Satcom Terminal.

scratch [C,G&PS] Slang for some form of money; something of value.

screw 1. [LE] Archaic, a jail or prison correctional officer. 2. Someone who gives others a hard time.

script [C,G&PS] Slang for a (medical/drug) prescription.

scripter [LE] Slang for an individual who has legitimate prescriptions for narcotics or drugs and offers them for sale.

script mill [C,G&PS] Slang for a source who is able to produce prescriptions for narcotics or drugs.

scrub [US] Naval aviation voice brevity code meaning to erase a contact designation.

SCU [LE] Abbreviation for Street Crime Unit.

SDAC [US] Abbreviation for Seismic Data Analysis Center.

SDCU [C3I] Abbreviation for Satellite Delay Compensation Unit.

SDI [C3I] Abbreviation for Strategic Defense Initiative, also known as Star Wars.

SDIO [M] Abbreviation for Strategic Defense Initiative Organization.

SDLC [C3I] Abbreviation for Synchronous Data Line Control.

SDMA [C3I] Abbreviation for Space Diversity Multiple Access.

SDMS [US] Abbreviation for Shipboard Data Multiplex System.

SDNS [C3I] Abbreviation for Secure Data Network System.

SDS 1. [US] Abbreviation for Satellite Data System. 2. [C3I] Abbreviation for Space Defense System. 3. [TRG] Abbreviation for Students for a Democratic Society, a radical group that began conducting terrorist acts in the late 1960s as a protest to the war in Vietnam. The group bombed a number of facilities in the United States, mostly government office buildings and National Guard facilities. In the 1970s its activities tapered off as members grew older. The SDS has all but disappeared from the active terrorist scene.

SE Specialty code for security.

SEAD [M] Abbreviation for Suppression of Enemy Air Defenses.

seafarer [US] Code name for ELF, a submarine communications system.

SEALS [M] Abbreviation for Navy Sea, Air, and Land Teams, the equivalent to the U.S. Army Green Berets.

SEAL Team 6 [M] The special arm of the SEALS trained as deep-water combat swimmers. Members of SEAL Team 6 are assigned to Delta Force and support that group on antiterrorist missions.

search and rescue dedicated frequencies See EMERGENCY/DISTRESS FREQUENCIES WORLDWIDE.

seaspray [I] Designation for the CIA/US Army clandestine aviation unit.

SEC 1. Background code for security. 2. Specialty code for security and premises protection.

SECAM [C3I] Designation for sequential color with memory.

SECDEF [M] Acronym for SECretary of DEFense.

Seconal [LE] Brand name of secobarbital, a controlled substance that is a sedative. (See QUICK REFERENCE.)

secret [US] A security classification for information that is not authorized for disclosure to uncleared individuals and might affect the national security of the United States.

secret writing [I] Sophisticated chemicals (sometimes simple processes) that appear under certain conditions. The most simple is the juice from a lemon that dries clear when used as an "ink" but turns brown when heat is applied.

seek bus [US] Designation for jam-resistant digital tactical communications system.

seek talk [US] Designation for secure communications system.

seeley [US] Code name for short-range wide-band radio.

seggy [LE] Slang for various barbiturates, the exact identification of which is unknown.

seismograph An instrument that detects and records seismic waves caused by earthquakes and nuclear explosions. Most seismographs contain a weight that stays still while the rest of the instrument moves. The motion is recorded by a vibrating pen on a moving strip of paper. (See RICHTER SCALE.)

SEK [LE] Designation for *Speziale-insatz Kommando*, the West German police commando unit that responds to incidents much like police SWAT units in the United States.

seldon [US] Code name for modular record traffic terminal.

self-employs [C,G&PS] Slang for drug dealers who are doing business outside any gang.

semtex [M] A widely used (military) plastic explosive that is a favorite of terrorist bomb builders. Semtex is rust-(orange) colored and can be formed into sheets or molded into shapes. It can be made to look like almost anything, which is an advantage to terrorist operations. Formed around a drinking glass to create a cup, the terrorist can then place the open end against the surface to be penetrated and have, in effect, a shaped charge that directs the majority of the explosive energy in one direction. Czechoslovakia is the only country where Semtex is produced. Syria and Libya are known to be large quantity buyers of this plastic explosive. Semtex has appeared in many shapes, including children's candy.

SEN [C3I] Abbreviation for Small Extension Node.

Sendero Luminuso [TRG] A Peruvian terrorist group, also known as the Shining Path. It is a Marxist guerrilla organization that travels in the jungles of Peru seeking converts to its cause. Members of the group have attacked villages and outposts where they are known to have committed atrocities against the Peruvian peasants. They have a vast communications system that mixes new radio technology with hand-written coded messages. Their weapons are mostly from the Soviet Union. The group is also known as the Sendero Luminoso.

sensitive [I] Of or referring to certain materials requiring special protection from disclosure. Sensitive material, if somehow compromised, can cause great embarrassment or a threat to security.

Serax [LE] Brand name of oxazepam, a controlled substance that is a minor tranquilizer. (*See* QUICK REFERENCE.)

SERE [M] Abbreviation for Survival, Escape, Resistance, and Evasion, the training given to members of the U.S. Army Special Forces.

set **1.** [C,G&PS] The neighborhood subsets under an umbrella gang tag, for example, Hoover Crips are the Crips set on Hoover Street while Bounty Hunters are the creation of an off-shoot set of the Bloods street gang. **2.** [C,G&PS] The hardware and related paraphernalia used for the injection of drugs.

SETA [C3I] Abbreviation for System Engineering Technical Assistance.

SEWS [C3I] Abbreviation for Satellite Early Warning System.

SF [US] Abbreviation for Special Forces.

SFC [A] Abbreviation for Specific Fuel Consumption, that is, the fuel flow rate per unit of thrust.

SFJ [M] Abbreviation for Standforward Jamming.

SFOD-D *See* DELTA FORCE.

SFOD-Delta *See* DELTA FORCE.

shades [C,G&PS] Slang for sunglasses.

shake [LE] Slang term meaning to break a drug or narcotics habit.

shaped charge [M] Term for the Munro Effect. Munro had been an explosives tester for the U.S. Naval arsenal around 1900, and noticed that when he exploded a test piece of cordite (a smokeless powder composed of nitroglycerin, guncotton, and a petroleum substance) on a steel plate he found *U.S. Navy* etched on the plate in mirror writing. Each piece of cordite had been stamped underneath with *U.S. Navy* and it had been the hollows thus created that somehow focused the explosive effect. The effect was merely a curiosity for many years, but ultimately its potential was realized, and the 'shaped charge' resulted. In its simplest form this consisted of a block of explosive with a cone-shaped hollow on one face, the surface of the cone being thinly lined with metal. If the charge is exploded in contact with armor plate, the metal liner is converted into an extremely hot tongue emerging from the axis of the cone, which proceeded to drill a deep hole in the plate. The Munro Effect is in common usage by almost every firm in the world today who produce weapon systems.

sheep-dipped [I] The intelligence term used to describe members of the U.S. military who have been discharged and then hired by the NSA or CIA. The term also relates to aircraft, documents, files, or unaccountable funds that have been sanitized. (*See* SANITIZED.)

SHELF [US] Acronym for Super Hard ELF System.

Sheremetyevo [USSR] An airport outside Moscow. It is a familiar name in every spy story about the CIA besting the KGB.

sherms [C,G&PS] Slang for Nat Sherman brown

cigarettes that have been dipped in PCP. Sherms are sold primarily by the Hispanic gangs.

SHF [C3I] Abbreviation for Super High Frequency, 3 GHz-25 GHz/microwaves.

Shin Beth [I] The Israeli domestic counterintelligence arm of the Mossad, the Office of Intelligence and Special Missions.

shining path *See* SENDERO LUMINUSO.

shipyard confetti [TRG] Slang term used by terrorist/radical groups for the metal fragments caused by the explosion of a pipe bomb.

shit [C,G&PS] Slang term for dope, usually meaning heroin, cocaine, or marijuana, or drugs that turn out to be of an inferior quality.

shiv [C,G&PS] Slang for a knife used for protection or killing.

shoe [I] Slang for a false passport.

shoot [C,G&PS] To inject drugs.

shooter [C,G&PS] Slang for a professional killer, that is, a hit man.

shoot hoops [C,G&PS] A term used in a conversation meaning to inject narcotics, as in "Want to go over to Joe's place and shoot some hoops?"

shooting gallery [LE] Slang for a building or some part of a complex where drug users inject narcotics. In such a situation, drugs usually are purchased out of funds gathered by the group and needles are shared with other addicts as drugs are injected.

shooting up [C,G&PS] Injecting intravenous drugs.

SHORAD-C2 [M] Designation for Short-Range Air Defense Command and Control.

short [LE] Slang for an automobile, usually stolen or loaned.

short barrel [LE] Slang for a sawed-off shotgun.

short eyes [LE] Slang for a child molester.

short-timer [C,G&PS] An individual who has only a short time remaining on a prison or jail sentence.

shot [C,G&PS] Slang for an injection of drugs.

shotgun [C,G&PS] A method used by marijuana smokers to get more smoke into their lungs. A lighted marijuana cigarette is placed into the mouth of a smoker, lighted end first. A second smoker then holds the butt end in his mouth. The first smoker blows hard while the second smoker inhales. The result is that the second smoker receives the resulting smoke under added pressure.

SHP [M] Abbreviation for Shaft Horse Power, a naval term.

shrewd sands [US] Code name for a proposed plan to orbit four giant sand-filled satellites as a part of the Strategic Defense Initiative (SDI) program, one to guard each border of the continental United States. In the event of nuclear attack, the satellites would spray their contents into space, thus creating a "shield of silicon" that would break up other incoming missiles in the outer atmosphere.

shriek [C,G&PS] Slang for distilled and concentrated heroin.

SI [I] Abbreviation for Special Intelligence, the classification of data that relates to intelligence sources.

SIAM [C3I] Acronym for Submarine Intercept of Air Missile.

sick [C,G&PS] The feeling one has from the withdrawal from narcotics.

sidewalk servers [C,G&PS] Slang for dope pushers who are selling drugs, marijuana, and narcotics from street side to people in automobiles.

Sierra [A,LE,MIL] Designation for the letter *S*.

SIF [I] Abbreviation for Selective Identification Feature.

SIGINT [C3I] Acronym for SIGnal INTelligence, intelligence information collected by any and all electronic methods.

signal 1. [I] Slang for a field agent, for example, our signal is in the red shirt. 2. [I] An agent's ID number and/or radio callsign.

sign-of-life signal [I] A signal or radio transmission made by an undercover agent, covert operator, or field agent conducting extensive surveillance that will somehow signify that they are safe. The lacking of a SOLS signal generally means that the agent is Shit Out Of Luck (SOOL) and maybe in some sort of trouble.

SIGSEC [M] Acronym for SIGnal SECurity.

silencer [LE] *See* SUPPRESSER.

simplex system [C] In voice communications using radio, a system in which messages received and messages transmitted are on a single frequency. This system has been adopted by some law enforcement agencies for this reason.

SINCGARS-V [C3I] Abbreviation for SINgle Channel Ground and Airborne Radio (communications) System (VHF).

Sindicato Texas [LE] Mexican for Texas Syndicate. *See* TEXAS SYNDICATE.

single-letter identifiers [I] Identifiers are used by agencies of law enforcement and intelligence agents in surveillance operations to clearly identify a person, place, or thing. The following is a list of identifiers:

A	ALFA
A	Saturday
B	BRAVO
B	Base Station
C	CHARLIE
C	Cocaine
D	DELTA
E	ECHO
E	Electric Field Intensity
F	FOXTROT
F	Friday
G	GOLF
G	Acceleration due to gravity
H	HOTEL
H	Thursday
H	Heroin
H	Blister Agent (Mustard Gas)
I	INDIA
I	Interstate highway
J	JULIETT
J	A marijuana cigarette
J	Jamming (communications)
K	KILO
L	LIMA
L	Blister Agent (Lewisite)
M	MIKE
M	Monday
M	Morphine
M	Mach (number)
M	Mobile Units
N	NOVEMBER
O	OSCAR
O	Opium
P	PAPA
P	Power
Q	QUEBEC
Q	Cocaine
R	ROMEO
R	Residence
S	SIERRA
S	Sunday
T	TANGO
T	Tuesday
U	UNIFORM
V	VICTOR
V	Frequency varies
W	WHISKEY
W	Wednesday
X	X-RAY
X	Female
Y	YANKEE
Z	ZULU

singleton [I] Slang for an undercover police officer or intelligence agent who lives in a target area or in a country other than his own and works alone.

sinker [US] Naval aviation voice brevity code meaning a disappearing radar contact.

Sinn Fein [TRG] Political arm of the Irish Republican Army; also known as the IRA.

sinsemilla Spanish for "without seeds." *Sinsemilla* is sometimes spelled *sensamaya* and is a hybrid species of marijuana grown in Mexico. Like most marijuana plants, sinsemilla has a few seeds that are removed during the drying process.

SIOP [M] Abbreviation for Single Integrated Operational Plan.

SIR **1.** [C] Abbreviation for Signal to Interference Ratio. **2.** [NASA] Abbreviation for Shuttle Imaging Radar.

SIS [I] Abbreviation for British Secret Intelligence Service.

sister 1. [LE] Slang for a black female. 2. [LE] Slang for a very young female prostitute.

Site 300 The Lawrence Livermore Laboratory, a research facility of the University of California located near San Francisco, is known as the major design center in the United States for the development of nuclear weapon systems. At site 300, west of the facility, explosive testing and electromechanical triggering devices are evaluated. Overflights by aircraft are restricted. Emergency radio frequencies used at Site 300 include: 154.280, 164.325, 164.375, 164.475, and 166.275.

SIT REP [M] Abbreviation for Situation Report.

six pack [C,G&PS] Slang for the six individuals who are in a police lineup.

sixteenth [C,G&PS] Slang for one-sixteenth of an ounce, usually used when measuring out heroin.

SJ [M] Abbreviation for Support Jamming.

S/J [M] Abbreviation for Signal to Jamming ratio.

skag [C,G&PS] Slang for heroin. (*See* QUICK REFERENCE.)

skee [C,G&PS] Slang for opium. (*See* QUICK REFERENCE.)

skin burner [C,G&PS] Slang term for heroin considered to be the very best (top) quality.

skin game [LE] Slang term for a trick women use to get money for sex.

skin popping [C,G&PS] Slang term meaning to inject heroin just under the surface of the skin instead of into a vein.

SKT Specialty code for Skiptrace.

Skunk [US] Naval aviation voice brevity code meaning an unidentified surface contact, assumed to be hostile.

Skunk/ADP [M] Shortened form for the 'Skunk Works' Advanced Development Projects team at Lockheed-California where aircraft such as the U-2 high-altitude reconnaissance plane and the F-117 stealth aircraft were designed and developed.

skynet [UK] British military communications satellite system.

sky out [C,G&PS] Slang term meaning to leave the scene.

SL [C] Abbreviation for Sidelobe.

slammer [C,G&PS] Slang for a jail or prison.

SLAR [C3I] Abbreviation for Side-Looking Airborne Radar.

SLB [C] Abbreviation for Sidelobe Blanking.

SLBM [C3I] Abbreviation for Submarine-Launched Ballistic Missile.

SLC 1. [C] Abbreviation for Sidelobe Canceller. 2. [C3I] Abbreviation for Submarine Laser Communications system.

SLCM [C3I] Abbreviation for Submarine (Sea) Launched Cruise Missile.

sleep [C,G&PS] Slang for cocaine. (*See* QUICK REFERENCE.)

sleeper [I] An operator or agent in a foreign country or living in a certain area, perhaps with a job in a classified facility, who does not engage in intelligence activities until told to do so. A sleeper might not know his mission until called upon.

sleepers [C,G&PS] Slang for barbiturates. (*See* QUICK REFERENCE.)

sleeping pills [C,G&PS] Slang for barbiturates. (*See* QUICK REFERENCE.)

SLFCS [US] Abbreviation for Survivable Low-Frequency Communications System.

SLKT [M] Abbreviation for Survivability, Lethality, and Key Technologies.

slobs [C,G&PS] A derogatory term for members of the Bloods street gang.

slot [C,G&PS] Slang for slot machine.

slick [C,G&PS] Slang for an individual who appears to be clever.

slingers [C,G&PS] Slang for street dope pushers.

SM [M] Abbreviation for Standard Missile.

S-M [C,G&PS] Abbreviation for synthetic marijuana, such as PCP.

SMA [C3I] Abbreviation for Search Mode Acquisition.

smack [C,G&PS] Slang for heroin.

smacker [C,G&PS] Slang for an individual addicted to heroin.

SME [C3I] Abbreviation for Solar Mesosphere Explorer.

SMG [LE] Abbreviation for Submachine-Gun.

smiley [C,G&PS] One of several gangbanger nicknames. Smiley is notorious nationwide and indicates an individual who guns someone down while smiling, laughing, and seemingly enjoying the entire incident.

SMM [C3I] Abbreviation for Solar Maximum Mission satellite.

SMO [US] Acronym used by the U.S. intelligence community for the Soviet Military Office located on Massachusetts Avenue in Washington, D.C.

smoke [C,G&PS] Slang for marijuana. (*See* QUICK REFERENCE.)

smuggler [LE] An individual responsible for getting and transporting dope or contraband across a border, usually from Mexico into the United States. In 1989, law enforcement intelligence estimated that production of marijuana in the U.S. is between 4,350 and 4,850 tons—more than double the figure from 1988. Colombia remains the world's largest marijuana and cocaine producer, although vast amounts of money and manpower have been expended by the United States to aid the government of Colombia in stopping the process of growing marijuana and processing cocaine. The current law enforcement intelligence estimate is that marijuana production in Colombia is between 5,000 to 8,700 metric tons during any given 12-month period. Mexico is estimated to produce 4,720 metric tons yearly—most of it smuggled into the United States.

SMUN [US] Acronym used by the U.S. intelligence community for the Soviet Mission to the United Nations.

S/N [C] Designation for Signal-to-Receiver Noise Ratio.

SNA [C3I] Abbreviation for Systems Network Architecture.

SNF [M] Abbreviation for Short-range Nuclear Forces.

SNIE [I] Abbreviation for Special National Intelligence Estimate.

sniff [C,G&PS] Slang for cocaine. (*See* QUICK REFERENCE.)

sniffing [C,G&PS] Slang for injecting cocaine through the nose.

snitch [LE] Slang for an informer, one who shares information with law enforcement officers.

SNK (*Sovnarkom*) [USSR] Abbreviation for *Soviet Narodnykh Komissarov*, Council of People's Commissars.

snop [C,G&PS] Slang for marijuana. (*See* QUICK REFERENCE.)

snort [C,G&PS] Slang for cocaine. (*See* QUICK REFERENCE.)

snorting [C,G&PS] Slang for injecting cocaine through the nose.

snot [C,G&PS] Slang for a smokable methamphetamine. (*See* ICE.)

snow [C,G&PS] Slang for cocaine. (*See* QUICK REFERENCE.)

snowbird [C,G&PS] Slang for an individual who is addicted to cocaine.

SNU [LE] Abbreviation for Street Narcotics Unit.

SO [LE] Abbreviation for Special Operations.

soap bubbles [I] Slang for a voice (communications) scrambler.

soapies [C,G&PS] Slang for qualudes. (*See* QUICK REFERENCE.)

Social Security numbering index system Social Security numbers have an important role in personal identification in the United States. There was a time when every member of the U.S. military was given an individual serial number. The individual's Social Security number is now used for I.D., too. The first three numbers indicate where the card was issued. In the field, a police officer can confirm certain information supplied by a suspect by using the following guide:

Initial Three S.S. Numbers	State Where S.S. Number Was Issued
001–003	New Hampshire
004–007	Maine
008–009	Vermont
010–034	Massachusetts
035–039	Rhode Island
040–049	Connecticut

Initial Three S.S. Numbers	State Where S.S. Number Was Issued
050–134	New York
135–158	New Jersey
159–211	Pennsylvania
212–220	Maryland
221–222	Delaware
223–231	Virginia
232–236	West Virginia
237–246	North Carolina
247–251	South Carolina
252–260	Georgia
261–267	Florida
268–302	Ohio
303–317	Indiana
318–361	Illinois
362–386	Michigan
387–399	Wisconsin
400–407	Kentucky
408–415	Tennessee
416–424	Alabama
425–428, 587	Mississippi
429–432	Arkansas
433–439	Louisiana
440–448	Oklahoma
449–467	Texas
468–477	Minnesota
478–485	Iowa
486–500	Missouri
501–502	North Dakota
503–504	South Dakota
505–508	Nebraska
509–515	Kansas
516–517	Montana
518–519	Idaho
520	Wyoming
521–524	Colorado
525, 585	New Mexico
526–527	Arizona
528–529	Utah
530	Nevada
531–539	Washington
540–544	Oregon
545–573	California
574	Alaska
575–576	Hawaii
577–579	District of Columbia
580	Virgin Islands

Initial Three S.S. Numbers	State Where S.S. Number Was Issued
581–584	Puerto Rico
586	American Samoa, Guam, and all other Pacific Territories.
700	Railroad Employees under the Special Retirement Act.

SOCOM [M] Acronym for Special Operations Command.

SOD [M] Acronym for Special Operations (Detachment) Division, the specific group within the U.S. Army established to facilitate projects and the management of special (covert) operations in the Army.

softballs [C,G&PS] Slang for barbiturates. (*See* QUICK REFERENCE.)

soft film [I] Photographic film whose gelatin emulsion has been removed through a chemical process, the backing discarded, and the thin emulsion then dried flat, folded, or rolled into a tiny packet so it can be hidden in a small space.

SOG [M] Abbreviation for Special Operations Group.

SOJ **1.** [M] Abbreviation for Standoff Jamming. **2.** [TRG] Abbreviation for Second of June Movement, a terrorist group headquartered in West Germany.

SOLAS [C3I] Abbreviation for Safety Of Life At Sea.

Soldiers of Justice [TRG] A Lebanese underground terrorist organization with links to Iran. This group has mounted a campaign of terror against Saudi diplomats.

solo [LE] Slang for a law enforcement officer who is alone on an assignment.

sommnafac [LE] A controlled substance that is a sedative. (*See* QUICK REFERENCE.)

SOP [M] Abbreviation for Standard Operating Procedure.

Sopor [LE] Brand name of methaqualone, a controlled substance that is a sedative. (*See* QUICK REFERENCE.)

SORO [M] Abbreviation for Scan On Receive Only.

SOSUS [M] Acronym for SOund SUrveillance System.

SOT 1. [M] Abbreviation for Special Operations Training, training given to members of the SEALS, Special Forces, and Delta Force to equip them to deal with terrorist and their organizations. SOT includes profiles of terrorist/radical groups and their goals. 2. [LE] Abbreviation for Special Operations Team, a law enforcement group that operates along the same lines as a Special Weapon Action Team (SWAT).

SOTFE [M] Abbreviation for Special Operations, Task Force Europe.

sour [US] Naval aviation voice brevity code meaning receiving (radio transmission) poorly.

source [I] A person, device, system, or specific activity from which intelligence information is gathered.

space ranger [C,G&PS] Slang for an individual who uses amphetamines to excess.

spaced [C,G&PS] Slang term referring to an individual who shows the effects of a narcotic by his actions.

SPADATS [US] Acronym for SPAce Detection And Tracking System.

SPADOC [C3I] Acronym for SPAce Defense Operation Center.

SPANNER [US] Acronym for SPecial Analysis of Net Radio.

special, a [LE] Short for a special law enforcement tactical operation.

speed [C,G&PS] Slang for methamphetamine or methedrine.

speed ball [C,G&PS] Slang for pure cocaine that is blended with heroin.

speed freak [C,G&PS] Slang for an amphetamine user.

spike [C,G&PS] Slang for anything that can be used as a needle for drug injections.

spitfire [C,G&PS] Slang for a submachine gun.

SPLA [TRG] Abbreviation for Sudan People's Liberation Army, a rebel group headquartered in the southern Sudan of the African nation.

splash 1. [C,G&PS] Slang for methamphetamine. (*See* QUICK REFERENCE.) 2. [US] Naval aviation voice brevity code meaning enemy aircraft shot down.

splints [C,G&PS] Slang for marijuana cigarettes.

split [C,G&PS] Slang meaning to leave a location.

SPO [C3I] Abbreviation for System Program Office.

spook 1. [I] Slang term for a spy or covert agent, domestic or foreign. 2. [US] Naval aviation voice brevity code meaning unidentified surface contact, possibly enemy submarine.

spoon [C,G&PS] Slang for one-sixteenth of an ounce, usually of heroin.

sport of the gods [C,G&PS] Slang for the process of snorting cocaine.

SPOT [C3I] Acronym for Small Portable Operational Terminal, usually an electronic computer.

spot you [C,G&PS] Term used by drug/narcotic users meaning that they will pay first and take delivery at another time or place.

SPRINT [LE] designation for SPecial Police Radio INquiry.

SPU [USSR] Abbreviation for *Sekretno-politicheskoye Upravleniye*, or Secret Political Directorate.

spy-1 [M] Designation for a long-range naval shipboard radar system.

squad [M] A group of (usually armed) military troops or police officers.

squad car [LE] A law enforcement vehicle.

square 1. [LE] Slang for an honest police officer. 2. [C,G&PS] Slang for an individual in a drug or narcotics crowd who is not a user.

SR 1. [USSR] Abbreviation for Socialist Revolutionary Party. 2. [US] Abbreviation for Strategic Reconnaissance.

SR-71 [M] Designation for a high-altitude reconnaissance aircraft. The Air Force has always been reluctant to publicize anything concerning the SR-71, including its capabilities. Although the aircraft is scheduled to be retired soon from service, much of the information about the SR-71 is still classified. However, on July 27 and 28, 1976, the Air Force let three flight crews have a go at setting some new altitude and speed records. The three Air Force flight crews and planes flew from Beale Air Force Base in California, home to the 9th Strategic Reconnaissance Wing, and set the records at Edwards AFB. It is still not known whether the planes were pushed to the limit of their abilities for these record-setting efforts. People closely related to the SR-71 project have discussed in closed meetings that the aircraft is capable of traveling at four times the speed of sound. One of the thousands of interesting aspects of the SR-71 system is the fact that KC-135 tankers used to aerially refuel the SR-71s in flight are outfitted with a communications line within the refueling boom, allowing the planes to operate using a secure radio link with the tanker and maintain radio silence. (*See* BLACKBIRD; OX-CART.)

SR-71 world records The following are SR-71 world records:

Altitude in horizontal flight—July 28, 1976
Pilot: Capt. Robert C. Helt, USAF
Record: 85,068.997 ft.

Speed over a closed course—July 28, 1976
Pilot: Capt. Eldon W. Joersz, USAF
Record: 2,193.167 mph

Speed over a closed circuit—July 27, 1976
Pilot: Major Adolphus H. Bledsoe, USAF
Record: 2,092.294 mph

New York to London—September 1, 1974
Pilot: Major James V. Sullivan, USAF
Record Time: 1 hour and 55 minutes
Record Speed: 1,806.964 mph

London to Los Angeles—September 13, 1974
Pilot: Capt. Harold B. Adams, USAF
Record Time: 3 hours and 48 minutes
Record Speed: 1,435.587 mph

S&R [M] Abbreviation for Search & Rescue.

SRAM [C3I] Abbreviation for Short-Range Attack Missile.

SRHIT [C3I] Abbreviation for Small Radar Homing Intercept Technology.

SRT [US] Abbreviation for Standard Remote Terminal.

SS **1.** Specialty code for Store Shopping. **2.** Abbreviation for Stockholm Syndrome. **3.** Designation for Spanish.

SSAS [M] Designation for Surface Ship Advance Sonar.

SSBN [M] Designation for Ballistic (missile) submarine, nuclear powered.

SSBSC [C3I] Abbreviation for Single SideBand Suppressed Carrier.

SSC [C3I] Abbreviation for Software Steering Committee.

SSD [I] Designation for Ministry for Security and Intelligence for East Germany. The SSD is responsible for foreign and domestic counterintelligence, electronic intercepts, as well as military and strategic intelligence. It is directed in intelligence operations by the Politburo.

SSF **1.** [HRU] Abbreviation for Special Security Force, the Saudi Arabian counterterrorist and hostage rescue unit. **2.** [HRU] Abbreviation for Sultan's Special Force, the Special Forces unit of the country of Omani.

SSGN [M] Designation for cruise missile attack submarine, nuclear powered.

SSJ [M] Abbreviation for Self-Screening Jamming.

SSKP [LE] Abbreviation for Single-Shot Kill Probability.

SSMA [C3I] Abbreviation for Spread Spectrum Multiple Access.

SSN [M] Designation for Attack Submarine, Nuclear powered.

SSPA [C3I] Abbreviation for Solid-State Power Amplifiers.

SSPP [C3I] Abbreviation for System Safety Program Plan.

SSRO [M] Abbreviation for Sector Scan Receive Only.

SST [A] Abbreviation for Supersonic Transport.

SSTS [C3I] Abbreviation for Space Surveillance and Tracking System.

S & T [M] Abbreviation for Selection and Training.

STA Background code for state police, highway patrol, or equivalent.

stack [C,G&PS] Slang for a large quantity of packaged marijuana cigarettes.

stages [C,G&PS] Slang for a silencer used on a handgun.

staging area [LE] That area where law enforcement officers gather prior to a police action.

standard [LE] Of or referring to operating in the clear.

stand in [LE] Slang term referring to an accommodation arrest. When an individual is working with law enforcement and is involved in a criminal activity, that person might be arrested at a crime scene so his activities with the police will not become suspect. Law enforcement agents sometimes refer to an individual who is arrested to accommodate a *cousin*.

STARCOM [US] Acronym for STrategic ARmy COMmunications.

stardust [C,G&PS] Slang for cocaine. (*See* QUICK REFERENCE.)

START [GOV] Acronym for STrategic Arms Reduction Talks/Treaty.

stash [C,G&PS] Slang for stolen goods or narcotics in a hidden location.

stashcan [LE] Slang for a container, often made commercially, to appear as a soft drink can with a secret compartment for hiding narcotics.

state chicken [US] Naval aviation voice brevity code meaning fuel state requires recovery, refueling, or diversion.

state lamb [US] Naval aviation voice brevity code meaning inadequate fuel for both mission plus reserve to return to base.

state tiger [US] Naval aviation voice brevity code meaning sufficient fuel to complete mission and return to base.

status trip [LE] A successful dope operation can mean a great deal of hard cash on hand. The dealer or smuggler usually likes to show-off his or her success by buying heavy gold chains, flashy cars, and expensive clothes. This status trip is a manifestation that usually results in the dealer's downfall and makes who (what) he is obvious to law enforcement officials.

STB Designation for the state secret security of Czechoslovakia. The STB is directed by the Minister of the Interior of Czechoslovakia and is concerned with military and strategic intelligence, electronic intercepts, domestic counterintelligence and foreign counterintelligence.

STCICS [UK] Abbreviation for STrike Command Integrated Communications System.

STDL [US] Abbreviation for Submarine Tactical Data Link.

STDN [C3I] Abbreviation for Spaceflight Tracking & Data Network.

stealth aircraft An aircraft that is claimed to be almost invisible to enemy radar because of the extensive use of exotic composite materials, some of which absorb, rather than reflect radar waves; its lack of sharp surface angles; and a cross section that offers a very small profile to radar. (*See* IMPULSE RADAR.)

steamboat [C,G&PS] Slang for a marijuana cigarette holder.

steerer [C,G&PS] Slang for an individual who guides drug buyers to drug sellers.

Stelazine [LE] Brand name of a controlled substance that is a major tranquilizer. (*See* QUICK REFERENCE.)

STEM [C3I] Acronym for System Trainer and Exercise Module.

stepped on [C,G&PS] In the dope trade, of or referring to a product (cocaine/heroin) that has been cut. If heroin has been stepped on twice, it has been cut on two occasions.

sterile [I] Of or referring to an overt or clandestine action from which has been removed anything that can be identified as originating with a sponsoring nation or organization.

sterile funds [GOV] Money put to use by government intelligence agencies that has been obtained by roundabout means and methods, and in no way can be traced back to the original source.

STIC [C3I] Abbreviation for Security Threat Intelligence Cell.

stick 1. [C,G&PS] Slang for a marijuana cigarette. **2.** [C,G&PS] Slang term meaning to stab an individual with a knife or ice pick.

sticks [C,G&PS] Slang for useless twigs or sticks that have been mixed into a load of marijuana. (*See* LUMBER.)

stiff [C,G&PS] Slang for a dead body; a corpse.

stinking [C,G&PS] Slang referring to an individual who is under the influence of drugs or alcohol.

STN Specialty code for standards research.

STO [D] Abbreviation for *Service de Travail Obligatoire* (French).

Stockholm syndrome [LE] The psychological relationship between hostage and captor in which the hostage talks with the captor and begins to believe that the captor is more right than wrong in his motives for taking hostages and doing whatever it is the captor has done to get attention to his cause by the world press and others.

STOL [M] Designation for Short Takeoff and Landing (type) of aircraft.

stoned [C,G&PS] Slang term referring to being high and completely under the influence of narcotics.

stool [C,G&PS] Slang for an informer.

stool pigeon [C,G&PS] Slang for an individual who informs law enforcement of a criminal act about to happen, or a criminal activity involving some other individuals.

stoolie *See* STOOL; STOOL PIGEON.

STP [LE] Designation for a controlled substance that is a hallucinogen. (*See* QUICK REFERENCE.)

straight [C,G&PS] The feeling of well-being experienced after the use of narcotics.

straight man [C,G&PS] Slang for an individual who does not use drugs or narcotics.

stranger [US] Naval aviation voice brevity code meaning unidentified aircraft.

strangle [US] A U.S. military code meaning "switch off equipment indicated." (*See* IFF.)

strangle parrot [I] A code used by the U.S. military meaning "switch off identification friend or foe equipment." (*See* IFF.)

strategic intelligence [I] The various levels of intelligence information required for the development and formation of policies and plans as they relate to the military and at the national and international level.

straw [C,G&PS] Slang for marijuana. (*See* QUICK REFERENCE.)

strawberry [C,G&PS] Slang for a woman willing to give sex for drugs.

streamliner [US] Code name for secure intelligence transmission system.

street man [C,G&PS] Slang for an individual who sells narcotics directly to users.

street peddler [C,G&PS] Slang for a drug or narcotic pusher selling directly to users. A street peddler usually has a "stash" within reach, or near his location.

stressor [LE] Slang for some event that has resulted in murder.

stretch [C,G&PS] Slang term meaning to cut high-strength narcotics, thus reducing the potency.

stringer 1. [LE] Slang for an occasional law enforcement informant. **2.** [I] Slang for an occasional or freelance spy, not a formal employee of an intelligence agency.

strung out [C,G&PS] Slang for an individual who uses narcotics and is in need of drugs to support a dope habit.

STU [C3I] Abbreviation for Secure Telephone Unit.

stuff [C,G&PS] Slang for heroin. (*See* QUICK REFERENCE.)

stuffing [C,G&PS] Slang for the hiding of dope anywhere near at hand, usually in an emergency; that is, during a police raid.

stun grenade [LE] A device either thrown by hand or fired from a launcher that makes a loud explosion and creates a bright (blinding) flash to disorient terrorists during an assault. The device is so designed so as not to injure people.

Su [USSR] Abbreviation for Sukhoy, an aircraft designer.

Su-27 [USSR] designation for an advanced military jet fighter aircraft.

SUB Specialty code for subversive terrorist.

subject [LE] An individual who is under surveillance.

SUBROC [M] Acronym for SUBmarine ROCket.

SUBSAM [C3I] Acronym for SUBmarine Surface-to-Air Missile.

suey [C,G&PS] Term for a liquid preparation of opium.

sugar [C,G&PS] Slang for LSD. (*See* QUICK REFERENCE.)

sugared grass [C,G&PS] Slang for marijuana adulterated with sugar that tends to enhance the flavor for some. A sugared-water mix is sometimes added to bricks of marijuana to bind the weed into a hard and solid mass. This watering also adds weight to the bricks, thus benefiting the seller.

sugar lump [C,G&PS] Slang for a small amount of LSD on a cube of sugar.

Sumiyoshi-rengo [LE] The second largest *yakuza* (Japan's criminal underworld) group. Based in Tokyo, members of the *Sumiyoshi-rengo* operate much like the Mafia in the United States with their gangs involved in illegal acts.

Sunday habit [C,G&PS] Slang for occasional drug or narcotic usage.

sunshine [C,G&PS] Slang for LSD. (*See* QUICK REFERENCE.)

suppresser [LE] A noise-suppression device attached to a firearm, generally known as a silencer.

SUR Specialty code for Surveillance.

SURF [C3I] Acronym for Space Ultravacuum Research Facility.

surface [I] The public disclosure of an intelligence activity or operation.

SURTASS [M] Acronym for SURveillance Towed-Array Sonar System.

surveillance [I] A well-planned and systematic monitoring of a target individual, facility, or location.

SURVSATCOM [US] Acronym for SURVivable SATellite COMmunications system.

SV Specialty code for surveillance.

SVIP [C3I] Abbreviation for Secure Voice Improvement Program.

S.W. [LE] Abbreviation for a court-ordered search warrant.

swag [LE] Slang for stolen property.

swallow [LE] Slang for a female seducer. The term is used to identify a female lure who is involved in an intelligence-gathering operation.

swallower [C,G&PS] Slang for an individual who swallows drugs or narcotics, usually contained in a balloon, to get them past law enforcement or custom authorities.

SWAT **1.** [LE] Acronym for Special Weapons Action Team. **2.** [LE] Acronym for Special Weapons And Tactics (team). SWAT teams normally are a part of local police operations and specialize in hostage situations, gang-related incidents, and lone sniper operations.

sweat box [LE] Slang for the individual compartments in a patrol wagon used for prisoner transport.

sweated [C,G&PS] Slang term used when a young person is pressured by gang members to join up.

sweep [I] Slang term meaning to employ technical means to uncover a planted microphone, tape recorder, or some other surveillance device.

sweep jamming [I] A narrow band of electronic jamming that is swept back and forth over a relatively wide operating band of frequencies.

sweet [US] Naval aviation voice brevity code meaning receiving (radio transmission) well.

sweet lock [US] Naval aviation voice brevity code meaning receiving (radio transmission) well and locked on signal.

Sweet Lucy [C,G&PS] Slang for hashish. (*See* QUICK REFERENCE.)

sweets [C,G&PS] A street name for amphetamines.

swim   [USSR] English translation of the Soviet slang term meaning "travel" or "to travel."

swingman   [C,G&PS] Slang for an individual who supplies narcotics.

SWL   [US] Abbreviation for Signals Warfare Laboratory.

SWM   Specialty code for scuba, swimming, diving, pool injuries.

SWPS   [C3I] Abbreviation for Strategic War Planning System.

SWR   [C3I] Abbreviation for Standing Wave Radio.

sycamore   [FRANCE] Code name for intelligence and operational command data system.

syndicated acid   [C,G&PS] Slang for STP. (*See* QUICK REFERENCE.)

T

tab [C,G&PS] Slang for a narcotic in the form of a tablet.

tabs [C,G&PS] Slang for drugs that are in pill form.

tabbing [C,G&PS] Slang for the process of placing LSD on sugar cubes or small pieces of paper for ingestion.

TAC 1. [C3I] (USAF) Abbreviation for Tactical Air Command. 2. [M] Abbreviation for Tactical.

TACAMO [US] Designation for Airborne Strategic Communications System, also known as the airborne radio relay system.

TACAN [US] Acronym for TACtical Air Navigation, an ultrahigh frequency electronic air navigation system that provides a continuous indication of bearing and distance (slant range) to the TACAN station, the common components being used in distance and bearing determination.

TACS [C3I] Abbreviation for Tactical Air Control System.

TACSATCOM [US] Acronym for TACtical SATellite COMmunications.

TACSI [C3I] Abbreviation for Tactical Air Control System Improvement.

TACTAS [M] Abbreviation for TACtical Towed-Array Sonar.

TACTEC [US] Abbreviation for Totally Advanced Communications TEChnology.

tactical [I] Name for all forms of intelligence that support intelligence plans or operations at a military unit level.

tag [LE] Slang for a parking summons.

tail [I] Slang term meaning to conduct surveillance on an individual.

tailed [LE] Slang for being followed.

tail trip [LE] Slang for surveillance of a suspect by intelligence or law enforcement agents.

take 1. [LE] Term for a percentage of the money bet at a racetrack that is divided between the track and the state government. 2. [I] Slang for the intelligence fruits of spying.

take off 1. [C,G&PS] Slang meaning to use heroin. 2. [C,G&PS] Slang meaning to steal.

take out 1. [C,G&PS] A term used by criminal elements meaning to kill someone. 2. [LE] A term meaning to free a confined prisoner from jail or court jurisdiction. The term usually relates to an informant.

TALC [C3I] Abbreviation for Tactical Airborne Laser Communications.

tall kings [US] Department of Defense codename for long-wave early warning Soviet radar designed to reduce the penetration of U.S. Stealth aircraft into Soviet airspace. (*See* BISTATIC RADAR.)

tally ho [US] Naval aviation voice brevity code meaning I have visual contact—follow me.

Tango [A,LE,MIL] Designation for the letter *T*.

TAOC [C3I] Abbreviation for Tactical Air Operations Center.

tapping [I] Electronically intercepting telephone calls or radio transmissions.

tar [C,G&PS] Slang for opium. (*See* QUICK REFERENCE.)

TARADCOM [US] Designation for Army Tank-Automotive Research And Development COMmand.

TARCOM [US] Designation for Army Tank-Automotive Material Readiness COMmand.

TARE [NATO] Abbreviation for Telegraph Automatic Routing Equipment.

target 1. [I] Slang for an individual who is under surveillance. A target also can be a facility, agency, area, or country where intelligence operations are undertaken with a specific subject in mind. **2.** [LE] Slang for the possible victim of a crime. **3.** [LE] An individual or organization against which an intelligence or covert operation is conducted. This term also can refer to hardware, documentation, photographs, or even an individual that an agency wants to somehow obtain.

targeting [I] As it relates to COMINT, the intentional selection and/or collection of telecommunications for intelligence purposes.

target of opportunity [I] An individual, installation, political organization, or entity that becomes accessible to an intelligence agency by chance.

TARIF [UK] Abbreviation for Telegraph Automatic Routing In the Field.

TAS Abbreviation for True Air Speed, which equals ground speed under zero wind conditions.

TASI [C3I] Abbreviation for Time Assignment Speech Interpolation.

task force-160 [M] Designation for the transportation arm of the counterterrorist effort of the Joint Special Operations Command (JSOC). The aircraft and helicopter unit for United States commando operations is based at Fort Campbell, in southwestern Kentucky. Its slogan is "Death Waits in the Dark."

taste [C,G&PS] Slang for a small amount of drugs or narcotics.

TAV [NASA] Abbreviation for Trans-Atmospheric Vehicle.

TBC [LE] Abbreviation for To Be Clean, which means being free from drugs/narcotics.

TBO [A] Abbreviation for Time Between Overhauls, for example, for an aircraft engine module.

t/c [A] Abbreviation for Thickness/Chord ratio for an experimental aircraft airfoil section.

TCAC [US] Abbreviation for Tactical Control and Analysis Center.

TCCF [US] Abbreviation for Tactical Communications Control Facility.

TCP [US] Abbreviation for Technological Capabilities Panel.

TCS [US] Abbreviation for Tactical Computer System.

TCT [US] Abbreviation for Tactical Computer Terminal.

TDD [US] Abbreviation for Target Detection Device.

TDHS [C3I] Abbreviation for Time Domain Harmonic Scaling.

TDM [C3I] Abbreviation for Time Division Multiplex.

TDMA [C3I] Abbreviation for Time Division Multiple Access.

TDRS [I] Abbreviation for Tracking and Data Relay Satellite. There are a half-dozen or so TDRS, that have been placed in orbit for military communications—at least one for every two flights of the space shuttle under its current schedule. The first TDRS was launched from *Challenger* in 1983, and *Challenger* was carrying a second one that was destroyed along with the seven-person crew in the disaster of January 28, 1986. With its seven antennas, a TDRS can transmit to the ground station at White Sands, N.M., the equivalent of a 20-volume encyclopedia in one second.

TDY [M] Designation for Temporary Duty.

tea [C,G&PS] Slang for marijuana. (*See* QUICK REFERENCE.)

tea blower [C,G&PS] Slang for a user of marijuana.

tea head [C,G&PS] Slang for an individual who uses marijuana.

tea man [C,G&PS] Slang for a user of marijuana.

tea party [C,G&PS] Slang for a marijuana party.

teal ruby [I] Code name for a shuttle-mounted sensor system that looks down toward the earth during orbit and detects cruise missiles or other aircraft in flight.

tecata [C,G&PS] Slang for heroin. (*See* QUICK REFERENCE.)

TECHINT [I] Acronym for TECHnical INTelligence.

TECOM [US] Designation for Army Test and Evaluation COMmand.

TED [C3I] Acronym for Threshold Extension Demodulator.

Teflon [LE] *See* COP KILLERS.

Tekiya [LE] One of the three major Japanese street gangs, the criminal element of street peddlers throughout Japan. The *Gurentai* and *Bakuto* operate more along the lines of strongarm gangsters. All three gangs are involved in blackmarket activities, drugs, and prostitution in the major cities of Japan.

TELINT [US] Acronym for TELemetry INTelligence.

TELO [TRG] Abbreviation for Tamil Eelam Liberation Organization, a terrorist/radical group headquartered and active in Sri Lanka.

tempest [I] Name of a highly classified shield process applied to computer hardware systems. (*See* F-3.)

TENCAP Abbreviation for Tactical Exploitation of National CAPabilities.

ten cents [C,G&PS] Slang for $10.

ten-cent pistol [C,G&PS] Slang for a bag or container of narcotics or drugs that contains poison.

Ten-Code The standard 10-Codes are used by most law enforcement, state, and federal agencies including the United States military. Certain agencies have introduced modifications to the code to meet their specific needs. The listener must interpret the codes by the way in which they are used. This listing serves as a general guide only. This listing does not represent the official Association of Public Safety (APCO) standard ten-code signals established by that organization. The 10-Codes that appear in TABLE T-1 are in the order they are most often used (with permission of DataPort).

tenley [US] Code name for secure voice system.

ten most wanted To get on the FBI's "10 Most Wanted" list, a criminal has to qualify on four counts: an official arrest warrant must exist; the individual must have a record of criminal activity; evidence must indicate that the criminal continues to be a threat to society; publicity to alert the public seems needed.

Tenuate [LE] Brand name for a controlled substance that is a stimulant. (*See* QUICK REFERENCE.)

terminate [C,G&PS] Slang term meaning to murder an individual.

TES [UK] Abbreviation for Transportable Earth Station.

TET [A] Abbreviation for Trailing Edge Tracking.

Texas syndicate [LE] A group of America-Mexican smugglers who have a major network established to transport tons of marijuana into the United States from Mexico, along the southern borders.

Texas tea **1.** [C,G&PS] Slang for hashish. (*See* QUICK REFERENCE.) **2.** [C,G&PS] Slang for marijuana. (*See* QUICK REFERENCE.)

TF [M] Abbreviation for Task Force.

TF-160 [M] Designation for Special Aviation Operation Army Task Force 160. This unit is one of the prime organizations in the U.S. military ready to move on a moments notice to where terrorist activities are taking place on United States territory.

TFA [C3I] Abbreviation for Transmit Frame Acquisition.

TFR [M] Abbreviation for Terrain-Following Radar.

TFW [M] Abbreviation for Tactical Fighter Wing.

TGCR [C3I] Abbreviation for Tactical Generic Cable Replacement.

TGSM [M] Abbreviation for Terminally Guided Submunitions.

Thai sticks [C,G&PS] Slang for cigarettes made from a high-quality marijuana.

THC [LE] Abbreviation for delta-9, tetrahydra cannabinol, the main psychoactive ingredient in marijuana. By measuring the THC content scientists have been able to determine that today's marijuana is much more potent than it was 10 years ago.

the "A" man [LE] Radio code word for the SWAT Commander, used when requesting him to respond to the crime scene.

Table T-1. Law Enforcement Ten-Codes

Code	Meaning
10−0	Caution
10−0	Chase in progress
10−1	Unable to copy or signal is weak
10−1	Unable to copy, change location
10−1A	Unable to copy, signal is breaking up
10−1B	Unable to copy, signal is very, very weak
10−1C	Unable to copy, signal is very noisy
10−1	Clear channel #1 traffic
10−1	Receiving poorly
10−1	Contact your command
10−1	Assist officer
10−1	In service (or back in service)
10−2	Signal good
10−2	Receiving well
10−2	Clear channel #2 traffic
10−2	Report of bomb threat at __(location)__
10−2	Report to your command
10−2	Larceny
10−2	Radio check
10−2	Out of service at __(location/telephone number)__
10−3	Stop transmitting
10−3	Estimated time of arrival (ETA) to landline __(time)__
10−3	Go ahead with your message
10−3	Officer in trouble
10−3	Contact the dispatcher by landline
10−3	Burglary
10−3	You are not needed, return to your post
10−4	Affirmative (OK) acknowledgment
10−4	Message received
10−4	Automobile accident
10−4	Repeat
10−5	Relay (To)
10−5	Automobile accident (injury)
10−5	Homicide
10−5	Repeat the message
10−5	Message is received and understood
10−5	Request to leave post on personal business
10−6	Busy—stand by
10−6	Excessive speeder or hot rod vehicle
10−6	Stand by
10−6	Remain in service
10−6	Kidnaping
10−6	Request coffee/meal break
10−7	Out of service (usually followed by the time)
10−7	Breaking and entering—or door found open
10−7	Criminal mischief

Table T-1. Continued

Code	Meaning
10−7	Request coffee/meal break
10−7G	Out of service—garage
10−7M	Out of service—meal
10−7R	Out of service—radio repair
10−7S	Out of service—bathroom
10−7T	Out of service—traffic control
10−7	Unable to read or copy transmission
10−7	Verify the message
10−8	In service (usually followed by the time)
10−8A	In service—at home (followed by the time)
10−8F	In service—on foot patrol
10−8	Breaking and entering in progress at *(location)*
10−8	Transporting prisoner—unable to use unit radio
10−8	Sick or injured
10−8	Off coffee/personal/meal break
10−9	Say Again (repeat)
10−9	Inhalator required at *(location)*
10−9	Contact *(person)* by telephone at *(phone number)*
10−10	Negative
10−10	Fight in progress
10−10	Transmission complete, standing by
10−10	Report of fire at *(location)*
10−10	Possible crime in progress (shots fired, etc.)
10−10	Is there a telephone where you can be reached?
10−10	On minor detail—subject to call
10−10	On the air and in service (followed by the time)
10−10	Out of service, subject to call
10−10	Bicycle stolen/recovered at *(location)*
10−10	Automobile accident at *(location)*
10−10	Contact your commanding officer
10−11	*(Person)* On Duty (followed by time)
10−11	Dog case
10−11	Dispatcher/reporting officer talking too rapidly
10−11	Alarm (specific type and location)
10−11	Stay in service
10−11	Contact headquarters by telephone
10−11	Report to command or as directed
10−12	Stand by (stop)
10−12	Officials or visitors present
10−12	On pager—no radio
10−12	Disregard last instructions you were given
10−12	Police officer is holding suspect
10−12	Check registration
10−12	Report to watch commander/chief/etc.
10−12	Acknowledge call from base (headquarters) radio
10−12	This unit is out of service at *(location)*

Table T-1. Continued

Code	Meaning
10−13	Existing conditions
10−13	Weather and road conditions
10−13	Check for outstanding traffic citations
10−13	Assist police officer
10−13	Assist citizen
10−13	Advise of the conditions at your location
10−13	Contact by radio/telephone *(location)*
10−13	Pick up prisoner at jail and transport to *(location)*
10−14	Message/information
10−14	Request permission to take my meal break at *(location)*
10−14	Prowler report
10−14	Convoy or escort
10−14	Please terminate conversation
10−14	Stabbing or cutting incident at *(location)*
10−14	Stolen automobile
10−14	What is the correct time?
10−15	Message delivered
10−15	Civil disturbance
10−15A	Have additional personnel with me
10−15B	Have stolen/recovered/lost property in my possession
10−15C	Have prisoner in my custody
10−15D	Have documents/court papers in my possession
10−15	Give time check because prisoner/witness is in vehicle
10−15	Out of service at court
10−15	Call your home as soon as possible
10−15	Robbery
10−15	Hit plate, vehicle identification number (VIN) or want and warrant (automobile theft)
10−15	License number—verify if stolen (occupied or not)
10−16	Reply to message
10−16	Domestic problem—fight
10−16	Make pickup at *(location)*
10−16	Meet officer at *(location)*
10−16	Pick up prisoner/passenger or witness at *(location)*
10−16	Daily reports
10−16	NCIC check
10−16	Any traffic for us?
10−16	Disturbance
10−16	Vehicle/person on railroad crossing
10−16	Vehicle is abandoned (followed by) make, registration, VIN and year
10−16	Vehicle is reported stolen
10−17	En route
10−17	Meet complainant
10−17	Vehicle is not reported stolen
10−17	Arrest log information (followed by) name of subject, date of birth, Social Security number, etc.
10−17	Urgent business
10−17	Nothing for you

Table T-1. Continued

Code	Meaning
10–17	Pick up documents/court papers at *(location)*
10–17	Pick up officer/city official at *(location)*
10–17	Domestic problem (other than a fight) at *(location)*
10–17	Traffic hazard on highway at *(location)*
10–17	Vehicle/person off railroad crossing
10–18	Urgent
10–18	Complete assignment quickly
10–18	Livestock on highway at *(location)*
10–18	What is your location at this time?
10–18	Any assignments for us?
10–18	Dead body at *(location)*
10–18	Out of service (usually followed by the time)
10–19	(In) Contact
10–19	Return to *(location)* (or: return to station)
10–19	Nothing for you
10–19	Drunk person at *(location)*
10–19	Individual Driving Under the Influence (DUI)
10–19	Gone on arrival
10–20	Location?
10–20	Motor vehicle listing
10–20	Robbery has occurred at *(location)*
10–20	Drowning at *(location)*
10–20	Drunk driver
10–21	Contact *(person)* by telephone
10–21	Hit and run
10–21	Meet *(person)* at *(location)*
10–21	Request motor vehicle record check
10–21	Burglary has occurred at *(location)*
10–21	Check (license) plate for loss/theft
10–22	Disregard (or take no further action)
10–22	Larceny (specify from person, auto, etc.) occurred at *(location)*
10–22	Report in person to *(location)*
10–22	Complaint regarding dog at *(location)*
10–22	Unruly group
10–22	Check (license) plate for ownership
10–22	Give telephone number at location
10–23	Arrive at scene
10–23	Stand by—or stand by until no further interference
10–23	NCIC check (followed by subject identification)
10–23	Officer in trouble at *(location)*
10–23	Check for traffic congestion at *(location)*
10–23	Request permission to leave duty assignment (errand)
10–23	Request detective at the scene
10–23	Check (license) plate for registered owner
10–23	Radio reception interference. Go to channel *(number)*

Table T-1. Continued

Code	Meaning
10-24	Assignment completed
10-24	Trouble at station
10-24	Unwelcome visitor at *(location)*
10-24	Vehicle check
10-24	Clear, no traffic congestion at this time
10-24	All units in vicinity *(location)* report at once
10-24	Records indicate stolen or wanted
10-24	Make personal contact (time and location)
10-24	Assist *(name)* at the scene of a fire at *(location)*
10-24	Assault occurred at *(location)*
10-24	Fire
10-24	Criminal record check (followed by subject identification)
10-24	Check for want and warrants
10-25	Report to *(person)*
10-25	Can you contact *(person)* ?
10-25	Make contact with *(person)*
10-25	Traffic accident at *(location)*
10-25X	Traffic accident at *(location)* ; hit and run
10-25	Respond as a backup
10-25	Personnel who are on duty?
10-25	Have you made contact with *(person)* ?
10-25	Return to station immediately
10-25	There is a fire at *(location)*
10-25	Vehicle registration
10-25	Prowler/peeping tom at *(location)*
10-25	Pedestrian down at *(location)*
10-25	Disregard your last assignment
10-26	Estimated arrival time (ETA)
10-26	Detaining subject, expedite
10-26	Disregard last information
10-26	Do not use emergency equipment
10-26	Can you obtain vehicle registration information?
10-26	Make contact by radio or telephone
10-26	Motorist assist at *(location)*
10-26	There is a fight at *(location)*
10-26	Citizen requires escort from *(location)* to *(location)*
10-26	Check Vehicle Identification number (VIN) for lost or stolen
10-26	Fatal accident at *(location)*
10-27	License/permit information
10-27	(Drivers) license information
10-27	I am moving to channel *(number)*
10-27	Any answer at reporting party (RP) telephone number?
10-27	I have (need) a hospital report regarding *(person)*
10-27	Ambulance enroute/needed at *(location)*
10-27	Officer on duty at *(location)*
10-27	In service (usually followed by the time)
10-27	Any response regarding *(situation)*

Table T-1. Continued

Code	Meaning
10—28	Ownership Information
10—28	Vehicle registration information
10—28	Wrecker enroute/needed at *(location)*
10—28	Name check
10—28	Identify your station
10—28	Homicide at *(location)*
10—28	Out of service (usually followed by the time)
10—29	Records Check
10—29	Check records for wanted/stolen
10—29	Fire department enroute/needed at *(location)*
10—29	Time is up for contact
10—29	The crime of (specify) occurred at *(location)*
10—29	Juvenile complaint
10—29	Verification of (vehicle) registration
10—30	Danger/Caution
10—30	Construction at *(location)* ; traffic tie-up
10—30	Unnecessary use of radio
10—30	Does not conform to FCC Rules
10—30	Does not conform to regulations of the department
10—30	Person/vehicle is wanted
10—30	Larceny
10—30	Robbery in progress at *(location)*
10—30	Silent alarm
10—30	Missing person
10—30	Use a callbox to get your next assignment
10—31	Pick up
10—31	Crime in progress
10—31	Urgent—all units stay in service
10—31	Send for Justice of the Peace
10—31	Send for county attorney
10—31	Burglary in progress at *(location)*
10—31	Is lie detector technician available?
10—31	Check driver license information
10—31	Individual has police record in this city
10—31	Send wrecker to *(location)*
10—31	Lie detector/breathanalyzer operator report to *(location)*
10—31	Missing person—or found missing person
10—31	Bomb scare
10—31	Lost/kidnapped child
10—31	Request permission to go to headquarters
10—31	Contact headquarters
10—32	*(Number)* units needed (specific/number/type)
10—32	Person with a gun
10—32	Chase in progress; all units stand by
10—32	Emergency—keep this frequency (channel) clear
10—32	I will give you a radio check
10—32	Individual/vehicle is clear

Table T-1. Continued

Code	Meaning
10−32	Is breathanalyzer/drunkometer technician available?
10−32	Breathanalyzer/drunkometer required
10−32	Send ambulance (or medical assistance) to _(location)_
10−32	Report to headquarters in person
10−32	Larceny in progress (specify person, auto, etc.) at _(location)_
10−32	Message for _(person)_
10−32	Transportation of prisoner
10−32	Demonstration
10−32	Out of service—court (followed by time)
10−33	Help me quick
10−33	Emergency
10−33	Emergency traffic on this frequency (channel)
10−33	Person with weapon (gun, knife, club, etc.)
10−33	Chase in progress
10−33	Switch to mobile frequency (go direct)
10−33	Report of explosive (threat, suspected, device) at _(location)_
10−33	Clear channel (any emergency request)
10−33	Allow entry or exit at crime scene to _(location)_
10−33	Need assistance; trouble at this location
10−34	Time (check)
10−34	Riot
10−34	Bomb threat
10−34	Officer down (and) needs assistance
10−34	Trouble at this station, help needed
10−34	Trouble at _(location)_ ; all units respond
10−34	Clear this (channel) frequency for local dispatch
10−34	Exact type of complaint is unknown
10−34	Assault in progress at _(location)_
10−34	General broadcast—alert
10−34	Suspicious person/automobile/incident
10−34	Disturbance (unknown) at _(location)_
10−35	Reserved
10−35	Establish road block at _(location)_ ; stop all traffic
10−35	Major crime alert
10−35	Major crime occurred at _(location)_ ; establish roadblocks
10−35	Confidential information
10−35	Hit on NCIC, can you copy?
10−35	None of your business
10−35	Request permission to search
10−35A	Acknowledge—permission to search granted
10−35	Render assistance
10−35	What is your current location?
10−36	Reserved
10−36	Correct time
10−36	Security check
10−36	Assist police
10−36	Use caution; consider subject dangerous

Table T-1. Continued

Code	Meaning
10−36	Obstruction on highway/street
10−36	No further assistance required
10−36	Emergency notice—attention all units
10−36	Confidential information
10−36	Arrived at scene
10−37	Reserved
10−37	(Investigate) suspicious vehicle
10−37	Wrecker needed at _(location)_
10−37	Stopping at _(location and time)_
10−37	Who is the operator on duty?
10−37	No rush
10−37	Contact your supervisor by telephone at _(number)_
10−37	Intoxicated person
10−37	Person with mental problems at _(location)_
10−37	Official or visitor is present
10−37	Officer on duty (or) at post
10−38	Reserved
10−38	Stopping suspicious vehicle
10−38	Conditions of probation are _(details)_
10−38	Ambulance needed at _(location)_
10−38	Blood (human organ) relay
10−38	Send automobile mechanic to _(location)_
10−38	Computer down
10−38	Urgent—not an emergency
10−38	Urgent—respond quickly without lights or siren
10−38	Send relief unit
10−38	Station report satisfactory
10−38	Information is needed immediately
10−38	Investigating _(situation)_ at _(location)_
10−38	Property destruction
10−38	Completed last assignment
10−38	Request car-to-car communication with _(person)_
10−39	Reserved
10−39	Emergency, use lights and siren
10−39	Urgent, use lights and siren
10−39	Assisting officer _(person)_ with _(person)_ at _(location)_
10−39	Your message delivered
10−39	The number is _(number)_ ; deliver to addressee
10−39	Prowler at _(location)_
10−39	Military personnel are involved
10−39	Civil defense message to follow
10−39	Investigate suspicious vehicle
10−39	Request registration information; no VIN available
10−39	Any messages for this unit?
10−39	Request information on how to contact complainant
10−39	Crime (specify) in progress at _(location)_
10−39	Vehicle/individual escort required
10−39	Emergency currently in progress—stand by for information and your assignment

Table T-1. Continued

Code	Meaning
10−40	Silent run, no lights or siren
10−40	Fatality report
10−40	Notify watch commander
10−40	Do not divulge location
10−40	Proceed with the assignment (raid)
10−40	Crowd control needed
10−40	Acknowledge receipt of last radio transmission
10−40	Request permission to leave patrol area
10−40	Advise if officer _(person)_ is available to respond
10−40	Clear this channel for emergency transmission
10−40	Road is in need of repair at _(location)_
10−40	Recovered (stolen/lost) property
10−40	Drug/narcotic usage at _(location)_
10−40	Fight in progress at _(location)_
10−40	Transferring a prisoner who has not eaten
10−40	At scene, no assistance needed
10−40	Surveillance—observe subject but don't stop
10−41	Beginning tour of duty (usually followed by the time)
10−41	Please tune to channel _(number)_
10−41	Check suspicious person/vehicle at _(location)_
10−41	Civil defense test
10−41	Permission requested/granted for 10-40
10−41	Clear—no precipitation (weather)
10−41	Intoxicated individual
10−41	Female prisoner in patrol unit—mileage is _(number)_
10−41	Armed robbery
10−41	Bank holdup
10−41	Send wrecker to _(location)_
10−41	Request the assistance of one backup unit at _(location)_
10−41	Report of a prowler
10−42	Ending tour of duty (followed by the time)
10−42	Traffic accident at _(location)_
10−42	Call _(person)_ at _(number)_
10−42	Officer is now at _(residence/station, etc.)_
10−42	Partly cloudy to cloudy—no precipitation (weather)
10−42	Does not conform to department regulations
10−42	Change to radio (channel) frequency _(number)_
10−42	Unit number _(number)_ is stopped at his home
10−42	Complete drivers license record check
10−42	Robbery in progress at _(location)_
10−42	Bomb threat
10−42	Request the assistance of two backup units at _(location)_
10−42	Dog complaint
10−42	Stop immediately and advise of your location
10−43	Information is of special interest to intelligence
10−43	Chase in progress; in pursuit
10−43	Information (requesting/or for your information)
10−43	Traffic tie up at _(location)_

Table T-1. Continued

Code	Meaning
10–43	Shuttle
10–43	Officer *(person)* report to *(location)* for investigation
10–43	Intoxicated pedestrian
10–43	Meet the officer at *(location)*
10–43	Meet *(person)* at *(location)*
10–43	Drag-racing at *(location)*
10–43	Request supervisor at *(location)*
10–43	What telephone can you be reached at?
10–43	Cloudy—possible precipitation (weather)
10–43	Urgent, use siren and red lights
10–43	Advise of road and weather conditions
10–43	*(Person)* return to this station
10–43	Call your office
10–43	Drivers license check only
10–43	Shooting at *(location)*
10–43	You will relieve *(person)* who is at *(location)*
10–44	Permission to leave *(location)* for *(reason)*
10–44	I have a message for you or *(person)*
10–44	Stolen vehicle
10–44	Out of vehicle at *(location)* with *(person)*
10–44	Investigate vehicle at *(location)*
10–44	Suspicious person/vehicle at *(location)*
10–44	Possible mental case
10–44	Request impound of vehicle at *(location)*
10–44	Heavy rain or thunderstorm (weather)
10–44	Silent run
10–44	Message received and understood by all concerned
10–44	Driver's license is clear and valid
10–44	Units involved, acknowledge
10–44	Accident at *(location)* ; no injuries
10–44	Accident at *(location)* ; property damage
10–44	Check for record and wanted
10–44	Sex crime
10–44	Riot at *(location)*
10–45	Animal carcass at *(location)*
10–45	All units within range please report
10–45	Automobile accident at *(location)* ; property damage only
10–45	Accident at *(location)* ; injuries are involved
10–45	Domestic trouble
10–45	Patrol scene with another officer
10–45	Flooding conditions at *(location)* (weather)
10–45	Complete driver's license record check
10–45	Open door reported at *(location)*
10–45	Meet for coffee/discussion
10–45	Accident at *(location)* ; personal injury
10–45	Stolen automobile—or stolen/wanted vehicle
10–45	Investigate vehicle and occupants
10–45	Bomb threat

Table T-1. Continued

Code	Meaning
10–45	Request detectives at _(location)_
10–45	Warrant check
10–45	Listing of wants and warrants requested
10–46	Assist motorist
10–46	Automobile accident; injuries
10–46	Disabled motor vehicle at _(location)_
10–46	Investigate drunken driver
10–46	Breathanalyzer needed at _(location)_
10–46	Personal injury accident at _(location)_
10–46	Holding suspect, rush reply
10–46	Snow (light, moderate, or heavy) (weather)
10–46	I have a prisoner in custody
10–46	Confidential information
10–46	Check for fish and game violation
10–46	Meet for vehicle/drivers' license check
10–46	Emergency run to _(location)_
10–46	Bank alarm sounding at _(location)_
10–46	Wrecker requested at _(location)_
10–47	Explosion reported at _(location)_
10–47	Emergency road repair at _(location)_
10–47	Investigate suspicious vehicle
10–47	Illegally parked vehicle at _(location)_
10–47	Ambulance requested at _(location)_
10–47	Automobile accident with property damage
10–47	Urinalysis report; _(number)_
10–47	Property damage at _(location)_
10–47	Request medical examiner at _(location)_
10–47	Sleet (light, moderate, or heavy) (weather)
10–47	Subject/Victim injured (minor)
10–47	Subject in question might be armed/dangerous/wanted
10–47	Suicide/suicide attempt at _(location)_
10–47	Drunk driver at _(location)_
10–47	Complete assignment quickly
10–47	Suspect should be considered armed and dangerous
10–48	Traffic standard repair at _(location)_
10–48	Open garage door
10–48	Automobile accident with personal injuries
10–48	Unattended death
10–48	Disturbing the peace
10–48	Send wrecker to _(location)_
10–48	Stopping vehicle _(location and license number)_
10–48	Blood alcohol report; _(number)_ %
10–48	Emergency road conditions (supply details)
10–48	Request patrol (paddy) wagon or coroner car to pick up dead body
10–48	Subject/victim injured (severe)
10–48	NCIC hit; is it safe to transmit/copy information?
10–48	Suspicious vehicle at _(location)_ —or suspicious person

Table T-1. Continued

Code	Meaning
10−48	Speeder at _(location)_
10−48	Detaining subject, expedite backup units
10−48	Use caution with this subject
10−48	Fire reported at _(location)_
10−49	Traffic light out at _(location)_
10−49	Automobile blocking alley/driveway at _(location)_
10−49	Automobile accident with fatality
10−49	Driving under the influence (drunk)
10−49	Ambulance needed at _(location)_
10−49	Civil disturbance
10−49	Possible homicide
10−49	Subject/victim injured (fatal)
10−49	Back up traffic assignment at _(location)_
10−49	Assist with traffic control at _(location)_
10−49	Advise me of registration and amount paid for the size and weight of the unit (trucking)
10−49	Vice complaint at _(location)_
10−49	Auto racing at _(location)_
10−49	Any traffic for this unit?
10−49	Flooding reported at _(location)_
10−50	No traffic for your unit
10−50	Automobile accident:
	PD—property damage only
	PI—personal injury reported
	F—fatal injuries
10−50	Property damage accident at _(location)_
10−50	Police car involved in accident
10−50	Break channel, move to channel _(number)_
10−50	Send tow truck to _(location)_
10−50	Police vehicle in pursuit of _(vehicle/person)_
10−50	Request police department wrecker
10−50	Fatality
10−50	Homicide reported at _(location)_
10−50	Message from other jurisdiction
10−50	Break-in or theft reported
10−50	No traffic hazard at this location
10−50	Use extreme caution
10−50	Wanted person—or wanted felon
10−50	Now at scene
10−51	Wrecker needed
10−51	Body in automobile
10−51	Cutting or stabbing at _(location)_
10−51	Debris in the roadway
10−51	Rape reported at _(location)_
10−51	Industrial accident at _(location)_
10−51	Any answer at the telephone number supplied?
10−51	Driving without a license

Table T-1. Continued

Code	Meaning
10−51	Driving under the influence (DUI)
10−51	Can subject/suspect overhear this?
10−51	Pick up __(person)__ at __(location)__ and prepare for a roadblock assignment at __(location)__
10−51	Patrol (paddy) wagon is needed at __(location)__
10−51	Request a vehicle registration check
10−51	Bus inspection at __(location)__
10−51	Request washdown by fire department
10−51	Vehicle stopped at __(location)__
10−52	Ambulance needed
10−52	Burglary in progress at __(location)__ ; Alarm report
10−52	Arrest made at __(location)__
10−52	Send wrecker at owner's request
10−52	Personal injury accident at __(location)__
10−52	Drowning at __(location)__
10−52	Shooting at __(location)__
10−52	Armed robbery
10−52	Item number for assignment
10−52	Out of unit; conducting vehicle check at __(location)__
10−52	Speeder
10−52	Improperly parked automobile
10−52	Subject wanted (felony)
10−52	Establish a roadblock at __(location)__
10−53	Road blocked at __(location)__ or establish roadblock
10−53	Abduction reported at __(location)__
10−53	Traffic control
10−53	Officer (unit) is clear for assignment at __(location)__
10−53	Report for duty at __(location)__
10−53	Coroner required at __(location)__
10−53	Holdup or robbery at __(location)__
10−53	Individual is wanted for __(crime)__
10−53	Subject wanted (misdemeanor)
10−53	Unable to copy telephone caller
10−53	Discontinue roadblock by authority of __(person)__
10−53	Switch to another channel
10−53	Request large emergency (command) truck
10−53	Bomb threat at __(location)__
10−54	Untimely death reported at __(location)__
	A—accidental
	D—drowning
	N—natural causes
	S—suicide
10−54	Stand by for FAX/TWX
10−54	Livestock on highway
10−54	Change to channel __(number)__
10−54	Need electrician, traffic signal problem
10−54	District attorney needed at __(location)__

Table T-1. Continued

Code	Meaning
10–54	Drag racing
10–54	Individual *(M/F)* with handgun, knife, at *(location)*
10–54	Arrest individual and hold for *(crime)*
10–54	Send backup units
10–54	Direct traffic at *(location)*
10–54	Wanted status confirmed
10–54	Estimated Time of Arrival (ETA)
10–54	Correct date and time
10–54	Road-work/highway repairs at *(location)*
10–54	Hit and run
	PD—property damage only
	PI—personal injuries reported
	F—fatal injuries
10–54	Fatal accident at *(location)*
10–54	Meet *(person)* at *(location and time)*
10–54	Have vehicle stopped; occupants might be dangerous; the license number of the vehicle is *(number)*
10–55	Intoxicated driver
10–55	Funeral
10–55	Ambulance requested at *(location)*
10–55	Inspection of *(item)* is OK
10–55	Disabled communications repeater
10–55	Vehicle accident
10–55	Report for radar detail
10–55	Armed robbery in progress at *(location)*
10–55	Officer in trouble at *(location)*
10–55	Kidnapping
10–55	Rape in progress at *(location)*
10–55	Change to another frequency (radio channel)
10–55	Subject clear, but use caution
10–55	Surveillance activity
10–55	Request large towing unit for truck tow
10–55	Request permission to call or use channel *(radio channel)*
10–56	Intoxicated pedestrian
10–56	Investigate DUI/DWI
10–56	Burglar alarm sounding at *(location)*
10–56	Wrecker needed at *(location)*
10–56	Next message number?
10–56	Changing surveillance location
10–56	Vandalism at *(location)*
10–56	Assault against a person at *(location)*
10–56	Establish roadblock at *(location)* immediately
10–56	Request the telephone number of *(person)*
10–56	Request tow truck for disabled patrol car
10–57	Hit and run
10–57	Alert
10–57	Report for school crossing detail

Table T-1. Continued

Code	Meaning
10−57	Intoxicated or inebriated individual at *(location)*
10−57	Individual under the influence of drugs at *(location)*
10−57	Repeat message/transmission
10−57	Fight in progress at *(location)*
10−57	Ambulance needed at *(location)*
10−57	Vehicle exceeds roadway weight limits
10−57	Disregard, no further action required
10−57	Request drunkometer/breathanalyzer operator at *(location)*
10−57	Request light panel truck with photo/television for immediate surveillance
10−58	Direct traffic at *(location)*
10−58	Airplane crash
10−58	Prowler at *(location)*
10−58	Violent mental patient at *(location)*
10−58	Have you dispatched?
10−58	Public drunk
10−58	Larceny at *(location)*
10−58	Check for current driver's license/criminal record
10−58	Riot
10−58	Request permission to talk to *(person)*
10−58	Request explosives technician and bomb truck
10−58	Bank run
10−59	Convoy or escort
10−59	Reckless driver
10−59	Nonviolent mental patient at *(location)*
10−59	Person exposing himself at *(location)*
10−59	Assist motorist at *(location)*
10−59	Drunk person in a public place at *(location)*
10−59	Unsafe traffic conditions
10−59	Check for valid driver's license
10−59	Open door or window at *(location)*
10−59	Need radio repair/service/replacement
10−59	Request crime scene search unit at *(location)*
10−59	Individual with gun at *(location)*
10−59	Urgent response—use no red lights or siren
10−59	Attention all units
10−60	Squad/patrol car/other officers in the vicinity
10−60	Lost hunter
10−60	What is the next message (or incident) number?
10−60	Out of car on violator at *(location)*
10−60	Require transportation for prisoner/citizen at *(location)*
10−60	Check for suspension of operator's license (followed by state identification, name of operator, and the number on the license)
10−60	Emergency blood run to *(location)*
10−60	Tower lights are not operational
10−60	The next case number is *(number)*
10−60	Notify coroner
10−60	Brawl/fight reported at *(location)*

Table T-1. Continued

Code	Meaning
10−60	Have there been any messages for this unit?
10−60	Emergency—use red lights and siren
10−60	Request helicopter at _(location)_
10−60	Emergency assistance needed by this unit at _(location)_
10−61	Personnel in area
10−61	Motor inspection
10−61	Hunting accident
10−61	Fire call
10−61	Repeat your message and transmit slower
10−61	Clear for assignment
10−61	Assignment is outside my area
10−61	Request marine rescue unit at _(location)_
10−61	I need a case/file number for this incident
10−61	Illegal use of radio
10−61	Prisoner in custody
10−61	Domestic disturbance at _(location)_
10−61	Give following message to _(person)_ as soon as possible
10−61	Stopping a suspicious vehicle/person at _(location)_
10−61	Officer is sick and needs assistance
10−61	This officer has been injured
10−62	Reply to message
10−62	Repeat your message and speak louder
10−62	Unable to copy, use telephone
10−62	Drowning accident
10−62	Request permission car to car
10−62	City police unit involved in accident at _(location)_
10−62	Individual screaming at _(location)_
10−62	Have you completed your (radio) transmission?
10−62	Prison/jail break
10−62	Enroute to assignment
10−62	Motorist assisted at _(location)_
10−62	Transporting prisoner
10−62	Burglary/breaking and entering in progress at _(location)_
10−62	Shoplifter at _(location)_
10−62	Bomb threat at _(location)_
10−63	Prepare to make written copy
10−63	Net directly to _(person)_
10−63	Beating of woman or child at _(location)_
10−63	Illegal night hunting in progress at _(location)_
10−63	Out of unit serving warrant at _(location)_
10−63	Theft at _(location)_
10−63	Request explosive disposal unit
10−63	Advise telephone number of _(person)_
10−63	Dispatch coroner to _(location)_
10−63	Transporting citizen
10−63	Investigate _(crime)_ at _(location)_
10−63	Unit _(number)_ respond to radio call

Table T-1. Continued

Code	Meaning
10−64	Barricaded subject at *(location)*
10−64	Message for local delivery
10−64	Dog/deer complaint
10−64	Net clear
10−64	Assault at *(location)*
10−64	Vandalism
10−64	Dead body at *(location)*
10−64	Bomb threat
10−64	Your transmission is not clear
10−64	Prisoner/citizen transport complete
10−64	Station/unit clear
10−65	Net message assignment
10−65	Boating accident
10−65	Larceny at *(location)*
10−65	Juvenile problem
10−65	Mad dog
10−65	Respond to *(location)* to assist in investigation
10−65	I am clear for another assignment
10−65	Blockade
10−65	Armed robbery reported at *(location)*
10−65	Request SWAT unit at *(location)*
10−65	Radio check
10−65	Clear for item *(assignment)*
10−66	Message/assignment or cancellation
10−66	Clear for cancellation
10−66	Major crime alert
10−66	Bomb scare
10−66	Shots fired at *(location)*
10−66	Drag racing
10−66	Notify coroner and/or medical examiner
10−66	Photographer needed at *(location)*
10−66	Snowmobile accident
10−66	Vehicle requires service
10−66	Completed last assignment
10−67	Clear for net message
10−67	Request canine unit at *(location)*
10−67	All units comply
10−67	Rape at *(location)*
10−67	Station *(channel frequency)* carry this message
10−67	Prisoner is in custody
10−67	Investigate the report of a dead body at *(location)*
10−67	Out of service *(reason and location)*
10−68	Individual bailed or released
10−68	Restrict use of telephone system to absolute minimum
10−68	Dispatch information
10−68	Runaway juvenile

Table T-1. Continued

Code	Meaning
10–68	Kidnapping at *(location)*
10–68	Repeat dispatch
10–68	Give me a radio (test) check
10–68	Mental subject
10–68	Livestock on the roadway
10–68	Send additional assistance/backup to this location
10–69	Message received
10–69	Missing person
10–69	Has *(person)* been dispatched?
10–69	Drug related incident
10–69	I am detaining subject, rush your reply
10–69	Test (radio) with no modulation
10–69	Advise the telephone number at your location
10–69	Aircraft crash
10–70	Fire alarm
10–70	Net message
10–70	Missing person reported at *(location)*
10–70	Test (radio) intermittently with no modulation for *(number)* minutes
10–70	Civil disturbance
10–70	Is there traffic (radio) for this unit or station?
10–70	Stopping vehicle; might be dangerous; the license number of the vehicle is *(number)* and my location is *(place)*
10–70	Report of an improperly parked vehicle at *(location)*
10–70	Frequency (channel) is in use for special assignment—do not use for emergency messages
10–70	Crime in progress at *(location)*
10–70L	Lost person
10–70M	Missing person
10–70W	Wanted person
10–71	Advise nature of fire (exactly what is burning)?
10–71	Proceed with transmission
10–71	Proceed with radio traffic in sequence (busy here)
10–71	Test (communications system) continuously with tone
10–71	Records indicate individual/property is wanted/stolen
10–71	Request removal of *(property)*
10–71	Bomb threat
10–71	Out of service (to issue warrant)
10–71	Officer is clear from vehicle stop
10–71	Fish and game officer notified and enroute
10–71	Improper use of radio
10–72	Report progress of fire
10–72	Riot
10–72	Establish roadblock at *(location)*
10–72	Request jail matron/female police officer at *(location)*
10–72	Advise (communication system) signal strength
10–72	Fire alarm at *(location)*
10–72	Larceny
10–72	Dead body found at *(location)*

Table T-1. Continued

Code	Meaning
10−72	Out of service special detail ordered by *(person)*
10−72	Information incomplete—no action will be taken until full information is furnished; we need *(information)*
10−72	Have prisoner in custody
10−72	Transporting mental patient; my mileage is *(number)*
10−73	Smoke report
10−73	Speed trap at *(location)*
10−73	Advise (communication system) audio quality
10−73	Abandoned vehicle
10−73	Contact *(name)* funeral home
10−73	Trouble at station
10−73	Rape
10−73	Establish a roadblock
10−73	Out of gas at *(location)*
10−73	Break in
10−73	Use cellular telephone/radio scrambler
10−73	Out of service follow-up on case # *(number)*
10−73	Information is not in proper form—retransmit or rewrite
10−73	Mental subject
10−73	Lift roadblock at *(location)* ; the authority is *(person)*
10−74	Negative
10−74	Officer needs assistance (emergency)
10−74	Civil disturbance
10−74	Audio quality (communication system) is good
10−74	Emergency blood run to hospital
10−74	Contact emergency (hospital) room for *(reason)*
10−74	Theft
10−74	Armed robbery
10−74	Out of service (servicing equipment)
10−74	Escape—prison or jail break
10−75	In contact with *(person)*
10−75	You are causing interference (stand by)
10−75	Vehicle is reported stolen
10−75	Resume your patrol
10−75	Threat to *(person)* at *(location)*
10−75	Domestic problem
10−75	Aircraft crash
10−75	Emergency air clearance
10−75	Juvenile problem at *(location)*
10−75	Records indicate wanted or stolen vehicle
10−75	Shooting at *(location)*
10−75	Out of service (stakeout)
10−76	Enroute to *(location)*
10−76	Meet complainant at *(location)*
10−76	Do you have radio traffic for *(location)*
10−76	Dead on arrival (DOA)

Table T-1. Continued

Code	Meaning
10−76	Transmission (radio) is choppy
10−76	Prison/jail escape
10−76	Request permission to leave patrol area
10−76	Assault at *(location)*
10−76	Accident—seriousness of which is not known here
10−76	Prowler
10−77	Estimated time of arrival (ETA)
10−77	Negative contact
10−77	Return to *(location)*
10−77	Civil defense test
10−77	Prowler at *(location)*
10−77	Roadblock
10−77	Report existing conditions at your location
10−77	Vandalism
10−77	General (local) emergency—all units stand by
10−77	Attempted arson at *(location)*
10−77	Assist fire department with traffic control at *(location)*
10−78	Need assistance
10−78	Civil defense—federal agency reports probable attack
10−78	For your information
10−78	Transmitter (radio) quality is poor
10−78	Ambulance and Emergency Medical Services (EMS) needed
10−78	Meet a citizen at *(location)*
10−78	Officer is in danger
10−78	Bank hold-up alarm at *(location)*
10−78	Trespasser at *(location)*
10−79	Notify coroner
10−79	Transmit on an alternate (channel) frequency
10−79	Civil defense—actual attack
10−79	Prowler
10−79	Domestic disturbance at *(location)*
10−79	All clear
10−79	Out of service (end of shift)
10−79	Aircraft crash at *(location)*
10−80	Chase in progress
10−80	Streetlight burned out at *(location)*
10−80	Traffic light out at *(location)*
10−80	No record shown
10−80	Business/residence alarm at *(location)*
10−80	Any narcotics information?
10−80	Sex crime at *(location)*
10−80	Armed and dangerous
10−80	Suspicious person at *(location)*
10−80	I am leaving on assignment
10−80	Pick up your partner at *(location)*

Table T-1. Continued

Code	Meaning
10−81	Breathalyzer report
10−81	Contact dispatcher for house watch
10−81	Misdemeanor (bench) warrant outstanding
10−81	Report of smoke at _(location)_
10−81	Reserve hotel room for _(person)_
10−81	Officer _(name)_ is at _(location)_
10−81	Missing person
10−81	Meet me at _(location)_ so we can go over case _(case number)_
10−81	Meet victim or complainant at _(location)_
10−81	At scene
10−81	Bank alarm at _(location)_
10−82	Reserve lodging
10−82	Prisoner in custody
10−82	Request you make me a room reservation
10−82	Contact dispatcher for telephone number
10−82	Burglary in progress at _(location)_
10−82	Domestic violence at _(location)_
10−82	Stopping suspicious vehicle at _(location)_
10−82	Officer will be late to appointment
10−82	Meal break—conditionally available
10−82	Leaving scene for hospital
10−83	Work school crossing at _(location)_
10−83	Confidential information
10−83	Undercover investigation at _(location)_
10−83	Roadway is blocked at _(location)_
10−83	Contact dispatcher for information
10−83	Vehicle requires repair
10−83	Fight at _(location)_
10−83	Disturbance at _(location)_
10−83	Writing report—conditionally available
10−83	At hospital
10−83	Traffic violation
10−84	If meeting _(person)_ advise estimated time of arrival
10−84	Advise telephone number at your location
10−84	My telephone number is _(number)_
10−84	Visitors present
10−84	Request radio repair
10−84	Leaving hospital—returning to post
10−84	Advise how to contact _(person)_
10−84	Assault on person at _(location)_
10−84	Crime in progress at _(location)_
10−84	Informant in unit at _(location)_
10−84	Police personnel in the area
10−84	Checking vehicle/building/person
10−84	Check local records
10−84	Report to _(location)_ for information/assignment

Table T-1. Continued

Code	Meaning
10–85	Delayed due to ___(reason)___
10–85	Alarm sounding at ___(location)___
10–85	My address is ___(location)___
10–85	Victim's condition
	A—Fair
	B—Critical
	C—Poor
	D—Possible fatality
	E—Fatality
10–85	Keep vehicle/individual under surveillance, do not stop or detain
10–85	Not needed—return to post
10–85	Knifing/stabbing at ___(location)___
10–85	Fire alarm at ___(location)___
10–86	Officer/operator on duty—or on post
10–86	Advise me of the correct time
10–86	Crime in progress
10–86	Out of vehicle at ___(location)___ subject to call
10–86	Armed robbery at ___(location)___
10–86	Open door or window at ___(location)___
10–86	Pickup your partner at ___(location)___
10–87	Pick up/distribute paychecks
10–87	Stopped at the pistol range
10–87	Can you meet ___(person)___ at ___(location)___
10–87	Abandoned car
10–87	Request permission to leave my patrol district
10–87	Stopping at my residence
10–87	Shooting at ___(location)___
10–87	Aircraft assignment, location, and time
10–88	Officer needed assistance
10–88	Present telephone number of ___(person)___
10–88	Out of my car and on portable (radio)
10–88	Man with gun
10–88	See complainant at ___(location)___
10–88	Another squad (police officer/vehicle) in vicinity
10–88	Package for ___(person)___
10–88	What telephone number shall we call to make direct contact with officer/agent?
10–88	Advise telephone number for station-to-station call
10–89	Bomb threat
10–89	Use caution
10–89	Traffic check; radar/scales/traffic sign
10–89	Radio repairman needed at ___(location)___
10–89	Felony warrant outstanding
10–89	Homicide at ___(location)___
10–89	This unit (vehicle) needs repairs
10–89	Escort
10–89	___(Person)___ is trying to contact you

Table T-1. Continued

Code	Meaning
10−90	Bank alarm at _(location)_
10−90	Unable to give information over the air
10−90	Hold traffic—passenger/prisoner in vehicle
10−90	Civil disturbance
10−90	Subject has scanner
10−90	Prepare to receive information
10−90	Officer welfare contact (usually on surveillance)
10−90	Police aircraft in trouble; we are going down
10−90	Crime in progress at _(location)_
10−91	Pick up prisoner/subject
10−91	Talk closer to mike
10−91	What officer is on duty at that location?
10−91	Police aircraft forced to make an emergency landing
10−91	Burglary
10−91	Return to _(location)_
10−91	Your transmission is weak, talk closer to mike
10−91	Meet at _(location)_
10−91	Call your residence—not an emergency
10−91	Oil spill at _(location)_
10−91	Jail/prison break in progress
10−92	Meet at command post
10−92	Felony pickup of subject, no warrant
10−92	Police aircraft closing flight plan at _(location)_
10−92	Improperly parked vehicle
10−92	Your transmitter appears to be out of adjustment
10−92	Your signal is too loud, talk further from mike
10−92	Theft
10−92	Car service at _(location)_
10−92	Armed robbery in progress at _(location)_
10−92	Need a radio technician at _(location)_
10−92	Repair traffic sign at _(location)_
10−92	Your transmission (radio) has interference
10−92	Money escort (from business to bank)
10−92	Delayed due to _(reason)_
10−93	Meet at major crime scene
10−93	Police aircraft in adverse weather conditions; our present position is _(location)_
10−93	Active warrant for subject
10−93	All units in area respond Code 3
10−93	Blockade
10−93	Check my frequency on this channel
10−93	Bank alarm at _(location)_
10−93	Unnecessary use of radio
10−93	Traffic violation
10−93	Message received
10−94	Respond to scene with shotguns and vests
10−94	Drag racing

Table T-1. Continued

Code	Meaning
10-94	Bomb threat at _(location)_
10-94	Police aircraft switching to FAA frequency _(channel)_
10-94	Active warrant for subject or vehicle
10-94A	Please give me a long count
10-94B	Transmit a carrier tone without voice
10-94	Contact your home
10-94	Personal relief—I need to go to the bathroom
10-94	Radio test with no modulation
10-94	Attention all units—general broadcast
10-94	Armed, dangerous, mental, parolee, intelligence subject, militant, or individual(s) with criminal record
10-95	Respond to scene with jump suits and helmets
10-95	Police aircraft out of service at _(time and location)_
10-95	Prisoner/subject in custody
10-95	Transmit dead carrier for 5 seconds
10-95	Meal break (requested)
10-95	Fight in progress at _(location)_
10-95	Radio test with modulation
10-95	Pick up prisoner at _(location)_
10-96	Civil Defense 'Alert'
10-96	Undercover operation; marked units stay out of area
10-96	Unable to give location—surveillance operation
10-96	Respond in old clothes
10-96	Prowler reported at _(location)_
10-96	Mental subject
10-96	Bar/tavern check at _(location)_
10-96	Breathanalyzer operator available?
10-96	Unrest on school campus at _(location)_
10-97	Civil Defense 'Evacuate'
10-97	Request precision firearms team and equipment
10-97	Check (test) radio signal for transmission quality
10-97	Transport legislator
10-97	Domestic problem at _(location)_
10-97	On scene at _(location)_
10-97	Radio check
10-98	Civil Defense 'Take Cover'
10-98	Prison/jail break
10-98	Command to all units involved in activity
10-98	Aircraft hijacking
10-98	Make out field investigation report
10-98	Mass disturbance/riot at _(location)_
10-98	Assignment complete
10-98	Switch to regional channel _(frequency)_
10-99	Civil Defense 'Test'
10-99	Possible emergency situation—respond quietly

Table T-1. Continued

Code	Meaning
10–99	Prison/jail break at ____(location)
10–99	Wanted/stolen is indicated
10–99	Mission completed, all units secure
10–99	Emergency—all units respond
10–99	Traffic signal out at ____(location)
10–99	Night safety check
10–100	Riot conditions exist at ____(location)
10–100A	Rest room pause
10–101	Investigate disturbance at ____(location)
10–101	Suspect is known to be armed and dangerous
10–200A	Police needed at ____(location)
10–1000	Emergency radio silence

the "B" man   [LE] Radio code word for the crime scene technician (I.D. TECH).

the "C" man   [LE] Radio code word for the watch commander.

the "H" man   [LE] Radio code word for the hostage negotiator.

the ice man   [LE] Slang for the police officer responsible for the sealing off an area or building so a search can be conducted.

the man   [C,G&PS] Slang for a law enforcement/ police officer.

The Red Army   [TRG] A terrorist/radical group started in Japan, also known as *Sekigun*. Ideology and aims are supported by a very small number of Japanese students who have come to the United States for their education. Members are under FBI investigation as "most wanted."

thermal imager   [M] A device, used by military and law enforcement units to track the movements or location of people in remote locations such as wooded areas, that can define between an existing environment and body heat and measure the difference. As an example, if someone has been seated in a chair, hours later residue of his thermal image remains. In a wooded area, a thermal scan would quickly locate a person who is trying to hide.

thermal neutron recorder   A plastic-explosive detector. Airlines, the military, and law enforcement have never had a reliable method of detecting plastic explosives. The plastic explosives that have been used by terrorists to blow up airplanes in recent years are light, powerful, and almost impossible to detect without a hand search of all luggage. Cleverly hidden plastic bombs can elude even a hand search. Explosives called "plastic" are putty-soft and can be pressed into any shape. They are also transparent to X-ray detectors because the explosives are composed of light elements such as nitrogen, carbon, hydrogen, and oxygen—the same elements that comprise clothing, wood, water, and other organic substances. The thermal neutron (detector) recorder, a device created by Science Applications International Corp. of San Diego, represents the first large advance in practical plastic explosive detectors. It can reliably spot explosives because its beam of neutrons can pass through any material, including lead, almost as if it were not there. The machine takes advantage of the fact that all modern explosives contain unusually large amounts of nitrogen. Many other materials also contain nitrogen, and an average packed suitcase can contain the equivalent of $1/2$ pound of nitrogen. A 1-pound bomb (enough to disable an aircraft in flight) by itself would contain twice as much nitrogen as a suitcase filled with clothing and toilet articles. The thermal neutron (detector) recorder bombards a piece of luggage with neutrons. Because neutrons have no charge, they pass easily through other materials without reacting greatly. But nitrogen atoms absorb neutrons, then immediately emit gamma radiation. The gamma radiation that emerges from the suitcase has a unique signature that can be detected by the machine. The amount of radiation used by the thermal neutron (detector) recorder is small and has little effect on the suitcase or its contents. A thermal neutron recorder does not affect photographic film in luggage. (*See* NEUTRON RECORDER; TNA.)

things [C,G&PS] Slang for balloons or condoms that are filled with heroin. Rubber protects the heroin from moisture in case it must be swallowed.

Thorazine [LE] Brand name of chlorpromazine, a controlled substance that is a major tranquilizer. (*See* QUICK REFERENCE.)

Threatcon [M] There are three levels of Threatcon that indicate the terrorist threat to U.S. military facilities and personnel:

- *Threatcon white*—nonspecific threat of terrorism against U.S. military personnel of facilities in a general geographic area. (This threat can be based on information that terrorist elements in an area have general plans concerning military facilities).
- *Threatcon yellow*—Specific threat of terrorism against U.S. military personnel or facilities within a particular geographic area. (This threat can be based on information that terrorist elements are actively preparing for operations in a particular area).
- *Threatcon red*—Imminent threat of terrorist acts against specific U.S. military personnel or facilities. (This threat can be based on information regarding plans or preparations for terrorist attacks against specific persons or facilities).

three-d [M] Shortened form of Three Dimensional.

throwaway [LE] A term used by police to indicate clothing found at or near the scene of a crime that has been discarded by the criminal.

THS [C3I] Abbreviation for Tactical Hybrid Switch.

Thunderbolt II *See* A-10.

TI [LE] Abbreviation for Thermal Imaging.

TIARA [C3I] Acronym for Tactical Intelligence And Related Activities.

ticket [C,G&PS] Slang for LSD impregnated on a sugar cube or strip of paper. This combination is ingested.

tickling [EW] Of or referring to a situation wherein an electronic warfare aircraft of one country approaches the border of another country in an effort to determine the effectiveness of air and ground defenses. In certain instances, the electronic warfare aircraft go undetected, but on most occasions they are turned away. A major contender in the area of U.S. airborne electronic intelligence gathering is the RC-135 aircraft that often flies as closely as possible to Soviet airspace and the borders of the Soviet Union. The United States conducts surveillance of the Soviet Union from the airspace of and over Turkey.

TIE [C3I] Abbreviation for Time Internal Errors.

tie [C,G&PS] Slang for the rubber tubing that is used to reduce the circulation in an arm or leg. Once in place, veins will protrude making it easier to inject narcotics.

tighten me up [C,G&PS] A street term used by a drug/narcotic user asking another person to supply him with some form of drug or narcotic.

time [C,G&PS] The two-handed sign for the letter *T*, used by drug dealers to indicate they have some sort of narcotics they wish to sell to people in a passing automobile. Narcotics are usually hidden somewhere nearby. If the buyer also happens to be a police officer, the dealer is clean, so surveillance is usually undertaken by a law enforcement agency to first determine the location of the narcotic or drug stash.

time bomb   1. [LE] A bomb connected to a timer that can be set to explode at a specific time. **2.** [LE] A computer virus or worm triggered by the computer's internal clock when it reaches a certain date or time (*See* VIRUS.)

tin   [LE] Slang for the badge of a law enforcement officer.

tingle   [C,G&PS] Slang for a sensation felt in the abdomen or chest by a narcotics user.

tipped   [LE] Slang referring to an altered credit card.

TIS   Abbreviation for Travelers Information Stations, low-powered stations broadcasting on 530 and 1610 kHz (AM radio) and providing information to travelers on current road conditions, nearby historical sites, freeway off-ramps, and highway junctions. Highway signs usually indicate TISs are located nearby.

TK   [M] Abbreviation for Talent-Keyhole, the code name that applies to all satellite photography from the Keyhole (KH) series of photo-reconnaissance satellites in use by the United States intelligence community. (*See* KH-12.)

TM   1. [C3I] Abbreviation for Thermatic Mapper. **2.** [C3I] Abbreviation for Transverse Magnetic.

TMUX   [C3I] Acronym for Transmultiplexer.

TNA   [A] Abbreviation for Thermal Neutron Analysis, a system that bathes luggage in low-energy neutrons that chemically react to plastic explosives. That reaction triggers an alarm. (*See* NEUTRON RECORDER; THERMAL NEUTRON RECORDER.)

T/O   [A] Abbreviation for Take-Off.

TOA   [M] Abbreviation for Time Of Arrival.

toat   [C,G&PS] Slang meaning to smoke a marijuana cigarette.

to be clean   [C,G&PS] Slang for someone not using narcotics or drugs.

to be off   [C,G&PS] A term used to indicate the withdrawal from the usage of drugs or narcotics.

TOC   [US] Abbreviation for Tactical Operations Center.

to chip   [LE] Slang meaning to have a small drug or narcotic habit.

todies   [C,G&PS] Slang for the barbiturate Tuinal.

to dig   [C,G&PS] Slang meaning to be able to understand or agree with another person. The term also is used to indicate that someone likes something.

TO & E   [M] Abbreviation for Table of Organization and Equipment.

TOE   [M] Abbreviation for Table of Organization and Equipment.

toke   [C,G&PS] Slang meaning to take a drag (puff) on a marijuana cigarette.

Tom   [A,LE,MIL] Designation for the letter *T*.

tommy   [LE] Slang for a machine gun.

tooies   [C,G&PS] Slang for barbiturates. (*See* QUICK REFERENCE.)

tool   [C,G&PS] Slang for cocaine. (*See* QUICK REFERENCE.)

tools   [C,G&PS] Slang for the hardware used for the injection of a narcotic into the bloodstream.

toot   [C,G&PS] Slang for cocaine. (*See* QUICK REFERENCE.)

tooter   [C,G&PS] Slang for a device used for the sniffing of cocaine.

to the mouth   [LE] The term used to indicate that an individual has ingested narcotic or drug evidence. The term is most likely used by police who have a suspect under surveillance, and the suspect suddenly becomes aware of the police.

tootsie roll   [C,G&PS] Slang for distilled and concentrated heroin.

toot spoon   [C,G&PS] Slang for the spoon used to hold an individual dose of cocaine.

to plant   [LE] Slang term meaning to hide or conceal something.

tops   [C,G&PS] Term for the flowers of a marijuana plant.

torch up   [C,G&PS] Slang to light up a marijuana cigarette.

TOS   [US] Abbreviation for Tactical Operations System.

toss   1. [LE] Slang term meaning to search a location or individual. **2.** To frisk.

TOW   [M] Designation for Tube-launched, Optically tracked, Wire-guided anti-tank missile.

towa yuai jigyo kumiai   [LE] Name of a group known by law enforcement agencies in Asia and the United States as the East Asia Friendship Enterprise Association. The *towa yuai jigyo kumiai*, made up mostly of Koreans, is an arm of the *yakuza* (Japan's criminal underworld) and is very active in the five western states where Asians are a part of the business community.

tower   [A] Short for control tower.

TOX   Specialty code for toxic materials and hazardous waste.

toy   [C,G&PS] In opium usage, the smallest amount of the drug in prepared form.

TP   Specialty code for Trial Preparation.

TPA   [C3I] Abbreviation for Transistor Power Amplifier.

TPLA   [TRG] Abbreviation for Turkish People's Liberation Army. The TPLA is a Turkish/Marxist terrorist faction with close ties to Palestinians and Communist-run governments worldwide. The majority of its terrorist activities have taken place in Turkey, but the group is recognized as a party to terrorism that takes place elsewhere in the world. The major thrust of the group is to disrupt NATO activities and operations, including major thefts of military arms from NATO facilities.

TPLF   [TRG] Abbreviation for Turkish People's Liberation Front. Intelligence indicates that many members of the TPLF also are active in the TPLA terrorist organization. The goals of both groups are parallel.

TPU   [M] Abbreviation for Tactical Patrol Unit.

TRACALS   [C3I] Acronym for TRAffic Control And Landing System.

tracks   [C,G&PS] Slang for the needle scars resulting from the collapse of veins in the arms and legs of a drug user caused by constant injections.

trackwolf   [US] A signal collection and direction finding system highly classified for surveillance applications and developed for the Army by the Information Systems Division of TCI International in Mountain View, California. Trackwolf is used to locate and pinpoint movements of the enemy by their radio transmissions. Neither the Army nor manufacturer will discuss Trackwolf because of the issues of national security. The Drug Enforcement Administration and Coast Guard are evaluating the Trackwolf system for interception of radio communications between drug smugglers and specific in-flight aircraft locations. Trackwolf is a computerized system designed to—in seconds—pinpoint a transmitter once it has sent out a signal by actual direction and distance.

tradecraft   [I] A variety of very specialized techniques and methods used in the intelligence-gathering process. Tradecraft usually will refer to someone with a special skill such as building penetration, firearms, electronics, or photography.

TRADOC   [M] Acronym for TRAining and DOctrine Command.

traffic radar   [LE] The radar system used by police departments that has been accepted by law enforcement agencies for a number of years as a device to measure the speed of passing traffic. Sound enforcement decisions and the successful prosecution of speed violations where traffic radar is applied depends upon the officer's having measured the violator's speed accurately, first by estimating the speed of a vehicle, then confirming that estimate with radar. A number of factors can make traffic radar less than accurate in the hands of someone lacking the proper training.

tranquility   [C,G&PS] Slang for STP. (*See* QUICK REFERENCE.)

trap   [C,G&PS] Slang for a location where drugs/narcotics are hidden.

traps   [M] Term for composite materials used to build the airframe and construct the outer skin of Stealth airplanes. Traps are fashioned into honeycombs inside the aircraft to shield inner components that create radio frequency interference and would be detected by their emissions. Composites are naturally poor reflectors, and the honeycomb lattice "traps" the few reflections that take place by bouncing them from one surface to another instead of away from the aircraft. (*See also* STEALTH AIRCRAFT.)

travel agent   [C,G&PS] Slang for a drug supplier, usually an LSD supplier.

trey [C,G&PS] Slang for a $5 bag of heroin.

TRF [C] Abbreviation for Tuned Radio Frequency.

triads [LE] Various Chinese organized criminal syndicates that are known to be active in the drug operations of Thailand, Hong Kong, and Taiwan. Triads control all heroin sales in Southeast Asia and are considered by law enforcement agencies all along the Pacific Rim as the greatest danger and largest force involved in organized crime anywhere in the world.

triffid [UK] Code name for transportable UHF radio relay equipment.

trigger [C,G&PS] Slang term meaning to ingest LSD, then smoke marijuana. This process gives the user a double feeling of euphoria at different levels.

TRI-TAC [C3I] Acronym for Tri-Service Tactical Communications, also known as the Joint Tactical Communications System.

trip [C,G&PS] The experience of being under the influence of LSD.

TRK Specialty code for truck/trailer.

Trojan horse [GOV] Slang for an innocent-seeming computer program that has been deliberately infected with a virus or worm entry (program addition) and circulated publicly (See VIRUS.)

TRP Specialty code for trial preparation.

TRS [C3I] Abbreviation for Tele-operator Retrieval System.

truck [LE] A surveillance aircraft or helicopter with law enforcement officers, such as FBI Strike Force, DEA Agents, etc. on board.

truck drivers [C,G&PS] Slang for amphetamines, so called because many cross-country truck drivers occasionally use amphetamines to stay awake over long periods. (See QUICK REFERENCE.)

truck stop [LE] Slang for airport or landing area, used for drug smuggling.

Try Add Radar [I] Term for the Soviet radar supporting the Galosh/ABM-1B missile system. Try add radar directs aircraft interceptors and missiles to foreign targets that violate Soviet air space. The Try Add Radar soon will replace or supplement the Pushkino radar system. (See PUSHKINO RADAR.)

TS **1.** Abbreviation for Top Secret, the security classification used by the United States to protect national security information. The disclosure of top secret data could result in exceptionally grave damage to the interests of the U.S. (See Q; SECRET & CONFIDENTIAL.) **2.** [LE] Abbreviation for Telephone Switchboard.

TSARCOM [US] Designation for Army Troop Support and Aviation Materiel Readiness Command.

TSM [C3I] Abbreviation for TDMA System Monitor. (See TDMA.)

TSP [C3I] Abbreviation for Tracking Signal Processor.

TTBT [GOV] Abbreviation for Threshold Test Ban Treaty.

TTC&M [C3I] Abbreviation for Telemetry, Tracking, Control & Monitoring.

TTY [C3I] Abbreviation for Teletype.

Tuinal [LE] Brand name of amobarbital, a controlled substance that is a sedative. (See QUICK REFERENCE.)

Tupamaros [TRG] Name of a Uruguayan terrorist group that was most active in the 1960s. The majority of the membership was either killed or arrested and imprisoned by the government. On rare occasions this group is blamed for terrorist acts in Uruguay. In the 1970s, the Tupamaros were known as the *Movimiento de Liberation National* (MLN).

turkey [LE] Slang for nonnarcotics represented as genuine narcotics to a prospective buyer.

turkey trots [C,G&PS] Slang for needle tracks resulting from narcotic usage.

turned [I] Slang referring to an individual who has been persuaded or bribed to change sides.

turn on **1.** [C,G&PS] Slang for the introduction of drugs/narcotics to a first-time user. **2.** [C,G&PS] Slang term meaning to supply a first-time user with a dose or injection.

turned off [C,G&PS] Slang meaning withdrawn from the use of drugs.

turps [C,G&PS] Slang for codeine blended with terpin hydrate.

TV [B] Abbreviation for TeleVision.

TVM [M] Abbreviation for Track Via Missile.

TVRO [C3I] Abbreviation for TeleVision Receive Only.

tweaker [C,G&PS] Slang for a user seeking crack cocaine for personal consumption.

Twelve-Code Some law enforcement agencies have incorporated the 12-Code into their communications system for better security. The 12-Code topics are closely related to the basic commands used in the 10-Code system, but different enough to be obscure to the uninformed listener. Most common usage is shown in TABLE T-2.

twenty cents [C,G&PS] Slang for $20.

twenty-five [C,G&PS] Slang for LSD. This term was derived from the origin of LSD, known as LSD-25. (*See* QUICK REFERENCE.)

twep [LE] Acronym for terminated (murdered) With Extreme Prejudice.

twisted [LE] Slang term referring to an individual who is under the influence of a drug or narcotic.

two-D [2D] Abbreviation for two-dimensional.

TWRL [C] Abbreviation for Two-Way Radio Link.

TWS 1. [A] Abbreviation for Tail Warning System. 2. [M] Abbreviation for Track While Scan.

TWT [C] Abbreviation for Traveling Wave Tube.

TX [C] Abbreviation for Transmitter.

Table T-2. Twelve-Codes

Code	Meaning
12−1	In service
12−2	Mobile going out of service
12−3	Return to your office
12−4	Call this office by telephone
12−5	Repeat message
12−6	Meet at _(place)_
12−7	Motor vehicle registration
12−8	Motor vehicle registration and legal owner
12−9	Check Public Utilities Commission (PUC) status
12−10	Check for operator's license (truck driver)
12−11	Describe individual from operator's license
12−12	Unable to copy—change location
12−13	Prepare to write down following information
12−14	Relay the following to _(person)_
12−15	Locate _(person)_ for emergency message
12−16	Motor vehicle accident—no injuries/fatal
12−17	Motor vehicle accident—ambulance needed
12−18	Ambulance dispatched
12−19	Dispatch tow truck
12−20	Check for wanted or stolen
12−21	No record on file
12−22	Subject has prior misdemeanor record—not wanted
12−23	Subject has prior felony record—not wanted
12−24	Subject is wanted
	A—Felony
	B—Misdemeanor
12−25	Similar subject record—added information required
12−26	Base station going out of service
12−27	Call by radio when you arrive at station

Table T-2. Continued

Code	Meaning
12—28	Suspicious person
12—29	Disturbance
12—30	Reckless driver
12—31	Intoxicated driver
12—32	Intoxicated person
12—33	Emergency—all units remain silent
12—34	Resume normal radio traffic and operations
12—35	Abandoned motor vehicle
12—36	Illegal hunting in the area of *(place)*
12—37	Advise of road and weather conditions at *(place)*
12—38	Switch to channel *(frequency)*
12—39	Attention all units
12—40	Stand by
12—41	This traffic (information) is for you
12—42	No traffic (information) at this time
12—43	Disregard previous transmission
12—44	Accidental chemical spill/hazardous material
12—45	Burglar alarm sounding at *(place)*
12—46	What is the telephone number at your location?
12—47	Computer information is not available now
12—48	Computer information is available now
12—49	Death investigation (or possible homicide)
12—50	Message is confidential—do not use radio
12—51	Radio repairs required
12—52	Radio technician responding to your location
12—53	Power is out, we are operating on emergency power
12—54	Testing base transmitter
12—55	Transmitter test (unit)—Unit *(number)* count one/five
12—56	No help is immediately available—units dispatched
12—57	Disabled motorist
12—58	Narcotic activity
12—59	Advise my headquarters/residence
12—98	Officer needed at *(place)* —nonemergency
12—99	Officer needed at *(place)* —emergency
12—100	Nuclear attack

U-2R [US] Designation for the latest version of an aircraft designed for high-altitude photographic and electronic surveillance missions.

UAT [LE] Abbreviation for Unidad Anti-Terrorista, a joint antiterrorist unit of the government of Chile combining specialists from the Chilean Army and police.

UB [USSR] Abbreviation for *Urzad Bezpieczenstwa*, Office of Security of Polish Security Service.

U/C [A] Abbreviation for Undercarriage.

UC 1. Specialty code for Undercover. 2. [C3I] Abbreviation for Up Converter.

U.C. [LE] Abbreviation for undercover.

UDA [TRG] Abbreviation for Ulster Defense Association, a terrorist/radical group determined to keep Northern Ireland Protestant. This group is responsible for murders and bombings throughout Europe. The main base of operations for the UDA is in Northern Ireland.

UEI [HRU] Abbreviation for Unidad Especial de Intervencion, the Spanish Guardia Civil anti-terrorist and hostage rescue unit.

UEJ [C3I] Abbreviation for Unattended Expendable Jammer.

UFF [TRG] Abbreviation for Ulster Freedom Fighters, a subgroup of the Ulster Defense Association, (UDA) members of the UFF are known to be even more militant than the UDA and generally more active with a lower profile than other terrorist groups. The base of operations for the UFF is in Northern Ireland.

U-group [HRU] Designation for the public security force and counterterrorist unit of Bahrain.

UHF [C3I] Abbreviation for UltraHigh Frequency, which is 300 MHz-3 GHz.

U'ie, a [LE] A term used in law enforcement indicating a U-turn on a roadway.

ULCS [C3I] Abbreviation for Unit Level Circuit Switch.

UNAVEM [GOV] Abbreviation for United Nations Angola VErification Mission.

unborns [C,G&PS] Abbreviation for would-be gang members, ages 6-10.

UNBRO [GOV] Abbreviation for United Nations Border Relief Operation, a group active in Thailand and on the borders of Kampuchea.

uncle [I] Term used by Soviet-bloc countries to refer to an advisor—scientific, military, intelligence, or technical—from the Soviet Union.

UNDOF [GOV] Abbreviation for United Nations Disengagement Observer Force (Syrian Golan Heights).

UNDP [GOV] Abbreviation for United Nations Development Program.

UNFAO [GOV] Abbreviation for United Nations Food and Agricultural Organization.

UNFICYP [GOV] Abbreviation for United Nations Force In CYPrus.

UNGOMAP [GOV] Abbreviation for United Nations Good Offices Mission in Afghanistan and Pakistan.

UNHCR [GOV] Abbreviation for United Nations High Commission for Refugees.

UNICEF [GOV] Acronym for United Nations Children's Emergency Fund.

Unicom [A] A ground-to-air communications system that provides general flight service information.

UNIFIL [GOV] United Nations Interim Force located in Lebanon.

Uniform 1. [LE] In surveillance operations, referring to a vehicle that is driving straight ahead on a road. 2. [A,LE,MIL] Designation for the letter *U*.

UNIIMOG [GOV] United Nations (UN) Iran-Iraq Military Observers Group.

Table U-1. U.S. Secret Service Nationwide Frequency Network

Code Name	Type		Input	Output	Tone
Baker	Operations	1		165.7875	none
Charlie	Operations	2		165.3750	none
Mike	Tactical	3		165.2125	none
Tango	Tactical	4		164.6500	none
Romeo Charlie	Repeaters	5	165.9000	165.3750	none
Golf Charlie	Repeaters	6	166.4000	165.3750	none
Papa Charlie	Repeaters	7	164.4000	165.3750	none
Charlie	Repeaters	8	166.2000	165.3750	none
Romeo Bravo	Repeaters	9	165.9000	165.7875	none
Golf Bravo	Repeaters	10	166.4000	165.7875	none
Papa Bravo	Repeaters	11	164.4000	165.7875	none
Bravo	Repeaters	12	166.2000	165.7875	none

Union [A,LE,MIL] Designation for the letter *U*.

United States military installations *See* APPENDIX B.

United States Secret Service nationwide frequency network *See* TABLE U-1.

unkie [C,G&PS] Street slang for morphine.

UNTAG [GOV] Abbreviation for United Nations Transition Assistance Group (Namibia).

UNTSO [GOV] Abbreviation for United Nations Truce Supervision Organization (Palestine).

UOO [USSR] Abbreviation for *Upravleniye Osobykh Otdelov*, Armed Forces Counterintelligence-Directorate of Special Departments.

up [C,G&PS] Slang term meaning to be high on drugs or narcotics.

uppers 1. [C,G&PS] Slang for amphetamines. (*See* QUICK REFERENCE.) **2.** [C,G&PS] Slang for cocaine. (*See* QUICK REFERENCE.) **3.** [C,G&PS] Slang for psychedelic drugs.

UPS [C3I] Abbreviation for Uninterruptible Power System.

ups [C,G&PS] Slang for amphetamines. (*See* QUICK REFERENCE.)

ups and downs [C,G&PS] A slang term for amphetamines (stimulants) and barbiturates (depressant).

up tight [LE] Slang for an anxious, sometimes depressed feeling.

uptown [C,G&PS] Slang for cocaine. (*See* QUICK REFERENCE.)

U.S. government license plate identification table Undercover law enforcement vehicles used by government agencies generally use license plates issued by the state where they operate. To avoid detection, these plates usually are listed with the department of motor vehicles with a special code so as not to disclose the registered agency using the vehicle. Government agencies have a license plate prefix code that includes the following:

Prefix	Agency
A	Department of Agriculture
AF	United States Air Force
C	Department of Commerce
CE	U.S. Army Corps of Engineers
CPSC	Consumer Products Safety Commission
D	Department of Defense
DOT	Department of Transportation
EO	National Security Council & Executive Office of the President
EPA	Environmental Protection Agency
EPS	Executive Protection Service
FA	Federal Aviation Administration
FC	Federal Communications Commission
FR	Federal Reserve System
G	Interagency Motor Pool System General Services Administration (GSA)
GA	General Accounting Office
GP	Government Printing Office
GS	General Services Administration
H	Housing & Urban Development

Prefix	Agency
I	Department of the Interior
IC	Interstate Commerce Commission
J	Department of Justice
L	Department of Labor
N	United States Navy & Marines
NA	National Aeronautics and Space Administration (NASA)
NRC	Nuclear Regulatory Commission
NS	National Science Foundation
P	United States Postal Service
SI	Smithsonian Institution
T	Department of the Treasury
TV	Tennessee Valley Authority (TVA)
W	United States Army

U.S. military radio frequency band designations
See TABLE U-2.

US [US] Designation for the fifty United States.

USA 1. [M] Abbreviation for United States Army.
2. [GOV] Abbreviation for the United States of America.

USAF [M] Abbreviation for United States Air Force.

USAFE [M] Abbreviation for United States Air Forces in Europe.

Table U-2. U.S. Military Radio Frequency Band Designations

Band	Range	Old Designation
A	0–250 MHz	
B	250–500 MHz	
C	500 MHz–1 GHz	
D	1–2 GHz	
E	2–3 GHz	
F	3–4 GHz	
G	4–6 GHz	150–225 MHz
H	6–8 GHz	100–150 MHz
I	8–10 GHz	
J	10–20 GHz	
K	20–40 GHz	10.9–36 GHz
L	40–60 GHz	390 MHz–1.55 GHz
M	60–100 GHz	
P		225–390 MHz
Q		36–46 GHz
S		1.55–5.2 GHz
V		46–56 GHz
X		5.2–10.9 GHz

U.S. AID [GOV] Abbreviation for United States Agency for International Development.

USAREUR [M] Abbreviation for United States ARmy in EURope.

U-SB [NASA] Abbreviation for Unified S-Band.

user [C,G&PS] Slang for a drug or narcotic addict.

USIB [I] Abbreviation for United States Intelligence Board.

U.S. Marshal [LE] Abbreviation for United States Marshal Service. (*See* FEDERAL LAW ENFORCEMENT NATIONWIDE COMMUNICATIONS FREQUENCIES.)

USMC [M] Abbreviation for United States Marine Corps.

USN [M] Abbreviation for United States Navy.

USP [GOV] Abbreviation for The United States and all Possessions.

USTS [C3I] Abbreviation for UHF Satellite Terminal System.

UTC [C] Designation for Coordinated Universal Time (ex-GMT).

UTK [HRU] Abbreviation for Unit Timpaan Khas, the Royal Malaysian Police Special Strike Unit specializing in antiterrorist activities and hostage rescue.

UV [CW] Abbreviation for Ultraviolet.

UVF [TRG] Abbreviation for Ulster Volunteer Force, a militant Protestant group determined to keep Northern Ireland Protestant. The UVF has been responsible for bombings, murders, and specific acts of terrorism throughout Western Europe. This group is headquartered in Northern Ireland.

UW [M] Abbreviation for Unconventional Warfare.

Uzi [M] An Israeli-designed assault weapon that is a lightweight, compact submachine gun that has a folding and removable shoulder stock. The weapon is made in a variety of versions for various applications. When fired in the fully automatic mode, the Uzi has a firing rate of 600 rounds per minute. The standard (issued) magazine holds 32 rounds, although magazines with much larger capacities are available and more often used in combat situations.

uzooka   [LE] Term for the tar and residue resulting from once smoked (used) crack cocaine that has been scraped from a cocaine pipe, ground into a fine powder and is smoked a second time. The tars from used cocaine retain a high potency so uzooka is often mixed with cocaine.

V

V [C] Designation for frequency varies.

V8 cooker [C,G&PS] A steel V8 vegetable juice can that is used to heat cocaine. The can is drained and washed clean. A piece of rock cocaine then is dropped inside the can and the bottom of the can heated using a solid fuel, such as Sterno. Used in an automobile with the windows mostly closed, the effect on the occupants is overpowering. Law enforcement officers should note that the container is always steel, rather than an empty aluminum soft drink container (which would melt), and could be overlooked in a search and not considered important.

V-22 [US] Designation for the Air Force's Advanced Tactical Fighter being built by The Boeing Company in Seattle, Washington.

vaccine [M] A computer program used in government and law enforcement that watches for the typical things—a virus, worm, logic bomb, time bomb, or Trojan horse in a computer system. The vaccine halts them, and warns the computer operator. (*See* LOGIC BOMB, TIME BOMB, TROJAN HOUSE, VIRUS, WORM.)

Valium [LE] Brand name of diazepam, a controlled substance that is a minor tranquilizer. (*See* QUICK REFERENCE.)

valley [C,G&PS] That area of the human body inside the elbow. This is usually the first place where heroin addicts make a mainline injection.

Vallor [US] Code name for secure communications system.

Vampire [US] Naval aviation voice brevity code meaning injured personnel on board.

vatos locos [C,G&PS] A term used by Mexican drug dealers meaning "the guy is crazy," usually on dope.

V-band [NASA] Designation for 46,000 to 56,000 MCS.

VCP [M] Abbreviation for Vehicle Check Point.

Vd [A] Designation for Maximum Permitted Dive Speed.

verdin [US] Code name for secure communications system.

VFO [C] Abbreviation for Variable-Frequency Oscillator.

VFR [A] Abbreviation for Visual Flight Rules.

VGWO [M] Abbreviation for Velocity Gate Walk Off.

VH-60 [M] Designation for the Marine Corps helicopters manufactured by Sikorsky Aircraft and used by the U.S. President and Vice President. The VH-60 can fly at speeds of up to 345 miles per hour. The nine modified VH-60s used by the White House are equipped with tempest shielding to protect the electronic systems against the electromagnetic pulse from a nuclear blast.

VHF [C] Abbreviation for Very High Frequency, which is 30 MHz-300 MHz.

VHSD [C3I] Abbreviation for Very High Speed Data.

VHSIC [C3I] Abbreviation for Very High Speed Integrated Circuit.

vibes [C,G&PS] In the world of narcotics, feelings or an intuition about some person or a drug deal drug users "feel" is about to go bad.

victor 1. [C,G&PS] Slang for a stolen automobile.
2. [A,LE,MIL] Designation for the letter *V*.

VID Specialty code for videotape.

VIN [LE] Abbreviation for Vehicle Identification Number.

Vinson [US] Code name for tactical secure speech equipment.

VIP [GOV] Abbreviation for Very Important Person. Among the VIPs in the United States who receive special treatment are high-ranking military officers and government officials. When they travel, usually in specially equipped aircraft, they stay in touch with their offices and associates using the Mystic Star communications network. TABLE M-5 lists some of the Mystic Star frequencies most commonly used by the President of the United States and other VIPs. When a VIP is moving about within a specific state, the protection usually includes highway patrol or state police officers and frequencies they use. (*See* MYSTIC STAR FREQUENCIES; REPEATER.)

viper's weed   [C,G&PS] Slang for marijuana. (*See* QUICK REFERENCE.)

virgin   [C,G&PS] Slang for an individual who is using drugs or narcotics, but is not yet considered to be addicted.

virus   [M] Electronic sabotage in a computer system. Although virus and worm are sometimes used interchangeably, a *worm* generally refers to an invasion that does not damage a computer's data or operating system, while a virus can cause much wider havoc. Viruses operate in several stages, and usually are targeted at large computer installations such as those used in law enforcement and government. Here, step by step, is how a computer worm, virus, time bomb, logic bomb, or Trojan horse works:

- A brief message, only a few characters of computer code, arrive at a target machine by way of electronic mail and activate the debug system. This feature, known to relatively few users of the mail system, allows an operator at one computer to make changes in the core program of distant computers.

- The receiving machine, following instructions on the initial message, requests a second chunk of the virus or worm, a set of programming instructions. It arrives from the outside computer and goes directly into the operating system, or main set of instructions, of the computer.

- The newly arrived program, in a process called compiling and execution, turns itself on

and uses the mail system to reach the outside computer for one final batch of instructions that complete the transfer of the virus, logic bomb, or worm. The instructions are contained in up to 20 different files, or sets of memory, and are stored in the receiving computer's memory.

- The new files order new copies of the worm or virus to be made. They also scan the computer's data tables to find still more outside computers that can be reached through the electronic mail system. In addition, they are written in several different versions so that more than one kind of computer can be attacked by the intruder.

- More computers are contacted, and the process repeats itself.

- As the worm or virus spreads to many computers, infected machines eventually begin contacting each other. They become infected a second, third, and fourth time and on and on, if not recognized by the system vaccine (*see* VACCINE) and the process overloads the processing power of the infected computer's as they try to obey floods of commands. Eventually a portion of memory, called the system table, which keeps track of what the machine is doing, overflows and it shuts down one computer in the system after another. This can result in thousands of computer failures on a nationwide basis. There is no surefire defense against a computer virus or worm. Any network is vulnerable.

virus detection   [G] NASA's Goddard Space Flight Center developed the following six steps to follow if an MS-DOS computer user believes a virus has somehow entered the system:

- Back up all hard disk drives immediately.

- Check the size of all .COM and .EXE files. Infected files will be larger. All .COM files, except for COMMAND.COM, will grow by 1,168 or 1,280 bytes if infected. .EXE files that have been infected can be detected just as easily because they will have grown by approximately 1,514 bytes.

- Use MS-DOS DEBUG to scan .COM files. Infected .COM files increased by 1,168 bytes will contain the hexadecimal string EB00B40 ECD21B4. Those increased by 1,280 bytes will contain the hexadecimal string 00568 DB43005CD21.

- Put all suspicious files on an isolated computer system and reset the date on the internal clock to a date 30 to 60 days later. If a virus has somehow infected the system, it will be activated and a notice of some sort should appear on the computer screen, followed by a notice about data being destroyed.

- Use antivirus software tools.

- Before restoring files to a suspect computer diskette, do a low-level format.

virus foiling   [G] A computer virus in your system has no chance for survival with the following four steps in place:

- Use software from reputable sources. Many virus programs are spread by using software transmitted on electronic bulletin boards, or by swapping floppy disks with other users.
- Make frequent copies of data files—the most frequent virus targets. Experts usually can help virus victims restore data from a backup disk or tape.
- Check for infections with a virus-scanning program, which looks for unusual increases in program size and signs of known viruses. Some also eradicate viruses.
- Some viruses are programmed to start on a specific date, such as Halloween. To check for viruses that are time-triggered, place a copy of all software on an isolated computer. Advance

the system's clock until after a suspected trigger date to see if any virus is activated.

VLA   [M] Abbreviation for Vertical Launch ASROC. The VLA is an instrumentated rocket.

VLF   [C3I] Abbreviation for Very Low Frequency, 0 kHz-150 kHz.

VLS   [NASA] Abbreviation for Vertical Launch System.

VLSI   [C3I] Abbreviation for Very Large Scale Integration.

Voice of Liberty   [I] A clandestine radio station operating out of apartments in Panama City, Panama, and funded by the CIA. Intelligence indications are that broadcasts have been made from apartments in Panama City because the U.S. military's Southern Command, which maintains a dozen bases in Panama, refused to allow such transmissions from its facilities on the grounds that they would violate the Panama Canal Treaties and potentially jeopardize U.S. base rights in countries other than Panama. Another short-lived covert CIA transmitter operated in Panama City was an FM station called *Radio Constitucional*.

vonce   [C,G&PS] Slang for the remaining butt of a marijuana cigarette.

Vortex   [US] A surveillance satellite system used for eavesdropping on communications.

VOW   [C3I] Abbreviation for Voice Order Wire.

VPK   [USSR] Abbreviation for *Voyenno-promyshlennaya Komissiya*, Military Industrial Commission.

VPR   [TRG] Abbreviation for *Vanguarda Popular Revolucionaria*, a radical and terrorist group active throughout Brazil.

VR-55   [CW] Designation for a nerve agent developed by the Soviet Union.

VS   Specialty code for Voice Stress.

VSNKh   [USSR] Abbreviation for *Vysshego Soveta Narodnogo Khozyaystva*, the Supreme Council of National Economy.

V/STOL   [A] Abbreviation for Vertical or Short Take-Off and Landing.

VSWR   [C] Abbreviation for Voltage Standing Wave Ratio.

VTsIK [USSR] Abbreviation for *Vserossiyskiy Tsentral'nyy Ispolnitel'nyy Komitet*, (the All-Russian Central Executive Committee of the Congress of Soviets).

VX [CW] Designation for a nerve agent, soman. This chemical warfare agent developed by the United States has many of the same characteristics as the cholinestase inhibitor GB or VR-55 developed by the Soviet Union. A container of VX is triggered just before usage by the insertion of a sulfur bar that begins a chemical reaction to create a poisonous agent.

wacked [C,G&PS] Slang term referring to drugs or narcotics that have been cut into smaller portions.

wafer [C,G&PS] Slang for methadone. (*See* QUICK REFERENCE.)

wagon [LE] Slang for a surveillance truck or van.

wake up [C,G&PS] Slang for a morning injection of narcotics.

wake ups [C,G&PS] Slang for amphetamines. (*See* QUICK REFERENCE.)

walk-in [I] Slang for an individual who voluntarily offers his or her services or information to an intelligence agent or law enforcement agency. A walk-in offers whatever he has to give to an intelligence operation or foreign country without any invitation by the group/country contacted.

walking the dog [LE] Slang for a law enforcement officer who is following an individual on foot during a surveillance operation.

Walburn [US] Code name for secure communications equipment.

wannabes [C,G&PS] Slang for young people trying to gain initiation into a gang of their choice.

warthog [M] *See* A-10.

war wagon [LE] Slang for a surveillance truck or van that also is an armored vehicle.

washed up [C,G&PS] Slang for an individual withdrawing from drug usage.

wasted **1.** [C,G&PS] Slang term referring to an individual who is under the influence of narcotics. **2.** [C,G&PS] Slang term referring to someone with an extreme narcotic or drug habit who always appears in a state of euphoria.

watchers [LE] Experienced experts who keep a group, individual, or facility under surveillance.

watch list [I] A specific list of words, such as names, or phrases, that are used in a computer database to select required information from a mass of data, such as information concerning export of a classified product.

wavell [UK] Code name for mobile information distribution system.

WBL [C] Abbreviation for WideBand Limiting.

WCCS [C3I] Abbreviation for Wireless Crew Communications System.

W/D [USSR] Abbreviation for War of Diversion, the carefully planned sabotage of factories and industrial installations in Western countries. There have been instances of this level of sabotage which, at present, tend to be more of a test of security, or lack of it, than an act of destruction.

weathermen [TRG] A radical/terrorist group that operated in the United States in the early 1960s.

Weather Underground [TRG] A militant group most active during the Vietnam War. Members were suspected of a number of terrorist acts, but like the more skilled groups in Europe, they often did not take responsibility. The group is known to have a close association with black militant groups in the U.S., and with the FALN in Puerto Rico. It is suspected by U.S. federal agencies that follow terrorism that certain members still might be active in acts of industrial sabotage in the U.S.

WEB [USSR] Designation for West European Bureau of the Communist Intelligence Network (Cominternet).

wedges [C,G&PS] Slang for LSD. (*See* QUICK REFERENCE.)

weed [C,G&PS] Slang for marijuana. (*See* QUICK REFERENCE.)

weed head [C,G&PS] Slang for an individual who uses hashish or marijuana as a way of life.

weeds [C,G&PS] Slang for hashish or marijuana in loose (grass) form.

weekend habit [C,G&PS] Slang for an individual with an occasional drug or marijuana habit.

weekend warrior [C,G&PS] Slang for an occasional drug or narcotic user.

WEFAX [C3I] Abbreviation for WEather FACSimile.

Wehrsportgruppe [TRG] A terrorist/radical group that started in Germany. Ideology and aims are supported by a limited number of people in the U.S. Members remain on the most wanted list of the FBI. This organization is active in West Germany.

weight [C,G&PS] Slang for a very large quantity of drugs.

wet job [USSR] Slang for an intelligence operation where someone is killed or blood is shed.

wetwash [C] Code name for the undersea communications cable between Nha Trang in Vietnam and the Philippine Islands.

W.F.P. [GOV] Abbreviation for World Food Program.

What's happening? [C,G&PS] A question asked by users meaning "Do you have any narcotics?"

What's your twenty? [LE] A question meaning where are you, exactly? (*See* 10-20.)

WHCA [US] Abbreviation for White House Communications Agency, a department of the White House staffed with communications personnel from the various military agencies. It operates out of the basement facilities of the White House and maintains the primary link between the U.S. President and the military. When the President travels, staff of the WHCA travel with him to maintain that link. Most communications involving a United States President are secure, but personnel of the WHCA have a special communications system they use as they travel with the president or vice president. Those frequencies they use are listed in TABLE W-1.

wheel [C,G&PS] Slang for the driver of an escape vehicle used in the commission of a criminal act.

wheels [C,G&PS] Slang for any form of transportation.

Table W-1. White House Communications Agency Frequencies

Code	Use	Frequency
Alpha	WHCA technicians	32.230
November	WHCA frequency 1 Protection	166.7000
Sierra	WHCA frequency 2 Command	166.5125
Oscar	WHCA frequency 3 Protection	164.8875
Whiskey	WHCA frequency 4 Paging	167.0250
Yankee	SAM telephone, ground-air	162.6875
Zulu	SAM telephone, air-ground	171.2875

Whiskey [A,LE,MIL] Designation for the letter W.

white boy [C,G&PS] Slang for heroin. (*See* QUICK REFERENCE.)

white girl [C,G&PS] Slang for heroin, usually meaning a stronger or better quality.

white horse [C,G&PS] Slang for heroin. (*See* QUICK REFERENCE.)

White House protection frequency hopping cache *See* TABLE W-2.

white lady 1. [C,G&PS] A West Coast term for heroin. 2. [C,G&PS] An East coast term for cocaine.

white lightning [C,G&PS] Slang for LSD. (*See* QUICK REFERENCE.)

white stuff [C,G&PS] Slang for morphine or heroin.

whites [C,G&PS] Slang for any form of amphetamines.

WHT Specialty code for white collar crime.

William [A,LE,MIL] Designation for the letter W.

WiN [USSR] Abbreviation for *Wolnosc i Neipodleglosc*, Freedom and Independence, a remnant of Polish Home Army.

Table W-2. White House Protection Frequency Hopping Cache

408.625	408.725	408.825	408.925
408.650	408.750	408.850	408.950
408.675	408.775	408.875	408.975
408.700	408.800	408.900	409.000

windex [C,G&PS] Slang for the narcotic Numorphan.

window pane [C,G&PS] Slang for a small square of paper soaked with LSD.

wings [C,G&PS] Slang for the first injection of heroin.

wire [LE] Slang for a body transmitter used to keep track of a person. It is sometimes an open transmitter that picks up sound or sends out a tone for tracking, much like a bumper beeper.

WIS [C3I] Designation for WorldWide Military Command and Control (WWMCCS) Information Systems. (*See* WWMCCS.)

wise guy [LE] An individual linked with a crime family. The terms tends to refer to "one of the boys" or "he is one of us."

WKR Specialty code for Workers' Compensation.

W/ [C] Abbreviation for "with."

WORKS **1.** [C,G&PS] A hypodermic needle used by narcotic addicts. **2.** [C,G&PS] Hardware used for injecting drugs.

worm [GOV] A computer program designed to infect systems with commands that make them "sick." (*See* VIRUS.)

wormer [I] Slang for an individual who creates a computer virus or worm and infects a system with unwanted commands that cause damage. (*See* TROJAN HORSE, VIRUS, and WORM.)

WS Specialty code for Watchman Service.

WWMCCS [C3I] WorldWide Military Command and Control System.

WWSVA [US] WorldWide Secure Voice Architecture.

WXR [GOV] Weather.

X **1.** [LE] Designation meaning to control the gambling, illegally, in a given city or state. **2.** [US] The regular prefix to designate experimental aircraft. **3.** [LE] Designation for female. **4.** [US] Designation for submersible craft, self-propelled, a device used by SEAL Team 6. (*See* SEAL TEAM 6.)

X-axis **1.** [NASA] The horizontal axis in a system of rectangular coordinates. **2.** That line on which distances to the right or left (east or west) of the reference line are marked, especially on a map, chart, or graph.

XCVR [NASA] Designation for transceiver.

XFD [NASA] Designation for crossfeed.

XFER [NASA] Designation for transfer.

X/L [NASA] Designation for X-axis of spacelab.

XLTN [NASA] Designation for translation.

XMT [NASA] Designation for transmit.

XMTR [C3I] Designation for transmitter.

XO [NASA] Designation for orbiter structural reference, X-axis.

X/O [NASA] Abbreviation for X-axis of orbiter.

XP [NASA] Designation for payload structural body reference, X-axis.

X/P [NASA] Abbreviation for X-axis of Payload.

XPNDR [NASA] Designation for transponder.

X-ray [A,LE,MIL] Designation for the letter *X*.

XRP [NASA] Abbreviation for X-Ray Polychromator.

X/S [NASA] Designation for X-axis of solid rocket booster.

X-scale [I] Designation for the scale along a line parallel to the true horizon on an oblique photograph.

X/T [NASA] Designation for X-axis of external tank.

XTAL [NASA] Designation for crystal.

Y

Y 1. [US] Designation for prototype. 2. [NASA] Designation for out-of-plane velocity.

YAG [US] Designation for miscellaneous self-propelled auxiliary ship.

yakuza [LE] Japan's criminal underworld, which extorts protection money from Japanese businessmen entering into American commerce under the threat of injury to them or their family. The trend in Japanese business is to not trust law enforcement officials for fear that certain business practices might be exposed. The result is that even in the United States, of the *yakuza* usually gets away with extortion of Japanese businessmen. In Japan, members of the *yakuza* are referred to as *boryokudan*, literally "violence groups." More than 2,500 rival *yakuza* gangs exist in Japan. The seat of *yakuza* power has traditionally been in Osaka, Japan's second city, but as drug and narcotic sales expand into the culture of Japanese life these organizations are becoming established in other major cities of Japan. Japan's National Police Agency estimated 120,000 *yakuza* members were active throughout Japan in early 1990.

Yamaguchi-Gumi [LE] The largest and most powerful crime syndicate in Japan. Members belong to the *yakuza*, Japan's criminal underworld; and all deal in every illegal activity ranging from drugs and narcotics to prostitution and extortion. The 20,000-plus members of the *Yamaguchi-Gumi* have held sway for centuries in Japan and have kept other *yakuza* families in check. This syndicate is very active in Europe and the United States and is deeply involved in extortion activities directed toward Japanese businessmen in those countries.

Yankee [A,LE,MIL] Designation for the letter *Y*.

yardstick [US] Naval aviation voice brevity code meaning the distance to the target; i.e., "The yardstick is ten miles."

yaw 1. [M] The rotation of an aircraft, ship, or missile about its vertical axis so as to cause the longitudinal axis of the aircraft, ship, or missile to deviate from the flight line or heading in its horizontal plane. 2. The rotation of a camera or a photograph coordinate system about either the photograph Z-axis or the exterior Z-axis. 3. The angle between the longitudinal axis of a projectile at any moment and the tangent to the trajectory in the corresponding point of flight of the projectile.

Y-axis 1. [NASA] The vertical axis in a system of rectangular coordinates. 2. That line on which distances above or below (north or south) the reference line are marked, especially on a map, chart, or graph.

YCV [US] Designation for aircraft transportation lighter.

YD [US] Designation for floating derrick.

YDT [US] Designation for diving tender.

yellow jackets [C,G&PS] Slang for the barbiturate Nembutal.

yellow rain [CW] Slang for a nerve agent, a compound that can cause severe bleeding when it comes into contact with human skin, and rapid death. Yellow rain compounds have been developed by the Soviet Union and the United States and remain on highly classified lists.

yellows [C,G&PS] Slang for phenobarbital sodium.

yen [C,G&PS] Slang for the craving for a narcotic injection.

yen hock [C,G&PS] Slang for the hardware used by opium smokers.

yen shee [C,G&PS] Slang for the ash (residue) from opium smoking.

yen shee suey [C,G&PS] Slang for wine that contains opium.

yen sleep [C,G&PS] The condition following opium usage—usually restlessness as the effect of opium wears off.

YF [US] Designation for covered lighter, self-propelled ship.

YFB [US] Designation for ferryboat/launch, self-propelled ship.

YFD [US] Designation for yard floating (dry) dock.

YFND [US] Designation for dry-dock companion craft.

YF-22A [I] Designation for Advanced Tactical (Stealth) Fighter (ATF), currently under development by the Lockheed Aeronautical Systems, General Dynamics Corp. and Boeing Advanced Systems Company. Flight testing of the YF-22A (code named red winner) is designed to fly on the very edge of space, will be able to go into orbit for very short periods (48 to 72 hours) and stay on station over a location for purposes of surveillance. Ground testing is scheduled to begin, at the Palmdale facility of Lockheed Advanced Systems (Skunk Works) located in the California desert north of Los Angeles, in the mid-1990s. Seven hundred and fifty ATFs are scheduled for manufacture. (*See also* STEALTH AIRCRAFT.)

YHLC [US] Designation for Salvage Heavy Lift Craft.

yield *See* NUCLEAR YIELDS.

YL [LE] Designation for female.

Y/L [NASA] Designation for Y-axis of spacelab.

YM 1. [US] Designation for dredge, self-propelled. 2. [NATO] Designation for prototype missile.

YMLC [US] Designation for Salvage Medium Lift Craft.

YMP [NATO] Designation for Motor Mine Planter.

Y/O [NASA] Designation for Y-axis of orbiter.

YOGN [US] Designation for gasoline barge.

yoke 1. [LE] To mug a victim. 2. [C,G&PS] Slang term meaning to have a job. 3. [C,G&PS] Slang for an illegal method of raising money for drugs.

YON [US] Designation for fuel oil barge.

YOS [US] Designation for oil storage barge.

Young [A,LE,MIL] Designation for the letter *Y*.

YP [US] Designation for Patrol Craft.

Y/P [NASA] Designation for Y-axis of payload.

YPD [US] Designation for Floating Pile Driver.

YR [US] Designation for floating workshop.

YRB [US] Designation for repair and berthing barge.

YRST [US] Designation for salvage craft tender.

Y-scale [I] On an oblique photograph, the scale along the line of the principal vertical, or any other line inherent or plotted which, on the ground, is parallel to the principal vertical.

Y/S [NASA] Designation for Y-axis of solid rocket booster.

Y-T [NASA] Designation for Yaw Trim.

Y/T [NASA] Designation for Y-axis of external tank.

YT [NASA] Designation for station identification symbol.

YTB 1. [US] Designation for harbor tug, big. 2. [NATO] Designation for sea-going tugboat.

YTL [US] Designation for harbor tug, little.

YTM [US] Designation for harbor tug, medium.

YTT [US] Designation for torpedo testing barge.

yubitsume [LE] A ritual act with the Japanese yakuza (Japan's criminal element) that involves the cutting off of part of the little finger. The act is a gesture of atonement for mistakes made. The error might result in the loss of both little fingers.

yuen [C,G&PS] Slang for an individual who craves narcotics.

YVV-1 [NASA] Designation for program (range) safety officer.

YVVS [NASA] Designation for DOD mission support.

Z

Z [GOV] Designation for Zulu (Greenwich Mean Time—GMT).

Z-1 [US] Designation for Zone 1 (nuclear), a circular area determined by using minimum safe distance (1) as the radius and the desired ground zero as the center, from which all armed forces are evacuated. If evacuation is not possible or if a commander elects a higher degree of risk, maximum protective measures will be required.

Z-2 [US] Designation for Zone 2 (nuclear), a circular area (less than Zone 1) determined by using minimum safe distance 2 as the radius and the desired ground zero as the center, in which all personnel require maximum protection. Maximum protection denotes that armed forces personnel are in "buttoned up" tanks or crouched in foxholes with improvised overhead shielding.

Z-3 [US] Designation for Zone 3 (nuclear), a circular area (less than Zones 1 and 2) determined by using minimum safe distance 3 as the radius and desired ground zero as the center, in which all personnel require minimum protection. Minimum protection denotes that armed forces personnel are prone on open ground with all skin covered with an overall thermal protection at least equal to that provided by a two-layer uniform.

Zacatecas purple [C,G&PS] Name for a type of marijuana grown in Zacatecas, a mountainous state in central Mexico. (*See* PURPLE.)

ZANLA [I] Abbreviation for Zimbabwe African National Liberation Army.

ZANU [I] Abbreviation for Zimbabwe African National Union.

Zapatista [TRG] Name of a terrorist/radical/bandit gang based in the desert areas of Mexico that robs and kills tourists to support itself. Members have a deep-rooted view of the politics they follow based on their leader, Frente Urbana Zapatista.

ZAPU [I] Abbreviation for Zimbabwe African People's Union.

ZCG [NASA] Designation for impedance cardiogram.

Zebra [A,LE,MIL] Designation for the letter Z.

zen [C,G&PS] Slang for LSD. (*See* QUICK REFERENCE.)

ZFW [A] Abbreviation for Zero Fuel Weight, maximum aircraft weight without fuel on board.

ZGT [NASA] Abbreviation for Zero Gravity Trainer.

ZI [NASA] Abbreviation for the Zone of Interior, continental USA.

ZIM [GOV] Abbreviation for Zimbabwe.

zinger [LE] Slang for a summons issued by the court.

zip gun [LE] Slang for a homemade, hand-crafted gun, usually of a small caliber, and single shot variety.

zippers [M] Slang for target dawn and dusk combat air patrols.

ZIPRA [I] Abbreviation for ZImbabwe People's Revolutionary Army.

Z/L [NASA] Designation for Z-axis of spacelab.

ZLV [NASA] Abbreviation for Z Local Vertical, Payload Bay toward the Earth.

Z/O [NASA] Designation for Z-axis of orbiter.

zona roja [LE] The redlight (prostitution) area of a town or city in Mexico.

zone of fire [US] An area within which a designated ground unit or fire support ship delivers, or is prepared to deliver, fire support.

zonked [C,G&PS] Slang for a state of unconsciousness caused by narcotic or drug usage.

Z/P [NASA] Designation for Z-axis of Payload.

ZP [NATO] Designation for lighter-than-air aircraft.

Z/S [NASA] Designation for Z-axis of solid rocket booster.

ZSI [NASA] Abbreviation for Z Solar Inertial, payload bay facing away from the sun.

Z/T [NASA] Designation for Z-axis of external tank.

Zulu [A,LE,MIL] Designation for the letter Z.

Zulu time [GOV] Designation for Greenwich Meridian (Mean) Time.

zunked [C,G&PS] Slang term referring to an individual who is addicted to the use of hard drugs.

Appendix A

Law Enforcement Agencies and Related Organizations

Worldwide Law Enforcement Agency Network

(With special appreciation to INTERPOL)

Afghanistan (Democratic Republic of Afghanistan/*De Afghanistan Democrateek Jamhuriat*) Local appointed officials supported and armed by the military.

Albania (Peoples Socialist Republic of Albania/*Republika Popullore Socialiste e Shqiperise*) Local military personnel (trained by the USSR) are the law enforcement authority in Albania.

Algeria (Democratic and Popular Republic of Algeria. *al-Jumhuriya al-Jazairiya ad-Dimuqratiya ash-Shabiya*) Local police personnel appointed by the military and given military assistance.

American Samoa The majority of the Samoan people are United States nationals. Until 1951, the U.S. Navy was the sole law enforcement force on the seven islands of American Samoa. Today, the Police Department, Fire Department, and Department of Corrections (prison system) are all under the Department of Public Safety headquartered in Pago Pago.

Andorra (Principality of Andorra/*Principat d' Andorra*) Andorra is located in the Pyrenees Mountains. There is a single police force for the entire country—the Andorran Police. Uniquely, Catalan is the official language of Andorra, but Spanish and French also are spoken, so the majority of police officers are multilingual.

Angola (People's Republic of Angola/*Republica Popular de Angola*) Angola is located in southwest Africa on the Atlantic coast. The police force of the country is made up of locally appointed government officials backed by the military. Law enforcement officials have organized their force nationwide into units that work closely together across the more isolated parts of the country.

Anguilla Anguilla joined with the islands of Nevis and St. Kitt in 1967 to form a state. The police force is administered by a commissioner who is appointed by the Queen of England. The state is policed by the Anguilla Police Force.

Antigua The British associated state of Antigua has a police force divided into four specific territorial divisions. The Special Branches are concerned with crime, traffic control, the court system, and state security. The Royal Police Force of Antigua is responsible for the protection and law enforcement of a population slightly in excess of 70,000. Firearms are not issued to the police force.

Argentina (Argentine Republic/*Republica Argentina*) The Minister of the Interior heads the principal law enforcement agency in Argentina, the *Policia Federal*. This agency is responsible for investigations that relate to violations of the federal law of Argentina. Each province of the country has a small police force made up of the *Gendarmeria Nacional*, Maritime Police, and the *Policia Federal Argentina*.

Australia   The first law enforcement agency head-quartered in Australia was formed in 1789 when 12 convicts were given the authority to deal with crimes in New South Wales. Law enforcement agencies in Australia now include: The New South Wales Po-lice, the South Australia Police Department, The Victoria Police, Tasmania Police, Western Australia Police, The Queensland Police Force, Northern Ter-ritory Police, The Commonwealth Police Force, and the Australian Capital Territory Police. All agencies appear to be based along the lines of the British police organizations.

Austria   (Republic of Austria/*Republik Osterreich*) The Federal Security Guard is an armed and uni-formed paramilitary organization. It is responsible for police services in the major cities of Austria. The majority of officers are uniformed. The Federal Se-curity Guard has two main branches—the *Staatspo-lizei* (State Police) and *Verwaltungspolizei* (Adminis-trative Police). The *Austrian Gendarmerie* is an armed organization responsible for local enforce-ment of the laws. The Criminal Police of Austria is a plain clothes organization and operates at a level much like the FBI in the United States.

Bahamas   (The Commonwealth of the Bahamas) The single police agency for the more than 30 is-lands of the Bahamas is the Royal Bahamas Police Force. (*See* BAHAMIAN ISLAND.)

Bahrain   (State of Bahrain/*Dawlat al-Bahrayn*) Bahrain is located off the coast of Saudi Arabia, and is a major oil-producing state. The Bahrain Police and Public Security Department are responsible for all police/fire services, including immigration, the prison system, and airport security. The Bahrain Police also has at its disposal the special skills of The Emergency Squad (a SWAT-like organization) that deals with disasters, major criminal investiga-tions, and civil disorders.

Bangladesh   (People's Republic of Bangladesh)

Local civil authorities appointed by the government and backed by the military.

Barbados   The Island of Barbados is located in the Atlantic Ocean near Grenada and Trinidad. The Royal Barbados Police Force has three territorial divisions to maintain law and order, a headquarters division, a criminal investigation division and a band. Members of the Royal Barbados Police Force usually are unarmed on duty except for special occa-sions.

Belgium   (Kingdom of Belgium/*Koninkrijk Belgie* (*Dutch*), *Royaume de Belgique* (*French*)) The *Na-tional Gendarmerie* is one of the armed forces of Belgium. It is not a part of the army, but has juris-diction over the entire kingdom. In each of the 345 major towns in Belgium a Municipal Police force is in place. The 245 smaller country towns have one or more constables appointed by the governor of the province. The Criminal Police, made up of 22 bri-gades, deals exclusively with violations of the crimi-nal law. The Belgian Criminal Police also is the National Central Bureau of Interpol. (*See* INTER-POL.)

Belize   Belize, formerly called British Honduras, is located on the eastern coast of central America. With an estimated population of more than 179,000, the Belize Police Force is uniformed, with the ex-ception of plain clothes investigators and members of the Security Branches.

Benin   (People's Republic of Benin/*Republique Populaire du Benin*) The government of Benin is Marxist-Leninist. Law enforcement activities are conducted by the People's Republic Police and the military forces of this country with a population in excess of 4,500,000.

Bermuda   The Bermudas consist of 360 small islands, 20 of which are inhabited. The Bermuda Police are not armed and carry an ordinary police nightstick. Patrols are made by boat, helicopter, and aircraft. The United States has air and naval bases and a NASA tracking station in the island chain and maintains a small military force to protect these installations.

Bolivia   (Republic of Bolivia/*Republica de Bolivia*) Four principal organizations make up the national police. The *Guardia Nacional* is the uniformed body concerned with public order. The plain clothes detective force is known as the National Investigation Department (DIN). The Public Order Department (DOP) deals with defensive intelligence, antiterrorism, political crimes, and state security. The military also has an active role in law enforcement and the security of the state.

Botswana   (Republic of Botswana) Botswana is located in southern Africa. The Botswana Police is a civilian authority based upon the British military. The Police Mobile Unit (PMU) is responsible for the national defense and internal security of the Republic. Law enforcement training of recruits takes place within the PMU before constables are assigned to general police duties.

Brazil   (Federative Republic of Brazil/*Republica Federativa do Brasil*) This country is made up of 21 individual states. Each state has one federal district and four territories. The format is generally the same throughout the Republic with the Uniformed Police (Police Militar) and the Civil Police (Policia Civil) being the frontline against crime. The Traffic Department (*Departmento de Transito*) is responsible for traffic control and the courts. The Federal Police Force is responsible for the protection of the capital, Brasilia, and the air and sea ports.

Brunei Darussalam   (State of Brunei Darussalam/ *Negara Brunei Darussalam*) The Royal Brunei Police is a paramilitary organization divided into three departments. Operations conducts all training and maintains the reserve units. The main force protects the air and sea ports and all public places. The administration department is responsible for communications, transportation, and civilian personnel. The third department conducts criminal investigations and maintains the records division.

Bulgaria   (People's Republic of Bulgaria/*Narodna Republika Bulgaria*) Law enforcement activities are conducted by the Internal Security Police, much like the KGB of the Soviet Union. A public Militia is in place handling general law enforcement responsibilities.

Burma   (Socialist Republic of the Union of Burma/ *Pyidaungsu Socialist Thammada Myanma Nain-gngandaw*) A paramilitary law enforcement group formed by the government maintains law and order throughout Burma. Officials that head the paramilitary forces are appointed by the government. Those officials create a following to enforce the laws.

Burundi   (Republic of Burundi/*Republika y'Uburundi*) A branch of the military enforces the law. Government officials handle the administration of power by supporting various factions.

Cambodia   (Cambodian People's Republic/*Kampuchea*) Military rule is the foundation for law enforcement in Cambodia. Police powers are given by appointment to members of collectives (specific areas) and those officials administrate a mix of military and civil authority.

Cameroon   (Republic of Cameroon) Law enforcement in the Cameroon Republic is along the lines of the French Police Nationale. Known as the *Surete Federale*, law enforcement responsibilities are divided into district (commissariats) that handle general police assignments and the regional *Police Judiciaire*, the criminal police.

Canada   The Royal Canadian Mounted Police is responsible for the administration of the Canadian criminal justice codes. The RCMP is divided into 12 divisions with headquarters in each of the provincial capitals of Canada. Each province of Canada has a civil police force that handles general law enforcement responsibilities and constabularies maintain a municipal police force.

Cayman Islands   The Cayman Islands has a population of less than 12,000 people. The Cayman Islands, located in the West Indies, are a British dependency. The entire police force consists of less than 150 constables, enlisted officers, and policewomen.

Central African Republic *(Republique Centrafricaine)* A military force supported by the central African government maintains law and order in this republic of almost 4 million.

Channel Islands The Channel Islands support two law enforcement groups—the State of Jersey Police Force and the Island Police.

Chile (Republic of Chile/*Republica de Chile*) The *Los Carabineros de Chile* is responsible for law enforcement throughout the entire country of Chile. The country is divided into six zones. In each of those zones specialized branches exist that are responsible for general enforcement, investigations, and security.

China (People's Republic of China/*Zhonghua Renmin Gonghe Guo*) The People's Police is the major law enforcement agency in China. It operates on three specific levels: The police station (*Pai chu so*) is responsible for an area approximately a mile square and is manned by 15 to 20 officers. The divisional headquarters (*Fen chu*) is the base of operations for a 10- to 15-square-mile area while the main headquarters (*Kung an chu*) directs police activities in an entire province, usually 20 to 50 square miles. A local Militia exists in certain areas of China but their power, responsibility, and ability to enforce regulations tends to vary depending on the need seen by the People's Police in a given area.

Colombia (Republic of Colombia/*Republica de Colombia*) Many cities and municipalities within Columbia have local police agencies that operate under a variety of names. On a broader basis, the Colombian National Police are responsible for patrolling highways and the protection of government facilities. At the government level, police operations are conducted by the Department of the Minister of Defense.

Comoro Islands (Federal Islamic Republic of the Comoros/*Jumhuriyat al-Qumur al-Itthadiyah al-Islamiyah*) Law enforcement activities are conducted on this archipelago in the Indian Ocean by a single detachment of the *French Gendarmerie Nationale.*

Congo (People's Republic of the Congo/*Republique Populaire du Congo*) Local Militia trained and supported by the People's Republic government are commanded by ranking military officers.

Costa Rica (Republic of Costa Rica/*Republica de Costa Rica*) Military police rule with local Militia groups.

Cuba (Republic of Cuba/*Republica de Cuba*) The police of Cuba are patterned along the lines of the Ministries for the Preservation of Public Order of the Soviet Union (MOOP). The police, by sheer forces of numbers, have maintained a law and order environment throughout Cuba. Senior officers and intelligence specialists are known to have received training at the hands of the Soviet KGB.

Cyprus (Republic of Cyprus/*Kibris Cumhuriyeti* (*Turkish*); *Kypriaki Dimokratia* (*Greek*) The Cyprus Police Force maintain law and order.

Czechoslovakia (Czechoslovak Socialist Republic/*Ceskoslovenska Socialisticka Republika*) The word *police* is not used in describing law enforcement functions in Czechoslovakia. Activities to maintain law and order are conducted by The National Security Corps (SNB). An Auxiliary Public Security Guard (PSVD) consists of volunteer citizens.

Denmark (Kingdom of Denmark/*Kongeriget Danmark*) The Danish Police operate under state controls set forth by a central police administration and headed by a law enforcement commissioner (*Rigspolitichefen*) appointed by the King of Denmark.

Djibouti (Republic of Djibouti/*Jumhouriyya Djibouti*) Military police, supported by local Militia, maintain law and order.

Dominican Republic (*Republica Dominicana*) The National Police Force is responsible for law enforcement. Special divisions include the Highway and Traffic Police, Criminal Police, Internal Security Service, and Bureau of Prisons. The National Police Force is very powerful and operates along the lines of a military force.

Dubai The Dubai Police are responsible for all law enforcement activities in the second largest state in the United Arab Emirates.

East Germany (German Democratic Republic/ *Deutsche Demokratische Republik*) The People's Police (*Die Volkspolizei*) has overall law enforcement authority in East Germany. Police personnel who are assigned at the local level are *Abschnittsbevollmachtigten* or sector agents (ABV). These sector agents live and patrol in the same area and are expected to be fully aware of all that goes on and maintain law and order.

Ecuador Military police rule with local government-appointed Militia groups.

Egypt (Arab Republic of Egypt/*Jumhuriyah Misr al-Arabiya*) Under the control of the Minister of the Interior, law enforcement responsibilities are assigned by the government. There are five divisions that maintain law and order: General Directorate of Investigations; General Directorate of Organization and Administration; Department of Public Affairs; General Directorate of State Security, and General Directorate of Officers' Affairs.

Eire The *Garda Siochana*, Guardians of the Peace, is a national force in southern Ireland (Eire) to maintain law and order anywhere in the country.

El Salvador (Republic of El Salvador/*Republica de El Salvador*) The El Salvador National Police is paramilitary in makeup and is comprised of the *Policia de Linea* (town police), *Policia de Caminos* (highway patrol), *Departamento de Investigacions* (criminal investigations), *Cuerpo de Vigilantes Nocturnos y Bancarios* (night patrols and special surveillance), and *Policia de Transito* (traffic police).

Ethiopia (People's Democratic Republic of Ethiopia/*Ye Etiyop'iya Hezbawi Dimokrasiyawi Republek*) Headquartered in Addis Ababa, the Regular Police (RP) maintain law and order in the 14 provincial capitals of Ethiopia. A paramilitary Emergency Strike Force Police unit patrols the borders and concerns itself with a public uprising.

Falkland Islands The Falklands, or *Islas Malvinas*, include about 200 islands, an estimated area of approximately 4,700 miles. While a number of small villages exist, there is only one town, Stanley, on all the islands located on East Falkland Island. The police force is made up of five constables, one sergeant, and a superintendent of police and operates along the lines of the British law enforcement agencies.

Fiji (Dominion of Fiji) A British colony since 1874, Fiji became an independent parliamentary democracy on October 10, 1970. The Royal Fiji Police were formed when Fiji became a colony. The RFP operates along the lines of the British police. A Mobile Police Force consisting of approximately 150 constables and officers is in place to support local operations in any part of Fiji.

Finland (Republic of Finland/*Suomen Tasavalta*) The Finnish National Police is a division of the national government. It operates under the Minister of the Interior. The Minister appoints a chief of police for all of Finland. Under his immediate control are the Central Criminal Police, the Security Police, and the Mobile Police. The General Police maintain law and order under the local city governments. The police chief of a General Police unit is directly responsible to the area inspector for the Finnish National Police.

France (French Republic/*Republique Francaise*) France has two major law enforcement agencies: the *Gendarmerie Nationale*, responsible for maintaining law and order in the rural areas and smaller towns, and the *Police Nationale*, which operates throughout the entire country. A plain clothes division of the National Police is known as the *Police Judiciaire—*

the criminal police—and are involved with the serious crimes in France ranging from fraud to terrorism.

French Guiana Located on the northeast coast of South America, French Guiana is famous for the penal colony known as Devil's Island. The government of French Guiana is administered by France and law enforcement is maintained as if French Guiana were a metropolitan part of France by a detachment of the *French Gendarmerie Nationale*.

French Polynesia The *French Gendarmerie Nationale* oversee law enforcement responsibilities over the 130 islands of French Polynesia. The French Gendarmerie Nationale are headquartered in Papeete, Tahiti and administers the laws of France over the 1,544-square-mile area that has a population of approximately 185,000.

Gabon (Gabonese Republic/*Republique Gabonaise*) Gabon is a French protectorate. Law enforcement is maintained by the *Gendarmerie Nationale*.

Gambia (Republic of The Gambia) The country of Gambia is divided into four specific divisions for the purpose of law enforcement by the Gambia Police Force. The capital town of Banjul is one of those divisions. With approximately 190 people for every square mile of the country, the other three divisions are mostly mobile in their patrols, using aircraft, boat, and land vehicles rather than manning individual police stations. A military Field Force is responsible for internal security of the republic.

Ghana (Republic of Ghana) The Ghana Police is a national force headquartered in the capital city of Accra with nine regions of the republic administrated from local police stations.

Gibraltar Gibraltar is a British dependency located on the southern coast of Spain. Gibraltar is 2.75 miles long and three-quarters of a mile wide. In 1966 the Spanish government called upon Britain to relinquish a "substantial sovereignty" of Gibraltar to Spain. In 1967 the residents voted to remain under British rule. All law enforcement is conducted by

the Gibraltar Police and operates along the lines of the United Kingdom.

Gilbert Islands The Gilbert Islands are policed by the Gilbert Islands Police. The force also is responsible for both domestic and airport fire fighting services.

Greece (Hellenic Republic/*Elliniki Dimokratia*) Greece maintains two police forces—the *Greek Gendarmeria* and the City Police. The City Police are responsible for law enforcement in the major cities of Greece while the *Gendarmeria* services the rest of the country. Together these enforcement agencies support the Criminal Investigative Services and the National Security Service. The *Gendarmeria* is responsible for the Emergency Squad, a unit much like special weapons and tactics (SWAT) units operating elsewhere in the world, the Security and Traffic Police, and the Market and Tourist Police.

Grenada (State of Grenada) The entire police force of Grenada is made up of West Indians and is patterned after the French colonial methods of law enforcement. The force is approximately 300 men strong for the population of 87,000 and is responsible for an area of about 133 square miles—or twice the size of Washington, D.C.

Guatemala (Republic of Guatemala/*Republica de Guatemala*) The Guatemala National Police was formed in 1881. A former member of the New York City Police was appointed as its deputy director. In 1955 the organization became the National Police. Operating on the lines of a paramilitary unit, the National Police functions with an initial year-long training program for all officers. This training includes jungle warfare, map reading, and antiterrorism instruction. The 6,500-man force is responsible for an exploding population of 9,412,000.

Guinea (Republic of Guinea/*Republique de Guinee*) Guinea is located on the coast of western Africa. Law enforcement is conducted by agencies of the government on a paramilitary basis. Within the capital city of Conakry, population approximately 656,000, local law enforcement officers appointed by the government maintain a police presence supported by military troops and plain clothed officers.

Guinea-Bissau (Republic of Guinea-Bissau/*Republica da Guine-Bissau*) Portuguese mainers explored the area known as Guinea-Bissau in the mid-15th century. Guinea-Bissau covers almost 15,000 square miles, is located on the Atlantic coast of western Africa, and is mostly a swampy coastal plain. Beginning in the 1960s an independent movement by the population of (now) more than 930,000 waged a guerrilla war and formed their own government. Full independence came on September 10, 1974, after the Portuguese regime was overthrown. Law enforcement is carried on in a paramilitary manner by troops loyal to the government.

Guyana (Co-operative Republic of Guyana) The Guyana Police is responsible for maintaining law and order in this area located on the north coast of South America. The country is about the size of Idaho and is divided into seven individual police divisions, each commanded by a group of senior officers. The Commissioner of Police maintains his headquarters at Georgetown, Guyana and under his command is a force of 3,200 men and women officers.

Haiti (Republic of Haiti/*Republique d'Haiti*) Paramilitary law enforcement maintains law and order.

Honduras (Republic of Honduras/*Republica de Honduras*) Paramilitary law enforcement with local officials and ranking officers appointed by the government. Troops come from the ranks of the military or are conscripted civilians familiar with certain areas of the country.

Hong Kong Based on the operating principals of the London Metro Police, the Royal Hong Kong Police Force has four major divisions of responsibility: Hong Kong Island, New Territories, (mainland) Kowloon, and in the Marine Patrol Districts. There are three divisions of police in the Marine district, six headquartered in Kowloon, four on Hong Kong Island, and five in the Territories. Each of the districts has a headquarters facility and supports a criminal investigation department.

Hungary (Hungarian People's Republic/*Magyar Nepkoztarasag*) The Hungarian Police is operated by the state and is paramilitary in formation. Local authorities are appointed by the Minister of Internal Affairs, and the ranking of police officers is a military one. Hungary remains under a communist government and a part of the Soviet bloc.

Iceland (Republic of Iceland/*Lyoveldio Island*) All police officers in Iceland are employed by the state. District chiefs of police report directly to the Minister of Justice. Because Iceland has no military, the police have been organized along the lines of a civilian force. The Icelandic Police maintain a Criminal Investigation Department in the city of Reykjavik as well as a Traffic Branch, Narcotics Surveillance Section, Mobile Police Corps, and Police Training College. The Icelandic National Central Bureau of Interpol is a part of the division headed by the Minister of Justice.

India (Republic of India/*Bharat*) The police of the country are organized on a state basis. The Police of India is the major protector of law and order although the Constitution of India mandates that certain special police functions are central to the government including the Border Security Force, Railway Protection Force, and Central Industrial Security Force. Local police have nothing to do with these responsibilities.

Indonesia (Republic of Indonesia/*Republik Indonesia*) Located southeast of Asia near the Equator, Indonesia is one of the most densely populated areas of the world. There are approximately 1,500 people located within the confines of every square mile of the country. The Indonesian National Police, with a total strength of more than 110,000 men and women, operate under the direction of the Minister of Defense.

Iran (Islamic Republic of Iran/*Jomhori-e-Islami-e-Iran*) Police powers are given to appointees by the government. Individuals are selected to serve under the appointed leader to enforce the law. Because all of Iran is an armed camp, killings are frequent and the right and wrong of any act is left open to interpretation by a variety of factions. Iran has had strong laws against drug traffic since the eighteenth century. Today, much of the genuine police work is directed toward drugs and smugglers. The penalty for drug possession, without exception to sex or age, is death.

Iraq (Republic of Iraq/*al Jumhouriya al Iraqia*) Iraq is governed by a ruling council known as the Revolutionary Command Council. Law enforcement is conducted at a strictly military level and the entire country is at a status closely related to marshall law.

Isle of Man The Isle of Man is a 227-square-mile area located in the Irish Sea, 20 miles from Scotland. The island is independently governed and has its own laws. The Isle of Man Constabulary was founded in 1863 and today consists of approximately 150 constables and officers.

Israel (State of Israel/*Medinat Israel*) Israel is located on the eastern end of the Mediterranean Sea. Its neighbors are Lebanon on the north, Syria and Jordan on the east, and Egypt on the west. The Israeli military currently occupies the West Bank and Gaza Strip; protesters and Israeli troops clash frequently. The Israel Police have been involved in a dual role since 1974, conducting the usual tasks of a police force on one hand while maintaining the security of the state. The 7,847 square miles that make up the triangular-shaped country of Israel is on a constant alert against terrorist activities from outside its boundaries. The majority of the population are on a war footing.

Italy (Italian Republic/*Repubblica Italiana*) The *Vigili Urbani* (City Police) are stationed in most major cities of Italy. The *Corpo delle Guardie di Pubblica Sicurezza* is responsible for the security of public places and the *Arma der Carabinieri* is a paramilitary force protecting the harbors, borders, airports, and all public officials.

Ivory Coast (*Republique de la Cote d'Ivoire/Cote*

d'Ivoire) Ivory Coast is located on the south coast of West Africa. Cities of the Ivory Coast have a *Police Municipale* (Municipal Police) whose sole responsibility is to police the market areas. The *Gendarmerie Nationale* conduct general police duties while the *Police Nationale* operates at a state level and conducts a majority of the criminal investigations.

Jamaica The country, located in the West Indies, is covered by mostly mountainous terrain. In the rural areas, private citizens are appointed as district constables. Although these citizens have no formal law enforcement training, they are expected to act as police officers when criminal acts are committed within their district. The island of Jamaica covers over 4,235 square miles. The Jamaica Constabulary Force comprised of approximately 5,000 officers and constables (men and women) enforce the laws.

Japan (Nippon) Japan is made up of four large islands and more than 500 smaller islands. Law enforcement is carried out by the *Todo-Fuken Keisatsu* (Prefectural Police) which operates on a local level in every district of the country but remains under the control of the *Keisatsucho* (National Police Agency). The National Police Agency is divided into five special bureaus: Criminal investigation, traffic, administration, state security, and communications. The State Security division is the watch group for terrorist activities that might originate in Japan.

Jordan (Hashemite Kingdom of Jordan/*Al Mamlaka al Urduniya al Hashemiyah*) The Jordanian Public Security Department is divided into three specific levels of administration: The Auxiliary Police are responsible for communications, supplies, training, and personnel. The Judicial Police conduct all investigations and are responsible for harbor and airport security. The Administrative Police maintain the vehicle licensing bureau, prisons and jails, and criminal records department.

Kenya (Republic of Kenya/*Jamhuri ya Kenya*) Kenya covers an area of approximately 224,960 square miles. It is slightly smaller than Texas. The

Kenya Police have local officials to maintain the law and order of an area and are supported by an Air Wing, criminal investigation division, airport, railway, and harbor agencies.

Korea (North) (Democratic People's Republic of Korea/*Chosun Minchu-chui Inmin Konghwa-guk*) Local appointed officials supported by a paramilitary police and military forces are responsible for law enforcement.

Korea (South) (Republic of Korea/*Taehan Min' guk*) South Korea is very mountainous with a very rugged east coast. The Korean National Police force has more than 45,000 officers and men and is headquartered in Seoul.

Kuwait (State of Kuwait/*Dowlat al-Kuwait*) The Kuwait Police has a number of specialized departments, most having to do with the internal security of the country. The KP is considered by most law enforcement authorities to be paramilitary in nature and purpose.

Laos (Lao People's Democratic Republic/*Sathalanalat Paxathipatai Paxaxon Lao*) Military rule is the basis for all law enforcement in Laos, with local officials appointed by the government.

Lebanon (Republic of Lebanon/*al-Jumhouriya al-Lubnaniya*) Lebanon is located on the eastern end of the Mediterranean Sea. It covers approximately 4,015 square miles. In the late 1950s all local police forces were placed under a central umbrella that came to be known as the Internal Security Forces. The present law enforcement force in Lebanon is paramilitary backed by military troops and sophisticated weapon systems.

Lesotho (Kingdom of Lesotho) Lesotho is located in southern Africa and is completely surrounded by the Republic of South Africa. Policing is conducted by the Lesotho Mounted Police. The force is headquartered in Maseru, the capital, and because officers of the LMP are spread so thin, an air patrol flies to various parts of the country to pick up criminals.

Liberia (Republic of Liberia) A paramilitary force

enforces the laws of Liberia. The entire country is in a state of marshal law resulting from rampant corruption in government that caused an Army Redemption Council of enlisted men and the police to stage a bloody predawn coup on April 12, 1980. President Tolbert was killed and replaced as head of state by Army Sgt. Samuel Doe. Doe was chosen president of Liberia in a disputed election, and survived a subsequent coup in 1985.

Libya (Socialist People's Libyan Arab Jamahiriya/ *al-Jamahiriyah al-Arabiya al-Libya al-Shabiya al-Ishtirakiya*) Libya is on the Mediterranean coast of North Africa. Information on the current law enforcement system is limited, although intelligence sources report that a national police force organized along British lines exists, along with a separate traffic force. Patrols are conducted using civil-type light aircraft in the desert areas, and by automobile, camels, and horses in more occupied areas. Because of political conditions, in Libya is considered an armed state with arms flowing into the country daily from the U.S.S.R and other eastern countries.

Liechtenstein (Principality of Liechtenstein/*Furstentum Liechenstein*) The Principality of Liechtenstein covers approximately 62 square miles. The Rhine Valley occupies about one-third of the entire country, while the Alps cover the rest. The Liechtenstein Security Corps consists of less than 40 regular officers and approximately 30 auxiliary officers.

Luxembourg (Grand Duchy of Luxembourg/ *Grand-Duche de Luxembourg*) The *Gendarmerie Grand-Ducale*, which includes the *Surete Publique*, maintains law and order in this country of 369,000. Luxembourgian, German, and French are the principal languages. The *Gendarmerie* is responsible for law enforcement throughout Luxembourg, while the *Corps de la Police* is active in towns with a population of more than 5,000. The *Surete Publique* conducts all criminal investigations.

Madagascar (Democratic Republic of Madagascar/*Repoblika Demokratika Malagasy*) About the same size as Texas, with a population of almost 12 million, the current regime closed French military outposts and a U.S. space tracking station in 1972. Since then, Madagascar has received military aid from China and the Soviet Union. Law enforcement is conducted by the military, that has an on-going program of arrests and expulsion of foreigners.

Malawi (Republic of Malawi) The government of Malawi operates under the one-party system. Law enforcement is conducted by a military force in this country, with a population of 8 million. Local police activities are conducted by individuals and groups appointed by the government headquartered in Lilongwe.

Malaysia (Federation of Malaysia) Neighboring on Thailand and Indonesia, Malaysia is marshy on the west coast, sandy desert on the east, and swampy in the coastal plain. With interior jungles, law enforcement in this spectrum of environments is based on a single federal police force, the Royal Malaysia Police. Police Field Forces of the RMP make frequent expeditions into the jungle to suppress uprisings and terminate criminal activities.

Mali (Republic of Mali/*Republique du Mali*) Located in the interior of west Africa, Mali has a small defense force supporting local government-appointed law enforcement officials.

Malta (*Repubblika Ta' Malta*) Located in the center of the Mediterranean Sea, the Island of Malta covers approximately 95 square miles. Law enforcement is conducted by the Malta Police consisting of approximately 1,500 constables, officers, and police women. The police force is deployed at 80 stations. For special occasions, the Malta Police Guard of Honor participates at official functions.

Mauritania (Islamic Republic of Mauritania/*Republique Islamique de Mauritanie*) Mauritania is located in west Africa and occupies a territory larger than the states of California and Texas combined. Law enforcement is under military rule.

Mauritius The government of Mauritius is a parliamentary democracy. The head of state is Queen Elizabeth II, who is represented by a Governor General. English and French are the common languages, and the Mauritius Police is made up of constables representing both nationalities.

Mexico (United Mexican States/*Estados Unidos Mexicanos*) With the avalanche of marijuana and brown heroin grown in the provinces of Chihuahua, Guerrero, Veracruz, San Luis Potosi, Hidalgo, Durango, Oaxaca, Sonora, Zacatecas, and Baja California, the Mexican federal and state police are daily faced with all levels of drug smuggling and drug-related murders on an ever-growing scale. Current intelligence indicates that not only is the purity of Mexican heroin up, but that the price is down. This has traditionally meant that there is an abundance of brown heroin for distribution into the illicit markets of the United States and an uphill battle for the police and border patrols.

Monaco (Principality of Monaco) Monaco is located on the northwest coast of the Mediterranean. The country is completely surrounded by France and has a population of less than 30,000. The Principality of Monaco occupies 0.6 square miles of the port area and hillside. The *Monaco Surete Publique* is divided into three principal commands: The *Police Urbaine*, which is the uniformed branch, the *Police Judiciaire*, responsible for criminal investigations, and the Police Administrative Section (PAS) which handles licensing and other activities that are not criminal in nature.

Mongolia (Mongolian People's Republic/*Bugd Nayramdakh Mongol Ard Uls*) Mongolia is one of the world's oldest countries. A Mongolian-Soviet mutual assistance pact was signed between the two countries in 1966. Since then, Soviet troops have been based in the country. Law enforcement activities are mainly conducted by the military with local government-appointed officials active in the countryside.

Montserrat The Island of Montserrat has a population of approximately 12,000. Montserrat is a self-governing British possession with a police force consisting of less than 100 constables and officers. Law enforcement is administrated along the lines of the British Colonial Police.

Morocco (Kingdom of Morocco/*al-Mamlaka al-Maghrebia*) Located on the northwest coast of Africa, Morocco became an independent country on March 2, 1956. At that time a National Police Force was formed along paramilitary lines. In 1980, *Polisario*, a guerrilla movement, proclaimed the entire region independent and launched attacks against government troops with Algerian support. In response, Morocco accepted U.S. military and economic aid. Military and law enforcement advisors currently reside in Morocco. After years of bitter fighting, government troops and the National Police Force control the main urban areas, but the *Polisario* Front's guerrillas move freely in the vast and sparsely populated desert regions.

Mozambique (People's Republic of Mozambique/*Republica Popular de Mocambique*) The 1974 revolution in Portugal paved the way for the orderly transfer of power to Frelimo (Front for the Liberation of Mozambique). The new government promised a gradual transition to a communist system. Since then, private schools have been closed, and rural collective farms and private homes nationalized. Law enforcement is conducted by the communist paramilitary government forces.

Nepal (Kingdom of Nepal/*Sri Nepala Sarkar*) The Ranas family rules all of Nepal and has kept the kings of the country as virtual prisoners. The Ranas family has a private police force as bodyguards and protectors of their vast holdings. Nepal is linked to India and Pakistan by air service and roads, but remains virtually closed to the outside world.

Netherlands (Kingdom of the Netherlands/*Konindrijk der Nederlanden*) The National Police Corps (*Korps Rijkspolitie*) is responsible for law enforcement in the entire country and is equipped with as many patrol boats for the waterways as are the automobiles used by police in major U.S. cities. Patrol motorcycles are painted a bright fluorescent orange,

and the police cars are unusually fast and powerful models.

New Caledonia New Caledonia and its dependencies are a group of islands located in the Pacific ocean. New Caledonia is one of the world's largest nickel producers. Other minerals found are iron, chrome, cobalt, manganese, silver, gold, copper, and lead. Some of the larger commercial mines have private security forces in place to prevent theft. The *New Caledonian Gendarmerie* consists of a force of approximately 450 officers and men and is responsible for all criminal investigations, public order, and the national defense. The *Noumea Commissariat of Police* operates along the same lines as the *New Caledonian Gendarmerie* in local areas and on individual islands.

New Zealand New Zealand comprises North Island, 44,035 square miles; South Island, 58,305 square miles; Stewart Island, 674 square miles, and Chatham Island 372 square miles. This entire area, with a population of more than 3 million, is patrolled by the New Zealand Police, which consists of a force of approximately 4,550 officers, policewomen, and constables.

Nicaragua (Republic of Nicaragua/*Republica de Nicaragua*) Located in Central America and about the size of Iowa, relations with surrounding countries as well as the United States have been strained because of Nicaragua's government and military aid to the leftist guerrillas groups in El Salvador and the backing of anti-Sandinista contra guerrilla groups by the United States. Law enforcement is conducted throughout the country by the military forces.

Niger (Republic of Niger/*Republique de Niger*) Niger became independent in 1960. In 1961 it signed a bilateral agreement with France. Law enforcement is on a paramilitary basis.

Nigeria (Federal Republic of Nigeria) After 13 years of military rule, Nigeria experienced a peaceful return to a civilian government in 1979. Military rule returned to Nigeria in late 1983 as a coup ousted the democratically elected government. Currently, a number of law enforcement groups are active in Nigeria. All police organizations are paramilitary in nature.

Norway (Kingdom of Norway/*Kongeriket Norge*) The Norwegian State Police is a force approximately 5,900 strong with a reserve force of more than 4,800. Norway also has a police officer known as a Lensmann who is much like a Sheriff's officer in the western United States. The Lensmann is responsible for the collection of taxes, and the processing of court orders.

Oman (Sultanate of Oman/*Saltanat 'Uman*) The Royal Oman Police, organized along British lines, is responsible for law enforcement throughout the country.

Pakistan (Islamic Republic of Pakistan) In December, 1970, Zufikar Ali Bhutto, leader of the Pakistan People's Party, became president. Bhutto was overthrown by a military coup in 1977. He was convicted of complicity in a 1974 political murder and executed in April 1979. His daughter returned from exile in Europe in 1986 in an effort to relaunch the Pakistan People's Party. Her return created riots and mass public violence. The country remains in a state of unrest with law and order being maintained by the Pakistan Police.

Panama (Republic of Panama/*Republica de Panama*) The president of Panama was ousted by the National Assembly in 1988 when he tried to fire the head of the Panama Defense Forces, General Manuel Noreiga. Noreiga has been indicted by two federal grand juries in the United States on drug and narcotics charges. The Panamanian National Guard is a paramilitary organization that combines the function of the police with the various military groups including the air force, navy, and the Army of Panama.

Papua New Guinea Papua New Guinea is slightly larger than California. It has a population estimated at 3,613,000 with many native tribes living in almost complete isolation with mutually unintelligible languages. The Royal Papua New Guinea Constabulary comprises a force of 4,563 officers and constables to maintain law and order.

Paraguay (Republic of Paraguay/*Republica del Paraguay*) One of the landlocked countries of South America, a wide variety of law enforcement organizations exist in this republic, which is under authoritarian rule. All police operations, aside from those controlled by the military, function under a law formulated in 1951 that defines the various responsibilities, procedures, and authority for the separate forces.

Peru (Republic of Peru/*Republica del Peru*) The Republican Guard is responsible for maintaining the peace and law and order in the republic. They also administrate the prison system, and supply security forces to patrol public places and private facilities that hold some importance nationally. The Peruvian Civil Guard has been trained along paramilitary lines. Personnel of the Civil Guard are experienced in keeping the peace where armed military intervention is not required. This includes criminal investigations, traffic control, and the interdiction of drugs. The Peruvian Investigative Police is the State Security force.

Philippines (Republic of the Philippines) All natural resources of the Philippines belong to the state, so it naturally follows that the Philippines Integrated National Police (INP) is the primary law enforcement body. In outlying areas, the Philippine military and paramilitary groups maintain law and order. Certain officials who head these groups are appointed by the government.

Poland (Polish People's Republic/*Polska Rzeczpospolita Ludowa*) The Republic of Poland has been under martial law from time to time over the last ten years. The government is Communist and law enforcement is patterned along the lines of the USSR with paramilitary and military forces making up the backbone of government security. Poland has an unarmed Militia responsible for local law enforcement activities.

Portugal (Republic of Portugal/*Republica Portuguesa*) In the late 1970s, the democratic parties of Portugal scored a 64% victory despite the Soviet-supported Communist party increasing its influence in government circles. Policing of the country is by a paramilitary force, while the Public Security Police (*Policia de Seguranca Publica*) is the law enforcement agency for cities and towns in Portugal.

Puerto Rico (Commonwealth of Puerto Rico/*Estado Libre Asciado de Puerto Rico*) The island of Puerto Rico is the easternmost of the West Indies group called the Greater Antilles, of which Jamaica, Cuba, and Hispaniola are the larger islands. The estimated population of Puerto Rico is 3,286,000. The Puerto Rico Police is divided into two separate groups. The Bureau of Criminal Investigation operates much like a state police organization, while the uniformed division is responsible for general law enforcement.

Qatar (State of Qatar) Qatar is located on a peninsula occupying 4,247 square miles of the Persian Gulf. It declared itself independent from the British rule of government in 1971. The Qatar State Police Force was organized in 1948 and expanded in the mid-1970s. The force currently includes the Coast Guard and a Marine Division, while the uniformed police have been riot trained and are responsible for fire fighting and local fire protection. The Qatar State Police Force has ample funding and is supported by a sizable mounted group, high-speed patrol boats, and armed helicopters.

Romania (Socialist Republic of Romania/*Republica Socialista Romania*) A small unarmed local Militia protected the smaller cities and towns of Romania, while a paramilitary organization is responsible for law enforcement on a country-wide basis.

Rwanda (Republic of Rwanda/*Republika y'u Rwanda*) Rwanda is one of the most densely populated countries in Africa. It is located in central Africa with a population in excess of 7 million. Law enforcement forces are paramilitary in formation with authorities coming from the government for local enforcement.

St. Helena, Ascension, and Tristan Da Cunha St. Helena is an island 1,200 miles off the west coast of Africa; Tristan da Cunnha is half way between the Cape of Good Hope and South America. Ascension Island is 700 miles northwest of St. Helena and is a communications relay station for Great Britain. The United States has a major satellite tracking center on Ascension Island. The law enforcement organization responsible for Ascension, St. Helena, and Tristan da Cunnha is the St. Helena Police force consisting of less than 40 constables and six police women.

St. Lucia Columbus landed on the island of St. Vincent and explored the Grenadines in 1498. The Royal St. Lucia Police Force was founded in 1834 and now maintains law and order on this 238 square mile island with a force of approximately 725 constables and officers. The force is currently comprised of the Special Reserve Police, (SRP) the Port Authority Constabulary, and the Rural Constabulary (RC).

San Marino (Most Serene Republic of San Marino/*Serenissima Republica di San Marino*) San Marino is completely surrounded by Italy and claims to be the oldest state in Europe. The Corps of Urban Police carries out all law enforcement in the republic.

Saudi Arabia (Kingdom of Saudi Arabia/*al-Mamlaka al-Arabiya as-Sa'udiya*) The government in Saudi Arabia is a monarchy supported by a council of ministers. Billions of dollars of advanced weapons have been purchased from the United States, Britain, and France. The United States supplied five airborne warning and control systems (AWACS) aircraft to Saudi Arabia in 1981. Since the early 1980s the French, British, and United States have assisted in the formation of a well-rounded law enforcement organization by sending experts to the country to conduct training. Currently, the major force is paramilitary in makeup.

Senegal (Republic of Senegal/*Republique du Senegal*) Senegal is located at the western extreme of Africa. French methods of law enforcement influence the law and order of the republic. Police organizations are formed and operated along paramilitary lines. The officers of the *Senegal Gendarmerie Nationale* (the uniformed force) are unarmed, while the *Surete Nationale of Senegal* operates as a State Security and is responsible for the borders and ports as well as criminal investigations.

Seychelles (Republic of Seychelles) The Seychelles are a group of 86 islands located in the Indian Ocean. The capital city is Victoria, where a police presence is maintained by the Seychelles Police. Permanent police units are stationed on the islands of La Digne, Mahe, and Praslin.

Sierra Leone (Republic of Sierra Leone) Sierra Leone is located on the west coast of west Africa. Freetown, the capital, was founded in 1787 by the British government as a haven for freed slaves. The Sierra Leone Police Force conducts the day-to-day responsibilities of a state-wide police agency.

Singapore (Republic of Singapore) Singapore, located off the tip of the Malayan Peninsula, is one of the world's largest port cities. The harbor area is protected by the Singapore Marine Police, (SMP) while other divisions of this paramilitary force are made up of a Gurkha Contingent, Traffic Police, Dog Unit, and Internal security (Criminal) Branch.

Somalia (Somali Democratic Republic/*Jamhuriyadda Dimugradiga Somaliya*) Located on the eastern horn of Africa, Somalia has laid claim to Goaden, the huge eastern region of Ethiopia. For a number of years, Somalia received financial assistance from the Soviet Union. In the late 1970s, Soviet military forces were expelled from Somalia in retaliation for Soviet support of the government of Ethiopia. Cuban troops with Soviet weapons defeated Somalia army troops in 1978. Guerrilla fighting continues in many parts of Ogaden. Law enforcement is administrated on a paramilitary basis by the Somalia government.

South Africa (Republic of South Africa/*Republiek van Suid-Afrika*) South Africa was formally part of the British Empire. The South African Police Force is a semimilitary force presently responsible for the whole of the Republic as well as southwest Africa. The total police contingency operates along the British lines of law enforcement with a base force of approximately 36,500 constables and police women.

Spain (Espana) Three principal police divisions are active in Spain: the uniformed (*Policia Armada*) responsible for the urban and business areas; the plain clothes (*Cuerpo General de Policia*), which conducts all criminal investigations; and the *Guardia Civil*, which is a uniformed force in the rural areas. The *Policia Gubernativa* is a uniformed group that works closely with investigators from the *Cuerpo General de Policia*.

Sri Lanka (Democratic Socialist Republic of Sri Lanka/*Sri Lanka Prajathanthrika Samajavadi Janarajaya*) Based upon the lines of the British Colonial Police the Ceylon Police Force of Sri Lanka is responsible for law enforcement throughout this country of more than 17 million.

Sudan (Republic of the Sudan/*Jamhuryat as-Sudan*) The northern Sudan was once ancient Nubia, settled by the Egyptians. Sudan is located at the east end of the Sahara desert. This country of more than 25 million has a police force of almost 30,000 officers and men. The Sudan Police Force is the primary law enforcement agency for the country. The force is comprised of a semimilitary division that handles criminal investigations; the Sudan Camel and Motorized Corps; and the Civil Police Corps (CPC) responsible for law enforcement in urban areas.

Suriname (Republic of Suriname) Suriname is located on the north shore of South America. Suriname has a paramilitary police force with civilian officials appointed by the government.

Swaziland (Kingdom of Swaziland) Swaziland is located in southern Africa near the Indian Ocean. The Swazis, a Bantu people, were driven to Swaziland from lands to the north by the Zulus in 1820.

Britain guaranteed their autonomy in 1903, and independence came in 1968. The king repealed the constitution of Swaziland in 1973 and assumed full power. According to intelligence sources, under the present constitution of Swaziland, political parties are totally forbidden. The role of the parliament is limited to advice and debate. The Royal Swaziland Police comprises a force of 1,348 constables and 98 policewomen. The commander of the force is the Prime Minister of Swaziland.

Sweden (Kingdom of Sweden/*Konungariket Sverige*) The Swedish State Police (*Rikspolis*) is controlled by the National Police Board (NPB) headquartered in Stockholm. Law enforcement throughout the country is maintained by the *Rikspolis*, with special investigations being conducted by the NPB.

Switzerland (Swiss Confederation) Switzerland has maintained an armed neutrality since 1815. Every able bodied male Swiss citizen must have basic military training by the age of 18. In addition, he must attend regular training sessions for the rest of his life. Law enforcement responsibilities are distributed among the *Gendarmerie Vaudoise*, the uniformed *Gendarmerie*, the Criminal Police Department (*Surete*), and individual police organizations in the rural and urban areas of Switzerland.

Syria (Syrian Arab Republic/*al-jamhouriya al Arabia as-Souriya*) Syria is located at the eastern end of the Mediterranean Sea. It has a Socialist government and a number of paramilitary semi-law-enforcement organizations.

Taiwan (Republic of China/*Chung-hua Min-kuo*) Taiwan (also called Formosa) is considered to be an integral part of China. Taiwan has rejected mainland China's efforts at reunification, but unofficially business activities between the mainland and Taiwan have grown more flexible. The Taiwan Police act as a state authority and are backed by the military.

Tanzania (United Republic of Tanzania/*Jamhuri ya Mwungano wa Tanzania*) Tanzania is located on the coast of east Africa. The law enforcement authority is paramilitary in nature.

Thailand (Kingdom of Thailand/*Muang Thai* or *Prathet Thai*) The police of Thailand is divided into two distinct administrations: the Central administration and the Provincial administration. The responsibility of the Provincial Police Bureau (PPB) is to maintain the peace throughout the countryside. The Central Police operate in the urban areas of Thailand with the Central Investigation Bureau (CIB) having jurisdiction over the entire country.

Togo (Republic of Togo/*Republique Togolaise*) Togo is located on the south coast of western Africa. Law enforcement is administrated by a paramilitary faction of the government with local officials appointed by the Office of the Prime Minister.

Tonga (Kingdom of Tonga/*Pule 'anga Tonga*) Tonga is comprised of 169 volcanic and coral islands, 45 of them inhabited. The less than 200 officers that make up the Tonga Police are unarmed and use many law enforcement methods patterned after the British.

Trinidad and Tobago (Republic of Trinidad and Tobago) Trinidad and Tobago are located off the eastern coast of Venezuela. The People's National movement party has held control of the government since 1956. The Tobago Police Force (TPF) maintains a Special Police Reserve Force (SPRF) and are supported in the countryside by the Rural Police. All of the law enforcement agencies are paramilitary organizations.

Tunisia (Republic of Tunisia/*al Jumhuriyah at-Tunisyah*) About the size of Missouri, the Republic of Tunisia is located on the north coast of Africa. Law enforcement is carried out by the *Garde Nationale*, a paramilitary organization that is patterned after the *French Gendarmerie*.

Turkey (Republic of Turkey/*Turkiye Cumhuriyeti*) Turkey occupies Asia Minor, between the Mediterranean and Black Seas. It borders on Bulgaria and Greece on the west, the Soviet Union (Georgia, Armenia) on the north, Iran on the east, and Syria and Iraq on the south. The *National Gendarmerie* are responsible for law enforcement in the rural areas of the country. The National Police are semimilitary in formation and divided into administrative, judicial (criminal) and political (state security) forces.

Turks and Caicos Islands Located at the southeast end of the Bahama Islands, The Turks and Caicos Islands are a separate possession of about 30 islands, 6 being inhabited. The population is estimated at slightly more than 9,000 in an area of 193 square miles. These 30 islands are a British dependency with a police force with a British commissioner, approximately 80 constables and 6 policewomen.

Tuvalu New Zealand and Britain provide extensive economic aid to this 10-square mile area near Samoa on the southeast, with Fiji to the south. Policing is done by a small force made up of six constables and eight policewomen.

Uganda (Republic of Uganda) Located in east central Africa, the Republic of Uganda is a high plateau slightly smaller than Oregon. Law enforcement is carried out by an assigned force of military troops, with officials appointed by the government acting as local authorities.

Ulster The Royal Ulster Constabulary is the single police force responsible for all of Northern Ireland. Patterned after the British form of law enforcement, they protect 16 territorial divisions, 6 of which are located in the Greater Belfast area. The Royal Ulster Constabulary is backed by an armed force of British troops because of the religious fighting between the Protestant and Catholic factions.

United Kingdom of Great Britain and Northern Ireland Organized police services in many parts of the world have been patterned after the Metropolitan Police of London, created by the British Prime Minister, Sir Robert Peel in 1829. Until then, law enforcement had been less than adequate in most parts of the world with the policeman as a single local entity with few affiliations outside his own community. Because of this, it was easy for a criminal to escape detection by simply moving on to another community. The Metropolitan Police changed all

that forever by forming a law enforcement network with constables working together. Today, each police force in the United Kingdom and Northern Ireland is commanded by a senior (chief) constable. This commander is responsible for all law enforcement in his area. The headquarters for all Metropolitan Police and related agencies of law enforcement for the United Kingdom is at New Scotland Yard located in London.

Uruguay (Oriental Republic of Uruguay/*Republica Oriental del Uruguay*) Located in southern South America on the Atlantic Ocean, its neighbors are Argentina to the west and Brazil to the north. The Uruguay National Police are semimilitary in formation and are in their greatest force in and around the capital city of Montevideo. That area alone is filled with over one million inhabitants requiring a force of over 3,500 officers. In the rural areas of the country, small detachments of police maintain law and order.

Union of Soviet Socialist Republics (USSR) (*Soyuz Sovetskykh Sotsialisticheskikh Respublic*) The USSR is the largest country in the world. The USSR is nominally a federation consisting of 15 union republics, the largest being the Russian Soviet Federated Socialist Republic. The nearest organization to a police force in the Soviet Union is the Militia. The Militia is currently managed by the Chief Administration of the Militia (GUM) for the Soviet Union and the Ministries for the Preservation of Public Order (MOOP). The Militia is responsible for all law enforcement activities. Certain criminal investigations are conducted by the Soviet State Security—*Komitet Gosudarstvennoy Bezopasnosti* (KGB).

United States of America (USA) Most cities in the United States have an independent metropolitan police force that range in size from one or two officers to thousands of police officers in major cities. The various police agencies in the United States are organized on five law enforcement levels: the small townships and rural areas, cities, counties, states, and the federal government. Those smaller towns and rural areas lacking a local law enforcement agency receive protection from a county constable or sheriff's department. The constables and sheriff's usually are responsible for law and order in a specific county of one of the 50 states. Local police departments work within the limits of cities and have at their disposal (for extensive criminal investigations) the resources and scientific laboratories of the county constable or sheriff, as well as even larger facilities of the state police and federal government agencies. The state police protect state property, facilities and officials. At the federal level is the FBI, responsible for the investigation of certain violations of federal statutes of the law. The military have their own internal police organizations and criminal justice system, including prisons. State prisons are operated in each of the 50 states for violations of civil crimes within the state. Federal prisons have been established at various sites within the United States to incarcerate prisoners convicted of violations of federal crimes.

Venezuela (Republic of Venezuela/*Republica de Venezuela*) The Republic of Venezuela is located on the Caribbean coast of South America. The Metropolitan Police force of Venezuela is known as *La Policia Metropolitana*. The force of almost 5,000 officers has limited authority and deals mostly with traffic, public health, and public law and order. In rural areas of the country, police operations are conducted by officials and groups appointed by the Metropolitan Police, the Judicial Police, or the National Guard. The Judicial Police act as a federal police force and is responsible to the Minister of Justice. The National Guard performs both law enforcement and military functions.

Vietnam (Socialist Republic of Vietnam/*Cong Hoa Xa Hoi Chu Nghia Viet Nam*) Vietman is located on the east coast of the Indochinese Peninsula in southeast Asia. Law enforcement activities are the responsibility of a paramilitary force appointed by officials of the government.

Virgin Islands (St. John, St. Croix, St. Thomas) The Virgin Islands are 3 large and 50 small islands and cays in the south and west of the Virgin Island group. The Royal Virgin Island Police Force was established in 1967. The force is unique in the fact that the Chief of Police must be appointed from a list of applicants for his professional police and management skills, and can come from anywhere in the world, while constables must be natives of the West Indian Islands or the Virgin Islands.

Western Samoa (Independent State of Western Samoa/*Malotuto'atasi o Samoa i Sisifo*) Western Samoa was an occupied German colony from 1899 to 1914, when troops of the New Zealand Army landed and took over this country that is about the size of Rhode Island. All police activities are conducted by the Western Samoa Police. Their methods and dress are patterned after the British and New Zealand police.

West Germany The Federal Republic of Germany is made up of 10 provinces that include Baden-Wurttemberg, Bavaria, Bremen, Schleswig-Holstein, Hesse, Rhineland, Hamburg, Palatinate, North Rhine-Westphalia, and Saarland. Each province has a separate law enforcement agency in place. The uniformed police (*Schutzpolizie*) and plain clothes criminal police (*Kriminalpolizie*) officers do most of the routine police work. Traffic enforcement is conducted by officers in police cars and on motorcycles (*Motorisierte Verkehrspolizie-Staffein*), while the *Kriminalpolizei* (criminal police) conduct crime scene investigations and intelligence. In a role somewhat akin to Special Weapons and Tactics units in the United States, the *Spezialeinsatkommandos* are in reserve as a law enforcement arm of the German police. The central headquarters for federal police services in Germany is the *Landeskriminalamt*, which maintains the criminal laboratory for the republic and the criminal records. The Border Police (*Bundesgrenzschutz*) are responsible for protection of the airports, harbors, and borders of the country.

North Yemen (Yemen Arab Republic/*al-Jumhuriyat al-Arabiyah al-Yamaniyah*) Policing is based on paramilitary forces with strict enforcement and harsh punishment.

South Yemen   (People's Republic of Yemen/*Jumhuriyat al-Yaman ad-Dimuqratiyah ash-Sha'biyan*) Law enforcement is conducted along paramilitary lines. In 1986 the government was overthrown in a bloody coup that was followed by an escalation in civil war with factions fighting each other.

Yugoslavia   (Socialist Federal Republic of Yugoslavia/*Socijalisticka Federativna Republika Jugoslavija*) Law enforcement in Yugoslavia is patterned after the Soviet police. Much of the actual enforcement (criminal) is conducted by a military force.

Zaire   (Republic of Zaire/*Republique du Zaire*) Zaire is located in central Africa. The country has serious economic difficulties. For years this country, about one-fourth the size of the United States, has been charged with corruption in government. To this day, those same charges filter down to the police agencies of Zaire. Law enforcement is semimilitary in nature with torture commonplace in the prisons and jails.

Zambia   (Republic of Zambia) Located in southern central Africa, Zambia is mostly high plateau country covered with dense forests. Policing is done by the Zambia Police Force. The headquarters for the force is located in Lusaka, the capital city. The Zambia Police Force is patterned after British law enforcement. The police are unique in that they are responsible for the prison system as well as individuals who are convicted felons and who are on probation or parole. Jungle patrols by groups of police to maintain law and order are common in the rural areas of Zambia.

Zimbabwe   Located in southern Africa, Zimbabwe is high plateau country with a population of almost 10 million. Zimbabwe was formerly known as Southern Rhodesia and under British rule until the early 1970s, when the Rhodesian Government declared Rhodesia an independent republic. This declaration was not accepted by the British Government. The government is now operated as a one-party socialist state. Law enforcement is now conducted by a paramilitary group in the outlying regions, while the South Africa Police is an unarmed force.

Organizations/Associations Related to Law Enforcement

The purpose of this listing is to make the reader aware of the wide variety of law enforcement organizations and associations in the northern hemisphere. Because these organizations are known to move to larger facilities as they expand, the best resource for current or last known address for anyone of these groups is to contact the author of this book (see last page) for further details and information. Please enclose a self-addressed, stamped business-size envelope (SASE) with your request. Limit: One request per envelope.

Academy of Criminal Justice Sciences

Afro-American Patrolmen's League

Airborne Law Enforcement Association

Alliance of Nongovernmental Organizations on Crime Prevention and Criminal Justice

American Academy of Forensic Sciences

American Academy for Professional Law Enforcement

American Association of Correctional Officers

American Association of Correctional Psychologists

American Association of Criminology

American Association of Police Polygraphists

American Association of Wardens & Superintendents

American Correctional Association

American Criminal Justice Association (Lambda Alpha Epsilon)

American Defense Preparedness Association

American Federation of Police

American Law Enforcement Officers Association

American Pistol and Revolver Association

American Polygraph Association

American Prison Ministry

American Society of Criminology

American Society of Forensic Odontolgy

Americans for Effective Law Enforcement

Americans for Human Rights and Social Justice

Associated Public Safety Communications Officers

Association of Federal Investigators

Association of Former Intelligence Officers

Association of Paroling Authorities

Association of State Correctional Administrators

Canadian Association for the Prevention of Crime

Canadian Association of Police Chiefs

Canadian Society of Forensic Science

Center for Community Justice

Center for Studies in Criminal Justice

Center for Studies in Criminology and Criminal Law

Citizens Committee for the Right to Keep & Bear Arms

Citizens Committee for Victim Assistance

Committee on Uniform Crime Records

Correctional Education Association

Correctional Service Federation

Evidence Photographers International Council

Federation of Postal Security Police

Federal Probation Officers Association

Fraternal Order of Police, Grand Lodge

Friends of the FBI

International Association of Arson Investigators

International Association of Chiefs of Police

International Association of Credit Card Investigators

International Association for Identification

International Association of Voice Identification

International Association of Women Police

International Benchrest Shooters

International Center for Comparative Criminology

International Criminal Justice Association

International Federation of Senior Police Officers

International Footprint Association

International Juvenile Officers Association

International Law Enforcement Stress Association

International Narcotic Enforcement Officers Assoc.

International Probation Organization

International Union of Police Associations

Justice System Training Association

National Association of Citizens Crime Commissions

National Association of Criminal Justice Planners

National Association of Extradition Officials

Nat. Assoc. of Federally Licensed Firearms Dealers

Nat. Assoc. of Police Community Relations Officers

National Association of Police Laboratories

National Association of Training Schools and Juvenile Agencies

National Association on Volunteers in Criminal Justice

National Black Police Association

National Board for the Promotion of Rifle Practice

National Clearinghouse for Justice Planning and Architecture

National Community Crime Prevention League

National Correctional Recreational Association

National Council on Crime and Delinquency

National Crime Prevention Association

National Crime Prevention Institute

National Criminal Justice Councils

National Institute on Crime and Delinquency

National Jail Association

National Jail Managers Association

National Juvenile Detention Association

National Military Intelligence Association

National Police and Firefighters Association

National Police Officers Association of America

National Police Reserve Officers Association

National Rifle Association of America

National Sheriffs Association

North American Association of Wardens and Superintendents

North American Police Work Dog Association

Parole and Probation Compact Administrators Assoc.

Police Marksman Association

Society of Former Special Agents of the Federal Bureau of Investigation

Society for the Prevention of Crime

Society of Professional Investigators

Sporting Arms and Ammunition Manufacturers Institute

United States Police Canine Association

United States Revolver Association

Women's Prison Association

Appendix B
U.S. Military Bases, Stations, and Related Installations Worldwide

Alabama	Maxwell Air Force Base (Air Force)
	+ Anniston Army Depot (Army)
	Fort McClellan (Army)
	Fort Rucker (Army)
	+ Redstone Arsenal (Army)
Alaska	Eielson Air Force Base (Air Force)
	Elmendorf Air Force Base (Air Force)
	Fort Greely (Army)
	Fort Richardson (Army)
	Fort Wainwright (Army)
	Adak Naval Station (Navy)
Arizona	− Davis-Monthan Air Force Base (Air Force)
	Luke Air Force Base (Air Force)
	Williams Air Force Base (Air Force)
	− Fort Huachuca (Army)
	− Navajo Depot Activity (Army)
	+ Yuma Proving Ground (Army)
	Marine Corps Air Station, Yuma (Marines)
Arkansas	+ Ira Eaker Air Force Base (Air Force)
	Little Rock Air Force Base (Air Force)
Azores	Lajes Field (Air Force)
Belgium	Supreme Headquarters Allied Powers in Europe
Bermuda	Bermuda Naval Air Station (Navy)
California	+ Beale Air Force Base (Air Force)
	Castle Air Force Base (Air Force)
	Edwards Air Force Base (Air Force)
	− George Air Force Base (Air Force)
	Los Angeles Air Force Base (Air Force)

+ Scheduled to be upgraded
− Scheduled to be cut back or closed

- March Air Force Base (Air Force)
- Mather Air Force Base (Air Force)
+ McClellan Air Force Base (Air Force)
- Norton Air Force Base (Air Force)
  Onizuka Air Force Base (Air Force)
  Travis Air Force Base (Air Force)
  Vandenberg Air Force Base (Air Force)
  Fort Irwin National Training Center (Army)
  Fort Ord (Army)
  Presidio of Monterey (Army)
- Presidio of San Francisco (Army)
- Hamilton Army Airfield (Army)
  Barstow Marine Corps Logistics Base (Marines)
  Camp Pendleton (Marines)
  El Toro Marine Corps Air Station (Marines)
  San Diego Marine Corps Recruit Depot (Marines)
  Twentynine Palms Marine Corps (Marines)
  Air Ground Combat Center (Marines)
  Alameda Naval Air Station (Navy)
  China Lake Naval Weapons Center (Navy)
  Concord Naval Weapons Station (Navy)
  Coronado Naval Amphibious Base (Navy)
  El Centro Naval Air Facility (Navy)
- Hunters Point Naval Station, San Francisco (Navy)
  Lemoore Naval Air Station (Navy)
  Long Beach Naval Hospital (Navy)
  Mare Island Naval Complex (Navy)
  Miramar Naval Air Station (Navy)
  Moffett Field Naval Air Station (Navy)
  Naval Construction Battalion Center, Port Hueneme (Navy)
  Naval Postgraduate School (Navy)
  North Island Naval Air Station (Navy)
  Oakland Naval Medical Command, Northwest Region/Naval Hospital (Navy)
  Pacific Missile Test Center, Pt. Mugu (Navy)
  San Diego Naval Station (Navy)
  San Diego Naval Training Center (Navy)
- Salton Sea Test Base (Navy)
  Skaggs Island Naval Security (Navy)
  Group Activity (Navy)
  Treasure Island Naval Station (Navy)

+   Scheduled to be upgraded
—   Scheduled to be cut back or closed

Colorado	+ Lowery Air Force Base (Air Force)
	Peterson Air Force Base (Air Force)
	United States Air Force Academy (Air Force)
	NORAD Cheyenne Mountain Complex (Air Force)
	Fitzsimons Army Hospital (Army)
	+ Fort Carson (Army)
	− Pueblo Army Depot (Army)
Connecticut	New London Naval Submarine Base (Navy)
Delaware	Dover Air Force Base (Air Force)
Diego Garcia	Diego Garcia Naval Communications Station (Navy)
District of Columbia	The Pentagon Building (Joint Chiefs of Staff)
	United States Soldiers' and Airmen's Home (Joint Military)
	Bolling Air Force Base (Air Force)
	Fort Lesley J. McNair (Army)
	Walter Reed Army Medical Center (Army)
	Washington Navy Yard (Navy)
England	RA Alconbury (Air Force)
	RAF Bentwaters-Woodbridge (Air Force)
	RAF Chicksands (Air Force)
	RAF Fairford (Air Force)
	RAF Greenham Common (Air Force)
	RAF Lakenheath (Air Force)
	RAF Mildenhall (Air Force)
	RAF Upper Heyford (Air Force)
Florida	Eglin Air Force Base (Air Force)
	Homestead Air Force Base (Air Force)
	Hurlburt Field (Air Force)
	Kennedy Space Center (NASA)
	MacDill Air Force Base (Air Force)
	Patrick Air Force Base (Air Force)
	Tyndall Air Force Base (Air Force)
	Cecil Field Naval Air Station (Navy)
	Jacksonville Naval Air Station (Navy)
	Key West Naval Air Station (Navy)
	Mayport Naval Station (Navy)
	Orlando Naval Training Center (Navy)
	Pensacola Naval Air Station (Navy)
	Whiting Field Naval Air Station (Navy)

+   Scheduled to be upgraded
−   Scheduled to be cut back or closed

Georgia	Moody Air Force Base (Air Force)
	Warner Robins Air Force Base (Air Force)
	Fort Benning (Army)
	Fort Gordon (Army)
	− Fort McPherson (Army)
	Fort Stewart (Army)
	Albany Marine Corps Logistics Base (Marines)
	Atlanta Naval Air Station (Navy)
	Kings Bay Naval Submarine Base (Navy)
	Navy Supply Corps School (Navy)
Germany	Bitburg Air Base (Air Force)
	Hahn Air Base (Air Force)
	Hessisch Oldendorf Air Station (Air Force)
	Rhein-Main Air Base (Air Force)
	Sembach Air Base (Air Force)
	Spangdahlem Air Base (Air Force)
	Tempelhof Central Airport (Air Force)
	Ansbach Military Community (Army)
	Armed Forces Recreation Centers (Army)
	Berchtesgaden
	Chiemsee
	Garmisch
	Aschaffenburg Military Community (Army)
	Augsburg Military Community (Army)
	Babenhausen Subcommunity (Army)
	Bad Kreuznach Military Community (Army)
	Bad Toelz Military Community (Army)
	Bamberg Military Community (Army)
	Baumholder Military Community (Army)
	Bremerhaven Military Community (All Corps)
	Dolan Barracks (Army)
	Frankfurt Military Community (Military/Civilian)
	Fulda Military Community (Army)
	Giessen Military Community (Army)
	Goppingen Military Community (Army)
	Grafenwoehr Training Area (Army)
	Heidelberg Military Community (Army)
	Herzogenaurach Artillery Base (Army)
	Kaiserslautern Military Community (Army)
	Kitzingen Military Community (Army)
	Landstuhl Army Medical Center (Army)

+   Scheduled to be upgraded
−   Scheduled to be cut back or closed

                 Mannheim Military Community (Army)
                 Miesau Army Depot (Army)
                 Nurnberg Military Community (Army)
                 Schweinfurt Military Community (Army)
                 Storck Barracks (Army)
                 Stuttgart Military Community (Army)
                 United States Military Command, Germany (Army)
                 Vilseck Combined Arms Training Center (Army)
                 Wiesbaden Military Community (Air Force)
                 Zweibrucken Military Community (Air Force)

Greece
                 Hellenikon Air Base (Air Force)
                 Iraklion Air Station, Crete (Air Force)
                 Naval Communications Station, Nea Makri (Navy)

Guam
                 Andersen Air Force Base (Air Force)
                 U.S. Naval Forces, (NAVFAC) Guam (Navy)

Hawaii
                 Hickam Air Force Base (Air Force)
                 Wheeler Air Force Base (Air Force)
                 Armed Forces Recreation Center, Hawaii (Army)
                 Schofield Barracks (Army)
                 Tripler Army Medical Center (Army)
                 Kaneohe Bay Marine Corps Air Station (Marines)
                 Barbers Point Naval Air Station (Navy)
              + Pearl Harbor (Navy)

Iceland
                 Keflavik Naval Station (Navy)

Idaho
              + Mountain Home Air Force Base (Air Force)

Illinois
              − Chanute Air Force Base (Air Force)
                 Scott Air Force Base (Air Force)
              − Fort Sheridan (Army)
                 Rock Island Arsenal (Army)
                 Glenview Naval Air Station (Navy)
                 Great Lakes Naval Training Center (Navy)

Indiana
                 Grissom Air Force Base (Air Force)
              + Fort Benjamin Harrison (Army)
              − Jefferson Proving Ground (Army)

Italy
                 Aviano Air Base (Air Force)
                 San Vito Dei Normanni Air Station (Air Force)
                 Camp Darby (Army)

+   Scheduled to be upgraded
−   Scheduled to be cut back or closed

	Caserma Ederle, So. European Task Force (Army)
	La Maddalena Naval Base, Sardinia (Navy)
	Sigonella Naval Air Station, Sicily (Navy)
	U.S. Naval Support Activity (NSA), Naples (Navy)
Japan	Misawa Air Base (Air Force)
	Yokota Air Base (Air Force)
	Camp Zama (Army)
	Marine Corps Air Station, Iwakuni (Marines)
	Atsugi Naval Air Facility (Navy)
	Fleet Activities, Sasebo (Navy)
	Fleet Activities, Yokosuka (Navy)
Kansas	McConnell Air Force Base (Air Force)
	Fort Leavenworth (Army)
	Fort Riley (Army)
Kentucky	Fort Campbell (Army)
	+ Fort Knox (Army)
Korea	Kunsan Air Base (Air Force)
	Osan Air Base (Air Force)
	Suwon Air Station (Air Force)
	Taegu Air Station (Air Force)
	Camp Ames (Army)
	Camp Carroll (Army)
	Camp Casey (Army)
	Camp Hialeah, Pusan (Army)
	Camp Howze (Army)
	Naija Armed Forces Recreation center, Seoul (Army)
	Taegu Military Community (Army)
	U.S. Army Garrison, Seoul (Army)
Louisiana	Barksdale Air Force Base (Air Force)
	England Air Force Base (Air Force)
	Fort Polk (Army)
	− Lake Charles Naval Station (Navy)
	− New Orleans Naval Air Station (Navy)
Maine	Loring Air Force Base (Air Force)
	Brunswick Naval Air Station (Navy)
	Cutler Naval Communications Unit (Navy)
Maryland	Andrews Air Force Base (Air Force)
	+ Fort Detrick (Army)

+   Scheduled to be upgraded
−   Scheduled to be cut back or closed

— Fort Holabird (Army)
— Fort Meade (Army)
Fort Ritchie (Army)
Patuxent River Naval Air Station (Navy)
United States Naval Academy (Navy)

Massachusetts   Hanscom Air Force Base (Air Force)
+ Army Material Technology Laboratory (Army)
— Fort Devens (Army)

Michigan   K.I. Sawyer Air Force Base (Air Force)
+ Wurtsmith Air Force Base (Air Force)
+ Detroit Arsenal Tank Plant (Army)

Mississippi   Columbus Air Force Base (Air Force)
+ Keesler Air Force Base (Air Force)
Gulfport Naval Construction Battalion Center (Navy)
Naval Air Station, Meridian (Navy)
United States Naval Home (Navy)

Missouri   Whiteman Air Force Base (Air Force)
+ Fort Leonard Wood (Army)

Montana   Malmstrom Air Force Base (Air Force)

Nebraska   Offutt Air Force Base (Air Force)

Netherlands   Camp New Amsterdam (Air Force)

Nevada   + Nellis Air Force Base (Air Force)
Fallon Naval Air Station (Navy)

New Hampshire   Portsmouth Naval Shipyard (Navy)
— Pease Air Force Base (Air Force)

New Jersey   McGuire Air Force Base (Air Force)
— Fort Dix (Army)
— Fort Monmouth (Army)
Military Traffic Management
Command, Bayonne (Army)
Lakehurst Naval Air Engineering Center (Navy)

New Mexico   + Cannon Air Force Base (Air Force)
Holloman Air Force Base (Air Force)
+ Kirtland Air Force Base (Air Force)
— Fort Wingate (Army)
White Sands Missile Range (Army)

+   Scheduled to be upgraded
—   Scheduled to be cut back or closed

New York	Griffiss Air Force Base (Air Force)
	+ Plattsburgh Air Force Base (Air Force)
	Fort Drum (Army)
	Fort Hamilton (Army)
	Seneca Army Depot (Army)
	United States Military Academy, West Point (Army)
	− Naval Station New York (Navy)
	+ Naval Station Staten Island (Navy)
North Carolina	Pope Air Force Base (Air Force)
	Seymour Johnson Air Force Base (Air Force)
	Fort Bragg (Army)
	Camp Lejeune (Marines)
	Cherry Point Marine Corps Air Station (Marines)
North Dakota	Grand Forks Air Force Base (Air Force)
	Minot Air Force Base (Air Force)
Ohio	Wright-Patterson Air Force Base (Air Force)
Okinawa	Kadena Air Base (Air Force)
	U.S. Marine Corps Installation, Okinawa (Marines)
Oklahoma	Altus Air Force Base (Air Force)
	Tinker Air Force Base (Air Force)
	Vance Air Force Base (Air Force)
	Fort Sill (Army)
Oregon	− Umatilla Army Depot (Army)
Panama	Albrook Air Force Station (*)
	Howard Air Force Base (Air Force)
	U.S. Naval Security Group, Galeta Island (Navy)
	U.S. Naval Station, Panama Canal (Navy)
	Rodman Naval Station & Support Unit (Navy)
	Fort Amador (*)
	Fort Clayton (Army)
	Fort Davis (Army)
	Fort Kobbe (Army)
	Fort Sherman (Army)
	Fuerte Espinar [Formerly Fort Gulick](*)
	(*) NOTE: U.S. bases turned over to Panamanian Defense Forces
Pennsylvania	Carlisle Barracks (Army)

+ Scheduled to be upgraded

− Scheduled to be cut back or closed

Fort Indiantown Gap (Army)
Philadelphia Naval Base (Navy)
− Naval Hospital Philadelphia (Navy)
Willow Grove Naval Air Station (Navy)

Philippines
Clark Air Base (Air Force)
U.S. Naval Facilities, Subic Bay (Navy)

Puerto Rico
Fort Buchanan (Army)
Roosevelt Roads Naval Station (Navy)

Rhode Island
Naval Education & Training Center (Navy)

Scotland
Naval Communications Station, Thurso (Navy)

South Carolina
Charleston Air Force Base (Air Force)
Myrtle Beach Air Force Base (Air Force)
Shaw Air Force Base (Air Force)
+ Fort Jackson (Army)
Beaufort Marine Corps Air Station (Marines)
Parris Island (Marines)
Charleston Naval Base (Navy)

South Dakota
Ellsworth Air Force Base (Air Force)

Spain
Torrejon Air Base (Air Force)
Zaragoza Air Base (Air Force)
U.S. Naval Station, Rota (Navy)

Tennessee
Arnold Air Force Base (Air Force)
Memphis Air Station (Navy)

Texas
+ Bergstrom Air Force Base (Air Force)
Brooks Air Force Base (Air Force)
+ Carswell Air Force Base (Air Force)
Dyess Air Force Base (Air Force)
+ Goodfellow Air Force Base (Joint Military)
John Space Center (NASA)
—formerly Marshall Space Center
Kelly Air Force Base (Air Force)
Lackland Air Force Base (Air Force)
Laughlin Air Force Base (Air Force)
Randolph Air Force Base (Air Force)
Reese Air Force Base (Air Force)
+ Sheppard Air Force Base (Air Force)
− Fort Bliss (Army)

+   Scheduled to be upgraded
−   Scheduled to be cut back or closed

Fort Hood (Army)
Fort Sam Houston (Army)
− Naval Station Galveston (Navy)
+ Naval Station Ingleside (Navy)
Chase Field Naval Air Station (Navy)
Corpus Christi Naval Air Station (Navy)
Kingsville Naval Air Station (Navy)

Turkey   Incirlik Air Base (Air Force)

Utah   Hill Air Force Base (Air Force)
− Fort Douglas (Army)
Dugway Proving Ground (Army)

Virginia   Langley Air Force Base (Air Force)
+ Fort Belvoir (Army)
− Cameron Station (Army)
Fort Eustis (Army)
+ Fort Lee (Army)
Fort Monroe (Army)
Fort Myer (Army)
Vint Hill Farms (Army)
Quantico Marine Base (Marines)
Norfolk Naval Base (Navy)
Oceana Naval Air Station (Navy)
Yorktown Naval Weapons Station (Navy)
− Defense Mapping Agency

Washington   + Fairchild Air Force Base (Air Force)
+ McChord Air Force Base (Air Force)
Fort Lewis (Army)
Bangor Naval Submarine Base (Navy)
+ Everett Naval Station (Navy)
Puget Sound Naval Shipyard (Navy)
− Sand Point Naval Station (Navy)
Whidbey Island Naval Air Station (Navy)

Wyoming   F.E. Warren Air Force Base (Air Force)

+ Scheduled to be upgraded
− Scheduled to be cut back or closed

Appendix C

Publications

There are a variety of specialized publications that will be of interest to readers of this book. The latest worldwide information regarding intelligence, aviation, communications, and law enforcement can be found in the following publications:

Access Report/FYI
Monitor Publishing Co.
1301 Pennsylvania Avenue
Suite 1000
Washington, D.C. 20004

Afrique Defense
Available From: Afrique Defense
11 rue de Teheran
75008 Paris, France

Air Force Magazine
Air Force Association
1501 Lee Highway
Arlington, VA 22209, USA

APCO Bulletin
Associated Public Safety Communications
    Officers, Inc.
Post Office Box 669
New Smyrna Beach, FL 32070, USA

APCO-IS
Associated Public Safety Communications
    Officers Information Service
(communications resource and reference service)
(Ask for list of documents available)
APCO-IS
930 Third Avenue
New Smyrna Beach, FL 32070, USA

Armada International
Post Office Box 139
CH8035
Zurich, Switzerland

Armed Forces Journal
Army and Navy Journal, Inc.
1414—22nd Street NW, Suite 104
Washington, DC 20037, USA

Armed Forces Journal International
Army and Navy Journal, Inc.
1414—22nd Street NW, Suite 104
Washington, DC 20037, USA

Arms Control Today
Arms Control Association
11 Dupont Circle, N.W.
Washington, D.C. 20077-5848, USA

Army
Association of the US Army
2425 Wilson Boulevard
Arlington, VA 22201, USA

Army Communicator
Department of Defense Publications
US Army Signal Center
Fort Gordon, GA 30905, USA

Asian Defence Journal
Post Office Box 836
61B Jalan Dato Haji Eusoff
Kuala Lumpur, Malaysia

Aviation Week & Space Technology
1221 Avenue of the Americas
New York, NY 10020, USA

Big SISter
Oasis Publications
Post Office Box 1666
Wellington, Aotearoa
New Zealand

COMBROAD
Commonwealth Broadcasting Association
CBA Secretariat
Broadcasting House
London W1A 1AA, U.K.

CRB Research Books, Inc.
(various communication books in print)
CRB Research Books, Inc.
Post Office Box 56
Commack, NY 11725, USA

CRYPTO
(Government Frequency Update (GFU) on
    microfiche and printed frequency updates)
DataPort Technologies
Post Office Box 3172
Ygnacio Valley Station
Walnut Creek, CA 94598, USA

Counterpoint
Ickham Publications Ltd.
Westonhanger, Ickham
Canterbury CT3 1QN, England

Covert Action Information Bulletin
Post Office Box 50272
Washington, D.C. 20004

Danish Clandestine Station Directory
(contains frequency listing for stations, military
operations and aircraft flights in Europe and the
Soviet Union as well as signals to the eastern U.S.
coast)
DSWCI
Tavleager 31
DK-2670 Greve Strand, Denmark

Defence & Armament
48 Boulevarddes Batignolles
75017 Paris, France

Defence Attache
Bedford Row House
58 Theobalsds Road
London, WC1X 8SF, England

Defense Electronics
1170 East Meadow Drive
Palo Alto, CA 94303, USA

Defense and Foreign Affairs
1777 "T" Street, NW
Washington, DC 20009, USA

Defense Management Journal
Department of Defense Publications
OASD (MRA&L)
Cameron Station
Alexandria, VA 22314, USA

Defense Science & Electronics
300 Orchard City Drive, Suite 234
Campbell, CA 95008, USA

DX Listening Digest
Post Office Box 1684
Enid, OK 73702, USA

Espionage
Leo 11 Publications
Post Office Box 1184
Teaneck, NJ 07666

First Principles
Center for National Security Studies
122 Maryland Avenue NE
Washington, D.C. 20002

Foreign Intelligence Literary Scene
National Intelligence Study Center
1800 K Street NW
Washington, D.C. 20006

Future Products
(electronics, computers, etc.)
Global Knowledge Ltd.
86 Sycamore Road, Amersham, Bucks
HP6 5DR England

Geheim
Lutticher Strasse 14
5000 Koln 1
Federal Republic of Germany

Government Radio Systems
Mobile Radio Resources
2661 Carol Drive
San Jose, CA 95125, USA

GRAFEX
Australian Government
Department of Administrative Services
Grafex Predictions
IPS Radio and Space Services
Post Office Box 702
Darlinghurst NSW 2010
Australia

Intelligence and National Security
Frank Cass & Company Ltd.
Gainsborough House
11 Gainsborough Road
London E11 1RS, England

Intelligence/Parapolitics
Association pour la Droite a l'information
16 rue des Ecoles, 75005
Paris, France

Intelligence Quarterly
Michael Speers Publishing
Post Office Box 232
Weston, VT 05161

Interbooks
International Communications Reference Books
(i.e., aircraft, Interpol, military, news agencies, etc.)
RD2, Stanley, Perth
PH1 4QQ, Scotland

Interface Europe
(Technology Transfer [participation] Programs)
Global Knowledge
86 Sycamore Road, Amersham, Bucks
HP6 5DR, England

International Code Transmissions (ICT)
Morsum Magnificat
c/o Tony Smith
G4FAI, 1 Tash Place
London, England N11 1PA

International Countermeasures Handbook
1170 East Meadow Drive
Palo Alto, CA 94303, USA

International Defence Review
86 Avenue Louis Casai
Geneva, CH12-16 Switzerland

*International Journal of Intelligence and
    Counterintelligence*
Intel Publishing Group
Post Office Box 188
Stroudsburg, PA 18360

Jane's Defence Review
Jane's Publications
238 City Road
London EC1, England

Journal of Electronic Defense
Association of Old Crows
The AOC Building
1000 North Payne Street
Alexandria, VA 22314-1696, USA

Law Enforcement News
John Jay College of Criminal Justice
444 West 56th Street
New York, NY 10019, USA

Lobster
Lobster Publishing
17C Pearson Avenue
Hull HU5 2SX, England

Marine Corps Gazette
Marine Corps Association
Post Office Box 1775
Quantico, VA 22134, USA

Military Intelligence (quarterly)
Superintendent of Documents
U.S. Government Printing Office
Washington, D.C. 20402

Military Logistics Forum
15 Ketchum Street
Westport, CT 06881, USA

Military Research Letter
Post Office Box 3751
Washington, DC 20007, USA

Military Technology
Heilsbachstrasse 26
D-5300 Bonn 1, West Germany

Miltronics
Miltronics Publications
50 High Street
Eton, Berkshire, England SL4 6BL

Monitoring Times
Grove Enterprises, Inc.
Post Office Box 98
Brasstown, NC 28902, USA

National Defense
Rosslyn Ctr., Suite 900
1700 N. Moore Street
Arlington, VA 22209, USA

National Intelligence Book Center Catalog
National Intelligence Book Center
1700 K Street—Sixth Floor
Washington, D.C. 20006, USA

National Intelligence Study Center newsletter/books
National Intelligence Study Center
1800 K Street, Suite 1102
Washington, D.C. 20006, USA

NATO's Sixteen Nations
International Press Centre
1 Boulevard Charlemagne
b-140 Brussels, Belgium

Navy Times
Springfield, VA 22159

Nightwatch (free)
Security and Intelligence Foundation
1010 Vermont Avenue, Suite 1020
Washington, D.C. 20005

Police—The Law Officer's Magazine
Hare Publishing
6300 Yarrow Drive
Carlsbad, CA 92009, USA

Popular Communications
76 North Broadway
Hicksville, NY 11801, USA

RADEX
European confidential frequency listings
    & reference books
RADEX Publishing
Post Office Box 726
251 07 Helsingborg, Sweden

Radio Data Base International
International Broadcasting Services
Post Office Box 300
Penn's Park, PA 18943, USA

RCMA Newsletter
Radio Communications Monitoring Assoc.
Post Office Box 4563
Anaheim, CA 92803, USA

SCIP Newsletter
Washington Researchers, Ltd.
2612 P Street
Washington, DC 20007
(See SCIP)

Sea Power
Navy League Association
2300 Wilson Boulevard
Arlington, VA 22201, USA

Signal
AFCEA Association
5641 Burke Centre Parkway
Burke, VA 22015, USA

SPYBASE
Microcomputer index & database software
Micro Associates
Post Office Box 5369
Arlington, VA 22205, USA

TAB BOOKS
Scientific/technical books on aviation, communications, and electronics. A wide selection of high-quality reference books
TAB BOOKS
13311 Monterey Avenue
Blue Ridge Summit, PA 17294-0850, USA

Telecommunication Journal
ITU, Place des Nations, 1211
Geneva, 20, Switzerland

The National Reporter
Post Office Box 21279
Washington, D.C. 20009

U.S. Naval Institute Proceedings
225 Park Avenue
New York, NY 10017, USA

U.S. Scanner News
Bob's Publications
Post Office Box 1103
Vancouver, WA 98666, USA

USSR High Frequency Broadcast Newsletter
USSR High Frequency Newsletter
Post Office Box 232
McLean, VA 22101, USA

Wisconsin Police Journal
Wisconsin Professional Police Association
7 North Pinckney Street
Madison, WI 53703, USA

WRTH Downlink
Billboard Publications, Inc.
1515 Broadway
New York, NY 10036, USA

Publication note: The purpose of this listing is to supply readers with comprehensive sources for the various levels of communication material and information on related topics currently available on a worldwide basis. We suggest that you direct a letter to the circulation editor of those publications listed and request subscription information. Be sure to enclose a self-addressed and stamped envelope (SASE).

Appendix D

Resources

There are a variety of resources that allow the reader of this reference guide to keep abreast of the codes used by law enforcement agencies, the military, and surveillance organizations. Following are the services that will assist you most, along with a comprehensive description of what the resources offer. Contact them individually and include a stamped, self-addressed envelope for your reply. Information concerning recently declassified records can be found in two government publications. The U.S. Monthly Catalog Reference System produces the *Declassified Documents Reference System*, a collection of documents declassified under executive orders. It includes materials from a number of agencies and departments of government, including the CIA, Department of State, the Department of Defense, and the White House. Another listing of declassified documents, many concerned with communications and electronic warfare, can be found in the rear section of *Prologue*, a quarterly National Archives publication. Most major public libraries receive one or both of these publications.

National Security Archive
1755 Massachusetts Ave., NW
Suite 500
Washington, DC 20036
202-797-0882

The National Security Archive is a public/privately held depository of documents that have been created in the military/intelligence and foreign policy sector. These documents and their indexes serve as an excellent resource for activities involving the government of the United States since 1960. A letter to the National Security Archive describing what you are seeking along with a self-addressed stamped envelope will result in a prompt reply. When asking for information, try to be as specific as possible.

Council for Inter-American Security
122 C St., NW
Washington, DC 20001
202-543-6622

The CIAS offers a monthly newsletter, *Westwatch*, that discusses terrorist acts. The major motive of the organization is to oppose Soviet influence supported by terrorism. Enclose a stamped self-addressed envelope along with your request for information.

National Intelligence Book Center
1700 K St., NW, Suite 1007
Washington, DC 20006
202-797-1234

Data Memory Systems
Historical Evaluation & Research Organization
10392 Democracy Lane, 2nd Floor
Fairfax, VA 22030
703-591-3674

Data Memory Systems compiles research databases on terrorism, conventional warfare, and low intensity conflicts worldwide. Be specific in your request for the services they offer.

DataPort C/S
5525 Olinda Rd.
El Sobrante, CA 94803 USA
415-223-3658
FAX: 415-233-1924

Radiofrequency microfiche, produced by the FCC, of government, military, commercial and aircraft frequencies is available. Hard to find data with original microfiche (4×6 inch) films also are available. Also privately produced microfiche on popular (special) topics and frequency newsletter.

National Defense Council Foundation (NDCF)
108 South Columbus St., Suite 101
Alexandria, VA 22314
703-836-3443

The NDCF offers internships in such topics as terrorism, low-intensity foreign and domestic conflicts, and military activities worldwide.

National Intelligence Study Center
1800 K St., Suite 1102
Washington, DC 20006
202-466-6029

The NISC has information available on current espionage activities, and surveillance and intelligence operations in the United States.

A Final Note

If you are an IBM compatible computer user, you'll want to own a menu-driven frequency database on diskette to use in conjunction with *Latest Intelligence*. Features of this unique software program include the ability to add frequencies to the data files, edit entries already entered, and delete entries that are no longer desired. Frequencies also can be printed out. This is not a commercially produced product. The database includes hundreds of nationwide frequencies already entered so it's ready to use. Send a self-addressed stamped envelope (SASE) to the second address listed below, along with the diskette format you'll require (3.5 or 5¼, DD/HD, etc.), and I'll respond promptly.

Although a good share of the material in this book comes from working professionals in the business of law enforcement, the military, and government, and agencies foreign and domestic involved in areas of intelligence and communications, one of our very best resources will always be the readers of this reference guide. Do you have something special in your files that fits into the context of this book you'd like to share and see in the next edition of this book?

The author welcomes such material and suggestions you have for additional data. I, of course, invite your comments, too. Send your correspondence to: James E. Tunnell, c/o TAB BOOKS, Blue Ridge Summit, PA 17294 or P.O. Box 3172 Ygnacio Valley Station, CA 94598, USA.

Pleasant Listening

Other Bestsellers of Related Interest

THE BEGINNER'S HANDBOOK OF AMATEUR RADIO—3rd Edition—Clay Laster

Get your amateur radio license and get on the air as quickly as possible, with the help of this classic handbook. This volume includes radio communication theory, fundamentals of radio transmitters and receivers, descriptions of key radio components, and the latest information on the Novice License privileges. 400 pages, 291 illustrations. Book 2965, $18.95 paperback, $24.95 hardcover.

PRACTICAL ANTENNA HANDBOOK
—Joseph J. Carr

This is the most comprehensive guide available on designing, installing, testing, and using communications antennas. Carr provides a unique combination of theoretical engineering concepts and the kind of practical antenna know-how that comes only from hands-on experience in building and using antennas. He offers extensive information on a variety of antenna types (with construction plans for 16 different types), including high-frequency dipole antennas, microwave antennas, directional beam antennas, and more. 416 pages, 351 illustrations. Book No. 3270, $21.95 paperback, $32.95 hardcover.

UNDERSTANDING DIGITAL ELECTRONICS
—2nd Edition—R.H. Warring
and Michael J. Sanfilippo

This revised edition of the bestselling guidebook to digital electronics is the perfect tool to help you keep up with the growth and change in technology. It's a quick and complete resource of all the principles and concepts of digital circuits, providing coverage of important areas such as binary numbers, digital logic gates, Boolean algebraic theorems, flip-flops and memories, number systems, and arithmetic logic units (including the 74181 ALU). 196 pages, 172 illustrations. Book No. 3226, $14.95 paperback, $22.95 hardcover.

TROUBLESHOOTING AND REPAIRING AUDIO EQUIPMENT—Homer L. Davidson

When your telephone answering machine quits . . . when your cassette player grinds to a stop . . . when your TV remote control loses control . . . or when your compact disc player goes berserk . . . you don't need a degree in electronics or even any experience. Everything you need to troubleshoot and repair most common problems in almost any consumer audio equipment is here in a servicing guide that's guaranteed to save you time and money. 336 pages, 354 illustrations. Book No. 2867, $18.95 paperback, $25.95 hardcover.

600 LOW-COST ELECTRONIC CIRCUITS
—David M. Gauthier

Need just the right circuit—FAST? Then look no further! This "nuts and bolts" resource tool is packed with illustrations, schematics, and hundreds of the most current application circuits. The author has compiled over 600 practical circuits that you can build or adapt to your own electronic projects. And, most of these useful circuits can be built for $25 or less! All of the circuits use between one and 10 hobby-type ICs, and their applications range from digital gates to FM receivers. 350 pages, 698 illustrations. Book No. 3219, $18.95 paperback, $27.95 hardcover.

SOUND SYNTHESIS: Analog and Digital Techniques—Terence Thomas

This authoritative guide gives you access to the most up-to-date methods of sound synthesis—the information and guidance you need to plan, build, test, and debug your own state-of-the-art electronic synthesizer. You'll also find out how to modify or interface an existing unit to gain better synthesized sound reproduction. Packed with diagrams, illustrations, and printed circuit board patterns, this practical construction manual is designed for anyone serious about producing the most advanced synthesized sound possible. 176 pages, 149 illustrations. Book No. 3276, $14.95 paperback, $22.95 hardcover.

THE DIGITAL IC HANDBOOK—Michael S. Morley

This book will make it easier for you to determine which digital ICs are currently available, how they work, and in what instances they will function most effectively. The author examines ICs from many major manufacturers and compares them not only by technology and key specification but by package and price as well. If you've ever been overwhelmed by the number of choices, this book will help you sort through the hundreds of circuits and evaluate your options. 624 pages, 273 illustrations. Book 3002, $49.50 hardcover only.

Prices Subject to Change Without Notice.

Look for These and Other TAB Books at Your Local Bookstore

To Order Call Toll Free 1-800-822-8158
(in PA, AK, and Canada call 717-794-2191)

or write to TAB BOOKS, Blue Ridge Summit, PA 17294-0840.

Title	Product No.	Quantity	Price

☐ Check or money order made payable to TAB BOOKS

Charge my ☐ VISA ☐ MasterCard ☐ American Express

Acct. No. _____ Exp. _____

Signature: _____

Name: _____

Address: _____

City: _____

State: _____ Zip: _____

Subtotal $ _____

Postage and Handling
($3.00 in U.S., $5.00 outside U.S.) $ _____

Add applicable state and local
sales tax $ _____

TOTAL $ _____

TAB BOOKS catalog free with purchase; otherwise send $1.00 in check or money order and receive $1.00 credit on your next purchase.

Orders outside U.S. must pay with international money order in U.S. dollars.

TAB Guarantee: If for any reason you are not satisfied with the book(s) you order, simply return it (them) within 15 days and receive a full refund.   BC